GED Math Ultimate Study Guide:
For the Math-Phobic

By:

Daniel Eiblum, MSEd., Editor-in-Chief

Eaton Chong Lee, M.S., Editor

Michael Forman, M.S., Editor

Neil Mann, Ph.D., Editor

Harrison Agrusa, M.S.

Michelle Kaplan-Cohen, B.S.

William Miller, Ph.D.

Ramya Vishnubhotla, Ph.D.

Danny Zheng, M.S.

Copyright © 2022 Superlative Press
All rights reserved
ISBN 978-0-578-38612-6

CONTENTS

Author Biographies 4
Introduction to Book 6
GED Test Information 7
How to Use this Book 8
Diagnostic Test I 10
How to Interpret Your Score 25

Elementary Math
Chapter 1: Arithmetic 26
Chapter 2: Numbers - Miscellaneous Topics 40
Chapter 3: Negative Numbers 49
Chapter 4: Fractions and Mixed Numbers 60
Chapter 5: Exponents and Roots 73
Chapter 6: Order of Operations 82

Algebra
Chapter 7: Simplifying Expressions 90
Chapter 8: Solving Equations and Manipulating Expressions ... 98

Word Problems
Chapter 9: Word Problems Using Equations 113
Chapter 10: Rates, Ratios, and Proportions 123
Chapter 11: Percentages 132
Chapter 12: Simple Interest 144
Chapter 13: Speed, Distance, and Time Word Problems 149
Chapter 14: Units and Measurements 156

Geometry
Chapter 15: Lines 165
Chapter 16: Angles and Triangles 174
Chapter 17: Circles 184
Chapter 18: Perimeter, Area, Volume, and Surface Area 195

Statistics
Chapter 19: Probability and Statistics 211

Miscellaneous Topics
Chapter 20: Inequalities 224
Chapter 21: Geometry in the Coordinate Plane 234
Chapter 22: Interpretation of Graphs 251
Chapter 23: Scientific Notation 264
Chapter 24: Quadratic Expressions and Functions 271
Chapter 25: Functions 285

Practice Test II 299

Editors

Daniel Eiblum, MSEd., Editor in Chief, received a BA in Mathematics and Geophysical Sciences from the University of Chicago in 1988, and then earned his Master of Education degree from Johns Hopkins University in 2000. He earned a BS in Atmospheric Sciences in 2015 from the University of Maryland at College Park. He has over twenty years of tutoring experience in mathematics ranging from Pre-Algebra through Calculus, in addition to Math SAT and Praxis Core Math preparation. He founded a tutoring agency in 2000, called MathSmart Tutoring, which serves the Washington, D.C., area with math and science tutors. He is the editor in chief and coauthor of *Math SAT 800: How to Master the Toughest Problems*, *SAT Vocabulary Lightning*, *Praxis I Math: My Private Tutor*, *SAT Math 800: Challenge Yourself to the Perfect Score*, *Graphs for Algebra I & II: Understanding the "Y,"* and *How to Master GRE Vocabulary: A Verbal GRE Preparation*. He taught high school math at the Phelps School of Engineering in Northeast Washington, D.C., in an afterschool program. He wrote the math SAT curriculum for Education Unlimited, a summer preparatory camp.

Eaton Chong Lee, M.S., Editor, received a BS in Physics from the University of Maryland at College Park, and an M.S. in Medical Physics from Georgetown University. He has over 18 years of teaching experience in SAT Math, Calculus, and Physics. He is the editor of *SAT Math Prep 800: Challenge Yourself to the Perfect Score*.

Michael Forman, M.S., Editor, has both a B.S. and an M.S. in Physics and Applied Math from the University of Massachusetts at Lowell. He was a professional mathematician and physicist at NASA for 40 years and has published in several scientific journals. He began tutoring math and physics in 2005. Math courses include pre-algebra through calculus and Math SAT preparation. He is the editor of *Math SAT 800: How to Master the Toughest Problems,* and *SAT Math Prep 800: Challenge Yourself to a Perfect Score*.

English Editor

Neil Mann, Ph.D., holds a B.A. and Ph.D. in English from Oxford University. He has taught at university and high school level, and works as a teacher, editor, and translator. He is an editor and coauthor of *SAT Vocabulary Lightning* and *How to Master GRE Vocabulary: A Verbal GRE Preparation*.

Authors

Harrison Agrusa, M.S., is a Ph.D. student at the University of Maryland. He holds B.A. degrees in Physics and Astrophysics from the University of California, Berkeley, and an M.S. in Astronomy from the University of Maryland. He is a teaching assistant for University of Maryland's Astronomy Department and has taught classes on General Astronomy, Computational Astrophysics, and Asteroid Deflection. He was also a teaching assistant at UC Berkeley, where he taught courses on General Astronomy and the Solar System. He has tutored calculus and geometry for MathSmart Tutoring. Currently, he is working on his Ph.D., specializing in the orbital dynamics of near-Earth asteroids.

Michelle Kaplan-Cohen graduated cum laude with a B.S. in Physiology and Neurobiology from the University of Maryland. Over the past decade, Michelle tutored, while working primarily in the medical field. She performed targeted research on the role of the Akt/mTOR pathway in lung cancer, provided life-saving treatments as a charge EMT, and built and managed a successful healthcare start-up. However, while working in the emergency room last year, Michelle realized her love for education surpassed her interest in medicine; thus, she decided to exclusively dedicate her time to a career in education. Currently, she tutors elementary through college students in math, science, ACT/SAT/PSAT/SSAT test prep, and executive functioning skills. Michelle also specializes in working with students with ADD, ADHD, autism, dyscalculia, dyslexia, and learning disabilities.

Will Miller, Ph.D., has a B.S. in Chemistry from the University of Virginia. He worked as a nuclear engineer with the U.S. Navy, where he helped supervise the operations and maintenance of the nuclear reactors onboard the USS Harry S. Truman. He has a Ph.D. in Atmospheric and Oceanic Sciences from the University of Maryland at College Park, where he tutored students in Fluid Dynamics and Synoptic Meteorology. His Ph.D. research project focused on improving our understanding of both the unusual motion and rapid intensification of hurricanes using his own computer model simulations of two cases: Hurricane Wilma (2005) and Hurricane Joaquin (2015). Currently, he works as a postdoctoral researcher at the National Severe Storms Lab in Norman, Oklahoma.

Ramya Vishnubhotla, Ph.D., has a Ph.D. in Physics from the University of Pennsylvania and a B.S. in Physics and Astrophysics from Penn State. She was an ROTC Tutor at Penn State where she tutored undergraduates in Introductory Calculus and Physics. She has also tutored physics and science projects for MathSmart Tutoring.

Danny Zheng, M.S., has an M.S. in Applied Mathematics from Towson University and a B.S. in Mathematics from the California Polytechnic State University. He is a part-time Adjunct Professor of Mathematics at Montgomery College and Howard Community College. He is also a Data Scientist at the Department of Navy/Naval Facilities Engineering Command. He tutored mathematics through Calculus, and SAT and ACT math for over 10 years. He is coauthor of *SAT Math Prep 800: Challenge Yourself to the Perfect Score*.

Introduction

We wrote this book to provide you with the ultimate workbook to enable you to pass the test with flying colors. You might be dreading the test, fearful that you will never pass it and fail to realize your dream of getting a high school diploma. For this purpose, we try to make the book as easy as possible to use and understand.

Whether you have taken the test multiple times and were just shy of a passing score each time or are way behind and haven't a clue how to solve most of the problems, this book will help you develop the math skills you need to pass the test. If you work through this study guide diligently and give yourself sufficient time to study, you'll be on your way to obtaining your high school diploma and be more likely to get a high-paying job.

Our book starts off with the multiplication table and then delves into the very basics you once learned in elementary school. It will refresh your memory on middle school math and pre-algebra, and then help you through the torturous material in algebra I & algebra II, geometry, and statistics.

We cover the material in a cumulative fashion to make sure that you will understand each topic in succession. All the authors and math editors of this book have had teaching and/or tutoring experience in math, and most in test preparation. We have all mastered high school math and many of us have gone through brutal math preparation in college or graduate programs, so we empathize with your math anxiety! We all have one thing in common—we know how to break down complex topics to help math-phobic students quickly grasp the challenging material.

If you have a test scheduled soon, start working through this study guide right away—don't delay! But give yourself time to get through all the chapters. This workbook covers twelve years of math material, so you might find that you need to study for an entire semester to master the material. We begin our lessons with information about the test that you may not already know, followed by an assessment test to help you later gauge your progress.

We wish you much good luck in your studies and endeavors!

Daniel Charles Eiblum, MSEd.

GED Test Information

The purpose of the GED test is to demonstrate high school equivalency and readiness to pursue college and a career. It includes reading, writing, reasoning and problem-solving skills that are necessary for college programs and beyond as well as career requirements.

There are four sections in the test: Reasoning through Language Arts – 2.5 hours long, Mathematical Reasoning – 1 hour, 55 minutes long, Social Studies – 1 hour, 10 minutes, and Science – 1.5 hours.

Because this book covers the math section only, we provide below information about the GED Math test only.

There are two parts to the test:

Part I: Quantitative Reasoning, 18 Questions, (45%) and ;

Part II: Algebraic Reasoning and Geometry, 22 Questions, 55%.

Part I: Quantitative Reasoning. This section includes problems with:
   A. Whole numbers, decimals, and fractions
   B. Decimals and fractions
   C. Ratios, proportions, and percentages
   D. Data and Statistics
   E. Geometric measurements

Part I: Algebraic Reasoning. This section includes problems with:
   A. Expressions
   B. Polynomials
   C. Equations including linear and quadratic
   D. Inequalities
   E. Patterns and functions
   F. Graphs

Calculators are allowed to use, either a handheld or an online version of a scientific calculator. The exception is for the first five questions on the test. You may take up to 12 minutes with these questions.

Formula Sheet: A formula sheet is included in your test that has equations on volume and surface area of geometric solids, areas and perimeters of geometric figures, and formulas in algebra including slope of a line, forms of linear equations, the quadratic formula, the Pythagorean Theorem, simple interest, distance formula, and total cost.

There are both **multiple choice** questions as well as **fill-in-the blank** questions that will require you to type a numerical answer or to enter an equation. The latter is possible by clicking to open the symbol selector and then inserting the symbol into the box.

Using the TI-30XS MultiView™ Calculator

There are plenty of resources on how to use this calculator online. We recommend that you purchase this calculator and follow the manual that is included to familiarize yourself with its use. You will only need to use the numeric keypad to: A. enter numbers, the decimal point, and the negative sign, B. The operation keys allowing you to add, subtract, multiply, and divide, C. the 2nd functions above the keys. These include percent, exponent, and square root and others. D. Use may also use the four arrows to move the cursor around. E. You can also use the delete key to correct mistakes, F. The clear button to start a problem from scratch.

Wipe-Off Board

The testing center will provide you with a wipe-off board and dry erase marker. This can be used to take notes and solve problems.

Symbol Selector Toolbar

There will be some questions that will require you to use the Symbol Selector Toolbar that include symbols such as multiplication, division, plus-or-minus, square root, parentheses, greater than or equal to, equal to, etc.

To use this toolbar, you should click on the symbol to insert it in the correct location in an equation/inequality or an expression. After you enter the symbol, you should click on the "X" at the top of the window to close the window.

How to use this book

You are probably wondering how much time it will take you to work through this study guide. The answer depends on your situation, level of comfort with math, and how far behind you are. If you keep failing the test by just a few points, you probably have mastered the basics, including elementary and middle school math, and most of high school math. If so, this book will be a faster read.

After you take the practice test, check to see which problems stumped you. Go over the chapters that cover these problems first. It is quite possible that those chapters will be the only chapters you need to study. On the other hand, if you did poorly on most or all of the test, study each chapter in succession. This strategy will speed up your progress and help you pass the test in a shorter time.

If you are clueless or failing the practice tests you have taken, give yourself at least a semester to practice all the problems. To accomplish this, you will need to master approximately two chapters per week, with each practice test counting as one chapter.

Make sure to go through the chapters to prevent yourself from missing information that is necessary to understand the next chapter. If you are confused about the material presented in a chapter, go through the chapter once more until you are more comfortable with the material.

Planning Your Study Time

- Give yourself enough time to prepare for the test. Some students may require only a few weeks, whereas others may require a whole semester or two to study our workbook.
- Schedule a test that is far enough in the future for you to prepare for the test.
- Plan your study schedule according to the test date. You might find it easier to work backwards from the scheduled tests. For example, if you have fifteen weeks to take the test, you will need to cover almost two chapters of this study guide per week.
- Make sure your schedule of study is realistic. To be realistic, study a chapter or two and see how long it takes you to get through the material. Base the rest of your schedule on this preparation time.

Important Facts about the Test

- Your score is based on the number of questions you answer correctly, with no penalty for an incorrect response. This means that you should guess an answer if you do not know it, but first try to eliminate wrong answers if you can.
- You can skip questions and then come back to them later. If you skip a question, be sure to mark it to help you remember to answer it at the end, if you have time.

Smart Tips for Taking the Test

- Time yourself by looking at your watch or smartphone to make sure you have enough time to finish and then go back over the questions you left blank.
- If you cannot solve the problem when you return to a problem you skipped, try to eliminate answer choices, and then guess.
- Practice pacing yourself on the practice tests in this workbook. This will help you pace yourself on the actual test.
- Make sure to check all your answers if you have sufficient time at the end. And be sure to respond to every problem.

Diagnostic Test I

Number of questions: 40

Time: 115 minutes

Directions:

There are 40 questions on this test. You have 115 minutes to complete the test. You may fill in the ovals next to the correct answers or write your answers on a separate piece of paper. You MAY use a calculator.

Below is a formula sheet that appears on the actual GED® Test. You can refer to this page on Part II of this Pretest.

Area of a:

square	$A = s^2$
rectangle	$A = hw$
parallelogram	$A = bh$
triangle	$A = \frac{1}{2}bh$
trapezoid	$A = \frac{1}{2}h(b_1 + b_2)$
circle	$A = \pi r^2$

Perimeter of a:

square	$P = 4s$
rectangle	$P = 2l + 2w$
triangle	$P = s_1 + s_2 + s_3$
Circumference of a circle	$C = 2\pi r$ or $C = \pi d$; $\pi \approx 3.14$

Surface area and volume of a:

rectangular/right prism	$SA = ph + 2B$	$V = Bh$
cylinder	$SA = 2\pi rh + 2\pi r^2$	$V = \pi r^2 h$
pyramid	$SA = \frac{1}{2}ps + B$	$V = \frac{1}{3}Bh$
cone	$SA = \pi rs + \pi r^2$	$V = \frac{1}{3}\pi r^2 h$
sphere	$SA = 4\pi r^2$	$V = \frac{4}{3}\pi r^3$

(p = perimeter of base with area B; $\pi \approx 3.14$)

Data

mean	mean is equal to the total of the values of a data set, divided by the number of elements in the data set
median	median is the middle value in an odd number of ordered value of a data set, or the mean of the two middle values in an even number of ordered values in a data set.

Algebra

slope of a line	$m = \dfrac{y_2 - y_1}{x_2 - x_1}$
slope intercept form of the equation of a line	$y = mx + b$
point-slope form of the equation of a line	$y - y_1 = m(x - x_1)$
standard form of a quadratic equation	$y = ax^2 + bx + c$
quadratic formula	$x = \dfrac{-b \pm \sqrt{b^2 - 4ac}}{2a}$
Pythagorean theorem	$a^2 + b^2 = c^2$
simple interest	$I = Prt$ (I = interest, P = principal, r = rate, t = time)
distance formula	$d = rt$
total cost	total cost = (number of units) × (price per unit)

Provided by GED® Testing Service.

1. $$\frac{4x}{3} + \frac{5x}{2}$$
   The expression above can also be written as:

   A) $\frac{23x}{6}$

   B) $\frac{9x}{5}$

   C) $\frac{20x}{6}$

   D) $\frac{9x}{6}$

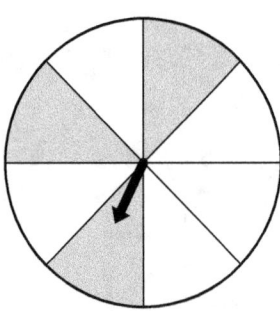

2. In the figure above, all 8 sections in the circle above have the same area. If the hand of the spinner is spun once, what is the probability that the spinner's hand will land on one of the shaded sectors?

   A) $\frac{1}{4}$

   B) $\frac{3}{8}$

   C) $\frac{1}{2}$

   D) $\frac{5}{8}$

3. If $(x+3)(x-4) = 0$, which of the following values of x would satisfy the equation?

   A) 3

   B) -3

   C) -4

   D) -12

4. Together, two pounds of tomatoes and three pounds of apples cost $9. Three pounds of tomatoes and two pounds of apples cost $8.50. How much would one pound of tomatoes and two pounds of apples cost?

   A) $3.00

   B) $4.50

   C) $5.00

   D) $5.50

5. Given the following two equations, what is the value of x?

   $$2x - y = 4.5$$
   $$3x + y = 11.75$$

   A) 2.5

   B) 2.75

   C) 3

   D) 3.25

6. Tickets at a movie theater cost $12 per adult admission and $9.50 for a child. If a family with 2 adults and 4 children were to buy movie tickets, how much would they pay in total?

   (A) $55
   (B) $60
   (C) $62
   (D) $66

7. James has some crayons in a drawer, some yellow, some blue, and some green. He selects one crayon from the drawer. If the probability of selecting a blue crayon is $\frac{1}{3}$, and the probability of selecting a yellow crayon is $\frac{5}{12}$, what is the probability of selecting a green crayon?

   (A) $\frac{1}{4}$
   (B) $\frac{5}{12}$
   (C) $\frac{1}{2}$
   (D) $\frac{2}{3}$

8. Peter has two cubes, one white and one black, with sides numbered 1 to 6 on each. If he tosses both cubes simultaneously, what is the probability that the top face of the black cube is a 4, and the top face of the white cube is an odd number?

   (A) $\frac{1}{36}$
   (B) $\frac{1}{18}$
   (C) $\frac{5}{12}$
   (D) $\frac{1}{12}$

$$3x - 7 \geq 11$$

9. Which of the following values of x would satisfy the inequality above?

   (A) 3.25
   (B) 3.95
   (C) 5.35
   (D) 6

10. Which of the following number lines represent the inequality $4 \leq x + 1 < 7$?

    (A) ●━━━○ 4   7
    (B) ○━━━● 4   7
    (C) ●━━━○ 5   8
    (D) ●━━━○ 3   6

11. What is the value of x if $3x - 18 = 33$?

    (A) $-\dfrac{17}{3}$

    (B) $\dfrac{17}{3}$

    (C) 15

    (D) 17

13. A retail store discounts the price of a television by 40%. The following week, the store raises the new price of the television by 20%. By what percent did the price of the television decrease from the original price ?

    (A) 15%
    (B) 20%
    (C) 24%
    (D) 28%

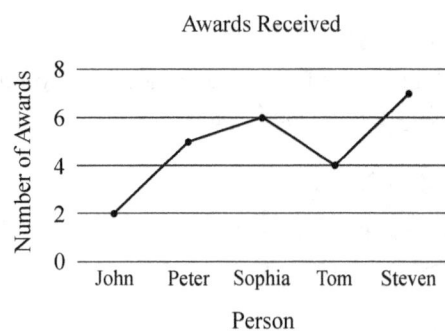

Awards Received

12. A math teacher in a middle school created a chart, shown above, that displays the number of awards each of five students in her class received during an academic year. What is the median number of awards they received?

    (A) 2
    (B) 4
    (C) 5
    (D) 6

Year	Population Country A
1965	1,200,000
1970	1,440,000
1975	1,728,000
1980	2,073,600
1985	2,488,320

14. The table above shows the population of Country A every five years from 1965–1985. If the population continued to grow at the same rate, what would the population be in 1990?

    (A) 2,650,788
    (B) 2,666,074
    (C) 2,708,320
    (D) 2,985,984

15. Find the mean of the data set below:

    {3, 6, 9, 12, 15}

    (A) 3
    (B) 9
    (C) 15
    (D) 18

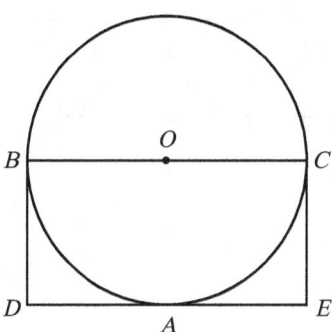

16. In the figure above, circle O has a diameter of 8 inches. Segments $\overline{DB}$, $\overline{EC}$, and $\overline{DAE}$ are tangent to circle. What is the area of rectangle $BCED$?

    (A) 16 in²
    (B) 24 in²
    (C) 32 in²
    (D) 12π in²

17. Bob and Jim received money from the sale of their business in a ratio of 75% to 25%, respectively. If Jim got $600,000, how much money did Bob and Jim collect in total?

    (A) $800,000
    (B) $1,000,000
    (C) $1,200,000
    (D) $2,400,000

18. Evaluate:

    $$(-2) \times (-2) + 5 \times 3 + 15 \times (-1)$$
    $$-16 \times (-1) + 7 \times 2 - 6 \times (1 + 3)$$

    (A) −5
    (B) −9
    (C) 10
    (D) 23

19. Simplify: $\dfrac{3}{10} - \dfrac{1}{4}$. Express your answer in simplest fraction form.

    (A) $\dfrac{1}{20}$
    (B) $\dfrac{1}{7}$
    (C) $\dfrac{3}{40}$
    (D) $\dfrac{1}{3}$

20. Simplify: $3\frac{2}{5} - 4\frac{1}{4}$

    A) $-\frac{21}{10}$
    B) $-\frac{9}{54}$
    C) $-\frac{17}{20}$
    D) $\frac{3}{20}$

21. If $x^2 = 169$, what could be the value of x?

    A) -84.5
    B) -13
    C) 17
    D) 84.5

22. Which of the following numbers is less than zero?

    A) 4^{-3}
    B) -10^{-2}
    C) $-16 \times (-3)^3$
    D) $\sqrt{16^{-2}}$

23. A blizzard causes snow to accumulate at 3.5 inches per hour. How many centimeters accumulate in one minute to the nearest hundredth? (1 inch = 2.54 cm)

    A) 0.04
    B) 0.09
    C) 0.15
    D) 0.19

24. The population of people in Country X increased by 850,000 in 2019. How fast did the population grow in people per hour to the nearest integer? (Year 2019 had 365 days.)

    A) 18
    B) 97
    C) 204
    D) 310

25. How is 0.00810 expressed using scientific notation?

    A) 1.00×10^{81}
    B) 810×10^{-3}
    C) 0.01×10^{-81}
    D) 8.10×10^{-3}

26. A circular bicycle trail has a radius of 3 miles. James biked around the trail 6 times. Approximately how many miles did James travel?

   A) 16π
   B) 26π
   C) 36π
   D) 46π

27. What is the least common multiple of 6, 15, and 21?

   A) 105
   B) 210
   C) 305
   D) 1890

28. Gregg drove his car from Chicago to Oklahoma City. The distance between those cities is 792 miles. The gas gauge in Jason's car was on full when he started. He filled his tank twice from empty to full during the trip. Once he arrived, it was empty again. His car's tank holds 12 gallons of gas. How many miles per gallon did the car average on the trip?

   A) 18
   B) 20
   C) 21
   D) 22

29. The exchange rate today is one dollar for 0.88 euros. How many dollars can Joseph get for 200 euros (rounded to the nearest dollar)?

   A) 164
   B) 176
   C) 206
   D) 227

30. A hat contains 10 colored marbles, 2 red, 3 orange, 1 white, 2 yellow, and 2 brown. If three marbles are drawn with replacement, what is the probability that the first two marbles are brown and the third one is orange?

   A) $\dfrac{6}{125}$
   B) $\dfrac{12}{50}$
   C) $\dfrac{3}{250}$
   D) $\dfrac{6}{25}$

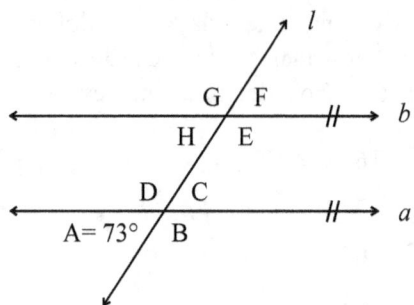

31. The figure above shows line *l* crossing two parallel lines *a* and *b*. If angle A has a measure of 73°, what is the measure of angle G?

   (A) 17°
   (B) 27°
   (C) 73°
   (D) 107°

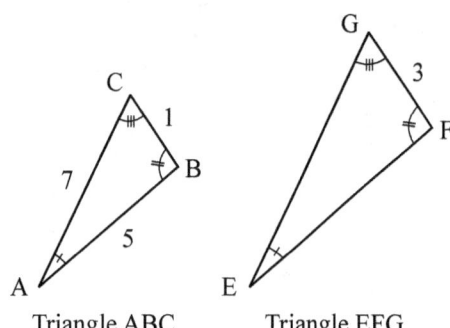

Triangle ABC   Triangle EFG

32. In the figure above, triangles ABC and EFG are similar triangles. Side AC = 7, side AB = 5, and side BC = 1. If side FG = 3, what is the length of EG?

   (A) 12
   (B) 14
   (C) 21
   (D) 24

33. Eight students in a math class took a quiz and scored an average of 78%. Six other students achieved an average score on their biology quiz of 84%. What is the average score of all the students?

   (A) 80.0
   (B) 80.6
   (C) 81.3
   (D) 81.6

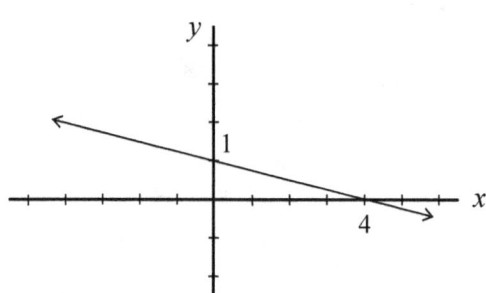

34. Which of the following equations represents the graph of the line above?

   (A) $y = x - \dfrac{1}{4}$
   (B) $y = \dfrac{1}{4}x + 1$
   (C) $y = -\dfrac{1}{4}x + 1$
   (D) $y = -4x - 1$

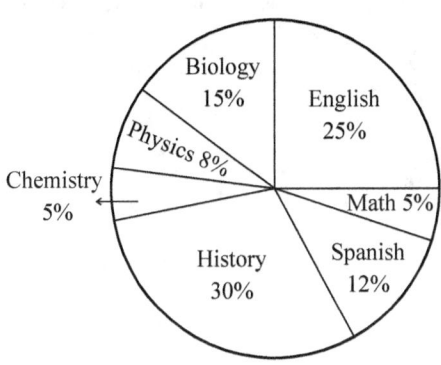

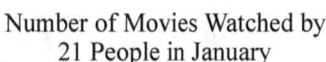
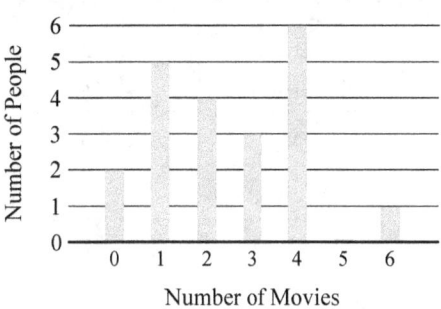

35. The graph above shows the distribution of students' favorite subjects at Woodward High School. If there are 1,250 students in the school, how many students prefer history over physics as their favorite subject?

A) 275
B) 288
C) 294
D) 302

37. Based on the graph above, what is the median number of movies watched by the 21 people surveyed?

A) 1
B) 2
C) 3
D) 4

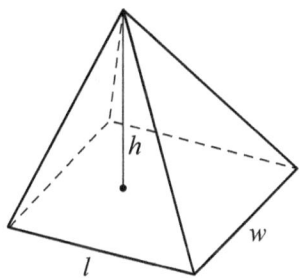

Figure not drawn to scale.

36. The volume of a rectangular pyramid can be expressed as $V = \frac{1}{3}lwh$, where l is the length of the base, w is the width of the base, and h is the height of the base. If the volume of the pyramid is 750 cm³, and the base is a square with sides of 5 cm what is the height of the pyramid?

A) 30 cm
B) 50 cm
C) 75 cm
D) 90 cm

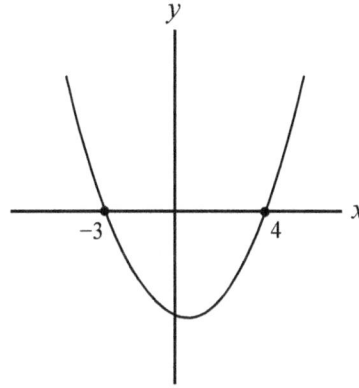

38. Given the graph of the equation, $y = x^2 - x - 12$, above, what is the solution set for $x^2 - x - 12 > 0$?

A) $x > -3$
B) $x < -3$ or $x > 4$
C) $x < -3$
D) $-3 < x < 4$

Size	Percentage
Small	20%
Medium	25%
Large	30%
X-Large	15%
XX-Large	10%

39. In a clothing store, 280 men's T-shirts come in five sizes, as shown by the distribution in the table above. How many shirts are large-sized?

   Ⓐ 30
   Ⓑ 84
   Ⓒ 114
   Ⓓ 140

40. Convert 0.15 to a fraction in simplest form.

   Ⓐ $\dfrac{3}{200}$
   Ⓑ $\dfrac{15}{100}$
   Ⓒ $\dfrac{3}{20}$
   Ⓓ $\dfrac{3}{2}$

Answers to GED Math Test 1

1. **(A)** The expression consists of like terms, so we can combine them into one term. We add the fractions $\frac{4}{3} + \frac{5}{2}$ together by first finding the lowest common denominator of 3 and 2, which is 6, and then multiply the resulting fraction by the variable, x.

   $$\frac{4}{3} + \frac{5}{2} = \frac{(4 \times 2) + (5 \times 3)}{6} = \frac{23}{6}$$

   Thus, we get $\frac{23}{6} \times x = \frac{23}{6}x$.

2. **(B)** The event in question is that the spinner's hand lands on a shaded sector. Because there are 8 possible outcomes (8 sectors) and 3 favorable outcomes (3 shaded sectors), the probability of the favorable event is 3 out of 8, or $\frac{3}{8}$.

3. **(B)** If $(x + 3)(x - 4) = 0$, then either $(x + 3) = 0$, in which case $x = -3$, or $(x - 4) = 0$, in which case $x = 4$.

4. **(D)** Let $T =$ price of tomatoes and $A =$ price of apples. Then, we can write: $2T + 3A = 9$ from the first statement, and $3T + 2A = 8.5$ from the second statement. Multiply the first equation by -3 to get:

   $$-6T - 9A = -27$$

   Multiply the second equation by 2 to get:

   $$6T + 4A = 17$$

   Add the two equations together to get rid of the variable T to get:

   $$-5A = -10$$

   Divide both sides of the equation by -5 to get $A = -10/-5 = 2$. Now we know that apples cost $2 a pound. Plug $2 for the price of apples into the first equation to get:

   $$2T + 3(2) = 9$$

   so $2T = 9 - 6$, to get $T = 1.5$. (We could have used the second equation just as well). One pound of tomatoes plus 2 pounds of apples, would be: $1(1.5) + 2(2) = \$5.50$.

5. **(D)** Add the two equations together to get

   $$\begin{aligned} 2x - y &= 4.5 \\ + \ 3x + y &= 11.75 \\ \hline 5x + 0 &= 16.25 \end{aligned}$$

   Divide both sides of the equation by 5 to get:

   $$x = \frac{16.25}{5} = 3.25$$

6. **(C)** Let $A =$ price of adult tickets and $C =$ price of child tickets. Then, the total price will equal $2(12) + 4(9.5) = \$62$.

7. **(A)** We know that the probability of exactly one of the three events occurring is 100% or 1. If the probability of selecting a blue crayon is $\frac{1}{3}$, and the probability of selecting a yellow crayon is $\frac{5}{12}$, then the probability of selecting a green crayon is

   $$1 - \frac{1}{3} - \frac{5}{12} = \frac{12}{12} - \frac{4}{12} - \frac{5}{12} = \frac{3}{12} = \frac{1}{4}$$

8. **(D)** The tossing of the black cube and the white cube are two independent events. The probability of two independent events, A and B, is $P(A \text{ and } B) = P(A) \times P(B)$, where P means probability, A is event A, and B is event B. Applying this rule to our problem, we get

   $$P(4 \text{ and } Odd) = P(4) \times P(Odd)$$
   $$= \frac{1}{6} \times \frac{3}{6} = \frac{3}{36} = \frac{1}{12}$$

9. **(D)** Solve for x by adding 7 to both sides of the equation to get $3x \geq 18$. Now divide both sides of the inequality by 3 to get $x \geq 6$. Any value of x greater than or equal to 6 satisfies the equation.

10. **(D)** Subtract 1 from $x + 1$ from both sides of the inequality to get $3 \leq x < 6$. So, x lies between 3, inclusive, to 6, exclusive. The number line in choice **D** shows this inequality visually.

11. **(D)** Add 18 to both sides of the equation to obtain $3x - 18 + 18 = 33 + 18$, so that $3x = 51$. Divide both sides of the equation by 3 to get $x = \dfrac{51}{3} = 17$.

12. **(C)** To find the median of the data points, we first need to order them from least to greatest. From the line graph, we see that the numbers when put in order are: 2, 4, 5, 6, and 7. The median is the middle of those numbers because there is an odd number of data points. Thus, the middle number is 5.

13. **(D)** Call the price of the television before the price changes, X. After the sale, the television costs $100\% - 40\% = 60\%$ of $X = 0.6X$, because $60\% = 0.6$. After the price increases, the new price of the television is 120%, or 1.2 times the price after the discount, and we can write it as $1.2 \times (0.6X) = 0.72X$. Therefore, the final price is 72 percent of the original price, and the price of the television decreased by $100 - 72 = 28\%$. If you chose **B**, you subtracted 20 from 40, and this is not the correct calculation. The logic behind this is that the television is being marked up by 20% of the new price, which is lower than before the discount.

14. **(D)** From a few simple calculations, we can see that the population increases by 20% every 5 years. To check the percent increase from 1980 to 1985, use the percent change formula:

$$\text{Percent Change} = \frac{\text{Final} - \text{Beginning}}{\text{Beginning}} \times 100\%$$

Plugging in 2,488,320 in 1985 for the final population and 2,073,600 for the beginning population in 1980, we get:

$$\frac{2{,}488{,}320 - 2{,}073{,}600}{2{,}073{,}600} \times 100\% = 20\%$$

To add 20% to the population of 1985, multiply the population in 1985 by 120%, or 1.2: $2{,}488{,}320 \times 1.2 = 2{,}985{,}984$.

15. **(B)** Using the formula for the mean, we obtain:

$$\text{Mean} = \frac{\text{The sum of the data points}}{\text{The number of data points}}$$
$$= \frac{3 + 6 + 9 + 12 + 15}{5} = \frac{45}{5} = 9$$

16. **(C)** Segment $\overline{BC}$ of the rectangle is the diameter of the circle, which is equal to 8 inches. The radius, r, of a circle is equal to one half of the diameter, so $r = 8/2 = 4$ inches. Since we now know segment $\overline{CE}$ (or $\overline{BD}$) and segment $\overline{BC}$ (or $\overline{DE}$), the area of the rectangle can be calculated as $L \times W = 8 \times 4 = 32$ in².

17. **(D)** The ratio of Bob's collection for his business to Jim's collection is 75 : 25, which simplifies to 3 : 1. So Bob collects three times as much money as Jim. Therefore, Bob collects $600{,}000 \times 3 = \$1{,}800{,}000$. Together they make $\$1{,}800{,}000 + \$600{,}000 = \$2{,}400{,}000$.

18. **(C)** Simplify as follows, following PEMDAS (parentheses, then exponents, then multiplication and division, then addition and subtraction):

$$4 + 15 - 15 + 16 + 14 - 6(4) = 10$$

19. **(A)** The lowest common denominator of 10 and 4 is 20. Therefore, simplify as follows:

$$\frac{6}{20} - \frac{5}{20} = \frac{1}{20}$$

20. **(C)** Convert both mixed numbers to improper fractions:

$$3\frac{2}{5} - 4\frac{1}{4} = \frac{17}{5} - \frac{17}{4}$$

Take the common denominator of 5 and 4, which is 20, and convert into fractions with denominator of 20:

$$\frac{17 \times 4}{20} - \frac{17 \times 5}{20} = \frac{68}{20} - \frac{85}{20} = \frac{-17}{20}$$

21. **(B)** Take the square root of both sides of the equation to get:

$$\sqrt{x^2} = \pm\sqrt{169} = \pm 13$$

To test the answers square 13 and −13 to see if they equal to 169.

$$13^2 = 169 \checkmark$$
$$(-13)^2 = 169 \checkmark$$

22. **(B)** Choice **A** is equal to $\frac{1}{4^3} = \frac{1}{64} > 0$.

    Choice **B** is equal to $-\frac{1}{10^2} = -\frac{1}{100} < 0$.

    Choice **D** is equal to $-16(-3)^3 = (-16) \cdot (-27) > 0$, since a negative number times a negative number is a positive number.

23. **(C)** Convert inches to centimeters and hours to minutes as follows:

    $$\frac{3.5 \text{ inches}}{\text{hour}} \times \frac{1 \text{ hour}}{60 \text{ minutes}} \times \frac{2.54 \text{ cm}}{1 \text{ inch}}$$
    $$= 0.15 \text{ cm/minute}$$

24. **(B)** Convert a year to days, then days to hours as follows:

    $$\frac{850,000 \text{ people}}{\text{year}} \times \frac{1 \text{ year}}{365 \text{ days}} \times \frac{1 \text{ day}}{24 \text{ hours}}$$
    $$= 97 \text{ people/hour}$$

25. **(D)** Move the decimal 3 spaces to right, to immediately after the 8 to get: 8.10×10^{-3}.

26. **(C)** To calculate the total distance James biked, we need to first find the circumference of the bicycle trail as follows:

    $$C = 2\pi r = 2\pi(3) = 6\pi \text{ miles}$$

This is how far he biked around a trail once. Now we multiply the circumference by 6:

$$6C = 6(6\pi) = 36\pi \text{ miles}$$

27. **(B)** Write 6, 15, and 21 in the factorized form:
    $$6 = 2 \times 3$$
    $$15 = 3 \times 5$$
    $$21 = 3 \times 7$$

    Select the factors 2 and 3 from the number 6, 5 from the number 15, and 7 from the number 21 to get $2 \times 3 \times 5 \times 7 = 210$.

28. **(D)** Gregg traveled 792 miles (given). He used up three gas tanks. Since the gas tank holds 12 gallons, Jason used a total of $3 \times 12 = 36$ gallons. So, he got 792 miles per 36 gallons. We write the ratio as:

    $$\frac{792 \text{ miles}}{36 \text{ gallons}} = 22 \text{ miles/gallon}$$

29. **(D)** We have $\frac{1 \text{ dollar}}{0.88 \text{ euro}} = \frac{x \text{ dollar}}{200 \text{ euro}}$.

    Multiply both sides of the equation by 200 to get: $x = \frac{1 \text{ dollar}}{0.88 \text{ euro}} \times 200 \text{ euro} = \$227$.

30. **(C)** "With replacement" means that after the first marble is drawn, it is put back into the hat before the second is drawn, and likewise with the third draw. Therefore, these three events are independent. The formula for the probability of two independent events occurring is:

    $$P(A \text{ and } B) = P(A) \times P(B)$$

    where P = probability, and A = event A, B = event B. This formula can be extrapolated to three events, where

    $$P(A \text{ and } B \text{ and } C) = P(A) \times P(B) \times P(C)$$

    In this case the probability of picking the first brown marble is 2/10. Likewise, because the first marble is put back into the hat, the probability of picking a brown one in the second draw is also 2/10. Finally, the probability of picking an orange marble is 3/10. Plugging these three fractions into our formula, we obtain:

$$\frac{2}{10} \times \frac{2}{10} \times \frac{3}{10} = \frac{1}{5} \times \frac{1}{5} \times \frac{3}{10} = \frac{3}{250}$$

31. **(D)** Angles A and D are supplementary, and therefore, ∠D = 180° − ∠A = 180° − 73° = 107°. Angles D and G are corresponding angles. Corresponding angles are equal, so angle G = angle D = 107°.

32. **(C)** Triangle ABC and triangle EFG are similar triangles because they have 3 equal pairs of angles, and therefore, the sides are proportional. Because side GF is 3 times the length of side CB, then side EG is 3 times the length of side AC. Therefore, side EG = 3 × 7 = 21.

33. **(B)** We need to first find the total score of all 14 students. This can be calculated as

$$78 \times 8 + 84 \times 6 = 1128$$

The rationale for this calculation is that the average score = total score / number of students, and therefore, total score = average score × number of students. In the above calculation, we are adding the two total scores of the two quizzes. Now that we have found the total score, we divide by the total number of students who took the test, 8 + 6 = 14. Therefore, the average score of 14 students = $\frac{1128}{14}$ = 80.6.

34. **(C)** The y-intercept is 1 and the slope is $-\frac{1}{4}$. Therefore, the equation of the line is $y = -\frac{1}{4}x + 1$.

35. **(A)** The percentage of students who prefer history over physics is 30% − 8% = 22%. Now take 22% of 1,250 students:

$$0.22 \times 1250 = 275 \text{ students}$$

36. **(D)** If the volume of the pyramid is 750 cm³ and the dimensions of the square base are 5 × 5 = 25 cm², then we have

$$V = \frac{1}{3}lwh$$

Since V = 750 cm³ and lw = 25 cm², we have: $750 = \frac{1}{3}h(25) = \frac{25}{3}h$. Multiply both sides by $\frac{3}{25}$ to get $h = 750 \times \frac{3}{25} = 90$ cm.

37. **(B)** The median number of movies people watched is found by first listing the number of movies watched in order from least to greatest, and then finding the middle value in the list. When the number of movies watched by each of the 21 people is ordered from least to greatest, the median is the 11th number of movies. The list is as follows: 0, 0, 1, 1, 1, 1, 1, 2, 2, 2, 2, 3, 3, 3, 4, 4, 4, 4, 4, 4, 6. The histogram indicates that the eleventh number (median) of movies watched is 2 because there were 11 people who watched between 0 to 2 movies, and 10 people who watched between 3 and 6.

38. **(B)** The question asks for what values of x is $x^2 - x - 12$ greater than zero. The graph shows the values of $x^2 - x - 12$ on the y-axis and the values of x on the x-axis. We can see that when $x > 4$, $x^2 - x - 12 > 0$ because the graph is above the x-axis, where the y values (in this case, $x^2 - x - 12$) are positive. We can see that this is also true when $x < -3$. When x is between −3 and 4, the points on the graph are below the x-axis, where the y values are negative. Therefore, the solution is

$$x < -3 \text{ or } x > 4$$

39. **(B)** Since 30% of the shirts are large-sized, simply multiply 30% by 280: 0.3 × 280 = 84.

40. **(C)** $0.15 = \frac{15}{100} = \frac{3}{20}$

How to interpret your score

We combined the two sections in the test in to one. But this change will not affect how you performed on the sample test. If you got less than 20 problems correct, you are unlikely to pass the test if you were to take the actual GRE Math test today. If you got 20-26 of the problems correctly, you may or may not pass the test. If you got between 27-29 of the problems correctly, you are somewhat likely to pass the test, and if you got 30+ problems correctly, you are very likely to pass the test if you were to take the test today. However, rather than take any chances, even in this case, try to review the sections in this book that cover the problems that you got wrong on the practice test. That way, you can be sure you will pass!

Chapter 1
Arithmetic

Arithmetic is the branch of mathematics that usually deals with nonnegative real numbers and includes the four fundamental operations: addition, subtraction, multiplication, and division.

Before you embark on making any arithmetic calculations, you should try to memorize the multiplication table below. This will help you invest more time in trying to comprehend the material presented in this workbook rather than in performing tedious calculations. Additionally, certain calculations involved in our chapters and on the actual test you take can be done faster in your head than by pressing buttons on the calculator.

Multiplication Table

$1 \times 1 = 1$	$1 \times 4 = 4$	$1 \times 7 = 7$	$1 \times 10 = 10$
$1 \times 2 = 2$	$1 \times 5 = 5$	$1 \times 8 = 8$	$1 \times 11 = 11$
$1 \times 3 = 3$	$1 \times 6 = 6$	$1 \times 9 = 9$	$1 \times 12 = 12$

$2 \times 1 = 2$	$2 \times 4 = 8$	$2 \times 7 = 14$	$2 \times 10 = 20$
$2 \times 2 = 4$	$2 \times 5 = 10$	$2 \times 8 = 16$	$2 \times 11 = 22$
$2 \times 3 = 6$	$2 \times 6 = 12$	$2 \times 9 = 18$	$2 \times 12 = 24$

$3 \times 1 = 3$	$3 \times 4 = 12$	$3 \times 7 = 21$	$3 \times 10 = 30$
$3 \times 2 = 6$	$3 \times 5 = 15$	$3 \times 8 = 24$	$3 \times 11 = 33$
$3 \times 3 = 9$	$3 \times 6 = 18$	$3 \times 9 = 27$	$3 \times 12 = 36$

$4 \times 1 = 4$	$4 \times 4 = 16$	$4 \times 7 = 28$	$4 \times 10 = 40$
$4 \times 2 = 8$	$4 \times 5 = 20$	$4 \times 8 = 32$	$4 \times 11 = 44$
$4 \times 3 = 12$	$4 \times 6 = 24$	$4 \times 9 = 36$	$4 \times 12 = 48$

$5 \times 1 = 5$	$5 \times 4 = 20$	$5 \times 7 = 35$	$5 \times 10 = 50$
$5 \times 2 = 10$	$5 \times 5 = 25$	$5 \times 8 = 40$	$5 \times 11 = 55$
$5 \times 3 = 15$	$5 \times 6 = 30$	$5 \times 9 = 45$	$5 \times 12 = 60$

$6 \times 1 = 6$	$6 \times 4 = 24$	$6 \times 7 = 42$	$6 \times 10 = 60$
$6 \times 2 = 12$	$6 \times 5 = 30$	$6 \times 8 = 48$	$6 \times 11 = 66$
$6 \times 3 = 18$	$6 \times 6 = 36$	$6 \times 9 = 54$	$6 \times 12 = 72$

$7 \times 1 = 7$	$7 \times 4 = 28$	$7 \times 7 = 49$	$7 \times 10 = 70$
$7 \times 2 = 14$	$7 \times 5 = 35$	$7 \times 8 = 56$	$7 \times 11 = 77$
$7 \times 3 = 21$	$7 \times 6 = 42$	$7 \times 9 = 63$	$7 \times 12 = 84$

$8 \times 1 = 8$	$8 \times 4 = 32$	$8 \times 7 = 56$	$8 \times 10 = 80$
$8 \times 2 = 16$	$8 \times 5 = 40$	$8 \times 8 = 64$	$8 \times 11 = 88$
$8 \times 3 = 24$	$8 \times 6 = 48$	$8 \times 9 = 72$	$8 \times 12 = 96$

$9 \times 1 = 9$	$9 \times 4 = 36$	$9 \times 7 = 63$	$9 \times 10 = 90$
$9 \times 2 = 18$	$9 \times 5 = 45$	$9 \times 8 = 72$	$9 \times 11 = 99$
$9 \times 3 = 27$	$9 \times 6 = 54$	$9 \times 9 = 81$	$9 \times 12 = 108$

$10 \times 1 = 10$	$10 \times 4 = 40$	$10 \times 7 = 70$	$10 \times 10 = 100$
$10 \times 2 = 20$	$10 \times 5 = 50$	$10 \times 8 = 80$	$10 \times 11 = 110$
$10 \times 3 = 30$	$10 \times 6 = 60$	$10 \times 9 = 90$	$10 \times 12 = 120$

$11 \times 1 = 11$	$11 \times 4 = 44$	$11 \times 7 = 77$	$11 \times 10 = 110$
$11 \times 2 = 22$	$11 \times 5 = 55$	$11 \times 8 = 88$	$11 \times 11 = 121$
$11 \times 3 = 33$	$11 \times 6 = 66$	$11 \times 9 = 99$	$11 \times 12 = 132$

$12 \times 1 = 12$	$12 \times 4 = 48$	$12 \times 7 = 84$	$12 \times 10 = 120$
$12 \times 2 = 24$	$12 \times 5 = 60$	$12 \times 8 = 96$	$12 \times 11 = 132$
$12 \times 3 = 36$	$12 \times 6 = 72$	$12 \times 9 = 108$	$12 \times 12 = 144$

Chapter 1: Arithmetic

Addition

Addition is the process of adding together two or more numbers. An addition sentence is a mathematical equation that includes two or more numbers, the **addends**, added together, and the answer, the **sum**.

Addition Sentence

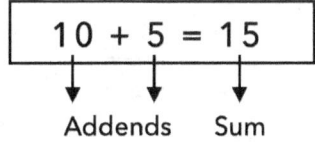

Addends Sum

This sentence is read as "10 plus 5 equals 15."

Addition problems can be solved using column addition. To set up column addition, write one number above the other so that the hundreds, tens, and ones place are lined up, and draw a line under the bottom number. Then, starting from the ones place digits, add together the numbers. If the sum of the numbers in the first column is greater than 10, write the ones place digit below the line and carry the tens place digit above to the next digit place to the left. This process of changing groups of ones into tens is called **regrouping**.

Example 1. What is $348 + 549$?

(A) 201
(B) 887
(C) 897
(D) 900
(E) 997

Answer: C.

$$\begin{array}{r} 1 \\ 348 \\ +\;549 \\ \hline 897 \end{array}$$

First, add the ones place digits together $(8 + 9 = 17)$. Since this yields an integer greater than 9, place the 1, from the tens place in 17, above the tens place column and write the 7, from the ones place in 17, below the line in the ones place column.

$$\begin{array}{r} 1 \\ 348 \\ +\;549 \\ \hline 7 \end{array}$$

Then, add the tens place digits together $(1 + 4 + 4 = 9)$, and write the 9 in the tens place column.

$$\begin{array}{r} 1 \\ 348 \\ +\;549 \\ \hline 97 \end{array}$$

Finally, add the hundreds place column $(3 + 5 = 8)$ and write the 8 in the hundreds place column.

Subtraction

Subtraction is the process of taking one number away from another. A subtraction sentence is a mathematical equation that includes one number that is to be subtracted from, the **minuend**, and the other number that is to be subtracted, the **subtrahend**, and the result of subtracting one number from another, the **difference**.

Subtraction Sentence

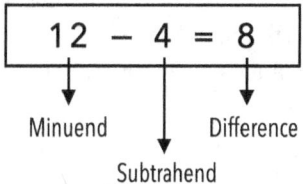

Minuend   Difference
    Subtrahend

This sentence is read "12 minus 4 equals 8."

Subtraction problems can be solved using column subtraction. To set up column subtraction, write down the minuend first and the subtrahend directly below it so that the ones places of both numbers are directly on top of one another, and then draw a line under the subtrahend. Then, starting from the ones place digits, subtract the subtrahend from the minuend. If the minuend is greater than the subtrahend, subtract the numbers and write the answer directly in the column below. If the subtrahend is greater than the minuend, "borrow" a digit from the next place over to the left by subtracting 1 from this number and adding 10 to the top number in the column directly to the right. Now the minuend will be greater than the subtrahend since a 1 from the tens place was borrowed from the number to the left, thus adding 10 to the minuend on the right. As a reminder, this process of changing groups of ones into tens is called regrouping.

Example 2. What is $523 - 282$?

(A) 231
(B) 241
(C) 251
(D) 341
(E) 351

Answer: B.

$$\begin{array}{r} 5\ 2\ 3 \\ -\ 2\ 8\ 2 \\ \hline 1 \end{array}$$

First, subtract the ones place digits. The minuend 3 in the ones place is greater than the subtrahend 2, so subtract the ones place digits $(3 - 2 = 1)$ and write the answer 1 below the line in the ones place column.

$$\begin{array}{r} {}^{4}\ {}^{12} \\ \cancel{5}\ \cancel{2}\ 3 \\ -\ 2\ 8\ 2 \\ \hline 4\ 1 \end{array}$$

Then, subtract the tens place digits. The minuend 2 in the tens place is smaller than the subtrahend 8, so "borrow" a digit from the next place over to

the left, the 5, by subtracting 1 from this number $(5 - 1 = 4)$ and adding 10 to the top number in the column directly to the right $(10 + 2 = 12)$. Now, subtract the subtrahend, 8, from new minuend 12, $(12 - 8 = 4)$ and write the answer 4 below the line in the tens place column.

$$\begin{array}{r} {}^{4}\ {}^{12} \\ \cancel{5}\ \cancel{2}\ 3 \\ -\ 2\ 8\ 2 \\ \hline 2\ 4\ 1 \end{array}$$

Finally, subtract the hundreds place column. The minuend 4 in the hundreds place is greater than the subtrahend 2, so subtract the hundreds place digits $(4 - 2 = 2)$ and write the answer 2 below the line in the hundreds place column.

Multiplication

Multiplication is the process of adding a number to itself a specified number of times. A multiplication sentence is a mathematical equation that includes one number, the **multiplicand**, that is multiplied by another number, the **multiplier**, and the answer that results from multiplying these numbers together, the **product**. Additionally, note that both the multiplicand and the multiplier are **factors** of the product. The multiplication sign can be written as ×, •, or *.

Multiplication Sentence

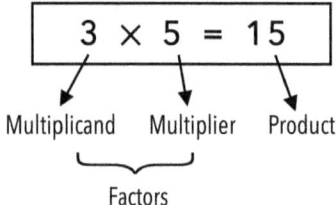

This sentence is read as "3 times 5 equals 15."

Multiplication problems can be solved using column multiplication. To set up column multiplication, write the second factor directly below the first factor so that the ones places of

Chapter 1: Arithmetic

both numbers are directly on top of one another and draw a line under the bottom number. Starting from the ones place digits of the multiplier, multiply this digit first by the ones place digit of the multiplicand, then by the tens place digit of the multiplicand, and finally by the hundreds place digit of the multiplicand. If the product of any of the factors is greater than 10 use regrouping to write the ones place digit below the line and carry the tens place digit to the next digit place to the left. This digit will be added to the next set of factors after they are multiplied. In the next line below, write a 0 in the ones place. Then, following all the same steps, multiply the tens place digit of the multiplier by the ones place digit of the multiplicand, then by the tens place digit of the multiplicand, and finally by the hundreds place digit of the multiplicand. Continue this pattern of placing 0's in the corresponding places on the multiplier that have already been multiplied until all digits of the multiplier have been multiplied by all digits of the multiplicand. Finally, add all of the products together to yield the final product of the multiplication problem.

Example 3. What is 841×134?

- (A) 3,364
- (B) 6,728
- (C) 25,230
- (D) 112,694
- (E) 672,800

Answer: D.

$$\begin{array}{r} 1 \\ 841 \\ \times\ 134 \\ \hline 3364 \end{array}$$

First, multiply the ones place digit of the multiplier 4 by the ones place digit of the multiplicand 1 $(4 \times 1 = 4)$ and write the product 4 below the line in the ones place column. Then, multiply the ones place digit of the multiplier 4 by the tens place digit of the multiplicand 4 $(4 \times 4 = 16)$. Since the product 16 is greater than 10 use regrouping to write the ones place digit 6 below the line in the tens place column and carry the tens place digit 1 to the next digit place to the left. Finally, multiply the ones place digit of the multiplier 4 by the hundreds place digit of the multiplicand 8 $(4 \times 8 = 32)$ and add the 1 that was carried $(32 + 1 = 33)$. Write this number 33 below the line in the hundreds place column.

$$\begin{array}{r} 1 \\ \cancel{1} \\ 841 \\ \times\ 134 \\ \hline 3364 \\ 25230 \end{array}$$

In the next line below write a 0 in the ones place. Now, follow all the same steps as previously described. First, multiply the tens place digit of the multiplier 3 by the ones place digit of multiplicand 1 $(3 \times 1 = 3)$ and write the product 3 below the line in the tens place column. Then, multiply the tens place digit of the multiplier 3 by the tens place digit of the multiplicand 4 $(3 \times 4 = 12)$. Since the product 12 is greater than 10 use regrouping to write the ones place digit 2 below the line in the hundreds place column and carry the tens place digit 1 to the next digit place to the left. Finally, multiply the tens place digit of the multiplier 3 by the hundreds place digit of the multiplicand 8 $(3 \times 8 = 24)$ and add the 1 that was carried $(24 + 1 = 25)$. Write this number 25 below the line in the thousands place column.

$$\begin{array}{r} \cancel{1} \\ \cancel{1} \\ 841 \\ \times\ 134 \\ \hline 3364 \\ 25230 \\ 84100 \end{array}$$

Now, in the next line below, write a 0 in the ones place and a 0 in the tens place. Again, follow all the same steps as previously described. First, multiply the hundreds place digit of the multiplier 1 by the ones place digit of multiplicand 1 $(1 \times 1 = 1)$ and write the product 1 below the line in the hundreds place column. Then, multiply the hundreds place digit of the multiplier 1 by the tens place digit of the multiplicand 4 ($1 \times 4 = 4$). Finally, multiply the hundreds place digit of the multiplier 1 by the hundreds place digit of the multiplicand 8 ($1 \times 8 = 8$) and write the product 8 in the ten thousands place column.

$$
\begin{array}{r}
\cancel{1} \\
\cancel{1} \\
8\,4\,1 \\
\times\ \ 1\,3\,4 \\
\hline
{}_1 3\,3\,6\,4 \\
2\,5\,2\,3\,0 \\
+\ \ 8\,4\,1\,0\,0 \\
\hline
1\,1\,2\,6\,9\,4
\end{array}
$$

Now that all digits of the multiplier have been multiplied by all digits of the multiplicand, the final step is to add all of the products together to yield the final product of the multiplication problem.

Multiplication with Decimals

The first step to multiply an integer by a decimal is to write the second factor directly below the first factor WITHOUT aligning the decimal points. Then, draw a line under the bottom number. Now, the multiplication process is the same as previously explained: starting on the right, multiply each digit in the top number by each digit in the bottom number, and then add the products together. The final step is to insert the decimal point in the answer by starting at the right of the answer and moving the same number of places as the number of places after the decimal point in the decimal.

Example 4. What is $16 \times 0.25 \times 200$?

Ⓐ 80

Ⓑ 400

Ⓒ 800

Ⓓ 1,600

Ⓔ 40,000

Answer: C.

$$
\begin{array}{r}
\cancel{3} \\
1\,6 \\
\times\ \ .2\,5 \\
\hline
{}_1 8\,0 \\
+3\,2\,0 \\
\hline
4.0\,0
\end{array}
$$

First, multiply 16×0.25. Write the second factor, 0.25, directly below the first factor, 16, without aligning the decimal points. Then, multiply the ones digits of the multiplier 5 by the ones digit of the multiplicand 6 ($5 \times 6 = 30$). Since the product is greater than 10, write the ones place digit 0 below the line and carry the tens place digit 3 to the next digit place to the left. Then, multiply the ones digit of the multiplier 5 by the tens digit of the multiplicand 1 ($5 \times 1 = 5$) and add the 3 ($5 + 3 = 8$). Write the answer 8 below the line. In the next line below write a 0 in the ones place. Then, repeat these steps until all the digits of the multiplier have been multiplied by all the digits of the multiplicand. Finally, add the products together ($80 + 320 = 400$). The final step is to insert the decimal point in the answer by starting at the right of the answer and moving the same number of places as the number of places after the decimal point in the decimal to yield the final product of the multiplication problem, 4.00.

$$
\begin{array}{r}
2\,0\,0 \\
\times\ \ \ \ \ 4 \\
\hline
8\,0\,0
\end{array}
$$

Now, multiply this number 4 by 200 ($4 \times 200 = 800$) to yield the final answer, 800.

Division

Division is the process of splitting a number into equal parts. A division sentence is a mathematical equation that includes one number, the **dividend**, that is divided by another number, the **divisor**, and the answer that results from dividing the dividend by the divisor, the **quotient**. The division sign can be written as ÷, /, or —.

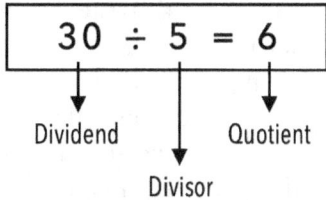

This sentence is read as "30 divided by 5 equals 6."

Division on the GED Math test can be easily done with a calculator, and so we will only do a couple of examples of simple division for the sake of completeness.

Example 5. Divide 132 by 12:

$$\begin{array}{r} 11 \\ 12\overline{)132} \\ \underline{12} \\ 12 \\ \underline{12} \\ 0 \end{array}$$

Here we asked ourselves, "how many times does 12 go into 13?" The answer is 1, so we put a 1 above the 3 in 132. We then multiplied 1 by 12 to get 12 and put the 12 underneath the 13. We subtracted 12 from 13 to obtain 1, then brought the digit 2 in 132 down and put it in front of the 1 on the bottom, to obtain 12. We asked ourselves, "how many times does 12 go into 12?" The answer is one, so we put a 1 in front of the 1 on top to obtain 11.

Sometimes we obtain a remainder when dividing a number by another number as the following example shows.

Example 6. Divide 289 by 7:

$$\begin{array}{r} 41 \\ 7\overline{)289} \\ \underline{28} \\ 9 \\ \underline{7} \\ 2 \end{array}$$

We get 41 plus a remainder of 2, which is equal to $41\frac{2}{7}$. In this problem, we ask ourselves, "how many times does 7 go into 28?" The answer is 4, so put a 4 on top. Bring down the 9. 7 goes into 9 once, so put a 1 above, after the 4. Now subtract 7 from 9 to obtain 2. Since 7 does not go into 2, we get a remainder of 2, which means that the answer is a combination of an integer and a remainder, in this case 41, and a remainder of 2. We can convert the remainder of 2 into a fraction of $\frac{2}{7}$.

We recommend that you use a calculator on the test for complicated calculations to avoid careless errors, but perform the operations in your head for simple calculations.

We also show you now a few division problems involving fractions.

Converting Fractions into Decimals

Fractions are a type of division problem. The line, —, or slash, /, in a fraction separating the **numerator** from the **denominator** can be replaced with a division symbol. The numerator is the top number of the fraction, and the denominator is the bottom number of a fraction. Then, use division to divide the numerator by the denominator in order to convert a fraction into a decimal. In a fraction, the numerator is the dividend and the denominator is the divisor.

To set up the long division problem, write the dividend on the right under the division symbol, $\overline{)}$, and the divisor on the left outside of the division symbol. The quotient will eventually go on top of the division symbol, above the dividend. In fractions, the dividend will always be smaller than the divisor, so it is necessary to add a decimal point with a trailing zero behind the dividend and a zero with a decimal point behind it in front of the quotient.

Begin the long division problem by determining how many times the divisor can go into the dividend with the trailing zero. Write this number behind the decimal point on top of the division symbol. Then multiply this number by the divisor. Write the product under the dividend and subtract. If the subtraction results in a number other than zero, add another zero behind the dividend and bring down this zero, repeating this process until either the subtraction yields an answer of zero or a digit or group of digits begins to repeat over and over again.

When the subtraction yields an answer of zero, or if a digit or group of digits begins to repeat endlessly, the problem is complete, and the fraction has been fully converted into its decimal form. Repeating decimals can be written by drawing a line over the part that repeats.

Example 7. What is $\frac{3}{8}$ as a decimal?

- (A) 0.00385
- (B) 0.027
- (C) 0.165
- (D) 0.375
- (E) 0.875

Answer: D.

```
      0 . 3 7 5
   8 ) 3 . 0 0 0
     - 2 4 ↓
         6 0
       - 5 6 ↓
           4 0
         - 4 0
             0
```

Set up the long division problem by writing the dividend 3 on the right under the division symbol and the divisor 8 on the left outside of the division symbol. Since with fractions the dividend will always be smaller than the divisor, add a decimal point with a trailing zero behind the dividend and a zero with a decimal point behind it, to the quotient. Now, determine how many times the divisor 8 can go into the new number 30. Write this number 3 behind the decimal point on top of the division symbol. Then multiply this number 3 by the divisor 8 ($3 \times 8 = 24$). Write the product 24 under the dividend and subtract ($30 - 24 = 6$). Since the subtraction results in a number other than zero, add another zero behind the dividend and bring down this zero, repeating this process until the subtraction yields an answer of zero. The quotient is 0.375.

Fractions are the most common form of division problems found on the GED Math test, so make sure you understand this section.

Example 8. What is $\frac{5}{6}$ as a decimal?

- (A) 0.03125
- (B) $0.08\overline{3}$
- (C) $0.\overline{1}$
- (D) $0.1\overline{6}$
- (E) $0.8\overline{3}$

Answer: E.

```
       0 . 8 3 3 3
    6 ) 5 . 0 0 0 0
      - 4 8 ↓
          2 0
        - 1 8 ↓
            2 0
          - 1 8 ↓
              2 0
            - 1 8
                2
```

Set up the long division problem by writing the dividend 5 on the right under the division symbol and the divisor 6 on the left, outside of the division symbol. Since with fractions the dividend will always be smaller than the divisor, add a decimal point with a trailing zero behind the dividend and a zero with a decimal point behind it to the quotient. Now, determine how many times the divisor 6 can go into the new number 50. Write this number 8 behind the decimal point on top of the division symbol. Then multiply this number 8 by the divisor 6 ($8 \times 6 = 48$). Write the product 48 under the dividend and subtract ($50 - 48 = 2$). Since the subtraction results in a number other than zero, add another zero behind the dividend and bring down this zero, repeating this process until it is clear that the answer is a repeating decimal since the digit 3 repeats over and over again. Write the repeating decimal by drawing a line over the part that repeats. The quotient is $0.8\bar{3}$.

Multiplication and Division Multistep Operations

Arithmetic problems can include a combination of operations, such as multiplying an integer by a decimal and then multiplying by another integer, dividing an integer by an integer and then multiplying by a decimal, and even multiplying an integer by an integer then dividing by an integer and finally multiplying by another integer. These problems can be tackled by performing one operation at a time, starting from the left and moving toward the right.

Additionally, recall that estimation is a strategic approach to take in order to be the most efficient with time management on the GED test. In multiplication and division multistep operations, use estimation to eliminate answer choices that are unreasonable and choose the answer choice that is the most reasonable.

Example 9. What is $1200 \div 16 \times 0.45$?

- (A) 0.3375
- (B) 3.75
- (C) 33.75
- (D) 337.5
- (E) 3,375

Answer: C.

$$
\begin{array}{r}
75 \\
16{\overline{\smash{\big)}\,1200}} \\
-112\downarrow \\
\hline
80 \\
-80 \\
\hline
0
\end{array}
$$

Set up the long division problem by writing the dividend 1,200 on the right under the division symbol and the divisor 16 on the left outside of the division symbol. Determine how many times the divisor 16 can go into 120. Write this number 7 on top of the division symbol. Then, multiply this number 7 by the divisor 16 ($7 \times 16 = 112$). Write the product 112 under the dividend and subtract ($120 - 112 = 8$). Next, bring down the next digit, 0, and repeat this process. The quotient is 75.

$$
\begin{array}{r}
\overset{2}{}\overset{2}{} \\
75 \\
\times\ .45 \\
\hline
375 \\
3000 \\
\hline
33.75
\end{array}
$$

Now, multiply this number 75 by 0.45 to yield the final answer, 33.75.

Estimation can also be used to solve this problem, as follows:

1,200 is about equal to 1,000
16 is about equal to 20

Start by rounding 1,200 down to 1,000 and 16 up to 20.

Then, divide 1,000 by 20.

$$1000 \div 20 = 50$$

Next, round 0.45 up to 0.5.

$$50 \times 0.5 = 25$$

Finally, multiply 50 by 0.5 to yield the estimate of 25.

Now, look for the answer choice which is closest to 25 and select answer choice (C), 33.75.

Example 10. What is $500 \times 15 \div 6 \times 12$?

- (A) 150
- (B) 1,250
- (C) 7,500
- (D) 15,000
- (E) 22,500

Answer: D. First, multiply 500 by 15 to yield 7,500 ($500 \times 15 = 7500$).

```
      5 0 0
    ×   1 5
    -------
      2 5 0 0
    + 5 0 0 0
    ---------
      7 5 0 0
```

Next, divide 7,500 by 6 ($7500 \div 6 = 1250$).

```
        1 2 5 0
      ┌─────────
    6 │ 7 5 0 0
      - 6 ↓
        ───
        1 5
      - 1 2 ↓
        ─────
            3 0
          - 3 0 ↓
            ─────
                0 0
              -   0
                ───
                  0
```

Finally, multiply 1,250 by 12 to yield the final answer, 15,000 ($1250 \times 12 = 15000$).

```
      1 2 5 0
    ×     1 2
    ─────────
      2 5 0 0
    1 2 5 0 0
    ─────────
    1 5 0 0 0
```

Therefore, answer choice (D) is correct.

Practice Problems

1. What is $297 + 934$?

    Ⓐ 1,121
    Ⓑ 1,131
    Ⓒ 1,221
    Ⓓ 1,231
    Ⓔ 1,331

2. What is $653 + 349$?

    Ⓐ 902
    Ⓑ 992
    Ⓒ 1,002
    Ⓓ 1,112
    Ⓔ 1,902

3. What is $389 + 462$?

    Ⓐ 741
    Ⓑ 751
    Ⓒ 841
    Ⓓ 851
    Ⓔ 951

4. What is $787 - 298$?

    Ⓐ 389
    Ⓑ 399
    Ⓒ 489
    Ⓓ 499
    Ⓔ 589

5. What is $825 - 247$?

    Ⓐ 478
    Ⓑ 578
    Ⓒ 588
    Ⓓ 678
    Ⓔ 688

6. What is $523 - 478$?

    Ⓐ 45
    Ⓑ 55
    Ⓒ 135
    Ⓓ 145
    Ⓔ 155

7. What is 745×345?

    Ⓐ 2,980
    Ⓑ 3,725
    Ⓒ 22,350
    Ⓓ 257,025
    Ⓔ 2,265,525

8. What is 883×24?

    Ⓐ 3,532
    Ⓑ 5,298
    Ⓒ 21,192
    Ⓓ 180,132
    Ⓔ 211,920

9. What is 254×63?

   (A) 762
   (B) 1,524
   (C) 16,002
   (D) 76,200
   (E) 160,020

10. What is 962×834?

    (A) 3,848
    (B) 14,430
    (C) 28,860
    (D) 802,308
    (E) 7,696,000

11. What is $\frac{7}{12}$ as a decimal?

    (A) 0.036
    (B) $0.038\overline{5}$
    (C) $0.058\overline{3}$
    (D) 0.385
    (E) $0.58\overline{3}$

12. What is $\frac{5}{9}$ as a decimal?

    (A) 0.045
    (B) $0.0\overline{45}$
    (C) $0.04\overline{5}$
    (D) $0.4\overline{5}$
    (E) $0.\overline{5}$

13. What is $\frac{13}{15}$ as a decimal?

    (A) $0.00\overline{86}$
    (B) 0.09
    (C) 0.12
    (D) $0.8\overline{6}$
    (E) $0.\overline{86}$

14. What is $\frac{1}{16}$ as a decimal?

    (A) 0.016
    (B) 0.0625
    (C) 0.16
    (D) 0.625
    (E) $0.6\overline{25}$

15. What is $30 \times 0.15 \times 175$?

    (A) 45
    (B) 78.75
    (C) 787.5
    (D) 2,625
    (E) 10,000

16. What is $1,800 \div 20 \times 0.85$?

    (A) 17
    (B) 76.5
    (C) 900
    (D) 30,600
    (E) 7,650

17. What is $850 \times 18 \div 12 \times 4$?

   (A) 510
   (B) 1,275
   (C) 5,100
   (D) 15,300
   (E) 734,400

18. What is $16 \times 0.0625 \times 40$?

   (A) 4
   (B) 40
   (C) 400
   (D) 4,000
   (E) 40,000

19. What is $2,208 \div 92 \times 0.875$?

   (A) 2
   (B) 21
   (C) 72
   (D) 240
   (E) 2,168

20. What is $316 \times 13 \div 4 \times 41$?

   (A) 25
   (B) 1,027
   (C) 4,108
   (D) 42,107
   (E) 673,712

Answers to Practice Problems

1. **(D)** Write one addend, 297, on top of the other addend, 934. Solve using column addition and regrouping to yield the sum 1,231.

2. **(C)** Write one addend, 653, on top of the other addend, 349. Solve using column addition and regrouping to yield the sum 1,002.

3. **(D)** Write one addend, 389, on top of the other addend, 462. Solve using column addition and regrouping to yield the sum 851.

4. **(C)** Write the minuend, 787, first and the subtrahend, 298, directly below it. Solve using column subtraction and regrouping to yield the difference 489.

5. **(B)** Write the minuend, 825, first and the subtrahend, 247, directly below it. Solve using column subtraction and regrouping to yield the difference 578.

6. **(A)** Write the minuend, 523, first and the subtrahend, 478, directly below it. Solve using column subtraction and regrouping to yield the difference 45.

7. **(D)** Write the second factor, 345, directly below the first factor, 745. Solve using column multiplication and regrouping. Alternatively, use rounding and estimation to eliminate wrong answers and select the correct answer 257,025.

8. **(C)** Write the second factor, 24, directly below the first factor, 883. Solve using column multiplication and regrouping. Alternatively, use rounding and estimation to eliminate wrong answers and select the correct answer, 21,192.

9. **(C)** Write the second factor, 63, directly below the first factor, 254. Solve using column multiplication and regrouping. Alternatively, use rounding and estimation to eliminate wrong answers and select the correct answer, 16,002.

10. **(D)** Write the second factor, 834, directly below the first factor, 962. Solve using column multiplication and regrouping. Alternatively, use rounding and estimation to eliminate wrong answers and select the correct answer, 802,308.

11. **(E)** Use long division to divide the numerator, 7, by the denominator, 12. Remember, repeating decimals can be written by drawing a line over the part that repeats. Alternatively, use estimation to eliminate wrong answers and select the correct answer, $0.58\overline{3}$.

12. **(E)** Use long division to divide the numerator, 5, by the denominator, 9. Remember, repeating decimals can be written by drawing a line over the part that repeats. Alternatively, use estimation to eliminate wrong answers and select the correct answer, $0.\overline{5}$.

13. **(D)** Use long division to divide the numerator, 13, by the denominator, 15. Remember, repeating decimals can be written by drawing a line over the part that repeats. Alternatively, use estimation to eliminate wrong answers and select the correct answer, $0.8\overline{6}$.

14. **(B)** Use long division to divide the numerator, 1, by the denominator, 16. Alternatively, use estimation to eliminate wrong answers and select the correct answer, 0.0625.

Chapter 1: Arithmetic

15. **(C)** First, multiply 30 by 0.15 using column multiplication and regrouping. Then, multiply the product 4.5 by 175 using column multiplication and regrouping to yield the final answer 787.5. Alternatively, multiply twice using rounding and estimation to eliminate wrong answers and select the correct answer.

16. **(B)** First, divide 1,800 by 20 using long division. Then, multiply the quotient 90 by 0.85 using column multiplication and regrouping to yield the final answer 76.5. Alternatively, divide and then multiply using rounding and estimation to eliminate wrong answers and select the correct answer.

17. **(C)** First, multiply 850 by 18 using column multiplication and regrouping. Then, divide the product 15,300 by 12 using long division. Finally, multiply the quotient 1,275 by 4 using column multiplication and regrouping to yield the final answer 5,100. Alternatively, multiply, divide, and then multiply using rounding and estimation to eliminate wrong answers and select the correct answer.

18. **(B)** First, multiply 16 by 0.0625 using column multiplication and regrouping. Then, multiply the product 1 by 40 to yield the final answer 40. Alternatively, multiply twice using rounding and estimation to eliminate wrong answers and select the correct answer.

19. **(B)** First, divide 2,208 by 92 using long division. Then, multiply the quotient 24 by 0.875 using column multiplication and regrouping to yield the final answer 21. Alternatively, divide and then multiply using rounding and estimation to eliminate wrong answers and select the correct answer.

20. **(D)** First, multiply 316 by 13 using column multiplication and regrouping. Then, divide the product 4,108 by 4 using long division. Finally, multiply the quotient 1,027 by 41 using column multiplication and regrouping to yield the final answer 42,107. Alternatively, multiply, divide, and then multiply using rounding and estimation to eliminate wrong answers and select the correct answer.

Chapter 2
Numbers - Miscellaneous Topics

In this chapter, we will talk about prime numbers, even and odd numbers, and definitions for natural, whole, real, irrational and rational numbers.

Natural and Whole Numbers

The **natural** (or **counting**) **numbers** are 1, 2, 3, 4, 5, 6, 7, 8, 9, 10, etc. There are infinitely many natural numbers.

The **whole numbers** are the natural numbers together with 0.

The sum of any two natural numbers is also a natural number, and the product of any two natural numbers is a natural number. This is not true for subtraction and division, though.

The Integers

The **integers** are the set of real numbers consisting of the whole numbers, and their additive inverse. The additive inverse of 1 is −1, the additive inverse of 5 is −5, etc. The sum, product, and difference of any two integers is also an integer. But this is not true for division.

The Rational Numbers

The **rational numbers** are those numbers which can be expressed as a ratio between two integers. For example, the fractions $\frac{10}{41}$ and $\frac{3}{13}$ are both rational numbers. All the integers are included in the rational numbers, since any integer can be written as the ratio. For example, 5, an integer, can be expressed as $\frac{10}{2}$, which is a ratio of two integers.

All decimals that terminate are rational numbers (since for example 824.56 can be written as 82556/100). Decimals which have a repeating pattern after some point are also rational. For example, 0.444444 is equal to $\frac{444444}{1000000}$. Another example is 0.123123123, since this number can be written as $\frac{123123123}{1000000000}$.

Given any two rational numbers, their sum, difference, product, and quotient is also a rational number (except for a division by zero).

The Irrational Numbers

An **irrational number** is a number that cannot be written as a ratio (or fraction). In decimal form, it never ends or repeats.

Examples of irrational numbers are square roots of numbers that are not perfect squares, for example, $\sqrt{2}, \sqrt{3}, \sqrt{5}$. The number pi, $\pi = 3.14159265...$ is also an irrational number. π is the circumference of a circle divided by its diameter.

Another example is Euler's Number,

$$e = 2.7182818284590452353...$$

which is an important number used in calculus.

Real Numbers

Real numbers represent the set of numbers containing all of the rational numbers and all of the irrational numbers. The real numbers are all the numbers on the number line. There are infinitely many real numbers.

Imaginary Numbers

Imaginary numbers include numbers such as $\sqrt{-1}, \sqrt{-4}$, etc. You will not be tested on imaginary numbers on the GED Math test, and therefore we will not discuss them any further in this book.

Odd and Even numbers

An **even number** is a number that can be divided evenly by 2. That is, after you divide an even number by 2, you get an integer. Even numbers are

$$... -8, -6, -4, -2, 0, 2, 4, 6, 8, ...$$

An even number can be represented as $2n$, where n is an integer. For example, 12 is an even number because $12 = 2n$, where $n = 6$.

An **odd number** is a number that cannot be divided evenly by 2.

The result of dividing an odd number by 2 would be a number that is not an integer. Odd numbers are

$$..., -5, -3, -1, 1, 3, 5, 7, 9, ...$$

An odd number can be represented as $2n + 1$, where n is an integer. For example, 11 is an odd number because $11 = 2n + 1$, where $n = 5$.

Example 1. The sum of two consecutive odd numbers is 100. What are these two odd numbers?

Answer: 49 and 51. Call the first odd number n, and the second one $n + 2$ (because the next odd integer is 2 more than the previous one). Note: You can use $2n + 1$ as your first odd number, but this is not necessary as the solution will work just as well if you use n as your first number. In fact, you can use n as your first number for an even number as well, as in example 2. So

$$n + (n + 2) = 2n + 2 = 100$$

yielding $n = \dfrac{98}{2} = 49$. The next odd number is $49 + 2 = 51$.

Example 2. The sum of 5 consecutive even numbers is 200. What is the first of those numbers?

Answer: 36. Call the first even integer n. The second even integer would be $n + 2$, then $n + 4$, then $n + 6$, and finally $n + 8$. Adding them up we get $5n + 20 = 200$. Solving for n, we get, $5n = 180$, so $n = 36$.

Example 3. What is the average of the first 11 natural odd numbers?

Answer: 11. The first natural odd number is 1, then 3, 5, 7, 9, 11, 13, 15, 17, 19, 21. The average value can be found by $\dfrac{1 + 21}{2} = 11$. You can look at the middle value of the 11 terms, which is the 6th term, and find that it is equal to 11. To understand this better, let's look at a simpler example. To find the average of 3 numbers, say 5, 7, and 9, we see that the average of the three numbers in the list is (5 + 7 + 9) / 3 = 7. 7 is also the middle number in the list. We state without rigorous proof that in a list of consecutive odd numbers, the average of the numbers is the middle number. Therefore, in this example, 7 is the average of the three numbers based on the middle value being 7. This works for all odd and even numbers. In fact, it works if 0 is in the list. For example, to take the average of −10, −8, −6, −4, −2, 0, 2, 4, 6, 8, 10, zero is the middle number in the list, and therefore the average of the numbers is zero.

Prime Numbers

A **prime number** is a natural number greater than 1 that is *not* a product of two smaller natural numbers. That is, it is divisible only by 1 and itself. The first prime number is 2 since 2 is the product of 1 and 2. Prime numbers include

2, 3, 5, 7, 11, 13, 17, 19, 23, etc.

15 is not a prime number since it is the product of 3 and 5, which are numbers different from 1 and itself (15).

A **composite number** is a whole number that can be made by multiplying other whole numbers. A composite number is any number that is not prime, other than 1, such as 4, 12, 25, etc. The number 1 is neither prime nor composite.

Example 4. Which of the following are composite numbers?

Choose all answers that apply.

   [A] 1
   [B] 2
   [C] 3
   [D] 6
   [E] 11

Answer: D. In choice **A**, 1 is neither prime nor composite. Choices **B**, **C**, and **E** are all prime. Choice **D** is correct because 6 is equal to 2 × 3.

Example 5. What is the sum of the first 5 prime numbers?

   (A) 18
   (B) 21
   (C) 23
   (D) 26
   (E) 28

Answer: E. The first 5 prime numbers are 2, 3, 5, 7, 11. Therefore 2 + 3 + 5 + 7 + 11 = 28.

Factors, Multiples, Divisors, and Denominators

The GED Math exam might ask you to find the greatest common divisor, greatest common factor, the least common multiple, or the smallest common denominator. The smallest common denominator (or least common denominator) is covered in chapter 4 on fractions. Let's review the other terms you are responsible for knowing on the exam.

The **greatest common divisor** or **greatest common factor** of two or more integers, which are not all zero, is the largest positive integer that goes into two or more integers without remainder. For example, the greatest common divisor of 16 and 24 is 8 because 8 is the largest number that goes into 16 and 24 without a remainder.

The **least common multiple** of two or more integers, also called **lowest common multiple**, or **smallest common multiple,** is the smallest positive integer that is evenly divisible by both those numbers.

Chapter 2: Numbers - Miscellaneous Topics

The above terms may be mistakenly interchanged since there are so many of them and they sound alike. Let's go over the difference:

The **least/lowest/smallest common multiple (LCM)** of numbers is the smallest number (excluding zero) that is a multiple of those numbers.

The **greatest common factor** or **greatest common divisor** of two or more numbers is the product of all the prime factors the numbers have in common.

Example 7. What is the greatest common divisor of 24 and 60?

(A) 4
(B) 6
(C) 12
(D) 20
(E) 24

Answer: C. Ask yourself what numbers go into 24 evenly (besides 1). They are 2, 4, 6, 8, 12, 24. What numbers go into 60 evenly? They are 2, 4, 5, 6, 10, 12, 15, 20, 30, 60. Which number is the greatest of those numbers that is common to 24 and 60? We see that 2, 4, 6, 12 are the only numbers that are common to both. Of those numbers, 12 is obviously the greatest number. Therefore 12 is the greatest common divisor.

Example 8. What is the greatest common factor of 16 and 44?

(A) 1
(B) 2
(C) 3
(D) 4
(E) 11

Answer: D. This example is asking for the same information as example 6 (applied to different numbers) except for the fact that the question asks for the term greatest common factor instead of greatest common divisor, which are identical terms. The factors of 16 besides 1 are 2, 4, 8, and 16. The factors of 44 are 2, 4, and 11. Which of those numbers is the greatest common number? 2 and 4 are common to both numbers. 4 is the greater of the two.

Example 9. Find the least common multiple of 24 and 60.

- (A) 12
- (B) 48
- (C) 60
- (D) 90
- (E) 120

Answer: E. To find the least common multiple of two numbers, first list the prime factors of each number:

$$24 = 2 \times 2 \times 2 \times 3$$
$$60 = 2 \times 2 \times 3 \times 5$$

Now, multiply each prime factor the greatest number of times it occurs in either number. If the same factor occurs more than once in both numbers, you don't have to include them twice.

For 24, we have 3 occurrences of 2, and in 60 we have 2 occurrences of 2. Therefore, we take the 3 factors of 2 in 24 and ignore the two factors of 2 in 60. Both 24 and 60 have one 3 in them, so we use the factor of 3, and in the number 60 we have an occurrence of 5. Therefore, we multiply three 2's by one 3 by one 5 to get

$$2 \times 2 \times 2 \times 3 \times 5 = 120$$

To check your answer, make sure both numbers go into your answer evenly. In this case check to see if 24 goes into 120 evenly and whether 60 goes into 120 evenly. They do in fact, so 120 is our answer.

Example 10. Find the smallest common multiple of 12, 18, and 24.

- (A) 24
- (B) 36
- (C) 48
- (D) 72
- (E) 96

Answer: D. The prime factors of 12, 18, and 24 are, respectively,

$$12 = 2 \times 2 \times 3$$
$$18 = 2 \times 3 \times 3$$
$$24 = 2 \times 2 \times 2 \times 3$$

We see that 2 is repeated three times in 24, so we pick those three 2's. We also see that there are two 3's in 18, so we pick two 3's. Thus we have

$$2 \times 2 \times 2 \times 3 \times 3 = 72$$

Example 11. Find the least common multiple of 9, 15, and 25.

- (A) 75
- (B) 135
- (C) 225
- (D) 275
- (E) 3375

Answer: C. The prime factors of 9, 15, and 25 are, respectively,

$$9 = 3 \times 3$$
$$15 = 3 \times 5$$
$$25 = 5 \times 5$$

Take both three 3's from the 9 and both 5's from the 25 to obtain

$$3 \times 3 \times 5 \times 5 = 225$$

Place Values

One last topic about numbers that could appear on your GED Math test is place values. The place value is the value of where a digit is in the number.

For example, in 485, the 8 is in the "tens" place, so its place value is 10.

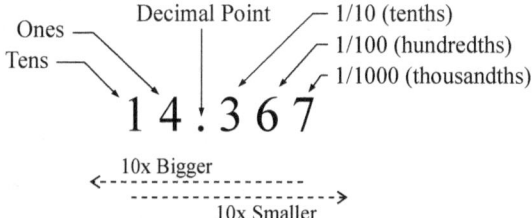

As another example, in 14.367, the 6 is in the hundredths place, so its place value is 0.01.

Example 12. What is the place value of 8 in 56.9782?

- (A) 0.0001
- (B) 0.001
- (C) 0.01
- (D) 0.1
- (E) 10

Answer: B. The 8 is in the thousandths place, so its place value is 0.001.

Example 13. What is the place value of 5 in 5042.67?

- (A) 100
- (B) 500
- (C) 1,000
- (D) 5,000
- (E) 10,000

Answer: C. The 5 is in the thousands place, so its face value is 1,000. Its place name is thousands.

Practice Problems

1. What is the product of the first 3 prime numbers?

   (A) 15
   (B) 24
   (C) 28
   (D) 29
   (E) 30

2. The sum of 5 consecutive odd integers is 75. What is the third integer?

   (A) 11
   (B) 13
   (C) 15
   (D) 17
   (E) 19

3. The sum of 4 consecutive even numbers is 20. What is their product?

   (A) 120
   (B) 164
   (C) 224
   (D) 384
   (E) 416

4. How many prime numbers are there between 1 and 50?

   (A) 12
   (B) 13
   (C) 14
   (D) 15
   (E) 16

5. What is the greatest common factor of 8, 12, 20, and 36?

   (A) 2
   (B) 4
   (C) 6
   (D) 8
   (E) 10

6. Find the least common multiple of 8, 12, and 36.

   (A) 2
   (B) 3
   (C) 24
   (D) 72
   (E) 144

7. Find the smallest common multiple of 12, 30, and 42.

    (A) 3
    (B) 4
    (C) 120
    (D) 240
    (E) 420

8. What is the greatest common factor of 16, 24, and 36?

    (A) 2
    (B) 4
    (C) 8
    (D) 72
    (E) 144

9. What is the place name of 6 in 467.048?

    (A) Tenths
    (B) Tens
    (C) Hundredths
    (D) Hundreds
    (E) Thousands

Answers to Practice Problems

1. **(E)** The first 3 prime numbers are 2, 3, and 5, and so the product is $2 \times 3 \times 5 = 30$.

2. **(C)** We can call the first odd integer n. The next 4 odd integers is $n + 2, n + 4, n + 6$, and $n + 8$. The sum is $5n + 2 + 4 + 6 + 8 = 5n + 20$. So we have $5n + 20 = 75$. Solving for n we get $5n = 55$, and so $n = 11$. The first odd integer therefore is 11. The second is 13, and the third is 15.

3. **(D)** We call the first even number n, and therefore the next 3 are $n + 2, n + 4$, and $n + 6$. The sum is

    $n + (n + 2) + (n + 4) + (n + 6) = 4n + 12$

    Therefore we have $4n + 12 = 20$. Solving for n we get $4n = 8$, so $n = 2$. The first even integer therefore is 2. The next 3 even integers are 4, 6, and 8. Therefore the product is $2 \times 4 \times 6 \times 8 = 384$.

4. **(D)** The prime numbers between 1 and 50 are 2, 3, 5, 7, 11, 13, 17, 19, 23, 29, 31, 37, 41, 43, 47. Thus, the total number is 15.

5. **(B)** 8 is divisible by 2, 4, and 8. 12 is divisible by 2, 3, 4, 6, and 12. 20 is divisible by 2, 4, 5, 10, and 20. 36 is divisible by 2, 4, 6, 9, 12, 18, and 36. The largest number that is common to those lists is 4.

6. **(D)** $8 = 2 \times 2 \times 2$, $12 = 2 \times 2 \times 3$ and $36 = 2 \times 2 \times 3 \times 3$. We pick the three 2's in 8 and the two 3's in 36 to get

    $2 \times 2 \times 2 \times 3 \times 3 = 72$

7. **(E)** $12 = 2 \times 2 \times 3$, $30 = 2 \times 3 \times 5$ and $42 = 2 \times 3 \times 7$. We pick two 2's in 12, one 3, one 5 and one 7 to get

    $2 \times 2 \times 3 \times 5 \times 7 = 420$

8. **(B)** The factors of 16 are 2, 4, 8, and 16. The factors of 24 are 2, 3, 4, 6, 8, 12, and 24. The factors of 36 are 2, 3, 4, 6, 9, 12, 18, and 36. The largest number that appears in all three lists is 4. If you got choice **E**, you calculated the least common multiple, not the greatest common factor.

9. **(B)** The place name of 6 is tens.

Chapter 3
Negative Numbers

In mathematics, every real number (other than zero) is positive or negative. Negative numbers are real numbers that are less than zero. The figure below shows a real number line.

Real Number Line

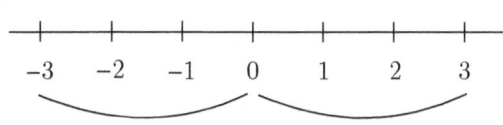

Figure 1

On a real number line, the negative numbers are located to the left of the zero, and the positive numbers are located to the right of the zero. Positive numbers are found to the right of zero and get larger and larger as you move farther rightward. Negative numbers are found to the left of zero and get smaller and smaller as you move farther leftward. Zero is always greater than negative numbers and less than positive numbers.

The sign > means greater than. The number to the left of the sign > is greater than the number to the right of the sign.

The sign < means smaller than. The number to the left of the sign < is smaller than the number to the right of the sign.

For example:

- $30 > 3$ because 30 is further from 0 than 3 on the number line.
- $-30 < -3$ because -3 is closer to 0 than -30 on the number line.
- $1000 > 0$ because 1000 is a positive number to the right of the zero on the number line.
- $-1000 < 0$ because -1000 is a negative number to the left of the zero on the number line.

Operations with Negative Numbers

The operations with negative numbers have more rules than the operations with positive numbers. The best way to master calculations using negative numbers is to treat positive and negative numbers as directed distances. For example, a positive number, 2, can be represented as a person moving two steps to the right of zero on a real number line. A negative number, -2, can be represented as a person moving two steps to the left of zero. Keep these rules in mind–we will continue to learn addition, subtraction, multiplication, and division of negative numbers.

1. Three Rules of Thumb for Addition

> **Rule 1:** When adding two positive numbers, the sum is positive.

Example: $2 + 3 = 5$

Explanation: A woman walks two steps to the right from zero and lands on +2. She continues to walk three to the right from 2 and ends up at +5. Positive direction has a sign, +.

> **Rule 2:** When adding two negative numbers, the sum is negative.

Example: $-2 + (-3) = -5$

Explanation: A woman walks two steps to the left from zero and lands on -2; she continues to walk three steps to the left from -2 and ends up at -5. Negative direction has a sign, $-$.

> **Rule 3:** When adding a positive and a negative number, the sum can either be positive or negative.

Example A: $2 + (-3) = -1$

Explanation: A woman walks two steps to the right from zero and lands on 2; she continues to walk three steps to the left from 2 and ends up at -1.

Example B: $-2 + 3 = 1$

Explanation: A woman walks two steps to the left from zero and lands on -2; she continues to walk three steps to the right from -2 and ends up at $+1$.

2. Three Rules of Thumb for Subtraction

With subtraction of two numbers, the most important thing to remember is to treat the subtraction as the **opposite direction**.

> **Rule 4:** When subtracting two positive numbers, the difference can be either positive or negative.

Example A: $(+2) - (+3) = -1$

Explanation: A man walks two steps to the right from zero and lands on +2; he continues to walk +3 in the opposite direction, which means three steps to the left from +2 and ends up at -1.

Example B: $(+3) - (+2) = +1$

Explanation: A man walks three steps to the right from zero and lands on +3; he continues to walk +2 in the opposite direction, which means two steps to the left from +3 and ends up at +1.

> **Rule 5:** When subtracting two negative numbers, the difference can either be positive or negative.

Example A: $(-2) - (-3) = +1$

Explanation: A man walks two steps to the left from zero and lands on -2; he continues to walk -3 in the opposite direction, which means three steps to the right from -2 and ends up at +1.

Example B: $(-3) - (-2) = -1$

Explanation: A man walks three steps to the left from zero and lands on -3; he continues to walk +2 in the opposite direction, which means two steps to the right from -3 and ends up at -1.

> **Rule 6:** When subtracting a positive and a negative number, the difference can either be positive or negative.

Example A: $(+2) - (-3) = +5$

Explanation: A man walks two steps to the right from zero and lands on $+2$; he continues to walk -3 in the opposite direction, which means three steps to the right from $+2$ and ends up at $+5$.

Example B: $(-3) - (+2) = -5$

Explanation: A man walks three steps to the left from zero and lands on -3; he continues to walk $+2$ in the opposite direction, which means two steps to the left from -3 and ends up at -5.

3. Three Rules of Thumb for Multiplication

> **Rule 7:** When multiplying two positive numbers, the product is positive.

Example: $2 \times 3 = 6$

$Positive\,(+) \times Positive\,(+) = Positive\,(+)$

> **Rule 8:** When multiplying two negative numbers, the product is positive.

Example: $(-2) \times (-3) = 6$

$Negative\,(-) \times Negative\,(-) = Positive\,(+).$

> **Rule 9:** When multiplying a positive and a negative number, the product is negative:

Example A: $(-2) \times 3 = -6$

$Negative\,(-) \times Positive\,(+) = Negative\,(-)$

Example B: $3 \times (-2) = -6$

$Positive\,(+) \times Negative\,(-) = Negative\,(-)$

4. Three Rules of Thumb for Division

> **Rule 10:** When dividing two positive numbers, the quotient is positive.

Example: $6 \div 2 = 3$

$Positive\,(+) \div Positive\,(+) = Positive\,(+)$

> **Rule 11:** When dividing two negative numbers, the quotient is positive.

Example: $(-6) \div (-3) = 2$

$Negative\,(-) \div Negative\,(-) = Positive\,(+)$

> **Rule 12:** When dividing a positive and a negative number, the quotient is negative.

Example A: $(-6) \div 3 = -2$

$Negative\,(-) \div Positive\,(+) = Negative\,(-)$

Example B: $6 \div (-3) = -2$

$Positive\,(+) \div Negative\,(-) = Negative\,(-)$

5. Rule of Thumb for Absolute Value

In mathematics, the **absolute value** of a number represents the distance between it and zero on the real number line. The absolute value has a symbol, | |, with two bars around a number. Absolute value of a number will remove any negative sign in front of the number, and the number will be positive. In other words, absolute value is the **magnitude** of a number.

Rule 13: Absolute value of a positive or a negative number is always positive.

Example: $|3| = 3$ or $|-3| = 3$

Explanation: 3 is 3 units away from zero on the real number line. Similarly, -3 is also 3 units away from zero on the real number line.

Example 1. Evaluate: $-11 - (-15)$.

- (A) -26
- (B) -4
- (C) 4
- (D) 26
- (E) 36

Answer: C. Imagine a person walking on a real number line, and first lands at -11. Since the sign is negative in front of -15, this means the opposite of -15 is 15. Then, the person continues to walk 15 to the right of the -11 and ends up at 4 (See Rule 5).

Example 2. Calculate: $\bigl((-8) \times 4\bigr) - \bigl((-5) \times 6\bigr)$.

- (A) -4
- (B) -2
- (C) 2
- (D) 4
- (E) 6

Answer: B.
Step 1: Calculate each parenthesis.
$$\bigl((-8) \times 4\bigr) - \bigl((-5) \times 6\bigr)$$
$$= (-32) - (-30)$$
Step 2: Opposite Rule (or Rule 5)
$$= (-32) + 30$$
Step 3: Addition Rule (or Rule 3)
$$= -2$$

Example 3. Stephanie overdrew $230 from her checking account for an emergency use after starting with a zero balance. Her bank charged her an overdraft fee of $20. She then deposited $550 on the next day. What is the new balance in her checking account?

- (A) $200
- (B) $230
- (C) $270
- (D) $300
- (E) $330

Answer: D. Since Stephanie overdrew $230, her checking account would show a negative balance, and she owed $230 to the bank. In mathematical representation, the negative balance is denoted as $-$230. In addition, the bank charged her an overdraft fee of $20, and we can denote it as $-$20. The next day, Stephanie deposited $550 into her checking account, to turn the negative into a positive balance. Therefore, in order to get the current balance, we can translate the words to $0 - $230 + (-$20) + $550 = 300 by Rule 2 and 3. In other words, Stephanie was not only repaying back the debt she owed to the bank; she deposited an extra $300 into her checking account.

Example 4. Which of the following is TRUE?

I. $25 \times (-6) < 180 \div (-3)$

II. $-6 - (-15) < -15 - (-6)$

III. $-1 < -3$

- (A) I only
- (B) II only
- (C) III only
- (D) I and II
- (E) I, II, and III

Chapter 3: Negative Numbers

Answer: A. From inequality I, calculate $25 \times (-6) = -150$ by Rule 9, and $180 \div (-3) = -60$ by Rule 12. Therefore, $-150 < -60$ is true because -60 is closer to 0 than -150. From inequality II, calculate $-6 - (-15) = -6 + 15 = 9$ and $-15 - (-6) = -15 + 6 = -9$ by Rule 5 and 6. Therefore, $9 < -9$ is false because a positive number is always greater than a negative number. From inequality III, we know -1 is closer to 0 than -3, so $-1 < -3$ is false.

Example 5. On Tina's credit card statement, the balance was $375. She then made a payment of $275 toward her balance. On the next day, she spent $25 on groceries, and received a refund of $35 from a clothing store, where she used her card earlier that same day. Then she spent $18 at the gas station. What is the new balance on Tina's credit card?

- (A) $92
- (B) $98
- (C) $108
- (D) $112
- (E) $132

Answer: C. In this problem, because Tina owed $375 on her credit card, we can use $-\$375$ to represent her debt. She then made a payment of $275 toward her balance, so we can use $+\$275$ to represent a credit. Since she continued to use her credit card, and spent $25 for groceries, she owed another $25 on her credit card account, so we can use $-\$25$ to represent her additional debt. She then received a refund $35, so we can use $+\$35$ to represent her refund. She then spent another $18 at the gas station, so we can use $-\$18$ to represent her charge. To get Tina's new credit card balance, we sum up all the debits and credits as

$-\$375 + \$275 + (-\$25) + \$35 + (-\$18) = -\$108$.

The $-\$108$ means she has a debt of $108, so the answer is **C**.

Example 6. Compute $(-2)(-2)(-2)/(2 \times 2)$.

- (A) -12
- (B) -10
- (C) -8
- (D) -4
- (E) -2

Answer: E. We know that $(-2) \times (-2) \times (-2) = -8$, and $2 \times 2 = 4$, so we have $-8 \div 4 = -2$.

Example 7: Order the following numbers from least to greatest:

$-4|5|, -2|-2|, -3|3|, 2|-10|, -4|-6|$

- (A) $2|-10|, -4|-6|, -4|5|, -3|3|, -2|-2|$
- (B) $-4|-6|, -4|5|, -3|3|, -2|-2|, 2|-10|$
- (C) $-2|-2|, 4|-6|, -3|3|, -4|5|, -2|-10|$
- (D) $2|-10|, -4|-6|, -4|5|, -3|3|, -2|-2|$
- (E) $-4|5|, 2|-10|, -3|3|, -2|-2|, 4|-6|$

Answer: B. First simplify all numbers in the order they appear: $-20, -4, -9, 20, -24$. Now rearrange to obtain: $-24, -20, -9, -4, 20$. Finally, match these numbers with the original form: $-4|-6|, -4|5|, -3|3|, -2|-2|, 2|-10|$.

Example 8. Which of the following is <u>greatest</u>?

- (A) $-27 \div 3$
- (B) $-14 + (-11)$
- (C) $-5 \times (-4) \times 3$
- (D) $14 - (-14)$
- (E) $-25 - (-23)$

Answer: C. According to negative operation rules, we obtain $-27 \div 3 = -9$ for (A). For **B**, $-14 + (-11) = -25$. For **C**, $-5 \times (-4) \times 3 = 20 \times 3 = 60$. For (D), $14 - (-14) = 28$. For **E**, $-25 - (-23) = -25 + 23 = -2$. The answer **C** is the greatest among all answer choices, since $-25 < -9 < -2 < 28 < 60$.

Example 9. John and Ruby are professional scuba divers. John is located 46 ft below the surface of the sea, and Ruby is 13 ft below John. How far is Ruby below the surface of the sea?

- (A) 22 ft below the surface of the sea
- (B) 33 ft below the surface of the sea
- (C) 49 ft below the surface of the sea
- (D) 59 ft below the surface of the sea
- (E) 65 ft below the surface of the sea

Answer: D. Since John is 46 ft below the surface of the sea, and Ruby is 13 ft below John, this means that Ruby is farther away from the surface of the sea. Therefore, use $46 + 13 = 59$ ft to obtain Ruby's position below the surface of the sea.

Example 10. If $p = -3$ and $q = 4$, what is the value of $-2p \times p \times p - 4q \times q$?

- (A) -10
- (B) -7
- (C) 5
- (D) 7
- (E) 10

Answer: A. Plug in -3 into p and 4 into q to get: $-2(-3)(-3)(-3) - 4(4)(4) = 54 - 64 = -10$.

Practice Problems

1. Evaluate: $-13 - (-18)$

   (A) -30
   (B) -5
   (C) -1
   (D) 5
   (E) 30

2. Calculate: $((-7) \times 2) - ((-4) \times 7)$

   (A) 10
   (B) 14
   (C) 18
   (D) 22
   (E) 26

3. If m is a negative number and n is a positive number, what is the sign of $\dfrac{m}{n}$?

   (A) Positive
   (B) Negative
   (C) Even
   (D) Odd
   (E) Cannot be determined from the information above.

4. John overdrew $115 from his checking account for an emergency after having a balance of $0. His bank charged him a one-time overdraft fee of $25. He then deposited $300 into his account on the next day. What is his current balance in his checking account?

   (A) $115
   (B) $130
   (C) $145
   (D) $160
   (E) $185

5. A statistician selected daily low temperature readings from a town in Pennsylvania. They were (in Celsius): $-3.1°$, $4.9°$, $2.2°$, $-4.3°$, $-6.1°$, $12.2°$, $-0.6°$. Given that the average of 7 numbers is equal to the sum of the 7 numbers, divided by 7, what was the average temperature on these seven days to the nearest degree?

   (A) $-4.7°$
   (B) $-2.1°$
   (C) $-1.1°$
   (D) $0.1°$
   (E) $0.7°$

6. Mary has a class project that required the students to convert a city's recorded temperatures from Celsius to Fahrenheit. Given that $F = \left(C \cdot \dfrac{9}{5}\right) + 32$, where F stands for Fahrenheit and C stands for Celsius, and that the city has a recorded temperature of $-10°$ Celsius, what is the temperature in degrees Fahrenheit for the city?

   (A) $-12°$
   (B) $-14°$
   (C) $12°$
   (D) $14°$
   (E) $50°$

7. Which of the following is TRUE?

   I. $30 \times (-6) > 180 \div (-3)$
   II. $-4 - (-12) < -12 - (-4)$
   III. $-1 > -3$

   (A) I only
   (B) II only
   (C) III only
   (D) I and II
   (E) I, II, and III

8. Which of the following is the most negative?

   (A) -55
   (B) $-54 - (-5)$
   (C) $-90 - (-40)$
   (D) $15 - 75$
   (E) $-1 - 70$

9. On Mary's credit card statement, the balance showed she owed $425. She made a payment toward her balance of $250. On the next day, she spent $37 for groceries and got a refund of $42 from a clothing store where she bought a dress earlier that day. Then she spent $22 at the gas station. What is the new balance on Mary's credit card?

   (A) $192
   (B) $202
   (C) $212
   (D) $222
   (E) $232

10. Which of the following is the closest to the number 0?

    (A) -3×-4
    (B) $-50 + 25$
    (C) $0 - 13$
    (D) $-25 - (-8)$
    (E) $-33 \div 3$

11. Compute: $|-23| - |-34|$

    (A) -60
    (B) -57
    (C) -11
    (D) 11
    (E) 57

12. Compute: $-5(11-15) + 2 \times 2 \times 2 \times 2$

    (A) 20
    (B) 24
    (C) 28
    (D) 32
    (E) 36

13. Tom and Mike are professional scuba divers. Tom is at 65 ft below the surface of the sea, and Mike is 14 ft above Tom. How far is Mike below the surface of the sea?

    (A) 51 ft
    (B) 57 ft
    (C) 79 ft
    (D) 82 ft
    (E) 91 ft

14. Mr. Williams was playing a game with his daughter for a point system. He earned 49 points in the first round, and then lost 18 points in the second round. Which of the following calculations would describe the total points earned by Mr. Williams?

    (A) $49 - (-18)$
    (B) $49 - 18$
    (C) $49 + 18$
    (D) $-49 - 18$
    (E) $-49 - (-18)$

15. Compute:
    $(-3)(-3)(-3)(-3)(-3) \div (3 \times 3 \times 3)$

    (A) -27
    (B) -18
    (C) -9
    (D) 9
    (E) 27

16. Which of the following is <u>smallest</u>?

    (A) $-16 \div 4$
    (B) $-15 + (-13)$
    (C) $-4 \times (-3) \times 2$
    (D) $13 - (-13)$
    (E) $-24 - (-22)$

17. Which of the following is <u>greatest</u>?

    (A) $-6 + (-9)$
    (B) $4 + (-20)$
    (C) 0
    (D) $6 - (-4)$
    (E) $15 + (-1)$

18. Let $p = -2$ and $q = 3$. What is the value of $-3p \times p \times p - 2q \times q$?

    (A) -9
    (B) -6
    (C) -1
    (D) 6
    (E) 9

Answers to Practice Problems

1. **(D)** Imagine a person walking on a real number line, landing on −13. The negative sign in front of −18 means the opposite of −18, which is +18. Then, the person continues to walk 18 units to the right of −13 and ends up at 5. Therefore, the answer is 5. (See Rule 5).

2. **(B)** Step 1: Calculate each parenthesis.
   $$\big((-7) \times 2\big) - \big((-4) \times 7\big) = (-14) - (-28)$$
   Step 2: Opposite Rule (or Rule 5)
   $$= -14 + 28$$
   Step 3: Addition Rule (or Rule 3)
   $$= 14$$

3. **(B)** Let m be an arbitrary negative number, $m = -8$. Let n be an arbitrary positive number, $n = 4$. By the division rule, or Rule 12, $\frac{m}{n} = \frac{-8}{4} = -2$, which has a negative sign.

4. **(D)** Since John overdrew $115, his checking account would show a negative balance of $115. In mathematical representation, the negative balance is denoted as −$115. In addition, the bank charged a penalty fee of $25 for overdraft, which is denoted as −$25. The next day, John deposited $300 into his checking account, to turn the negative balance to a positive balance. Therefore, in order to get the current balance, we can translate the words as
   $$0 - \$115 + (-\$25) + \$300 = \$160$$
   by Rule 2 and 3. In other words, John not only repaid back the debt to the bank, he also deposited an extra $160 into his checking account.

5. **(E)** In mathematics and statistics,
   $$\text{Average} = \frac{\text{Sum of a group of data points}}{\text{The number of data points}}$$
   Since the first week of January's daily temperatures are given, the sum of the temperatures is $-3.1° + 4.9° + 2.2° + (-4.3°) + (-6.1°) + 12.2° + (-0.6°) = 5.2°$ by Rule 2 and 3. To obtain the average temperature for the seven days, we divide by 7 (the number of data points) to obtain an average.
   $$\frac{5.2}{7} = 0.74° \approx 0.7°$$

6. **(D)** To convert Celsius to Fahrenheit, use the given formula, $F = \left(C \cdot \frac{9}{5}\right) + 32$. Mary should substitute −10° Celsius into the C of the given formula, to obtain
   $$F = \left(-10 \cdot \frac{9}{5}\right) + 32 = -18 + 32 = 14$$

7. **(C)** From inequality I, calculate $30 \times (-6) = -180$ by Rule 9 and $180 \div (-3) = -60$ by Rule 12; therefore, $-180 > -60$ is false because −60 is closer to 0 than −180. From inequality II, calculate $-4 - (-12) = -4 + 12 = 8$ and $-12 - (-4) = -12 + 4 = -8$ by Rule 5 and 6; therefore, $8 < -8$ is also false because a positive number is always greater than a negative number. From inequality III, we know −1 is closer to 0 than −3, so $-1 > -3$ is correct.

8. **(E)** For **A**, as shown −55. For **B**, $-54 - (-5) = -54 + 5 = -49$ by Rule 5 and 6. For **C**, $-90 - (-40) = -50$ by Rule 6. For **D**, $15 - 75 = -60$ by addition rule or Rule 4. For **E**, $-1 - 70 = -71$ by Rule 6. Once the answers are obtained from each, we can order them from least to greatest,
   $$-71 < -60 < -55 < -50 < -49$$
   Therefore, the most negative number is **E**.

Chapter 3: Negative Numbers

9. **(A)** In this problem, Mary owed $425 on her credit card, so we can use −$425 to represent her debit. She then made a payment of $250 toward her balance, so we can use +$250 to represent her payment toward her balance. Since she continued to use her credit card, and spent $37 for groceries, she owed $37 more on her credit card account, so we can use −$37 to represent her charge. She received a refund of $42, so we can use +$42 to represent her refund. She then spent another $22 at the gas station, we can use −$22 to represent her debit. To get Mary's new credit card balance, we sum up all the debits and credits as

   $-\$425 + \$250 + (-\$37) + \$42 + (-\$22)$
   $= -\$192$

10. **(E)** In choice **A**, $-3 \times -4 = 12$ by Rule 8. In choice **B**, $-50 + 25 = -25$ from rule 3. And for **C**, $0 - 13 = -13$ since -13 is 13 units below zero. In choice **D**, $-25 - (-8) = -25 + 8 = -17$ by Rule 5. In choice **E**, $-33 \div 3 = -11$ by Rule 12. Clearly, **E** is 11 units from zero, which is less than the other answer choices.

11. **(C)** From Rule 13, we know that absolute value of a number is always positive, hence,

    $|-23| - |-34| = 23 - 34 = -11$

12. **(E)** We can solve this problem by applying the operations of the negative number rules that were listed earlier in this chapter:

    $-5(11 - 15) + 2 \times 2 \times 2 \times 2$

    Step 1: Subtraction Rule 4
    $= -5(-4) + 2 \times 2 \times 2 \times 2$

    Step 2: Multiplication Rule 8
    $= 20 + 2 \times 2 \times 2 \times 2$

    Step 3: Addition Rule 1
    $= 20 + 16 = 36$

13. **(A)** Since Tom is 65 ft below the surface of the sea, and Mike is 14 ft above Tom, that means that Mike is closer to the surface of the sea. Therefore, use the calculation

    $-65 + 14 = -51$

    to obtain Mike's position below the surface of the sea.

14. **(B)** Since Mr. Williams received 49 points in the first round, we can use +49 to represent his points. Then, he lost 18 points in the second round, so we can use −18 to represent his loss in the second round. Finally, the total points accumulated can be calculated by summing up the points gained and lost,

    $+49 + (-18) = 49 - 18$

15. **(C)** We know that

    $(-3)(-3)(-3)(-3)(-3) = -243$

    and $3 \times 3 \times 3 = 27$, so

    $-243 \div 27 = -9$

16. **(B)** According to the negative operation rules, we get $-16 \div 4 = -4$ for **A**.

    For **B**, $-15 + (-13) = -28$.
    For **C**, $-4 \times (-3) \times 2 = 12 \times 2 = 24$.
    For **D**, $13 - (-13) = 26$.
    For **E**, $-24 - (-22) = -24 + 22 = -2$.

    The answer **B** is the smallest among all answer choices, since

    $-28 < -4 < -2 < 24 < 26$

17. **(E)** According to the negative operation rules, we get $-6 + (-9) = -15$ for **A**. For **B**, $4 + (-20) = -16$. For **C**, 0 is given. For **D**, $6 - (-4) = 10$. For **E**, we get $15 + (-1) = 14$. The answer **E** is the greatest among all choices since

    $-16 < -15 < 0 < 10 < 14$

18. **(D)** We have $-3(-2)(-2)(-2) - 2(3)(3) = 24 - 18 = 6$.

Chapter 4
Fractions and Mixed Numbers

A general fraction has the form $\frac{a}{b}$, where $b \neq 0$. (The symbol $\neq$ means "not equal to"). The variable a is the **numerator**, and b is the **denominator**. This fraction can also be considered "a parts out of b parts", or "a divided by b". The denominator specifies the number of parts in a whole, while the numerator tells how many parts you have out of the whole. An example of a fraction would be $\frac{3}{4}$. Here $a = 3$ and $b = 4$. This tells you, "3 parts out of 4."

An **improper fraction** such as $\frac{7}{3}$, is one in which the numerator is greater than the denominator, and indicates a fraction value greater than 1.

A **mixed number** contains both a whole number and a fraction, such as $3\frac{2}{3}$: three wholes, and 2 of 3 parts.

1. Simplifying Fractions

When simplifying fractions, we want to make sure that the fraction is always in its lowest terms. To write a fraction in lowest terms, we have to find the **common factors**. Take a look at example 1 below. To simplify $\frac{12}{27}$, we must find the common factors of 12 and 27 and cancel that factor out. Continue to do this until you cannot cancel/reduce anymore. Now, you have found the simplest form. It is important to try to find the largest factor of both the numerator and the denominator. We see that the largest common factor of 12 and 27 is 3. 3 goes into 12 and 27 evenly.

Example 1. Simplify $\frac{12}{27}$

Solution: $\frac{12}{27} = \frac{4 \cdot 3}{9 \cdot 3} = \frac{4 \cdot \cancel{3}}{9 \cdot \cancel{3}} = \frac{4}{9}$

Example 2. Simplify $\frac{28}{35}$

Solution: In example 2, 28 and 35 share a common factor of 7, since 7 goes into 28 and 35 evenly. Perform the operations as following:

$$\frac{28}{35} = \frac{\cancel{7} \cdot 4}{\cancel{7} \cdot 5} = \frac{4}{5}$$

2. Converting a Mixed Number to an Improper Fraction

Example 3. Convert $3\frac{2}{5}$ to an improper fraction.

Solution: To convert a mixed number to an improper fraction, multiply the whole number by the denominator, and add the result (the product) to the numerator. This is your new numerator. For this example, multiply 3 (the whole number) by 5 (the denominator) to find the product of 15. Add 2 to the numerator of the fraction to find the numerator of the improper fraction (15 + 2 = 17). The denominator does not change. The reason the denominator stays the same can be explained by the breakdown of $3\frac{2}{5}$.

$$3\frac{2}{5} = \frac{5}{5} + \frac{5}{5} + \frac{5}{5} + \frac{2}{5}$$

Notice that the denominator is all fifths; we are just simplifying the mixed number to make an improper fraction.

$$3\frac{2}{5} = \frac{3 \cdot 5 + 2}{5} = \frac{17}{5}$$

Example 4. Convert $2\frac{6}{7}$ to an improper fraction.

Solution: In example 4, the product of 2 and 7 is 14, and is then added to 6, to find the numerator of the improper fraction.

$$2\frac{6}{7} = \frac{(2 \times 7) + 6}{7} = \frac{14 + 6}{7} = \frac{20}{7}$$

3. Converting an Improper Fraction to a Mixed Number

In the examples above, we started with a mixed number and converted to an improper fraction. In the following examples, we start with an improper fraction and convert to a mixed number. To simplify, we see how many times the denominator goes into the numerator evenly. Then what is left becomes the fraction. The denominator will stay the same.

Example 5. Write $\frac{23}{7}$ as a mixed number.

Solution: To convert an improper fraction to a mixed number, divide the numerator by the denominator. We see that 7 does not go into 23 evenly, but 7 goes into 21 three times, with 2 left over. Put the remainder of the division operation over the original denominator to find the fraction portion of the mixed number. So 3 is our whole number (out front). The remainder is 2 (new numerator), and the denominator (7) remains the same.

$$\begin{array}{r} 3 \\ 7{\overline{\smash{\big)}\,2\;3}} \\ \underline{2\;1} \\ 2 \end{array}$$

Therefore, $\frac{23}{7} = 3\frac{2}{7}$.

Another way of solving the problem is using the following operation:

$$\frac{23}{7} = \frac{21 + 2}{7} = \frac{21}{7} + \frac{2}{7} = 3 + \frac{2}{7} = 3\frac{2}{7}$$

Example 6. Write $\frac{18}{11}$ as a mixed number.

Solution: Example 6 is solved the same way as example 5. 11 goes into 18 one time, with 7 left over (which is the remainder). Therefore 1 is the whole number, with 7 becoming the new numerator, and 11 remaining the denominator.

$$\begin{array}{r} 1 \\ 11{\overline{\smash{\big)}\,1\;8}} \\ \underline{1\;1} \\ 7 \end{array}$$

The result is $1\frac{7}{11}$.

4. Adding Fractions When the Denominators Are the Same

When adding fractions, we must pay attention to one important detail: the denominators of the fractions we are adding. This will tell us if the addition will be simple or more difficult.

To find the sum of two fractions with the same denominator, add the numerators and keep the denominator unchanged in the answer. In example 7, below, the numerators can be added to find the numerator of the answer since the denominators of the two fractions in the question are equivalent. The numerator of the sum will be $3 + 2 = 5$, and the denominator of the sum will be unchanged.

Example 7. Simplify $\dfrac{3}{7} + \dfrac{2}{7}$

Solution: $\dfrac{3}{7} + \dfrac{2}{7} = \dfrac{3+2}{7} = \dfrac{5}{7}$

In example 8, below, the addition is solved the same way, with the numerator of the answer equal to the sum of the original numerators. Since the answer is an improper fraction, it can be converted back to a mixed number as shown previously.

Example 8. Simplify $\dfrac{5}{9} + \dfrac{6}{9}$

Solution: $\dfrac{5}{9} + \dfrac{6}{9} = \dfrac{5+6}{9} = \dfrac{11}{9} = 1\dfrac{2}{9}$

5. Adding Fractions with Different Denominators

To find the sum of two fractions that have different denominators, find a common multiple of the denominators. A **common multiple** is a specific number that is a multiple of two or more numbers. For instance, 24 is a common multiple of the numbers 4 and 8 because both 4 and 8 go into 24 evenly. 16 is also a common multiple of 4 and 8 because both 4 and 8 go into 16 evenly. The **lowest common multiple** of two numbers is the smallest number both factors go into evenly. For example, 24 is the lowest common multiple of 8 and 6 because both 6 and 8 go into 24 evenly. There is no smaller number than 24 that both 6 and 8 go into evenly.

Another way to find a common denominator is by multiplying the two denominators together. This product will be a common multiple of the two (or more) individual denominators, as shown in Step 1 of the general example below. If you choose this method, you will probably have to simplify your fraction to lowest terms as shown in example 1 and example 2.

$$\dfrac{a}{b} + \dfrac{c}{d} = \dfrac{?}{b \cdot d} + \dfrac{?}{b \cdot d} \quad \text{(Step 1)}$$

$$= \dfrac{a \cdot d}{b \cdot d} + \dfrac{b \cdot c}{b \cdot d} \quad \text{(Step 2)}$$

$$= \dfrac{ad + cb}{bd} \quad \text{(Step 3)}$$

After step one, return to the fraction addition problem, and then multiply each denominator by the appropriate value to obtain a common denominator (the common multiple of the denominators), and also multiply the respective numerators by the same values (that the denominator was multiplied by), to obtain the fractions to be added, as shown in step 2 above. Then, follow the steps to add fractions with the same denominator, seen above in step 3.

In example 9 below, the denominators (6 and 9) are multiplied together to find the common denominator to be used, which is $6 \times 9 = 54$. The numerator 1 will also be multiplied by 9 to

Chapter 4: Fractions and Mixed Numbers

maintain equality, resulting in the fraction $\frac{9}{54}$. The numerator 2 of the second fraction will also be multiplied by 6, resulting in the fraction $\frac{12}{54}$. These two fractions, with common denominators, can be added according to the method described in examples 7 and 8 above. Notice that the answer $\frac{21}{54}$ will need to be simplified using a common factor of 3.

Example 9. What is $\frac{1}{6} + \frac{2}{9}$?

Solution: $\frac{1}{6} + \frac{2}{9} = \frac{1 \cdot 9}{6 \cdot 9} + \frac{6 \cdot 2}{6 \cdot 9} = \frac{9}{54} + \frac{12}{54}$

$= \frac{21}{54} = \frac{7 \cdot \cancel{3}}{18 \cdot \cancel{3}} = \frac{7}{18}$

Example 10 demonstrates a method of finding the sum of mixed numbers.

Example 10. Find the sum of $2\frac{3}{4} + 1\frac{3}{7}$.

Solution: $2\frac{3}{4} + 1\frac{3}{7} = \frac{11}{4} + \frac{10}{7}$

$= \frac{11 \cdot 7}{4 \cdot 7} + \frac{4 \cdot 10}{4 \cdot 7}$

$= \frac{117}{28} = 4\frac{5}{28}$

6. Finding the Least Common Denominator (LCD)

Example 11. Find the least common denominator of $\frac{3}{14}$ and $\frac{5}{32}$.

Solution:

Step 1: Find the prime factorization of each denominator in the addition or subtraction problem. Prime numbers are those numbers that only have factors of 1 and the number itself, such as 2,3,5,7, 11, 13, etc. Remember that 2 is the first prime number, not 1.

Factorize each denominator into primes as in the example below, first considering the smallest prime number (2) and trying larger primes if the smaller numbers are not factors of the given denominator. So let's find the prime factors of 14 and 32.

$$14 = 2 \times 7$$
$$32 = 2 \times 2 \times 2 \times 2 \times 2$$

Once the prime factorization of each denominator is complete, find the instances that each prime factor appears in the factorization of each denominator, as shown in Step 2 (below). Note the greatest number of times that each prime number appears for individual denominators.

Step 2: For 14, "2" appears once and "7" appears once. For 32, "2" appears five times.

Pick the greatest number of appearances of each prime number, and then multiply these prime numbers to produce the least common denominator, as shown in Step 3.

Step 3: Since "2" appears only once in the factorization of "14" and appears five times in the factorization of "32", "2" will be listed five times, and the 2 from the 14 can be ignored, since it doesn't appear more than five times. "7" appears once for "14", so we must use it even though it doesn't appear in 32. So, we have 2, 2, 2, 2, 2, and 7, all of which will be multiplied together to find the least common denominator. Therefore

$$2 \times 2 \times 2 \times 2 \times 2 \times 7 = 224$$

is the least common denominator of 14 and 32.

7. Multiplying Fractions

To find the product of fractions, multiply straight across the numerators to obtain the numerator of the answer, and multiply straight across the denominators to find the new denominator, as in Examples 12 and 13 below.

Example 12. Simplify $\dfrac{3}{7} \times \dfrac{2}{5}$

Solution: $\dfrac{3}{7} \times \dfrac{2}{5} = \dfrac{3 \times 2}{7 \times 5} = \dfrac{6}{35}$

Example 13. Simplify $\dfrac{2}{5} \times \dfrac{2}{9}$

Solution: $\dfrac{2}{5} \times \dfrac{2}{9} = \dfrac{2 \times 2}{5 \times 9} = \dfrac{4}{45}$

8. Cross Cancellation

Sometimes when two or more fractions are multiplied, there is a hard way and an easy way to perform the operations. Let's take an example:

Example 14. Multiply $\dfrac{121}{14} \times \dfrac{28}{11}$, then reduce to the lowest terms.

Solution: The hard way to solve the problem is to multiply 121 by 28, then divide it by the product of 14 and 11. But this involves tedious and time-consuming calculations. We can greatly simplify the calculation by performing cross cancellation. We notice that the denominator, 11, of the second fraction goes into the numerator of the first fraction evenly and the denominator of the first fraction, 14, goes into the numerator of the second fraction, 28, exactly two times. Therefore, we can divide 121 by 11 to obtain 11, and divide 28 by 14 to obtain 2. We are left with $11 \times 2 = 22$! The calculation is shown below:

$$\dfrac{\cancel{121}}{\cancel{14}} \times \dfrac{\cancel{28}}{\cancel{11}} = 11 \times 2 = 22$$

If there is a mixed number in the question, convert it to an improper fraction before finding the product, as in example 15.

Example 15. Find the product of $2\dfrac{3}{4}$ and $\dfrac{4}{7}$.

Solution: $2\dfrac{3}{4} \times \dfrac{4}{7} = \dfrac{11}{\cancel{4}} \times \dfrac{\cancel{4}}{7} = \dfrac{11}{7} = 1\dfrac{4}{7}$

8. Dividing Fractions

To find the quotient of two fractions, multiply the first fraction by the **reciprocal** (flip the fraction) of the second fraction, as shown in examples 16 and 17 below.

Example 16. Simplify $\dfrac{3}{7} \div \dfrac{2}{5}$.

Solution: To divide these fractions, we must change the operation to multiplication. To do this, we take the reciprocal of the second fraction, $\dfrac{2}{5}$, which is $\dfrac{5}{2}$. Then we can change the operation to multiplication. We can now follow our rules of multiplication to simplify the problem.

$$\dfrac{3}{7} \div \dfrac{2}{5} = \dfrac{3}{7} \times \dfrac{5}{2} = \dfrac{15}{14} = 1\dfrac{1}{14}$$

Example 17. Simplify $\dfrac{2}{5} \div \dfrac{1}{9}$.

Solution: $\dfrac{2}{5} \div \dfrac{1}{9} = \dfrac{2}{5} \times \dfrac{9}{1} = \dfrac{18}{5} = 3\dfrac{3}{5}$.

Chapter 4: Fractions and Mixed Numbers

9. Comparing Fractions

To find the fraction with the greatest value, cross multiply, as shown below. The larger fraction will correspond to the larger product obtained from the cross multiplication.

Example 18. Which fraction is larger, $\dfrac{5}{8}$ or $\dfrac{4}{7}$?

Solution: First, we cross multiply the numerator of the left fraction with the denominator of the right fraction. The product is $5 \times 7 = 35$. Write this value above the left fraction. Next, multiply the numerator of the right fraction by the denominator of the left, which gives us, $4 \times 8 = 32$. Write this value above the right fraction. The number above the fraction on the left is larger, therefore, $\dfrac{5}{8}$ is larger.

$$5 \times 7 = 35 \qquad 4 \times 8 = 32$$

$$\frac{5}{8} \quad > \quad \frac{4}{7}$$

Practice Problems

1. Find the least common denominator of the fractions $\frac{7}{9}$ and $\frac{1}{6}$.

   A) 9
   B) 12
   C) 18
   D) 48
   E) 54

2. Find the least common denominator of the fractions $\frac{3}{11}$ and $\frac{5}{8}$.

   A) 8
   B) 11
   C) 44
   D) 88
   E) 176

3. Add the fractions and write the answer in simplest form: $\frac{7}{9} + \frac{1}{6}$

   A) $\frac{17}{18}$
   B) $\frac{8}{15}$
   C) $\frac{18}{35}$
   D) $\frac{8}{54}$
   E) $\frac{47}{30}$

4. Add the fractions and write the answer in simplest form: $\frac{7}{6} + \frac{2}{5}$

   A) $\frac{9}{11}$
   B) $\frac{11}{15}$
   C) $\frac{9}{30}$
   D) $\frac{12}{30}$
   E) $\frac{47}{30}$

5. Add the fractions and write the answer in simplest form (no improper fractions): $2\frac{1}{9} + 3\frac{4}{5}$

   A) $5\frac{5}{14}$
   B) $5\frac{36}{45}$
   C) $5\frac{41}{45}$
   D) $6\frac{5}{45}$
   E) $6\frac{5}{14}$

Chapter 4: Fractions and Mixed Numbers

6. Subtract one fraction from the other and write the answer in simplest form (no improper fractions): $\frac{4}{9} - \frac{1}{3}$

   A) $\frac{1}{9}$
   B) $\frac{4}{27}$
   C) $\frac{1}{2}$
   D) $\frac{5}{6}$
   E) $\frac{15}{9}$

7. Subtract one fraction from the other and write the answer in simplest form (no improper fractions):

   $\frac{6}{7} - \frac{3}{14}$

   A) $\frac{9}{14}$
   B) $\frac{3}{7}$
   C) $\frac{18}{98}$
   D) $\frac{9}{49}$
   E) $\frac{3}{14}$

8. Subtract one fraction from the other and write the answer in simplest form (no improper fractions):

   $3\frac{2}{7} - 2\frac{1}{13}$

   A) $1\frac{1}{7}$
   B) $1\frac{1}{13}$
   C) $1\frac{19}{91}$
   D) $1\frac{38}{299}$
   E) $1\frac{19}{199}$

9. Multiply the fractions and write the answer in simplest form (no improper fractions):

   $\frac{5}{4} \times \frac{8}{25}$

   A) $\frac{13}{100}$
   B) $\frac{40}{29}$
   C) $\frac{1}{5}$
   D) $\frac{2}{5}$
   E) $\frac{13}{29}$

10. Multiply the fractions and write the answer in simplest form (no improper fractions):

    $\dfrac{6}{5} \times \dfrac{15}{18}$

    (A) 1

    (B) $\dfrac{21}{23}$

    (C) $1\dfrac{1}{2}$

    (D) $2\dfrac{1}{90}$

    (E) $3\dfrac{21}{23}$

11. Multiply the fractions and write the answer in simplest form (no improper fractions):

    $2\dfrac{1}{3} \times 1\dfrac{2}{5}$

    (A) $2\dfrac{1}{15}$

    (B) $2\dfrac{2}{15}$

    (C) $2\dfrac{3}{8}$

    (D) $3\dfrac{3}{15}$

    (E) $3\dfrac{4}{15}$

12. Divide the fractions and write the answer in simplest form (no improper fractions): $\dfrac{1}{4} \div \dfrac{1}{5}$

    (A) $\dfrac{1}{9}$

    (B) $\dfrac{1}{20}$

    (C) $1\dfrac{1}{4}$

    (D) $1\dfrac{1}{20}$

    (E) $1\dfrac{2}{9}$

13. Divide the fractions and write the answer in simplest form (no improper fractions): $\dfrac{3}{2} \div \dfrac{6}{8}$

    (A) $\dfrac{3}{4}$

    (B) $\dfrac{7}{8}$

    (C) 1

    (D) 2

    (E) 3

Chapter 4: Fractions and Mixed Numbers

14. Divide the fractions and write the answer in simplest form (no improper fractions):

    $2\frac{3}{8} \div \frac{3}{5}$

    (A) $1\frac{1}{7}$

    (B) $2\frac{1}{7}$

    (C) $3\frac{1}{2}$

    (D) $3\frac{23}{24}$

    (E) $5\frac{1}{10}$

16. Which of the following fractions is greater, $\frac{5}{8}$ or $\frac{4}{7}$, or are they equal?

    (A) $\frac{5}{8}$

    (B) $\frac{4}{7}$

    (C) They are equal

    (D) Cannot be determined from the information above

    (E) None of the above

15. Divide the fractions and write the answer in simplest form (no improper fractions):

    $3\frac{1}{2} \div 2\frac{1}{5}$

    (A) $1\frac{1}{10}$

    (B) $1\frac{5}{2}$

    (C) $1\frac{13}{22}$

    (D) $1\frac{2}{5}$

    (E) $3\frac{1}{10}$

17. Which of the following fractions is greater, $\frac{3}{7}$ or $\frac{6}{9}$, or are they equal?

    (A) $\frac{3}{7}$

    (B) $\frac{6}{9}$

    (C) They are equal

    (D) Cannot be determined from the information above

    (E) None of the above

18. Arrange the following numbers from smallest to greatest: $\frac{1}{2}, \frac{1}{3}, \frac{5}{8}, 1, 0, \frac{7}{6}, \frac{13}{6}$

   (A) $0, \frac{1}{2}, \frac{1}{3}, \frac{5}{8}, 1, \frac{13}{6}, \frac{7}{6}$

   (B) $0, \frac{1}{3}, \frac{1}{2}, 1, \frac{5}{8}, \frac{7}{6}, \frac{13}{6}$

   (C) $0, \frac{5}{8}, \frac{1}{3}, \frac{1}{2}, \frac{7}{6}, 1, \frac{13}{6}$

   (D) $0, \frac{1}{3}, \frac{5}{8}, \frac{1}{2}, 1, \frac{7}{6}, \frac{13}{6}$

   (E) $0, \frac{1}{3}, \frac{1}{2}, \frac{5}{8}, 1, \frac{7}{6}, \frac{13}{6}$

19. Convert $\frac{27}{11}$ to a mixed number.

   (A) $1\frac{7}{11}$

   (B) $1\frac{11}{27}$

   (C) $2\frac{5}{11}$

   (D) $2\frac{11}{27}$

   (E) $3\frac{5}{27}$

20. Convert $\frac{33}{4}$ to a mixed number.

   (A) $4\frac{1}{4}$

   (B) $4\frac{4}{33}$

   (C) $6\frac{1}{4}$

   (D) $8\frac{1}{4}$

   (E) $9\frac{4}{33}$

Chapter 4: Fractions and Mixed Numbers

Answers to Practice Problems

1. **(C)** We take the prime factors of each denominator to get the LCD (least common denominator). If any factors repeat, we take the factor(s) that appear(s) most often. We know that

    $9 = 3 \times 3$ and $6 = 2 \times 3$

    Notice how both denominators (6 and 9) have factors of 3, however 9 has two factors of 3 (3×3), so we use 3×3 as our factors for our LCD. We also see that 2 is a factor of 6, but not of 9, so 2 also belongs in the LCD. Therefore, the LCD $= 2 \times 3 \times 3 = 18$.

2. **(D)** The denominator 11 is a prime number and $8 = 2 \times 2 \times 2$, so 11 and 8 don't share any factors other than 1. Therefore, the LCD $= 2 \times 2 \times 2 \times 11 = 88$.

3. **(A)** We must first find a common denominator, which is 18. Then, we multiply the first fraction, $\frac{7}{9}$ by $\frac{2}{2}$, and the second fraction, $\frac{1}{6}$ by $\frac{2}{2}$. Thus,

    $$\frac{7}{9} + \frac{1}{6} = \frac{7 \cdot 2}{9 \cdot 2} + \frac{1 \cdot 3}{6 \cdot 3} = \frac{14}{18} + \frac{3}{18}$$
    $$= \frac{14 + 3}{18} = \frac{17}{18}$$

4. **(E)** The common multiple of 6 and 5 is 30. So we perform the operation as follows:

    $$\frac{7}{6} + \frac{2}{5} = \frac{7 \cdot 5}{6 \cdot 5} + \frac{2 \cdot 6}{5 \cdot 6} = \frac{35}{30} + \frac{12}{30} = \frac{47}{30}$$

5. **(C)** We are adding two mixed numbers, therefore, add the whole parts $3 + 2 = 5$. Add the fractions separately. The denominators are both factors of 45. This is the smallest number that 5 and 9 go into. Therefore, 45 is the LCD. Simplifying we obtain:

    $$2\frac{1}{9} + 3\frac{4}{5} = (2 + 3) + \left(\frac{5}{45} + \frac{36}{45}\right)$$
    $$= 5 + \left(\frac{5 + 36}{45}\right) = 5\frac{41}{45}$$

6. **(A)** We see that 3 is a factor of 9. Therefore, the LCD is 9. We only have to multiply the second fraction by 3 since the first fraction already has a denominator of 9.

    $$\frac{4}{9} - \frac{1}{3} = \frac{4}{9} - \frac{1 \cdot 3}{3 \cdot 3} = \frac{4}{9} - \frac{3}{9} = \frac{1}{9}$$

7. **(A)** We perform the operation as follows:

    $$\frac{6}{7} - \frac{3}{14} = \frac{12}{14} - \frac{3}{14} = \frac{9}{14}$$

8. **(C)** We perform the operation as follows:

    $$3\frac{2}{7} - 2\frac{1}{13} = (3 - 2) + \left(\frac{2}{7} - \frac{1}{13}\right)$$
    $$= 1 + \left(\frac{2 \cdot 13}{7 \cdot 13} - \frac{7 \cdot 1}{7 \cdot 13}\right)$$
    $$= 1 + \left(\frac{26 - 7}{91}\right) = 1\frac{19}{91}$$

9. **(D)** We can divide 4 into 8 and 5 into 25 to obtain,

    $$\frac{5}{4} \times \frac{8}{25} = \frac{5}{25} \times \frac{8}{4} = \frac{1}{5} \times \frac{2}{1} = \frac{2}{5}$$

10. **(A)** We see that 6 goes into 18 three times and 5 goes into 15 three times. Therefore,

    $$\frac{6}{5} \times \frac{15}{18} = \frac{6}{18} \times \frac{15}{5} = \frac{1}{3} \times \frac{3}{1} = 1$$

11. **(E)** First, we will change the mixed numbers to improper fractions. We will then multiply the fractions straight across.

$$2\frac{1}{3} \times 1\frac{2}{5} = \frac{7}{3} \times \frac{7}{5} = \frac{7 \cdot 7}{3 \cdot 5} = \frac{49}{15} = 3\frac{4}{15}$$

12. **(C)** To divide these fractions, take the reciprocal of the second fraction (flip the second fraction), and then take the product of the two fractions.

$$\frac{1}{4} \div \frac{1}{5} = \frac{1}{4} \times \frac{5}{1} = \frac{5}{4} = 1\frac{1}{4}$$

13. **(D)** Perform the operation as follows:

$$\frac{3}{2} \div \frac{6}{8} = \frac{3}{2} \times \frac{8}{6} = \frac{3}{6} \times \frac{8}{2}$$
$$= \frac{1}{2} \times \frac{4}{1} = \frac{4}{2} = 2$$

14. **(D)** First, change our mixed number into an improper fraction. Take the reciprocal of the second fraction, and then multiply the fractions together.

$$2\frac{3}{8} \div \frac{3}{5} = \frac{19}{8} \times \frac{5}{3} = \frac{19 \cdot 5}{8 \cdot 3} = \frac{95}{24} = 3\frac{23}{24}$$

15. **(C)** First, convert the mixed numbers to improper fractions, and then multiply the first fraction by the reciprocal of the second fraction. Lastly, multiply straight across.

$$3\frac{1}{2} \div 2\frac{1}{5} = \frac{7}{2} \div \frac{11}{5} = \frac{7}{2} \times \frac{5}{11}$$
$$= \frac{35}{22} = 1\frac{13}{22}$$

16. **(A)** To compare fractions and determine which is larger, cross multiply to compare $5 \times 7 = 35$ and $8 \times 4 = 32$. Place the 35 on the left over the $\frac{5}{8}$ and place the 32 over the $\frac{4}{7}$. The larger side is the largest fraction, so

$$5 \times 7 = 35 \quad 4 \times 8 = 32$$
$$\frac{5}{8} > \frac{4}{7}$$

17. **(B)** Cross multiply to obtain $7 \times 6 = 42$, and place it over the $\frac{6}{9}$, and multiply $3 \times 9 = 27$ and place it over the $\frac{3}{7}$. Since $42 > 27$,

$$6 \times 7 = 42 \quad 3 \times 9 = 27$$
$$\frac{6}{9} > \frac{3}{7}$$

18. **(E)** Determine first which fraction is larger than 2. The only fraction larger than 2 is $\frac{13}{6}$, since half of 13 is 6.5. Which fraction is larger than 1? $\frac{7}{6}$ is larger than 1, so, so far, we know 1, $\frac{7}{6}$, and $\frac{13}{6}$ are the last three fractions in the list, making only choices **D** and **E** possible. 0 is smallest, and we know $\frac{1}{3}$ is smaller than $\frac{1}{2}$. Is $\frac{5}{8}$ larger or smaller than $\frac{1}{2}$? Half of 8 is 4, so indeed $\frac{5}{8}$ is larger than $\frac{1}{2}$. Arranging the fractions from smallest to greatest, we obtain: $0, \frac{1}{3}, \frac{1}{2}, \frac{5}{8}, 1, \frac{7}{6}, \frac{13}{6}$.

19. **(C)** Divide 11 into 27. It goes into 27 twice, with a remainder of 5. Therefore

$$\frac{27}{11} = 2\frac{5}{11}$$

$$\begin{array}{r} 2 \\ 11{\overline{\smash{\big)}\,27}} \\ \underline{22} \\ 5 \end{array}$$

20. **(D)** Divide 4 into 33. 4 goes into 33 eight times, with a remainder of 1. Therefore

$$\frac{33}{4} = 8\frac{1}{4}$$

$$\begin{array}{r} 8 \\ 4{\overline{\smash{\big)}\,33}} \\ \underline{32} \\ 1 \end{array}$$

Chapter 5
Exponents and Roots

Exponents

A **power** or **exponent** refers to repeated multiplication of a number by itself. For example, in 2×2, the 2 is repeated twice. The number of times the number is multiplied by itself is determined by the value of the power. For example, 2 to the power of 3, or 2^3, is 2 multiplied by itself 3 times. That is:

$$2^3 = 2 \times 2 \times 2$$

In this example, 2 is called the **base**, and 3 is known as the power or exponent.

Squaring and Cubing a Positive Number

Any number, whether positive, zero, or negative can be squared, cubed, or raised to any power. The exception is zero raised to the zero power, which is undefined.

Let's take a look at what happens when you square a positive number:

Take for example the number 3^2. A common mistake among students is to multiply 3 by 2 to get 6. But this is incorrect. The exponent, 2, means that the base, 3, is to be multiplied by itself once, so that 3 is multiplied by 3 to get $3 \times 3 = 9$. The exponent, 2, means to have two 3's multiplied together. Another example would be $5^2 = 5 \times 5 = 25$. Again, be sure not to multiply 5 by 2 to get 10.

An example of cubing a number would be $2^3 = 2 \times 2 \times 2 = 8$. The exponent 3 means to have three 2's multiplied together. You will notice that $2^3 \neq 3^2$.

As a final example, let's look at 0^2. This means multiply 0 by itself to get $0 \times 0 = 0$. Similarly, $0^3 = 0 \times 0 \times 0 = 0$.

As stated earlier the exponent can be any number, like 4 or 5, or even a fraction, the later which will not be tested on the GED Math test.

Now let's look at what happens when a negative number is squared or cubed.

Note that there is a difference between $-x^2$ and $(-x)^2$. With $-x^2$ you square x to obtain x^2, then multiply by -1. With $(-x)^2$, you are squaring $-x$ to obtain $(-x) \times (-x) = +x^2$.

Examples:
$$(-2)^2 = (-2) \times (-2) = 4$$
$$\text{But } -2^2 = -(2 \times 2) = -4$$
$$\text{And } -(-2)^2 = -(-2 \times -2) = -(+4) = -4$$

As you will learn in chapter 6 on Order of Operations, the operation/s inside the parentheses is/are performed first before any other operation is performed, thus the results we obtained. If this is confusing to you, rest assured we will revisit these types of problems in chapter 6, and it will clarify things greatly.

Learn the following three rules about powers:

Any number when raised to the power of 1 equals that number.

Examples:
$$x^1 = x$$
$$2^1 = 2$$

Any non-zero number when raised to the power of zero equals 1.

Examples:
$$x^0 = 1$$
$$2^0 = 1$$

Any non-zero number when raised to a negative exponent equals one divided by that number raised to the positive exponent.

Examples:
$$x^{-2} = \frac{1}{x^{+2}}$$
$$2^{-3} = \frac{1}{2^{+3}} = \frac{1}{2 \cdot 2 \cdot 2} = \frac{1}{8}$$

Example 1. Which of the following is _smallest_?

- (A) 3^0
- (B) -3
- (C) 3^{-2}
- (D) 3^{-3}
- (E) 3^{-4}

Answer: B.

This problem applies the rules of powers discussed in this chapter. Let's go through each choice:

- **A.** $3^0 = 1$ by definition.
- **B.** -3 (given)
- **C.** $3^{-2} = \frac{1}{3^2} = \frac{1}{9}$
- **D.** $3^{-3} = \frac{1}{3^3} = \frac{1}{3 \cdot 3 \cdot 3} = \frac{1}{27}$
- **E.** $3^{-4} = \frac{1}{3^4} = \frac{1}{81}$

Answer choice **B** is the only negative number, all others are positive.

Example 2. Which of the following is _greatest_?

- (A) -3^0
- (B) 2^{-1}
- (C) 2^{-2}
- (D) 2^{-3}
- (E) 2^{-4}

Answer: B.

Choice **A** is equal to -1 because $-3^0 = -(3^0) = -1$. Remember any non-zero number raised to the zero power is equal to 1.

- **B.** $2^{-1} = \frac{1}{2^1} = \frac{1}{2}$
- **C.** $2^{-2} = \frac{1}{2^2} = \frac{1}{4}$
- **D.** $2^{-3} = \frac{1}{2^3} = \frac{1}{8}$
- **E.** $2^{-4} = \frac{1}{2^4} = \frac{1}{16}$

Looking at the answer choices, choice **A** is smallest because it is negative, and of all the other choices, **B** $\frac{1}{2}$ is greatest.

Chapter 5: Exponents and Roots

Example 3. Compute 9^{-2}

- Ⓐ -18
- Ⓑ 7
- Ⓒ $\dfrac{1}{7}$
- Ⓓ $\dfrac{1}{18}$
- Ⓔ $\dfrac{1}{81}$

Answer: E. $9^{-2} = \dfrac{1}{9^2} = \dfrac{1}{81}$

Multiplying Numbers by Adding Exponents

As we will see in chapter 7, simplifying expressions, a problem may require you to simplify an expression such as, $2^3 \times 2^4$. Here you see that the base, 2, is the same for both numbers we are multiplying. In such a case, we simply raise the base to the sum of the exponents to get, $2^3 \times 2^4 = 2^{3+4} = 2^7 = 128$.

As another example, let's simplify $4^1 \times 4^2 \times 4^2$.

Solution: Since the bases are equal, simply use the base 4 and raise it to the sum of the exponents:

$$4^1 \times 4^2 \times 4^2 = 4^{1+2+2} = 4^5$$

You can use a calculator to obtain 1,024.

Remember that to use our rule, the bases must be the same.

Square Roots

A **root** of a number is the opposite of a power or exponent. The symbol for a **square root** is the radical sign "$\sqrt{\ }$". The square root of a number is a number which, when multiplied by itself, yields that original number. For example, $2 \times 2 = 4$, so going backwards, the square root of 4 is 2.

Every positive number has only one square root, another positive number. However, consider the equation $x^2 = 4$. In this case, there are two square roots of x^2: one positive and one negative, namely 2 and -2. You solve for the two values of x by taking the square root of both sides of the equation.

$$\sqrt{x^2} = \sqrt{4}$$

The square root of 4 is 2, but note that the square root of x^2 is either $+x$ or $-x$ because

$$(+x)^2 = x^2 \text{ and } (-x)^2 = x^2$$

Therefore, when solving an equation such as the equation $\sqrt{x^2} = \sqrt{4}$, take the positive and negative square root. In this case,

$$\sqrt{x^2} = \sqrt{4}$$
$$\pm x = \sqrt{4}$$
$$x = \pm\sqrt{4} = \pm 2$$

MEMORIZE THIS TABLE!

Tables for Powers and Roots

x (number)	x^2 (power)	$\sqrt{x^2}$
1	1	1
2	4	2
3	9	3
4	16	4
5	25	5
6	36	6
7	49	7
8	64	8
9	81	9
10	100	10
11	121	11
12	144	12

Example 4. Which statement is true?

Choose all answers that apply.

[A] $\sqrt{2^2} = 2$

[B] $2^4 = 8$

[C] $\sqrt{2^4} = 4$

[D] $\sqrt{8^2} = 16$

[E] $\sqrt{1000} = 100$

Answer: A, C.

A. True because $\sqrt{2^2} = \sqrt{4} = 2$.

B. False because $2^4 = 2 \cdot 2 \cdot 2 \cdot 2 = 16$, not 8.

C. True. $\sqrt{2^4} = \sqrt{16} = 4$.

D. $\sqrt{8^2} = \sqrt{64} = 8$

E. $\sqrt{1000} \sim 31.62$, not 100.

Example 5. Compute $\sqrt{81}$

(A) 3

(B) 8

(C) 8.1

(D) 9

(E) 81

Answer: D.

Looking at the table, $\sqrt{81} = \sqrt{9^2} = 9$.

Example 6. Solve for x when $x^2 = 16$.

(A) -4

(B) 0

(C) 2

(D) 4

(E) -4 or 4

Answer: E. Take the square roots of both sides. $\sqrt{x^2} = \sqrt{16} = 4$, so x equal 4. But -4 is also a solution since $(-4)^2 = 16$ as well. Therefore, both $+4$ and -4 are solutions. Remember that when you take the square root of both sides of an equation $x^2 = c$, where $c > 0$, there are two solutions for x; one positive and one negative.

Example 7. Solve for x when $-1 + x^2 = 120$.

(A) -11

(B) 10

(C) 11

(D) 12

(E) 11 or -11

Answer: E. This problem is similar to example 6, except we must first add 1 to both sides of the equation to get

$$-1 + 1 + x^2 = 120 + 1$$
$$x^2 = 121$$
$$x = \pm\sqrt{121} = \pm 11$$

Example 8. Which of the following is <u>false</u>?

Choose all answers that apply.

[A] $\sqrt{144} = 12$

[B] $\sqrt{144} = -12$

[C] If $x^2 = 25$, $x = 5$ or $x = -5$.

[D] $\sqrt{250} = 50$

[E] $\sqrt{x^2} = x$ or $-x$

Answer: B, D. A is True. The square root of 144 equals 12. **B.** False. $\sqrt{144}$ cannot be a negative number, only a positive number. **C.** True. When $x^2 = 25$, there are two solutions for x, 5 or -5. **D.** False. $\sqrt{250} \sim 15.8$, not 50. **E.** True. For $x < 0$, $\sqrt{x^2} = -x$. For example, $\sqrt{(-4)^2} = \sqrt{16} = 4$, and $4 = -(-4)$.

Chapter 5: Exponents and Roots

Example 9. Which of the following is smallest?

(A) 0

(B) $\dfrac{1}{\sqrt{81}}$

(C) $\dfrac{1}{\sqrt{144}}$

(D) 3^{-3}

(E) $\sqrt{64}$

Answer: A.

This answer choice has the smallest value because all of the other answer choices are positive, including choice (D), because $3^{-3} = \dfrac{1}{3^3} = \dfrac{1}{27}$.

Example 10. Which of the following expressions is equal to a number smaller than zero?

(A) 5^{-2}

(B) $(-1)^0$

(C) $\left(\sqrt{100}\right)^{-2}$

(D) $(-2)^3$

(E) $\left(\sqrt{36}\right)^{-2}$

Answer: D.

A. $5^{-2} = \dfrac{1}{5^2} = \dfrac{1}{25} > 0$.

B. is equal to 1 since any non-zero number raised to the power of 0 is equal to one by definition.

C. is equal to $\dfrac{1}{\left(\sqrt{100}\right)^2} = \dfrac{1}{100} > 0$.

D. $(-2)^3 = (-2) \cdot (-2) \cdot (-2) = -8$.

E. is equal to $\dfrac{1}{\left(\sqrt{36}\right)^2} = \dfrac{1}{36} > 0$.

Let's revisit a problem type from the previous chapter on numbers, this time involving exponents.

Example 11. Adam claims that if you square a prime number and subtract one from it, the resulting number is never prime. Which of the following resulting numbers is proof that he is wrong?

(A) 3

(B) 8

(C) 24

(D) 48

(E) 120

Answer: A.

2 is the first prime number, so $2^2 - 1 = 3$, which is a prime number, which immediately conflicts with his claim, and so we can safely mark **A** as the correct answer. To check the other answer choices, however, in choice **B**, $3^2 - 1 = 8$, which is not prime. In choice **C**, $5^2 - 1 = 24$, which is not prime. In choice **D**, $7^2 - 1 = 48$, which is not prime, and in choice **E**, $11^2 - 1 = 120$, which is not prime. From the five answer choices, only choice A negates Adam's claim.

Practice Problems

1. Compute: $\left(\sqrt{64} + \sqrt{16}\right)^2$

   (A) 12
   (B) 80
   (C) 144
   (D) 149
   (E) 160

2. Which of the following is true?

   Choose all answers that apply.

   [A] $1^2 = 2$
   [B] $3^3 = 27$
   [C] $10^2 = \sqrt{100}$
   [D] $4^4 = 16$
   [E] $5^3 = 15$

3. Solve for x when $x^2 = \sqrt{1}$.

   (A) 1
   (B) 1 or -1
   (C) 2
   (D) 2 or -2
   (E) There are no solutions to the above equation.

4. Which of the following expressions are equivalent?

   Choose all answers that apply.

   [A] $5^0 = 6^0$
   [B] $1^5 = 5$
   [C] $7^{-2} = -49$
   [D] $\sqrt{49} = 7^2$
   [E] $\sqrt{144} = 11$

5. Compute: $\left(\sqrt{100} - \sqrt{81}\right)^2$

   (A) 1
   (B) 2
   (C) $\sqrt{19}$
   (D) 19
   (E) 19^2

6. Which of the following is greater than 0?

   Choose all answers that apply.

   [A] 2^{-2}
   [B] 2^0
   [C] 2^{-1}
   [D] $(-3)^{-1}$
   [E] 3^{-2}

7. Which of the following is false?

   Choose all answers that apply.

   [A] $(-4)^2 = 4^{-2}$

   [B] $5^1 = 1^5$

   [C] $3^3 = 9$

   [D] $5^0 = 0$

   [E] $(-3)^{-2} = -\dfrac{1}{9}$

8. Compute: $\left(\sqrt{64} + 3^3 + 2^{-2} + 2^{-4}\right)^0$

   (A) -21

   (B) 0

   (C) 1

   (D) 15

   (E) 22

9. Sam hired 2 new employees every day for 4 days. What is the equivalent expression below that represents the number of employees he has hired?

   (A) 2^4

   (B) 4^2

   (C) 2^3

   (D) 16

   (E) 6^2

10. Compute: $7^2 - 9^2 - 1^0$

    (A) -33

    (B) -4

    (C) 0

    (D) 4

    (E) 31

11. Which of the following is false?

    Choose all answers that apply.

    [A] $6^2 + 3^2 = 45$

    [B] $2^{-3} - 2^0 + 1 < 0$

    [C] $(-3)^3 = 3^{-3}$

    [D] $3^2 + 3^3 = 3^5$

    [E] $2^0 \times 3^1 = 6^1$

12. In which of the following are the two numbers equivalent?

    (A) $1^5 = 5$

    (B) $8^2 = \dfrac{1}{64}$

    (C) $\sqrt{11}^2 = \sqrt{11^2}$

    (D) $1^0 = 0$

    (E) $\dfrac{1}{4} = 4^{-2}$

13. Compute: $\dfrac{3^0}{2^3}$

    (A) 0

    (B) $\dfrac{1}{8}$

    (C) $\dfrac{1}{6}$

    (D) $\dfrac{3}{8}$

    (E) 1

Answers to Practice Problems

1. **(C)** First perform the operations within the parentheses and then perform the exponent operation outside the parentheses.
$$(\sqrt{64} + \sqrt{16})^2 = (8+4)^2 = 12^2 = 144$$

2. **(B)** A. False. $1^2 = 1 \times 1 = 1$. $1 \neq 2$, so these are not equivalent values. **B.** True. $3^3 = 3 \cdot 3 \cdot 3 = 27$. **C.** False. $10^2 = 100$, and $\sqrt{100} = 10$. These are not equivalent values. **D.** False. $4^4 = 4 \cdot 4 \cdot 4 \cdot 4 = 256$. **E.** False. $5^3 = 5 \cdot 5 \cdot 5 = 125$.

3. **(B)** $\sqrt{1} = 1$, so first simplify to get $x^2 = 1$. Take the square roots of both sides. $\sqrt{x^2} = \sqrt{1}$, which gives $x = \pm 1$. Therefore x can be either 1 or -1.

4. **(A)** $5^0 = 1$ and $6^0 = 1$. These are equivalent values. The applicable rule is that any non-zero number raised to the power of zero equals 1. **B.** $1^5 = 1 \cdot 1 \cdot 1 \cdot 1 \cdot 1 = 1 \neq 5$. **C.** $7^{-2} = \frac{1}{7^2} = \frac{1}{49} \neq -49$. The applicable rule is that any non-zero number when raised to a negative exponent equals one divided by that number raised to the positive exponent. **D.** $\sqrt{49} = 7 \neq 7^2 = 49$ **E.** $\sqrt{144} = 12 \neq 11$.

5. **(A)** $(\sqrt{100} - \sqrt{81})^2 = (10-9)^2 = 1^2 = 1$.

6. **(A), (B), (C), (E)** All answer choices are positive except choice **D**. **A.** $2^{-2} = \frac{1}{2^2} = \frac{1}{4}$, which is greater than zero. **B.** $2^0 = 1 > 0$. **C.** $2^{-1} = \frac{1}{2^1} = \frac{1}{2} > 0$. **D.** $(-3)^{-1} = -\frac{1}{3} < 0$. **E.** $3^{-2} = \frac{1}{3^2} = \frac{1}{9} > 0$.

7. **(A), (B), (C), (D), (E)**
A is False. $(-4)^2 = 16 \neq 4^{-2} = \frac{1}{16}$.
B is False. $5^1 = 5 \neq 1^5 = 1$.
C is False. $3^3 = 3 \cdot 3 \cdot 3 = 27 \neq 9$.
D is False because $5^0 = 1$.
E is False because $(-3)^{-2} = \frac{1}{(-3)^2} = \frac{1}{9}$.

8. **(C)** Any non-zero number raised to the 0 power is equal to 1. We only need to make sure that what value inside the parentheses is not equal to zero, which would make the expression undefined. Looking at what is inside the parentheses, all the numbers are positive, so the sum must be positive, ruling out a zero inside the parentheses. If you evaluated each expression inside the parentheses and then added the numbers together, you wasted valuable time.

9. **(C)** Sam has hired 8 employees, since $2 \times 4 = 8$. **A.** $2^4 = 2 \cdot 2 \cdot 2 \cdot 2 = 16$. **B.** $4^2 = 16$. **C.** $2^3 = 2 \cdot 2 \cdot 2 = 8$, which is the correct answer. **D.** 16 is not equal to 8, and **E.** $6^2 = 36$.

10. **(A)** $7^2 - 9^2 - 1^0 = 49 - 81 - 1 = -33$.

11. **(B), (C), (D), (E)**
A is True. $6^2 + 3^2 = 36 + 9 = 45$.
B. False. $2^{-3} - 2^0 + 1 = \frac{1}{8} - 1 + 1 = \frac{1}{8} > 0$.
C. False. $(-3)^3 = (-3)(-3)(-3) = -27$, while $3^{-3} = \frac{1}{3^3} = \frac{1}{27}$.
D. False. $3^2 + 3^3 = 9 + 27 = 36$, while $3^5 = 3 \cdot 3 \cdot 3 \cdot 3 \cdot 3 = 243$.
E. False. $2^0 \times 3^1 = 1 \times 3 = 3$.

12. **(C)** Both expressions are equal to 11.
A. $1^5 = 1 \cdot 1 \cdot 1 \cdot 1 \cdot 1 = 1 \neq 5$.
B. $8^2 = 64 \neq \frac{1}{64}$. D. $1^0 = 1$.
E. $4^{-2} = \frac{1}{4^2} = \frac{1}{16} \neq \frac{1}{4}$.

13. **(B)** $\frac{3^0}{2^3} = \frac{1}{2 \cdot 2 \cdot 2} = \frac{1}{8}$.

Chapter 6
Order of Operations

Order of Operations

The phrase Order of Operations refers to a set method for solving arithmetic expressions. This universal method helps to ensure that everyone goes about solving arithmetic expressions in the same order, thus arriving at the same solution. The following table represents the order of operations necessary for solving any arithmetic expression:

Order of Operations

1. Parentheses: First, complete all operations within parentheses.
2. Exponents and Roots: Second, simplify all exponents and roots beginning with those inside of the parentheses.
3. Multiplication and Division: Complete all multiplication and division operations from left to right, beginning with those inside of the parentheses.
4. Addition and Subtraction: Complete all addition and subtraction operations from left to right.

The order of operations, while seemingly complicated, is remarkably easy to remember. Teachers have created a mnemonic device for students to quickly and easily recall the intended order. That mnemonic device is **Please Excuse My Dear Aunt Sally**, or **PEMDAS**, where the **P** represents parentheses, the **E** represents exponents and roots, the **MD** represents multiplication and division, and the **AS** represents addition and subtraction. Using this simple mnemonic device, you should be able to quickly and easily arrive at the correct solution for any mathematical expression!

Example 1. Evaluate the expression:

$$12 \times 10 - 25 + 50 \div 10$$

- (A) 10
- (B) 15
- (C) 100
- (D) 150
- (E) 200

Answer: C. Following the order of operations, multiplication is done first in this problem, $12 \times 10 = 120$. Secondly, we will use division to simplify $50 \div 10$ which is 5. These operations are performed before the addition/subtraction according to **PEMDAS**. Now after performing multiplication and division we have $120 - 25 + 5$. Next, perform the addition and subtraction from left to right to arrive at an answer of 100.

Example 2. Evaluate the expression:
$$10 \times \left[(80 - 40) + 200\right] \div 20$$

- (A) 25
- (B) 40
- (C) 120
- (D) 160
- (E) 1200

Answer: C. First, perform operations inside of the inner most grouping symbols to result in the following,
$$10 \times \left[40 + 200\right] \div 20$$
Next, perform the operation inside of the brackets to get,
$$10 \times 240 \div 20$$
Finally, multiply and divide from left to right, to arrive at 120.

Example 3. Evaluate the expression:
$$\frac{12}{3} \times 15 \times 4 - 20 \cdot 5 + 100 - 15$$

- (A) 85
- (B) 95
- (C) 120
- (D) 225
- (E) 1185

Answer: D. Begin by simplifying all fractions as follows,
$$4 \times 15 \times 4 - 20 \cdot 5 + 100 - 15$$
Next, perform multiplication to obtain
$$240 - 100 + 100 - 15$$
Finally, add and subtract from left to right, to get the correct answer of **D**.

Example 4. Evaluate the expression:
$$(4 + 1) \times 125 + \frac{12}{6} + 13 \times 0$$

- (A) 0
- (B) 106.17
- (C) 144
- (D) 577
- (E) 627

Answer: E. Begin by performing the addition within the parentheses,
$$5 \times 125 + \frac{12}{6} + 13 \times 0$$
Then perform multiplication and division operations:
$$625 + 2 + 0$$
Remember, any number multiplied by 0 is 0. Next add the numbers to obtain 627.

Example 5. Evaluate the expression:
$$\left(9 \cdot \frac{7}{3} + 5 \cdot 6(1 + 3)\right) - 20 \cdot 2$$

- (A) 14
- (B) 30
- (C) 101
- (D) 242
- (E) 625

Answer: C. Begin by simplifying the inner parentheses to obtain
$$\left(9 \cdot \frac{7}{3} + 5 \cdot 6 \cdot 4\right) - 20 \cdot 2$$
Next perform the multiplication operations inside the parentheses: $21 + 120 - 20 \cdot 2$. Next perform the multiplication of $20 \cdot 2 = 40$ to obtain $21 + 120 - 40$. Then add from left to right to obtain 101.

Example 6. Evaluate the expression:

$$\frac{6^2}{4} + 4(3 + 5)$$

- (A) 18
- (B) 26
- (C) 35
- (D) 41
- (E) 48

Answer: D. First, perform the addition inside the parentheses to obtain $\frac{6^2}{4} + 4(8)$. Next evaluate the exponent to obtain $\frac{36}{4} + 4(8)$. Then perform the multiplication and division to obtain $9 + 32 = 41$.

Example 7. Evaluate the expression:

$$2 \times [(100 - 25) + 200] \div 10$$

- (A) 37.5
- (B) 55
- (C) 86
- (D) 195
- (E) 234

Answer: B. Begin by performing operations inside of the innermost grouping symbol,

$$2 \times [(75) + 200] \div 10$$

Next, perform the operation inside of the brackets,

$$2 \times 275 \div 10$$

Finally, multiply then divide from left to right, to arrive at 55.

Operations with Negative Numbers

PEMDAS remains true with negative numbers. Remember from chapter 3 on negative numbers that a negative times a negative equals a positive number, and a negative times a positive (or positive times a negative) equals a negative number.

Example 8. Evaluate the expression:

$$-4 + 8 \times \left(99 - 12^2 - 2 + \frac{45}{9}\right)$$

- (A) −1344
- (B) −647
- (C) −340
- (D) 1216
- (E) 1344

Answer: C. First, perform the exponent inside the parentheses to obtain

$$-4 + 8 \times \left(99 - 144 - 2 + \frac{45}{9}\right)$$

Next perform the division inside the parentheses:

$$-4 + 8 \times (99 - 144 - 2 + 5)$$

Next add and subtract inside the parentheses:

$$-4 + 8 \times (-42)$$

Next multiply, $-4 + (-336) = -340$.

Raising Negative Numbers to Exponents

When a negative number is raised to an even power, a positive number is obtained.

Example: $(-3)^2 = 9$

When a negative number is raised to an odd power, a negative number is obtained.

Example: $(-3)^3 = -27$

Chapter 6: Order of Operations

Also note the difference between -2^2 which equals -4 and $(-2)^2 = +4$. There is no difference between -3^3 and $(-3)^3$; both equal -27.

Example 9. Evaluate the expression:
$$-4^2 - 3^3 \times -4 + (-7 \times -8) - 3 \times (-4+5)$$

(A) -37
(B) -35
(C) 35
(D) 145
(E) 162

Answer: D. Perform all the operations inside the parentheses first:
$$-4^2 - 3^3 \times -4 + (56) - 3 \times (1)$$
Then perform the exponents to obtain
$$-16 - 27 \times -4 + 56 - 3(1)$$
Then perform the multiplication to get
$$-16 + 108 + 56 - 3 = 145$$

Example 10. Evaluate the expression:
$$-5^2 - 6(6^{(4-2)} - 30) + (-9)(-4-3)$$

(A) -124
(B) -102
(C) 2
(D) 102
(E) 634

Answer: C. Begin by simplifying
$$6^{(4-2)} = 6^2 = 36, \text{ and } -5^2 = -25$$
Then, evaluate all the expressions in the parentheses:
$$-25 - 6(36 - 30) + (-9)(-7)$$
Now perform the subtraction inside the parentheses:
$$-25 - 6(6) + (-9)(-7)$$
Now perform the multiplication operations:
$$-25 - 36 + 63$$
Now add to obtain 2.

Practice Problems

1. Evaluate: $8 + \dfrac{32}{4^2}$

   (A) 4
   (B) 6
   (C) 9
   (D) 10
   (E) 12

2. Evaluate: $-4(-5+7)^3 - 6(8-10)$

   (A) -20
   (B) -10
   (C) 2
   (D) 13
   (E) 15

3. Evaluate: $13 + \dfrac{18}{3-6} - 4(5-9)$

   (A) 19
   (B) 23
   (C) 145
   (D) 169
   (E) 224

4. Evaluate: $14 \times 12 - 3 \times 8\big(2 + 3(3-4)\big)$

   (A) 13
   (B) 145
   (C) 192
   (D) 193
   (E) 235

5. Evaluate: $3^2 - 5^2(-1-2) + 6^2 - 7^2$

   (A) 55
   (B) 69
   (C) 71
   (D) 73
   (E) 85

6. Evaluate: $4 \times (9 - 4^2) + 4(5 \quad 8)$

   (A) -130
   (B) -112
   (C) -92
   (D) -69
   (E) -40

Chapter 6: Order of Operations

7. Evaluate: $3 \times (7 - 12)^2 - 3 \times (3 - 5)^3$

    (A) 43
    (B) 51
    (C) 77
    (D) 99
    (E) 103

8. Evaluate: $6 + 2(4 - 3^2 - 5^2 + 11)$

    (A) −32
    (B) −28
    (C) 0
    (D) 14
    (E) 27

9. Evaluate: $-2 \times 3\left(4 - \dfrac{50}{5^2}\right) + 50$

    (A) −123
    (B) −38
    (C) −14
    (D) −2
    (E) 38

10. Evaluate: $\dfrac{3^3}{6 - 3^2} - 5(9 - 16)$

    (A) −35
    (B) −30
    (C) −26
    (D) 14
    (E) 26

11. Evaluate: $2(4 - 5)^2 + 3(4 - 5)^3$

    (A) −114
    (B) −100
    (C) −80
    (D) −1
    (E) 34

12. Evaluate: $3(5 - 6)^3 - 6(29 - 11 \cdot 3)$

    (A) 20
    (B) 21
    (C) 43
    (D) 123
    (E) 192

13. Evaluate: $2((-1)^3 - 4^2 \times (9-8))$

    Ⓐ −39
    Ⓑ −34
    Ⓒ 120
    Ⓓ 135
    Ⓔ 1296

14. Evaluate: $3(-2^3 + (-4)^2 - (-2)^2)$

    Ⓐ −3
    Ⓑ 0
    Ⓒ 12
    Ⓓ 36
    Ⓔ 234

15. Evaluate: $2(-4 - 3^2 + 14) - 2(9-3)$

    Ⓐ −455
    Ⓑ −35
    Ⓒ −22
    Ⓓ −12
    Ⓔ −10

Answers to Practice Problems

1. **(D)** $8 + \dfrac{32}{4^2} = 8 + \dfrac{32}{16} = 8 + 2 = 10.$

2. **(A)** $-4(-5+7)^3 - 6(8-10)$
   $= -4(2)^3 - 6(-2) = -4 \times 8 + 12$
   $= -32 + 12 = -20$

3. **(B)** $13 + \dfrac{18}{3-6} - 4(5-9)$
   $= 13 + \dfrac{18}{-3} - 4(-4) = 13 - 6 + 16 = 23$

4. **(C)** $14 \times 12 - 3 \times 8(2 + 3(3-4))$
   $= 168 - 3 \times 8(2 + 3(-1))$
   $= 168 - 3 \times 8(-1) = 168 + 24 = 192$

5. **(C)** $3^2 - 5^2(-1-2) + 6^2 - 7^2$
   $= 9 - 25(-3) + 36 - 49$
   $= 9 + 75 + 36 - 49 = 71$

6. **(E)** $4 \times (9 - 4^2) + 4(5-8)$
   $= 4 \times (9 - 16) + 4(5-8)$
   $= 4 \times (-7) + 4(-3) = -28 + (-12) = -40$

7. **(D)** $3 \times (7-12)^2 - 3 \times (3-5)^3$
   $= 3 \times (-5)^2 - 3 \times (-2)^3$
   $= 3 \times 25 - 3 \times (-8) = 75 + 24 = 99$

8. **(A)** $6 + 2(4 - 3^2 - 5^2 + 11)$
   $= 6 + 2(4 - 9 - 25 + 11) = 6 + 2(-19)$
   $= 6 + (-38) = -32.$

9. **(E)** $-2 \times 3\left(4 - \dfrac{50}{5^2}\right) + 50$
   $= -2 \times 3\left(4 - \dfrac{50}{25}\right) + 50$
   $= -2 \times 3(4 - 2) + 50 = -2 \times 3(2) + 50$
   $= -12 + 50 = 38.$

10. **(E)** $\dfrac{3^3}{6 - 3^2} - 5(9 - 16)$
    $= \dfrac{27}{6-9} - 5(-7) = \dfrac{27}{-3} - 5(-7)$
    $= -9 + 35 = 26$

11. **(D)** $2(4-5)^2 + 3(4-5)^3$
    $= 2(-1)^2 + 3(-1)^3 = 2(1) + 3(-1)$
    $= 2 - 3 = -1$

12. **(B)** $3(5-6)^3 - 6(29 - 11 \cdot 3)$
    $= 3(-1)^3 - 6(29 - 33) = 3(-1) - 6(-4)$
    $= -3 + 24 = 21$

13. **(B)** $2\big((-1)^3 - 4^2 \times (9-8)\big)$
    $= 2(-1 - 16 \times 1) = 2(-17) = -34$

14. **(C)** $3\big(-2^3 + (-4)^2 - (-2)^2\big)$
    $= 3(-8 + 16 - 4) = 3(4) = 12.$

    If you got $3(-8 + 16 + 4) = 36$, you erroneously multiplied a negative 1 by negative 2 to obtain positive 2, and then you squared it to obtain 4. But the correct order of operations is to first square -2 to obtain $+4$, and then multiply by -1 to obtain -4!

15. **(E)** $2(-4 - 3^2 + 14) - 2(9-3)$
    $= 2(-4 - 9 + 14) - 2(6) = 2(1) - 12 = -10$

Chapter 7
Simplifying Expressions

An algebraic expression is a mathematical phrase that contains letters and numbers. The letters are referred to as **variables**. The numbers that are attached to variables are referred to as **coefficients**, and the numbers that are not attached to variables are referred to as **constants**. For example, in the expression $3x + 6$, 3 is a coefficient, x is a variable, and 6 is a constant. Additionally, each part of the expression is called a **term**, which is separated from the next term by an addition or subtraction sign. A term is either: a stand-alone constant or a coefficient and variable pair with the variable raised to an exponent (including an exponent of 1). In the example $3x + 6$, there are two terms: $3x$, a coefficient and variable pair with the variable raised to the exponent of 1, and 6, a stand-alone constant.

$$\underbrace{3x}_{\text{Term 1}} + \underbrace{6}_{\text{Term 2}}$$

- 6 is the constant
- 3 is the coefficient
- x is the variable

Simplifying an expression means converting the expression into its most concise form. Problems involving simplifying expressions can be grouped into one of the four categories: adding and subtracting variables, multiplying variables, simplifying fractions, and applying the distributive property.

Adding and Subtracting Variables

Adding and subtracting variables is done by combining like terms. The first step is to identify the like terms. Like terms are terms of the same type, meaning sets of terms that include either all stand-alone constants (like $4 + 8$) or all of the same variable raised to the same exponent (like $2x^2 + 4x^2$) regardless of the coefficients. The second step is to combine, or add together, the like terms. The last step is to rewrite the expression in standard form. Standard form is the form in which the terms are written in order from the highest exponent term to the lowest exponent term.

Example 1. Which of the following sets contains all like terms?

- (A) $-8y^3, 2y^3, 160y^3$
- (B) x, y, z
- (C) $2x, 2x^2, 2x^4$
- (D) $100, 10, 1x$
- (E) $-3x, -3y, -3xy$

Answer: A. Here, 3 is the exponent that y is raised to, which is common to all the terms. Choice **A**, $-8y^3, 2y^3, 160y^3$, is the only choice that contains all like terms, since each term has the same variable (y) raised to the same exponent (3).

Example 2. Which of the following expressions can be simplified?

- (A) $2a + 2b$
- (B) $2a^3 + 3a^2$
- (C) $3a^3 + 2b^2$
- (D) $a + 3a$
- (E) $a^2 + 2a + 2$

Answer: D. When adding and subtracting variables, only expressions with like terms can be simplified. Choice **D**, $a + 3a$, is the only choice that contains all like terms since each term has the same variable (a) raised to the same exponent (1). The exponent common to both terms is 1 because $a^1 = a$.

Example 3. What is $33 + 8x^2 + 10 - 9x^2$ in simplest form?

- (A) $33 - x^2 + 10$
- (B) $-x^2 + 43$
- (C) $x^2 + 43$
- (D) $-x^4 + 43$
- (E) $17x^2 + 43$

Answer: B. First, identify like terms. There are two sets of like terms in this expression: $33 + 10$ and $8x^2 - 9x^2$. Second, combine the like terms: $33 + 10 = 43$ and $8x^2 - 9x^2 = -x^2$. Finally, rewrite the expression in standard form: $-x^2 + 43$.

Example 4. What is $-40 - 2x^5 - 12x^5 + 24$ in simplest form?

- (A) $-10x^5 + 16$
- (B) $-14x^5 - 16$
- (C) $10x^5 + 16$
- (D) $14x^5 - 16$
- (E) $-2x^5 - 16$

Answer: B. First, identify like terms. There are two sets of like terms in this expression: $-40 + 24$ and $-2x^5 - 12x^5$. Second, combine the like terms: $-40 + 24 = -16$ and $-2x^5 - 12x^5 = -14x^5$. Finally, rewrite the expression in standard form: $-14x^5 - 16$.

Multiplying Variables

Multiplying variables is done by multiplying the coefficients and then adding the exponents of like terms. For example,

$$2x^2 \times 9x = (2 \cdot 9) \times x^{2+1} = 18x^3$$

Example 5. What is $6x \times 2x^2$ in simplest form?

- (A) $12x^3$
- (B) $6x^3$
- (C) $6x^2$
- (D) $12x^2$
- (E) $12x$

Answer: A. Remember that $x = x^1$. Now multiply the coefficients: $6 \cdot 2 = 12$. Then, add the exponents and rewrite this number as the new exponent associated with the variable: $x^{1+2} = x^3$. The final answer is $12x^3$.

Example 6. What is $15x^7 \times 3x^2$?

- (A) $18x^9$
- (B) $45x^{14}$
- (C) $45x^9$
- (D) $45x^5$
- (E) $45x^{49}$

Answer: C. First, multiply the coefficients: $15 \cdot 3 = 45$. Then, add the exponents and rewrite this number as the new exponent associated with the variable: $x^{7+2} = x^9$. The final answer is $45x^9$.

Simplifying Fractions

Simplifying fractions is done by dividing the numerator and the denominator by the largest number possible that still results in a whole number.

Example 7. What is $\dfrac{3x}{9}$ in the simplest form?

- (A) $3x$
- (B) $9x$
- (C) 3
- (D) $\dfrac{x}{3}$
- (E) 9

Answer: D. Divide both the numerator and denominator by 3:
$$\frac{3x/3}{9/3} = \frac{x}{3}$$

Example 8. What is $\dfrac{36x}{6}$ in the simplest form?

- (A) 6
- (B) $6x$
- (C) $\dfrac{36x}{6}$
- (D) $\dfrac{x}{6}$
- (E) $36x$

Answer: B. Divide both the numerator and denominator by 6:
$$\frac{36x/6}{6/6} = \frac{6x}{1} = 6x$$

Remember that any number divided by 1 is itself, so the 1 in the denominator disappears.

Example 9. What is $\dfrac{16x}{4} + \dfrac{6x}{6}$ in the simplest form?

- (A) $\dfrac{4x}{4} + \dfrac{x}{6}$
- (B) $4x + 1$
- (C) $\dfrac{22x}{10}$
- (D) $\dfrac{11x}{10}$
- (E) $5x$

Answer: E. For the first term, divide both the numerator and denominator by 4:
$$\frac{16x/4}{4/4} = \frac{4x}{1} = 4x$$

For the second term, divide both the numerator and denominator by 6:
$$\frac{6x/6}{6/6} = \frac{x}{1} = x$$

Then add the terms: $4x + x = 5x$.

Chapter 7: Simplifying Expressions

Using the Distributive Property

The distributive property states that

$$a(b + c) = ab + ac$$

where a, b, and c are terms that are numbers, variables, or a combination of both. The distributive property is used to get rid of parentheses by multiplying each term inside the parentheses by the term outside the parentheses and then adding together the resulting products. The last step is to rewrite the expression in standard form. For example,

$$5(x^2 + 4) = (5 \cdot x^2) + (5 \cdot 4) = 5x^2 + 20$$

Example 10. What is $3(2x^3 + 9)$ in the simplest form?

- (A) $6x^3 + 9$
- (B) $6x^3 + 27x$
- (C) $6x^3 + 9x$
- (D) $6x^3 + 27$
- (E) $3x^3 + 27$

Answer: D.

Distribute the parentheses by multiplying each term inside the parentheses by the term outside the parentheses:

$$3(2x^3 + 9) = (3 \cdot 2x^3) + (3 \cdot 9) = 6x^3 + 27$$

Practice Problems

1. Simplify: $5x^2 \times 5x$

   (A) $25x$
   (B) $5x^3$
   (C) $25x^2$
   (D) $25x^3$
   (E) $10x^3$

2. Which of the following contains all like terms?

   (A) 8m, 2m, 2n
   (B) $18x^2$, $9x$, x
   (C) $3x$, $-11x$, $22x$
   (D) 18m, 18n, 18p
   (E) $3m^2$, $3n^2$, $6m^2n^2$

3. Simplify: $9x(x+9)$

   (A) $9x^2 + 81$
   (B) $81x^2 + 81$
   (C) $9x^2 + 9$
   (D) $9x + 81$
   (E) $9x^2 + 81x$

4. Which of the following is in simplest form?

   (A) $\dfrac{121}{11}$
   (B) $\dfrac{20x^2}{5}$
   (C) $\dfrac{45x^2}{2}$
   (D) $\dfrac{24x^2}{6}$
   (E) $\dfrac{80x}{2}$

5. Simplify: $8x + 9 - 2 + 8 + 5x - 1$

   (A) $13x + 14$
   (B) $27x$
   (C) $17x + 15 + 4x$
   (D) $13x + 18$
   (E) $12x + 16$

6. Simplify: $4(x^2 + 8)$

   (A) $2x^2 + 32$
   (B) $4x^2 + 32$
   (C) $4x + 32$
   (D) $2x^2 + 8$
   (E) $4x^2 + 8$

Chapter 7: Simplifying Expressions

7. Simplify: $4y^3 \times 7y^2$

    (A) $28y^5$
    (B) $28y^6$
    (C) $11y^5$
    (D) $11y^6$
    (E) $11y^9$

8. Simplify: $23 + 3x^4 - 2x^4 + 10$

    (A) $5x^4 + 33$
    (B) $5x^4 + 13$
    (C) $x^4 + 13$
    (D) $x^4 + 33$
    (E) $x^4 - 13$

9. Which of the following contains all like terms?

    (A) $4x, 4y, 4z$
    (B) $2x^2, 3x^3, 4x^4$
    (C) $2x^2, 2x^3, 2x^4$
    (D) $64x^2, 2x^2, 4x^2$
    (E) $4x^2, 4x, 4x^3$

10. Simplify: $2x^2 \times x^4$

    (A) $2x^6$
    (B) $3x^6$
    (C) $2x^8$
    (D) $2x^2$
    (E) $3x^2$

11. Simplify: $7x^4 \times 8x^2$

    (A) $15x^6$
    (B) $56x^8$
    (C) $56x^6$
    (D) $15x^8$
    (E) $15x^{16}$

12. Simplify: $5x^4(8x - 2)$

    (A) $8x^5 - 10x^4$
    (B) $40x^5 - 10x^4$
    (C) $40x^4 - 10x^4$
    (D) $40x^5 + 10x^4$
    (E) $40x^4 - 10$

13. Simplify: $\dfrac{24x}{3} + \dfrac{16x}{8}$

    (A) $10x^2$
    (B) 10
    (C) $8x^2$
    (D) $10x$
    (E) $12x$

14. Simplify: $10x^4 \times 2x^2$

    (A) $20x^8$
    (B) $20x^6$
    (C) $12x^6$
    (D) $12x^8$
    (E) $12x^2$

15. Which of the following is in simplest form?

    (A) $\dfrac{29x^3}{2}$
    (B) $\dfrac{2x}{10}$
    (C) $\dfrac{18x^2}{6}$
    (D) $\dfrac{20x^3}{5}$
    (E) $\dfrac{50}{5}$

Chapter 7: Simplifying Expressions

Answers to Practice Problems

1. **(D)** First, multiply the coefficients: $5 \times 5 = 25$. Then, add the exponents and rewrite this number as the new exponent associated with the variable: $x^{2+1} = x^3$. The final answer is $25x^3$.

2. **(C)** This is the only choice that contains all like terms since each term has the same variable (x) raised to the same exponent (1).

3. **(E)** Distribute the parentheses by multiplying each term inside the parentheses by the term outside the parentheses:
   $$(9x \cdot x) + (9x \cdot 9) = 9x^2 + 81x$$

4. **(C)** This is the only choice that cannot be simplified further by dividing the coefficients.

5. **(A)** First, identify like terms. There are two sets of like terms in this expression: $8x + 5x$ and $9 - 2 + 8 - 1$. Second, combine the like terms: $8x + 5x = 13x$ and $9 - 2 + 8 - 1 = 14$. Finally, rewrite the expression in standard form: $13x + 14$.

6. **(B)** Distribute the 4 to both terms inside the parentheses:
   $$(4 \cdot x^2) + (4 \cdot 8) = 4x^2 + 32$$

7. **(A)** First, multiply the coefficients: $4 \times 7 = 28$. Then, add the exponents and rewrite this number as the new exponent associated with the variable: $y^{3+2} = y^5$. The final answer is $28y^5$.

8. **(D)** First, identify like terms. There are two sets of like terms in this expression: $3x^4 - 2x^4$ and $23 + 10$. Second, combine the like terms: $3x^4 - 2x^4 = x^4$ and $23 + 10 = 33$. Finally, rewrite the expression in standard form: $x^4 + 33$.

9. **(D)** This is the only choice that contains all like terms since each term has the same variable (x) raised to the same exponent (2).

10. **(A)** First, multiply the coefficients: $2 \times 1 = 2$. Then, add the exponents and rewrite this number as the new exponent associated with the variable: $x^{2+4} = x^6$. The final answer is $2x^6$.

11. **(C)** First, multiply the coefficients: $7 \times 8 = 56$. Then, add the exponents and rewrite this number as the new exponent associated with the variable: $x^{2+4} = x^6$. The final answer is $56x^6$.

12. **(B)** Distribute the parentheses by multiplying each term inside the parentheses by the term outside the parentheses:
    $$(5x^4 \cdot 8x) - (5x^4 \cdot 2) = 40x^5 - 10x^4$$

13. **(D)** For the first term, divide both the numerator and denominator by 3:
    $$\frac{24x/3}{3/3} = \frac{8x}{1} = 8x$$
    For the second term, divide both the numerator and denominator by 8:
    $$\frac{16x/8}{8/8} = \frac{2x}{1} = 2x$$
    Then add the terms: $8x + 2x = 10x$.

14. **(B)** First, multiply the coefficients: $10 \times 2 = 20$. Then, add the exponents and rewrite this number as the new exponent associated with the variable: $x^{2+4} = x^6$. The final answer is $20x^6$.

15. **(A)** This is the only choice which cannot be simplified further by dividing the coefficients.

Chapter 8

Solving Equations and Manipulating Expressions

Algebraic manipulation is the process of manipulating and solving equations for an unknown quantity. An equation is an algebraic sentence with an equals sign such as,

$$3x - 5 = 8$$

It states that the value of both sides of the equals sign is the same. Algebra uses variables, usually letters such as x and y, to represent unknown quantities. When we solve equations, we find the value of the variable that makes the equation a true statement. For example, in the simple equation

$$2 + x = 5$$

the value of the variable x must be 3, because $2 + 3 = 5$, is a true statement.

The most important thing to remember when solving equations is that you must always do the same operation with the same quantity (number or variable) to both sides of the equation.
This way, the two sides of the equation remain equal. An equation is like a balance; if we subtract 5 ounces from one side of the scales, we must subtract 5 ounces from the other side for the two sides to balance.

Solving One-Step Equations Involving Addition and Subtraction

The first type of equation we will learn to solve is called a one-step equation because it only takes one step to solve it. One-step equations with a constant added to or subtracted from the variable are solved by adding or subtracting the constant term from both sides of the equation. We do the opposite operation so that the result will be zero.

Example 1. What is the value of x in the equation $x - 7 = 6$?

- (A) −1
- (B) 1
- (C) 6
- (D) 7
- (E) 13

Answer: E. Since the constant term 7 is subtracted from *x*, we do the opposite, and add 7 to each side of the = sign to get *x* all by itself on the left side, as follows:

$$x - 7 = 6$$
$$x - 7 + 7 = 6 + 7$$
$$x + 0 = 13$$
$$x = 13$$

Example 2. If $x + 11 = 15$, then what is the value of *x* ?

Ⓐ −4
Ⓑ 4
Ⓒ 11
Ⓓ 15
Ⓔ 26

Answer: B. Here the constant term is added to the variable, so we subtract 11 from both sides to get *x* all by itself on the left side of the equation:

$$x + 11 = 15$$
$$x + 11 - 11 = 15 - 11$$
$$x + 0 = 4$$
$$x = 4$$

Solving One-Step Equations Involving Multiplication

The other type of a one-step equation contains a constant multiplied by the variable such as

$$5x = 15$$

The *x* term is already isolated on the left side of the equation. So all we need to do is to make the coefficient of the *x* term a 1. We can do this by dividing each side of the equation by the coefficient of *x* (5 in this case), because any number divided by itself equals 1. Note that *x* is the same as 1*x* and we usually don't write the 1. Here are some examples and their solutions.

Example 3. What is the value of *x* in the equation $-3x = 18$?

Ⓐ −6
Ⓑ 6
Ⓒ 15
Ⓓ 21
Ⓔ 54

Answer: A. We solve this equation by dividing both sides of the equation by −3, so that the coefficient of *x* becomes 1.

$$\frac{-3x}{-3} = \frac{18}{-3}$$
$$1x = -6$$
$$x = -6$$

Example 4. Solve the following equation for *a*:

$$\frac{2a}{3} = 14$$

Ⓐ 7
Ⓑ 11
Ⓒ 21
Ⓓ 28
Ⓔ 42

Answer: C. In this equation the coefficient of the variable is a fraction. We want the coefficient to be a 1. So we multiply both sides of the equation by the reciprocal of $\frac{2}{3}$, which is $\frac{3}{2}$, because any number multiplied by its reciprocal is 1.

$$\frac{3}{2} \times \frac{2a}{3} = \frac{3}{2} \times 14$$
$$1a = 21$$
$$a = 21$$

Example 5. What is the value of the variable in the equation $\frac{z}{4} = -7$?

- (A) -28
- (B) -11
- (C) -3
- (D) $-\frac{7}{4}$
- (E) 28

Answer: A. In this equation the variable is divided by 4. But remember that z is equivalent to $1z$. So $\frac{z}{4}$ is the same as $\frac{1z}{4}$. Therefore, the coefficient of z is the fraction $\frac{1}{4}$, and this equation can be solved by multiplying by the reciprocal of the coefficient, just like in example 4. Note that the reciprocal of $\frac{1}{4}$ is $\frac{4}{1}$, which is the same as 4.

$$\frac{\cancel{4}}{\cancel{1}} \times \frac{\cancel{1}z}{\cancel{4}} = \frac{4}{1} \times (-7)$$
$$z = -28$$

Solving Two-Step Equations

Solving two-step equations is just a combination of solving the two types of one-step equations that we have solved so far. The process must always be done in a specific order. First, add or subtract any constant term that is on the same side of the equals sign as the variable term from both sides of the equals sign. This will isolate the variable term on one side of the equals sign (note that it does not matter which side). Next, make the coefficient of the variable term equal to 1 by dividing (if it is a whole number), or multiplying by the reciprocal (if it is a fraction).

So, adding or subtracting always comes first, then multiplication or division second. And all operations are always performed on both sides of the equation so that the sides remain equal.

Example 6. What is the value of x in the equation $8x + 9 = 33$?

- (A) 3
- (B) $\frac{33}{8}$
- (C) $\frac{33}{8}$
- (D) 13
- (E) 192

Answer: A. The first step in solving this equation is to subtract the constant term 9 from both sides of the equation. Then we divide by 8 to make the coefficient of the x term a 1.

$$8x + 9 - 9 = 33 - 9$$
$$\frac{\cancel{8}x}{\cancel{8}} = \frac{24}{8}$$
$$x = 3$$

Example 7. Solve the following equation for x:

$$14 - 2 = -\frac{3x}{8} + 17$$

- (A) -8
- (B) -5
- (C) $-\frac{15}{8}$
- (D) $\frac{5}{3}$
- (E) $\frac{40}{3}$

Chapter 8: Solving Equations and Manipulating Expressions

Answer: E. There are two constant terms on the left side of this equation. We need to combine these like terms (14 − 2 = 12), before proceeding with the two steps for equation solving. First, subtract 17 from both sides to isolate the x term.

$$12 = -\frac{3x}{8} + 17$$

$$12 - 17 = -\frac{3x}{8} + 17 - 17$$

$$-5 = -\frac{3x}{8}$$

Then multiply by −1 to cancel out the (−) sign.

$$5 = \frac{3x}{8}$$

Next, multiply by the reciprocal of $\frac{3}{8}$ to make the coefficient a 1. Notice that the variable is on the right side of this equation, but this does not change the solving process. We simply isolate the variable on the right side of the equation instead of the left.

$$\frac{8}{3} \times 5 = \frac{\cancel{8}}{\cancel{3}} \times \frac{\cancel{3}x}{\cancel{8}}$$

$$\frac{40}{3} = x$$

$$x = \frac{40}{3}$$

Solving More Complex Equations

Sometimes the equations we need to solve are more complex, involving fractions with variable expressions in them such as

$$\frac{x+5}{6} = 22$$

or expressions containing parentheses like

$$7(x + 4) = 35$$

The next two example problems will explain how to solve these types of equations.

Example 8. What is the value of x in the equation $\frac{x-7}{3} = -13$?

Ⓐ −39

Ⓑ −32

Ⓒ −18

Ⓓ $\frac{13}{3}$

Ⓔ 46

Answer: B. In this equation the variable x is contained within a fraction. To solve this type of equation we first need to eliminate the fraction. We do this by multiplying both sides of the equation by the denominator of the fraction. Then the equation is just a simple one-step problem that is solved by adding 7 to both sides.

$$\frac{x-7}{3} \times 3 = -13 \times 3$$

$$x - 7 = -39$$

$$x - 7 + 7 = -39 + 7$$

$$x = -32$$

Example 9. Solve the following equation for x:

$$3(x - 5) = 6$$

Ⓐ −3

Ⓑ 2

Ⓒ $\frac{11}{3}$

Ⓓ 7

Ⓔ 13

Answer: D. In this equation the variable x is contained within parentheses. To solve this type of equation we divide both sides of the equation by 3. Then we add five to both sides of the equals sign, to obtain $x = 7$.

$$3(x - 5) = 6$$
$$x - 5 = 2$$
$$x = 7$$

Solving an Equation for One Variable in Terms of Another

Sometimes an equation contains more than one variable. For example, the formula for converting degrees Fahrenheit to degrees Celsius contains two variables:

$$C = \frac{5}{9} \times (F - 32)$$

This equation is solved for C in terms of F because C is all by itself on one side of the equation. "In terms of F" means that we can't solve this equation for a numerical value for C; instead, we have an expression with the variable F in it. Once we know the value of F, we can plug it into the equation and get a numerical value for C. An equation containing two variables can be solved for either one of the variables by the same process we use to solve an equation with one variable. The variable you are solving for is isolated on one side of the equation, and the other variable is manipulated just like a constant term. This is illustrated in the following example.

Example 10. If $12x - 3y = 18$, what is the value of y in terms of x?

Ⓐ $4x - 6$
Ⓑ $12x - 8$
Ⓒ $3x + 12$
Ⓓ -2
Ⓔ $10x$

Answer: A. This equation contains two variables, x and y. We are asked to solve the equation for y in terms of x. Therefore, we want to isolate the y term. Since $12x$ is on the same side of the equation as $3y$, we subtract $12x$ from both sides, just like we would if it was a constant term. Note that the effect of this is that we now have the opposite of $12x$, or $-12x$, on the other side of the equation. This is why this process is sometimes referred to as moving the x term to the other side of the equation.

$$12x - 3y = 18$$
$$12x - 3y - 12x = 18 - 12x$$
$$-3y = -12x + 18$$

Next, we divide both sides of the equation by -3 to make the coefficient of the y term a 1. Notice that these are the same steps we used to solve single variable equations.

$$\frac{-3y}{-3} = \frac{-12x + 18}{-3}$$
$$1y = \frac{-12x}{-3} + \frac{18}{-3}$$
$$y = 4x - 6$$

Solving Equations for a Specific Expression

Equations can also be solved for a specific algebraic expression such as $(x - 4)$ or $(3a + 12)$. Our goal is to isolate the expression we are solving for on one side of the equation. We use the exact same methods as we have been using to solve equations for a single variable. However, when we are solving for an expression, we might not want the variable coefficient to be a 1, like we always do when solving for just one variable. For example, if we are solving for the expression $6b - 5$, then we want the variable coefficient to be a 6, not a 1. We will need to divide by the appropriate value to get the coefficient we want, as illustrated in the following example.

Chapter 8: Solving Equations and Manipulating Expressions

Example 11. If $4(y + 3) = 6x - 8$, then what is the value of $2y - 3x$?

- (A) -10
- (B) $-\dfrac{11}{2}$
- (C) 2
- (D) $\dfrac{5}{2}$
- (E) 20

Answer: A. First, notice that this equation contains two variables, x and y. We are asked to solve the equation for the expression $2y - 3x$. Order of operations tells us to take care of parentheses first, so our first step is to distribute.

$$4(y + 3) = 6x - 8$$
$$4y + 12 = 6x - 8$$

Next, we need to get both the x and y terms on the same side of the equation, and all constant terms on the other side. Remember, we can move terms around by adding or subtracting them from both sides of the equation.

$$4y - 6x = -8 - 12 = -20$$

Our last step is to divide both sides of the equation by 2 to get the desired coefficients for x and y. Notice that when we divide both sides of the equation by 2, that means we must divide each term on each side of the equation by 2.

$$\dfrac{4y - 6x}{2} = \dfrac{-20}{2}$$
$$2y - 3x = -10$$

Manipulating Equations Using Number Properties

We can manipulate equations using number properties such as the Commutative Property, the Associative Property, and the Distributive Property of Multiplication over Addition.

The **Commutative Property of Addition** means that when we add two quantities, we will get the same answer no matter what order we add them in. For example,

$$a + b = b + a$$

This property applies to multiplication as well, but not to subtraction or division.

The **Associative Property of Multiplication** states that we can change the grouping (parentheses), and not change the answer. For example,

$$a \cdot (b \cdot c) = (a \cdot b) \cdot c$$

In other words, we can multiply a times b first, then multiply by c, or we can multiply b times c first, then multiply by a, and we will get the same answer either way. The Associative Property applies to addition as well, but not to subtraction or division.

The **Distributive Property of Multiplication over Addition** states that

$$a(b + c) = ab + ac$$

The a is distributed through the parentheses and multiplies first times b and then times c.

We can use these properties to manipulate equations and determine if two equations are equal as shown in the example below.

Example 12. If x, y, and z are positive integers, which of the following equations must be true?

- (A) $x \cdot y + z = x + y \cdot z$
- (B) $x(y + z) = xy + xz$
- (C) $x + y + z = xy - xz$
- (D) $z - y + x = y - z + x$
- (E) $(x - y) - z = x + (y - z)$

Answer: B. To solve this problem we need to determine which equation makes correct usage of number properties, so that both sides are equal.

(A). False. This equation violates the order of operations.

(B). True. This equation demonstrates correct use of the distributive property. The x is distributed through the parentheses, multiplying first times the y and then times the z.

(C). False. There is no multiplication on the left side of this equation, so the distributive property has been incorrectly applied.

(D). False. The order of the z and y terms have been reversed, but this is not valid because the commutative property does not apply to subtraction.

(E). False. This is an attempt to apply the associative property, but the first subtraction sign was changed to addition. Also, the associative property does not apply to subtraction.

Solving Equations When the Variable Is in the Denominator

Now we can turn our attention to equations where the variable to be solved for appears in the denominator.

It should be noted that in a fraction, the denominator can't take a value of zero, in which case the fraction is *undefined*.

Example 13. Solve for x: $\dfrac{1}{x} = 2$

(A) $\dfrac{1}{4}$

(B) $\dfrac{1}{2}$

(C) 1

(D) 2

(E) 4

Answer: B. We can treat the 2 on the right as $\dfrac{2}{1}$ since dividing by 1 doesn't change the fraction. We obtain:

$$\frac{1}{x} = \frac{2}{1}$$

We can now cross multiply to obtain: $1 \times 1 = 2 \times x$, or $1 = 2x$. Now divide both sides of the equation by 2 to obtain $x = \dfrac{1}{2}$.

Example 14. Solve for x: $\dfrac{2}{x+2} = 3$

(A) $-\dfrac{3}{2}$

(B) $-\dfrac{4}{3}$

(C) $-\dfrac{2}{3}$

(D) 3

(E) 5

Answer: B. We cross multiply, treating the 3 as 3 over 1 to obtain: $3(x+2) = 2$. We distribute the 3 to obtain $3x + 6 = 2$. Subtract 6 from both sides to obtain $3x = -4$. Now divide both sides by 3 to get $x = -\dfrac{4}{3}$.

Example 15. Solve for x: $\dfrac{3}{x+4} = \dfrac{2}{x-4}$

(A) 0

(B) 1

(C) 4

(D) 8

(E) 20

Chapter 8: Solving Equations and Manipulating Expressions   105

Answer: E. Cross multiply to obtain:
$$3(x-4) = 2(x+4)$$
$$3x - 12 = 2x + 8$$
$$3x - 2x = 8 + 12$$
$$x = 20$$

Under normal circumstances, you must make sure that you can plug in 20 into the equation to avoid a denominator of zero. In this case $20 + 4$ does not equal 0 and $20 - 4$ does not equal zero, so 20 is a solution. If we had gotten an answer that would have made the denominator equal to zero, then we would have had no solution to the equation. However, on the GED Math exam, there will always be a solution, so you need not worry about this step.

Example 16. Which of the following expressions is equivalent to $\dfrac{1}{y} + \dfrac{1}{2y}$?

(A) $2y + 1$

(B) $\dfrac{1}{3y}$

(C) $\dfrac{2}{3}y$

(D) $\dfrac{3}{2}y$

(E) $\dfrac{3}{2y}$

Answer: E. We need to find the lowest common denominator, which is $2y$. The reason for this is that y and $2y$ go into $2y$ evenly. We combine fractions as we do with plain numbers (see chapter 4 on fractions):
$$\frac{1}{y} + \frac{1}{2y} = \frac{2+1}{2y} = \frac{3}{2y}$$

$$\frac{2}{3a} + \frac{4}{5b}$$

Example 17. Which of the following is equivalent to the expression above?

(A) $\dfrac{6}{3a + 5b}$

(B) $\dfrac{8}{3a + 5b}$

(C) $\dfrac{10b + 12a}{15ab}$

(D) $\dfrac{10b + 12a}{3a + 5b}$

(E) $10b + 12a$

Answer: C. Here we have two variables to combine. The common denominator of $3a$ and $5b$ is $15ab$ since both $3a$ and $5b$ go into $15ab$ evenly. We simplify as following:
$$\frac{2 \cdot 5b + 4 \cdot 3a}{15ab} = \frac{10b + 12a}{15ab}$$

Example 18. Which of the following expressions is equivalent to $\dfrac{3x}{x+1} - \dfrac{3}{y}$?

(A) $6x + x + y + 1$

(B) $3xy - 3x + 3$

(C) $3xy - 3x - 3$

(D) $\dfrac{3xy - 3x - 1}{xy + y}$

(E) $\dfrac{3xy - 3x - 3}{xy + y}$

Answer: E. We first find the common denominator of $x+1$ and y, which is
$$(x+1)y = xy + y$$

Then we combine the fractions:
$$\frac{3xy - 3(x+1)}{(x+1)y} = \frac{3xy - 3x - 3}{xy + y}$$

If you answered **D**, you didn't distribute the -3 to the 1 when simplifying $-3(x+1)$.

Practice Problems

1. What is the value of the variable in the equation $x + 8 = 15$?

    (A) -7

    (B) $\dfrac{15}{8}$

    (C) 7

    (D) 12

    (E) 23

2. Solve the following equation for x:
$$-6x = 24$$

    (A) -18

    (B) -4

    (C) 4

    (D) 18

    (E) 30

3. What is the value of x in the equation $\dfrac{-4x}{5} = 12$?

    (A) -48

    (B) -15

    (C) -3

    (D) 3

    (E) 15

4. If $4x - 11 = -3$, what is the value of x?

    (A) -12

    (B) -8

    (C) $-\dfrac{7}{2}$

    (D) 2

    (E) 8

5. What is the value of the variable in the equation $\dfrac{3x}{5} - 6 = 9$?

    (A) -5

    (B) 5

    (C) 9

    (D) 15

    (E) 25

6. Solve the equation $4(9 - 5x) = 16$ for x.

    (A) -20

    (B) $-\dfrac{7}{5}$

    (C) 1

    (D) $\dfrac{13}{5}$

    (E) 4

Chapter 8: Solving Equations and Manipulating Expressions

7. What is the value of x when

    $11x - 14 = 7x + 22$?

    (A) −7
    (B) −2
    (C) 2
    (D) 9
    (E) 36

8. If $9(x - 3) = 18$, what is the value of x?

    (A) −2
    (B) −1
    (C) 5
    (D) 21
    (E) 45

9. Solve the equation $-5(x - 6) = 10$ for x.

    (A) −8
    (B) −4
    (C) $-\dfrac{16}{5}$
    (D) 4
    (E) 16

10. What is the value of x in the following equation: $\dfrac{x + 17}{5} = 6$?

    (A) −11
    (B) −6
    (C) 7
    (D) 13
    (E) 43

11. What is the value of the variable in the following equation: $\dfrac{14}{x - 4} = 2$?

    (A) −6
    (B) $\dfrac{3}{7}$
    (C) 8
    (D) 11
    (E) 24

12. If $8x - 15 = 3(y - 7)$, then what is the value of $8x - 3y$?

    (A) −6
    (B) 3
    (C) 6
    (D) 8
    (E) 36

13. If $\dfrac{7}{x} + 6 = y$, what is the value of x in terms of y?

    (A) $\dfrac{y+6}{7}$

    (B) $7(y-6)$

    (C) $7y - 6$

    (D) $\dfrac{7}{y-6}$

    (E) $13y$

14. Solve the equation $8x - 2y + 7 = 21$ for y in terms of x.

    (A) $8x - 13$

    (B) $-4x + 14$

    (C) $4x - 7$

    (D) $8x + 7$

    (E) $2x - 21$

15. What is the value of $2x + y$ in the equation $6x + 3(y+4) = 27$?

    (A) -9

    (B) 5

    (C) 9

    (D) 14

    (E) 15

16. Solve for x in terms of y:

    $$\dfrac{3}{x} = 5y$$

    (A) $\dfrac{3}{5y}$

    (B) $\dfrac{5}{3y}$

    (C) $3 - 5y$

    (D) $15y$

    (E) $3 + 5y$

17. Solve for x: $\dfrac{7}{3x+2} = \dfrac{4}{2x-2}$

    (A) -4

    (B) -7

    (C) 7

    (D) 11

    (E) 20

18. Solve for x: $\dfrac{-3}{2x} + 3 = \dfrac{5}{2x}$

    (A) $-\dfrac{2}{3}$

    (B) $\dfrac{1}{4}$

    (C) $\dfrac{4}{3}$

    (D) 2

    (E) 3

$$\frac{2y}{x} - \frac{2x}{y}$$

19. Which of the following is equivalent to the expression above for $x \neq 0$ and $y \neq 0$?

   (A) $\dfrac{2y - 2x}{x - y}$

   (B) -1

   (C) $\dfrac{2y - 2x}{xy}$

   (D) $\dfrac{2y^2}{3xy}$

   (E) $\dfrac{2y^2 - 2x^2}{xy}$

$$\frac{2x - 3}{x} + 3x$$

20. Which of the following is equivalent to the expression above?

   (A) $\dfrac{3x^2 + 2x - 3}{x}$

   (B) $\dfrac{5x - 3}{x + 1}$

   (C) $3x^2 + 2x - 3$

   (D) $3x - 3$

   (E) $2x + 6$

Answers to Practice Problems

1. **(C)** This is a one-step equation involving addition because a constant term is added to the variable. We need to isolate x on the left side of the equation, so we subtract 8 from 8, giving us zero. And whatever we do to one side of the equation, we must do to the other side as well.

$$x + 8 = 15$$
$$x + 8 - 8 = 15 - 8$$
$$x = 7$$

2. **(B)** This is a one-step equation where the variable is multiplied by −6. We want the coefficient of x to be 1, so we divide both sides of the equation by −6.

$$\frac{-6x}{-6} = \frac{24}{-6}$$
$$x = -4$$

3. **(B)** This is a one-step equation where the coefficient of the variable is a fraction. We want the coefficient of x to be 1, so we multiply both sides of the equation by the reciprocal.

$$\frac{-4x}{5} = 12$$
$$\frac{-5}{4} \times \frac{-4x}{5} = \frac{-5}{4} \times 12$$
$$x = -15$$

4. **(D)** This is a two-step equation. First we isolate the x by adding 11 to both sides. Then we divide by the coefficient of x to make it a 1.

$$4x - 11 = -3$$
$$4x - 11 + 11 = -3 + 11$$
$$4x = 8$$
$$\frac{4x}{4} = \frac{8}{4}$$
$$x = 2$$

5. **(E)** This is a two-step equation with a fractional coefficient. First, we eliminate the constant term from the left side of the equation by adding 6 to each side.

$$\frac{3x}{5} - 6 + 6 = 9 + 6$$
$$\frac{3x}{5} = 15$$

Next, we multiply by the reciprocal of $\frac{3}{5}$, which gives us a coefficient of 1.

$$\frac{5}{3} \times \frac{3x}{5} = \frac{5}{3} \times 15$$
$$x = 25$$

6. **(C)** We divide both sides of the equation by 4, then subtract 9 from both sides, then divide by −5 to obtain $x = 1$.

$$\frac{4(9 - 5x)}{4} = \frac{16}{4}$$
$$9 - 5x = 4$$
$$-5x = 4 - 9 = -5$$
$$x = 1$$

7. **(D)** This equation contains variable terms and constant terms on both sides of the equation. So first we need to get all the x terms on one side, and all the constant terms on the other side. Then we can combine like terms on each side.

$$11x - 14 = 7x + 22$$
$$11x - 7x = 22 + 14$$
$$4x = 36$$

The last step is to make the coefficient of the x term a 1 by dividing both sides by 4

$$\frac{4x}{4} = \frac{36}{4}$$
$$x = 9$$

Chapter 8: Solving Equations and Manipulating Expressions

8. **(C)** We divide both sides of the equation by 9, then add 3 to both sides.

$$9(x - 3) = 18$$
$$x - 3 = 2$$
$$x = 5$$

9. **(D)** We divide both sides of the equation by -5, then add 6 to both sides.

$$-5(x - 6) = 10$$
$$x - 6 = -2$$
$$x = -2 + 6$$
$$x = 4$$

10. **(D)** In this equation the variable is contained within the numerator of a fraction. First we clear the fraction by multiplying both sides by the denominator. This leaves us with a simple one-step equation that is solved by subtracting 17 from both sides.

$$\frac{x + 17}{5} = 6$$
$$\frac{x + 17}{5} \times 5 = 6 \times 5$$
$$x + 17 = 30$$
$$x = 13$$

11. **(D)** In this equation the variable is contained in the denominator of a fraction. The first thing we need to do is eliminate the fraction by multiplying both sides of the equation by the denominator, which is the quantity $(x - 4)$. Notice that this expression is enclosed in parentheses to ensure that we multiply by the entire expression, not just the x term. Next we distribute, then isolate the variable term, followed by dividing by the variable coefficient.

$$\frac{14}{(x - 4)} \times (x - 4) = 2 \times (x - 4)$$
$$14 = 2x - 8$$
$$14 + 8 = 2x - 8 + 8$$
$$22 = 2x$$
$$x = 11$$

12. **(A)** We are asked to solve the equation for a specific expression, so we need to isolate this expression on one side of the equation. We start by distributing through the parentheses.

$$8x - 15 = 3(y - 7)$$
$$8x - 15 = 3y - 21$$

Then we move the y term over to the left side of the equation by subtracting $3y$ from both sides.

$$8x - 15 - 3y = 3y - 21 - 3y$$
$$8x - 3y - 15 = -21$$

Now we have the desired expression $8x - 3y$ on the left side of the equation, but there is also a constant term there. So we eliminate it from the left side by adding 15 (to both sides), and finish by combining like terms.

$$8x - 3y - 15 + 15 = -21 + 15$$
$$8x - 3y = -6$$

13. **(D)** This equation needs to be solved for one variable in terms of another. So we isolate the variable we are solving for (x), and treat the other variable (y) as we would a constant term. First we eliminate the constant term 6 from the left side of the equation by subtracting 6.

$$\frac{7}{x} + 6 = y$$
$$\frac{7}{x} = y - 6$$

Next we must get the variable x out of the denominator of the fraction by multiplying both sides by x.

$$\frac{7}{x} \cdot x = (y - 6) \cdot x$$
$$7 = (y - 6) \cdot x$$

Now we divide both sides by the expression $y - 6$ in order to get x all by itself.

$$\frac{7}{y - 6} = \frac{\cancel{(y - 6)}}{\cancel{(y - 6)}} \cdot x$$
$$x = \frac{7}{y - 6}$$

14. **(C)** This equation needs to be solved for y in terms of x. So we need to isolate the y term on the left side of the equation. We move the other two terms to the right side by adding their opposites to both sides of the equation.

$$8x - 2y + 7 = 21$$
$$8x - 2y + 7 - 7 = 21 - 7$$
$$8x - 2y = 14$$
$$8x - 2y - 8x = 14 - 8x$$
$$-2y = 14 - 8x$$

The final step is to divide by -2 to make the coefficient of y a 1.

$$\frac{-2y}{-2} = \frac{14 - 8x}{-2}$$
$$y = -7 + 4x$$
$$= 4x - 7$$

15. **(B)** We need to solve this equation for the expression $2x + y$, so that is what we need to isolate. First, distribute through the parentheses. Then bring the constant term to the right side of the equation, leaving us with just the x and y terms on the left side.

$$6x + 3(y + 4) = 27$$
$$6x + 3y + 12 = 27$$
$$6x + 3y + 12 - 12 = 27 - 12$$
$$6x + 3y = 15$$

Last, divide both sides by 3 to get the coefficients to equal the ones in the expression we are solving for.

$$\frac{6x + 3y}{3} = \frac{15}{3}$$
$$2x + y = 5$$

16. **(A)** Multiply both sides of the equation by x to obtain $3 = 5xy$. Now divide the sides of the new equation by $5y$ to obtain $x = \frac{3}{5y}$.

17. **(D)** Cross multiply to obtain:

$$7(2x - 2) = 4(3x + 2)$$

Then simplify:
$$14x - 14 = 12x + 8$$
$$14x - 12x = 8 + 14$$
$$2x = 22$$
$$x = 11$$

18. **(C)** Rewrite the expression as below:

$$\frac{-3}{2x} + \frac{3}{1} = \frac{5}{2x}$$

Then combine the fractions on the left side, with the common denominator of $2x$ and 1 equal to $2x$:

$$\frac{-3 + 6x}{2x} = \frac{5}{2x}$$

Since $2x$ appears in the denominators of both sides of the equation, we can simply write:

$-3 + 6x = 5$, which gives $6x = 8$, and therefore $x = \frac{8}{6} = \frac{4}{3}$.

19. **(E)** First find the common denominator, which is xy. Then combine the fractions as follows:

$$\frac{2y \cdot y - 2x \cdot x}{xy} = \frac{2y^2 - 2x^2}{xy}$$

Remember that $y \cdot y = y^2$, and the same goes for x.

20. **(A)** Treat the $3x$ as $\frac{3x}{1}$ to obtain:

$$\frac{2x - 3}{x} + \frac{3x}{1}$$

The common denominator of x and 1 is x, so combining fractions, we obtain:

$$\frac{2x - 3 + 3x \cdot x}{x} = \frac{3x^2 + 2x - 3}{x}$$

Chapter 9

Word Problems Using Equations

In the preceding chapter on algebraic manipulation, you learned how to solve linear equations. But on the GED Math exam, there will be a few word problems that will test your ability to actually create an equation or system of equations out of information given in a word problem, and then solve for an unknown quantity or price, as the following examples illustrate.

Creating an equation and substituting a number for a variable

In some problems, it is only necessary to set up an equation that enables you to calculate a total price or quantity, and then plug in one or two numbers as the following two examples show.

Example 1. Movie tickets in a theater cost $14 per adult and $10.50 per child. If a family of 2 adults with 3 children bought tickets to the movie, how much did they pay in total?

- (A) $39.50
- (B) $45.50
- (C) $57
- (D) $59.50
- (E) $63

Answer: D. Let adult tickets cost A dollars and children's tickets cost C dollars. Then the family must pay a total price, $T = 2A + 3C$. Plugging in the ticket prices for adults and children into our equation, we obtain:

$$T = 2(14) + 3(10.50) = \$59.50$$

Example 2. The telephone company charges $42 per month including tax and fees plus $0.12 a minute for phone calls. Maria used up 150 minutes in January. How much did her phone bill add up to in January?

- (A) $55.60
- (B) $60.00
- (C) $65.24
- (D) $68.48
- (E) $72.60

Answer: B. Let the fixed cost be F, and the charge per minute, be M. Then we have the equation for a total, $T = F + 150M$. Plugging in $42 for F and $0.12 for M, we obtain:

$$T = 42 + 150(0.12) = \$60$$

The problems on the GED Math test may be a bit harder, though, so equations need to be thought out more carefully as the following example shows.

Example 3. An internet café charges $5 for the first 30 minutes of use of a computer plus $1.80 for every 20 minutes after that. Jesse uses the computer for 1 hour and 30 minutes. How much must he pay the café for use of the computer?

- (A) $6.80
- (B) $8.80
- (C) $10.40
- (D) $13.10
- (E) $15.70

Answer: C. We'll call the total price to pay, C, the charge per 20 minutes, M, and the total time (in minutes), T. Then we have the equation:

$$C = 5 + \left[\frac{T-30}{20}\right]M$$

At first glance, this equation may look confusing. Let's analyze each part. We first add $5 because it is a fixed cost that does not depend on time of use. For $\frac{T-30}{20}$, we notice that Jesse only has to pay extra if he uses the computer for more than 30 minutes. We subtract 30 from T because $T-30$ is the time in excess of 30 minutes. If we do not subtract the first 30 minutes, we would be double counting them. We must divide the result by 20 because he gets charged per 20 minutes, not per minute. Finally, we multiply by M, which is the cost per 20 minutes.

Plugging in the values for T, 90 minutes, and M, $1.80, into the equation, we get:

$$C = 5 + \left[\frac{90-30}{20}\right](1.80)$$
$$= 5 + 3(1.8)$$
$$= \$10.40$$

Creating, Manipulating, and Solving One Linear Equation

Sometimes, after you set up the equation correctly, you might have to manipulate it in order to solve for the unknown variable, as the following three examples demonstrate.

Example 4. Rita received her monthly water bill that totaled $90. It included a monthly fee of $15 plus a fee per gallon of water. How much did one gallon of water cost her if she used 5,000 gallons?

- (A) 1.5 cents
- (B) 1.8 cents
- (C) 2.0 cents
- (D) 2.5 cents
- (E) 3.0 cents

Answer: A. The total water bill is $15 plus the number of gallons of water, 5000, times the price per gallon, x. So $90 = 15 + 5000x$.

To solve the equation, we perform the following steps:

$$15 + 5000x = 90$$
$$5000x = 90 - 15 = 75$$
$$x = \frac{75}{5000}$$
$$= 0.015.$$

Therefore $x = 1.5$ cents a gallon.

Example 5. James works as a waiter in an Italian restaurant. He earns $5/hr plus tips. If he earned $200 in tips this week and earned a total of $375, how many hours did he work for the week?

- (A) 15 hours
- (B) 20 hours
- (C) 25 hours
- (D) 30 hours
- (E) 35 hours

Answer: E. We write the equation $E = 5H + T$, where E is his earnings, H is the number of hours James worked, and T is his tips for the week. Plugging in the numbers for his earnings and tips, we obtain,

$$5H + T = E$$
$$5H + 200 = 375$$
$$5H = 175$$
$$H = \frac{175}{5}$$
$$= 35 \text{ hours}$$

Example 6. Dawn works for a telemarketing company, selling magazine subscriptions. She is paid $550 per week plus $4 per customer subscription. If her goal is to earn at least $850 for the week, what is the minimum number of subscriptions she must sell?

(A) 75
(B) 80
(C) 110
(D) 125
(E) 150

Answer: A. We use S to represent the number of subscriptions Dawn sells every week, and write the equation,

$$550 + 4S = 850$$

To understand the equation, she earns $850 if she sells the minimum number of subscriptions. If she does not sell any subscriptions (and remains employed), she will only make $550.

We subtract $550 from both sides of the equation, and then divide by 4:

$$4S = 850 - 550 = 300$$
$$S = \frac{300}{4}$$
$$= 75$$

Comparing Two Equations with Three Unknowns

You might encounter a problem that relates three variables, and then asks you to find the relationship between two of them, as the following example shows.

Example 7. If a is 30 more than b, and b is 4 less than c, how much greater or smaller is c than a?

(A) 22 more
(B) 26 less
(C) 26 more
(D) 34 less
(E) 34 more

Answer: B. We write the equations

$$a = 30 + b$$
$$b = c - 4$$

Then we substitute $c - 4$ into the first equation to obtain:

$$a = 30 + (c - 4) = c + 26$$

Therefore $c = a - 26$, or c is 26 less than a.

Solving Two Equations with Two Unknowns

In some problems, you will be given two equations with two unknown variables, and you will need to find the value of one or two of the unknown variables.

Example 8. If $3x + 2y = 12$ and $2x + 3y = 13$, what is the value of x?

(A) 0.5
(B) 1
(C) 1.5
(D) 2
(E) 3

Answer: D. We multiply the first equation by 3 and the second equation by 2:

$$9x + 6y = 36$$
$$4x + 6y = 26$$

We subtract the second equation from the first equation and eliminate y-term to get

$$9x + 6y = 36$$
$$-(4x + 6y = 26)$$
$$\overline{5x + 0 = 10}$$
$$x = 2$$

As you can see, we eliminated one of the variables, y to obtain the value of the other variable x. This method of solving a system of two linear equations is called the **method of elimination** (or **method of combination**). You must decide which variable you want to eliminate first, then multiply the first equation by the coefficient of the variable in the second equation, and multiply the variable in the second equation by the coefficient of the same variable in the first equation.

Remember to distribute the negative sign in the second equation to all three terms if you are subtracting one equation from the other.

In some word problems, instead of being given variables such as x and y, you will be given two items such as fruit, vegetables, or other items, and you will need to choose variable names for those items before solving the system of equations.

Example 9. Maria paid $13 for 2 pounds of apples and 3 pounds of tomatoes. If she can purchase 4 pounds of apples and 2 pounds of tomatoes for $14, how much more do tomatoes cost than apples per pound?

- (A) $0.75
- (B) $1
- (C) $1.25
- (D) $1.5
- (E) $1.75

Answer: B. Let A = price of apples, and T = price of tomatoes. Set up two equations:

$$2A + 3T = 13 \quad (1)$$
$$4A + 2T = 14 \quad (2)$$

First, divide both sides of the second equation by 2 to obtain

$$2A + T = 7$$

Now subtract the new second equation from the first:

$$2A + 3T = 13$$
$$-(2A + T = 7)$$
$$\overline{2T = 6}$$
$$T = 3$$

Now plug 3 into either the first equation or the second equation. Let's pick the first equation, arbitrarily, to get:

$$2A + 3(3) = 13$$
$$2A + 9 = 13$$
$$2A = 4$$
$$A = 2$$

So apples cost $2 per pound and tomatoes cost $3 per pound, and therefore tomatoes cost $1 per pound more than the apples do.

Example 10. Karen purchased 2 candy bars and 5 ice cream bars for $19, and 3 candy bars and an ice cream bar for $9. How much did the ice cream bar cost?

- (A) $1.5
- (B) $2.0
- (C) $2.5
- (D) $2.75
- (E) $3.0

Answer: E. We set up two equations as in example 9: Let C = price of a candy bar and I = price of an ice cream bar. Therefore,

$$2C + 5I = 19$$
$$3C + I = 9$$

Multiply the first equation by 3 and multiply the second equation by 2. Then subtract the second equation from the first to obtain:

$$6C + 15I = 57$$
$$-(6C + 2I = 18)$$
$$\overline{}$$
$$13I = 39$$
$$I = 3$$

Therefore the price of an ice cream bar was $3.

Practice Problems

1. Movie tickets in a theater cost $12 per adult and $9.50 per child. If a family of 2 adults with 2 children bought tickets for a movie, how much did they pay in total for the movie?

   A) $34
   B) $37.50
   C) $41
   D) $43
   E) $44.50

2. The telephone company charges $55 per month including tax and fees plus $0.09 a minute for phone calls. Maria used up 80 minutes in April. How much did her phone bill add up to in April?

   A) $60.00
   B) $62.20
   C) $67.40
   D) $78.00
   E) $82.60

3. An internet café charges $5 for the first 15 minutes of use of a computer plus $1.75 for every 15 minutes after that. José uses the computer for 1 hour and 15 minutes. How much must he pay the café for use of the computer?

   A) $9.25
   B) $11.75
   C) $12
   D) $87.5
   E) $134.25

4. Jennifer got her monthly water bill that totaled $33. It included a monthly fee of $12 plus a fee per gallon of water. How much did one gallon of water cost her if she used 2,100 gallons?

   A) 0.6 cents
   B) 0.7 cents
   C) 0.8 cents
   D) 0.9 cents
   E) 1 cent

5. Marlene works as a waitress in a French restaurant. She earns $7.50/hr plus tips. If she earned $400 in tips this week and earned a total of $550, how many hours did she work for the week?

   A) 20
   B) 22
   C) 25
   D) 35
   E) 40

6. Kathleen works for a telemarketing company, selling software. She is paid $750 per week plus $250 per each software package she sells. If her goal is to earn at least $2,250 for the week, what is the minimum number of packages she must sell that week?

   A) 2
   B) 3
   C) 6
   D) 8
   E) 12

Chapter 9: Word Problems Using Equations

7. If y is 18 more than x, and z is 13 less than x, what is the value of $y - z$?

    (A) 5
    (B) 31
    (C) 39
    (D) 50
    (E) 62

8. If $2x + 4y = 16$ and $2x + 3y = 13$, what is the value of $2x - y$?

    (A) -1
    (B) 0
    (C) 1
    (D) 2
    (E) 3

9. If $3a + 2b = -1$ and $4a - 2b = 8$, what is the value of $b + 4$?

    (A) -2
    (B) -1
    (C) 1
    (D) 2
    (E) 4

10. If $2a - 4b = -10$ and $3a + 4b = 25$, what is the value of $a + 2b$?

    (A) -7
    (B) -5
    (C) -1
    (D) 7
    (E) 11

11. Daphne paid $7.50 for 3 pounds of pears and 2 pounds of bananas. If she can purchase 4 pounds of pears and 4 pounds of bananas for $11, how much would it cost her to purchase 5 pounds of bananas?

    (A) $0.75
    (B) $2.25
    (C) $3.75
    (D) $5
    (E) $7.50

12. David purchased 4 chairs and a table for $325. The next day he bought 2 tables and 6 chairs at the same prices, for $550. How much did he pay for each chair?

    (A) $25
    (B) $35
    (C) $40
    (D) $50
    (E) $60

13. Scott took a taxi from the train station to a meeting. If he paid a total of $31 for a 14-mile drive, and paid the driver a $3 tip, how much does each mile of travel cost?

    (A) $1.25
    (B) $1.75
    (C) $2
    (D) $2.50
    (E) $3.25

14. Bob pays $1,150 for a television set and 2 computer monitors. He also pays $1,670 for two television sets and 3 computer monitors. Which set of equations would you use to find how much a television cost, if C represents a computer monitor and T represents a television?

    (A) $2C + T = 1150$
    $3T + C = 1670$

    (B) $C + 2T = 1150$
    $2T + 3C = 1670$

    (C) $T + 2C = 1150$
    $2T + 3C = 1670$

    (D) $2C - T = 1150$
    $2T - 3C = 1670$

    (E) $3C + T = 1150$
    $2T - 2C = 1670$

15. James mowed his lawn and cut 4 inches of grass yesterday. If G represents the length of grass in the lawn before he mowed the lawn, and C represents the length of grass after it was mowed, which equation would you use to calculate the length of grass in the lawn after it was mowed?

    (A) $C = G - 4$
    (B) $G + C = 4$
    (C) $C - G = 4$
    (D) $G = C - 4$
    (E) $G + C = -4$

Chapter 9: Word Problems Using Equations

Answers to Practice Problems

1. **(D)** Let A = price of adult tickets and C = price of child, then

    Total price = $2A + 2C$

    Plugging in the values for A and C, we get

    $2\,(\$12) + 2\,(\$9.50) = \$43$

2. **(B)** We create an equation,

    $55 + 0.09M$ = Total cost

    where M is the number of minutes she had used. Plugging in the number of minutes, 80 into M, we obtain

    $55 + 0.09(80) = \$62.20$

3. **(C)** Create an equation, calling the total cost C, and the charge per 15 minutes, M, and the total time, T. Then we have the equation:

    $C = 5 + \left[(T - 15)/15\right] \times (1.75)$

    Plugging the value for T into the equation, we get:

    $C = 5 + \left[(75 - 15)/15\right] \times (1.75)$
    $= 5 + 4 \times (1.75) = \$12$

4. **(E)** We create an equation that says that the total water bill, $T = \$12$ plus the number of gallons of water, 2,100, times the price per gallon, x. The equation is simply:

    $33 = 12 + 2100x$

    To solve the equation, we perform the following steps:

    $2100x = 33 - 12 = 21$
    $x = \dfrac{21}{2100}$
    $= 0.01$

    Therefore $x = 1$ cent a gallon.

5. **(A)** We write the equation $E = 7.5H + T$, where E is her earnings, H is the number of hours Marlene worked, and T is her tips for the week. Plugging in the numbers for her earnings, E, and tips, T, we obtain,

    $550 = 7.5H + 400$
    $550 - 400 = 7.5H$
    $H = \dfrac{150}{7.5} = 20$ hours.

6. **(C)** We use S to represent the number of softwares products Kathleen sells every week, and write the equation:

    $750 + 250S = 2250$

    We subtract $\$750$ from both sides of the equation, and then divide by 250:

    $250S = 1500$
    $S = \dfrac{1500}{250} = 6$

7. **(B)** We write $y = x + 18$ and $z = x - 13$. So,

    $y - z = (x + 18) - (x - 13)$
    $= x + 18 - x + 13$
    $= 31.$

    Don't forgot to distribute the negative sign to -13.

8. **(C)** Subtract the second equation from the first to obtain:

    $2x + 4y = 16$
    $-(\,2x + 3y = 13\,)$
    _____
    $y = 3$

    Now to find x, we plug in 3 for y in either equation. If we use the first equation, we obtain: $2x + 4(3) = 16$. Subtract 12 from both sides and divide the result by 2 to get:

    $x = \dfrac{16 - 12}{2} = 2$

    Therefore, $2x - y = 2(2) - 3 = 1$.

9. **(D)** We need to find b, then add 4 to it. We add the two equations together to obtain:

$$3a + 2b = -1$$
$$+4a - 2b = 8$$
$$\overline{7a + 0 = 7}$$
$$a = 1$$

Plug $a = 1$ into either equation. Using equation 1,

$$3(1) + 2b = -1$$
$$2b = -4$$
$$b = -2$$

So, $b + 4 = (-2) + 4 = 2$.

10. **(E)** Add the equations together to obtain:

$$2a - 4b = -10$$
$$+3a + 4b = 25$$
$$\overline{5a + 0 = 15}$$
$$a = 3$$

Plug 3 for a into either equation to find b. If we use the second equation, we get:

$$3(3) + 4b = 25$$
$$4b = 16$$
$$b = 4$$

So $a + 2b = 3 + 2(4) = 11$.

11. **(C)** We let P = pears and B = bananas. So

$$3P + 2B = 7.5 \text{ and } 4P + 4B = 11$$

Multiply the first equation by 2 to obtain $6P + 4B = 15$. Then subtract the second equation from new equation:

$$6P + 4B = 15$$
$$-(4P + 4B = 11)$$
$$\overline{2P + 0 = 4}$$
$$P = 2$$

Plugging 2 for P into the first equation we get $3(2) + 2B = 7.5$, so $2B = 1.5$, $B = 0.75$. For 5 pounds of bananas,

$$5B = 5(0.75) = \$3.75$$

12. **(D)** Let C and T be the price for a chair and a table, respectively. We set up the following equations:

$$4C + T = 325$$
$$6C + 2T = 550$$

Multiply the first equation by 2 to obtain $8C + 2T = 650$. Then subtract the second equation from the new equation to solve for C as follows:

$$8C + 2T = 650$$
$$-(6C + 2T = 550)$$
$$\overline{2C + 0 = 100}$$
$$C = 50$$

13. **(C)** We set up the following equation, with M = cost per mile, and solve for M:

$$3 + 14M = 31$$
$$14M = 28$$
$$M = \$2$$

14. **(C)** If he pays a total of $1,150 for a television set and 2 computer monitors, we get $1150 = T + 2C$. If he pays $1,670 for two television sets and 3 computer monitors, we get $1670 = 2T + 3C$. Therefore, the system of equations we will use is choice **C**.

15. **(A)** The grass is 4 inches shorter after it was mowed than before it was mowed, and therefore the equation is $C = G - 4$.

Chapter 10
Rates, Ratios, and Proportions

Ratios

Ratios represent the comparison of one quantity to another. Ratios are expressed as $c : d$, where c is one quantity and d is another.

Proportions

A proportion sets two ratios equal to one another. We see ratios and proportions every day all around us. Three dollars per gallon, $4.50 per pound, $30 per hour, and 10 cents per minute are all expressions involving ratios and proportions. When we use one of these known rates to find a specific unknown amount, we are using a proportion. For example, if a cell phone rate is 10 cents per minute, how much will I be charged for a 5-minute call? The answer, just by multiplying it, is 50 cents. This can be written in mathematical form as:

$$\frac{10}{1} = \frac{x}{5}$$

The terms on each side of the equal sign are ratios, or rates, and the entire mathematical equation is a proportion. To solve it, we cross multiply: $1 \times x = 5 \times 10$, and finally $x = 50$ cents. Every ratio, rate, and proportion word problem involves substituting the given values into equations similar to the one above.

Example 1. Jason traveled from Los Angeles to San Francisco by car. The distance between those cities is 396 miles. The gas gauge in Jason's car was on full when he started. He filled up his tank from empty to full twice during the trip. Once he arrived, it was empty again. His car's tank holds 11 gallons of gas. How many miles per gallon did the car average on the trip?

(A) 12
(B) 14
(C) 18
(D) 22
(E) 26

Answer: A. Jason traveled 396 miles (given). He used up three gas tanks. Since the gas tank holds 11 gallons, Jason used $11 \times 3 = 33$ gallons. So, he got 396 miles per 33 gallons. We write the ratio as:

$$\frac{396 \text{ miles}}{33 \text{ gallons}} = 12 \text{ miles/gallon}.$$

He got 12 miles per gallon. To solve using a proportion, we write:

$$\frac{396}{33} = \frac{x}{1}$$

So, $x = 396/33 = 12$ (miles).

Example 2. Jonathan bought three bags of apples, each weighing 4 pounds. The price of apples is $1.50 per pound. He paid the cashier $20 for the apples. How much change should he receive?

- (A) $0
- (B) $1
- (C) $2
- (D) $2.50
- (E) $3.49

Answer: C. Three bags weighing 4 pounds each total 12 pounds. Since the price of apples is $1.50 per pound, we set up the proportion:

$$\frac{1.5 \text{ dollars}}{1 \text{ pound}} = \frac{x \text{ dollars}}{12 \text{ pounds}}$$

$$x = 12 \times 1.5 = 18$$

We can read this equation as "If one has to pay $1.50 for one pound, how many dollars will one have to pay for 12 pounds?" So if he paid $20, and it cost him $18, he should get $2 back.

Example 3. Boneless chicken breasts at Fresh Meadows Foods are $3.69 per pound. Peter bought five 3-pound packages. He pays the cashier $60. How much change does he receive back?

- (A) $2.36
- (B) $3.67
- (C) $4.65
- (D) $8.02
- (E) $48.93

Answer: C. We set up the proportion:

$$\frac{3.69 \text{ dollars}}{1 \text{ lb.}} = \frac{x \text{ dollars}}{3 \text{ lb.}}$$

Multiply both sides of the equation by 3 to obtain

$$x = 3.69 \times 3 = \$11.07$$

He bought 5 packages, so in total he pays

$$5 \times \$11.07 = \$55.35$$

Since he pays $60, he gets

$$\$60 - \$55.35 = \$4.65$$

in change.

Example 4. Janet made a down payment of $75,000 on a house. If the house cost five times the down payment amount, and Janet paid for the house over a 10-year period with zero percent interest, how much were the monthly payments?

- (A) $1,925
- (B) $2,500
- (C) $3,000
- (D) $3,125
- (E) $5,500

Answer: B. The house cost five times the down payment, or $5 \times 75{,}000 = \$375{,}000$. Subtracting the down payment of $75,000, we obtain a mortgage of $300,000. Now since 10 years = 120 months, divide $300,000 by 120 months to obtain $2,500.

Example 5. On a map of Florida, a scale is used in which 3 inches equals 35 miles. If the distance on the map between Orlando and Miami is 20 inches, what is the actual distance between the two cities to the nearest mile?

- (A) 233
- (B) 236
- (C) 298
- (D) 302
- (E) 322

Chapter 10: Rates, Ratios, and Proportions

Answer: A. We set up the proportion:

$$\frac{35 \text{ miles}}{3 \text{ inches}} = \frac{x \text{ miles}}{20 \text{ inches}}$$

x will therefore be equal to $\frac{35}{3} \times 20 = 233$.

An alternative is to write:

$$\frac{20 \text{ inches}}{3 \text{ inches}} = \frac{x \text{ miles}}{35 \text{ miles}}$$

This proportion can be read as "the ratio between 20 inches on the map and 3 inches on the map is the same ratio as x actual miles to 35 miles on the scale." We cross multiply: $3x = 20 \times 35$, so

$$x = \frac{20 \times 35}{3} = 233$$

Ratios

As we said above, a ratio between two quantities represents the comparison of one quantity to the other. Let's look at a few problems involving ratios.

Example 6. There are 30 balloons in a bag. Twelve are red, eight are blue, and the rest are green. What is the ratio of green balloons to red balloons?

- (A) 1:4
- (B) 1:3
- (C) 1:2
- (D) 2:3
- (E) 5:6

Answer: E. If $12 + 8 = 20$ balloons are not green, and there are a total of 30 balloons, then there are $30 - 20 = 10$ green balloons. The ratio of green balloons to red balloons is $10:12$, or $5:6$.

Example 7. In Washington, DC, it snows an average of 18 days per year and it rains an average of 108 days per year. What is the ratio of snowy days to rainy days?

- (A) 1:6
- (B) 1:7
- (C) 2:9
- (D) 2:13
- (E) 3:14

Answer: A. The ratio is 18 snowy days : 108 rainy days, which is $1:6$.

Example 8. The ratio of number of men to number of women in a live talk show is $2:7$. If there are 882 people in the audience, how many men are there?

- (A) 142
- (B) 192
- (C) 196
- (D) 568
- (E) 686

Answer: C. If the ratio of men to women is $2:7$, then the ratio of men to the total number of people in the audience is $2:9$. This is because $2 + 7 = 9$. Since 2/9 people in the audience are men, and there is a total of 882 people, just multiply 2/9 by 882 to get:

$$\frac{2}{9} \times 882 = 196$$

Example 9. The ratio of dogs to cats staying in an animal hotel is $4:5$. If there are 216 dogs, how many dogs and cats are there in the hotel in total?

- (A) 328
- (B) 396
- (C) 486
- (D) 512
- (E) 528

Answer: C. Let D = number of dogs and C = number of cats. From the given ratio $4:5$, we have
$$5D = 4C$$
We know $D = 216$, so $5 \times 216 = 4C$. Dividing both sides of the equation by 4 we obtain $C = 270$. So there are $270 + 216 = 486$ cats and dogs staying at the hotel.

Example 10. The ratio of cars to vans at an automobile dealership is $4:3$. There are 336 cars and vans in the dealership. How many cars are there?

- (A) 144
- (B) 192
- (C) 198
- (D) 216
- (E) 228

Answer: B. If the ratio of cars to vans is $4:3$, then the ratio of cars to total number of vehicles is $4:7$. Therefore, simply multiply the total number of vehicles, 336 by 4/7 to get
$$336 \times \frac{4}{7} = 192 \text{ cars.}$$

Chapter 10: Rates, Ratios, and Proportions

Practice Problems

1. What is the value of $\dfrac{x}{y}$, if $\dfrac{x}{210} = \dfrac{y}{14}$?

    A) 15
    B) 20
    C) 25
    D) 30
    E) 35

2. 27 divided by 810 is the same as two-thirds of what number?

    A) $\dfrac{3}{10}$
    B) $\dfrac{3}{50}$
    C) $\dfrac{2}{25}$
    D) $\dfrac{1}{20}$
    E) $\dfrac{1}{15}$

3. A map of Switzerland is 6 inches long from east to west. If the scale of the map is 2 inches to 73 actual miles, how long is Switzerland from east to west in miles?

    A) 219
    B) 238
    C) 276
    D) 305
    E) 324

4. Broccoli is on sale for $1.69/lb. Corn costs $0.75 an ear. Martha paid $10.70 for broccoli and 3 ears of corn. How many pounds of broccoli did she purchase?

    A) 3.5
    B) 4.25
    C) 4.75
    D) 5
    E) 5.5

5. The exchange rate is one dollar for 0.92 euros. How many dollars can Joseph get for 184 euros?

    A) 150
    B) 160
    C) 175
    D) 192
    E) 200

6. A recipe calls for half a teaspoon of vanilla for every 4 eggs. The recipe also calls for 3 tablespoons of butter for every teaspoon of vanilla. If Maria uses 9 tablespoons of butter, how many eggs must she use?

    A) 15
    B) 18
    C) 21
    D) 24
    E) 28

7. If Alex read a third of a book on Monday and one fifth of the book on Tuesday, what is the ratio of the part of the book he read to the part he did not read?

    (A) 2 : 3
    (B) 8 : 7
    (C) 4 : 5
    (D) 3 : 4
    (E) 9 : 6

8. Jessica put a $50,000 down payment on a house valued at $400,000. What is the ratio of the down payment to the amount she still owes on her house?

    (A) 1 : 10
    (B) 1 : 9
    (C) 1 : 8
    (D) 1 : 6
    (E) 1 : 7

9. Jenny originally bought her car for $42,000. Four years later, she sold it to a used car salesman for $14,000. What is the ratio of the amount she sold it for to the amount that it depreciated by?

    (A) 1 : 2
    (B) 2 : 3
    (C) 3 : 4
    (D) 4 : 5
    (E) 5 : 6

10. Tim has a large credit card debt. He pays off a third of the outstanding balance. What is the ratio of the amount he still owes to the amount he paid off?

    (A) 1 : 1
    (B) 2 : 1
    (C) 3 : 1
    (D) 4 : 1
    (E) 5 : 1

11. The Washington Football Team lost the first three of five games in the beginning of the season. At that rate, how many more games will they have to play in order to win 90 games?

    (A) 145
    (B) 150
    (C) 155
    (D) 220
    (E) 225

12. At the University of Scottsbluff only 1 in 8 applicants were accepted for admission in 2018. At that rate, how many applicants will be rejected if 6,480 applied?

    (A) 810
    (B) 1,840
    (C) 5,670
    (D) 5,820
    (E) 5,996

Chapter 10: Rates, Ratios, and Proportions

13. In an international screenplay competition, 3,686 screenplays were entered. There were first, second, and third place awards in each of six genres and one grand prize winner. What is the ratio of winners to non-winners?

    (A) 1 : 92
    (B) 1 : 102
    (C) 1 : 141
    (D) 1 : 182
    (E) 1 : 193

14. In a room there are 18 red and blue balloons. If the ratio of blue balloons to red balloons is 5, how many red balloons are there?

    (A) 2
    (B) 3
    (C) 5
    (D) 12
    (E) 15

15. The ratio of boys to girls at Sherman High School was 5 : 6. If there were 4,400 students total, how many boys were there?

    (A) 1,600
    (B) 1,700
    (C) 2,000
    (D) 2,050
    (E) 2,400

Answers to Practice Problems

1. **(A)** Cross multiply to get $14x = 210y$, and then divide both sides by $14y$ to get:

$$\frac{14x}{14y} = \frac{210y}{14y}$$

$$\frac{x}{y} = \frac{210}{14} = 15$$

2. **(D)** We have $\frac{27}{810} = \frac{2}{3}x$. Multiply both sides of the equation by $\frac{3}{2}$ to obtain:

$$x = \frac{27}{810} \times \frac{3}{2} = \frac{1}{20}$$

3. **(A)** We are comparing 6 inches to 2 inches, and therefore, the length of Switzerland to 73 miles. So we have

$$\frac{6 \text{ inches}}{2 \text{ inches}} = \frac{x \text{ miles}}{73 \text{ miles}}$$

Multiplying both sides of the equation by 73, we obtain $x = 219$ miles.

4. **(D)** 3 ears of corn cost $3 \times \$0.75 = \$2.25$. Subtract $\$2.25$ from $\$10.70$, which is the total she paid for both broccoli and corn, to obtain $\$8.45$, the total amount she paid for broccoli only. Set up the proportion $\frac{8.45}{1.69} = \frac{x}{1}$ to obtain $x = 5$ lb.

5. **(E)** We have $\frac{0.92 \text{ euros}}{1 \text{ dollar}} = \frac{184 \text{ euros}}{x \text{ dollars}}$.

Cross multiply to obtain $x = \frac{184}{0.92} = 200$.

6. **(D)** If Maria used 9 tablespoons of butter, we set up the proportion:

$$\frac{3 \text{ tablespoons butter}}{1 \text{ teaspoon vanilla}} = \frac{9 \text{ tablespoons butter}}{x \text{ teaspoons vanilla}}$$

to obtain $x = 3$ teaspoons of vanilla. Next we set up the proportion:

$$\frac{3 \text{ teaspoons vanilla}}{x \text{ eggs}} = \frac{1/2 \text{ teaspoon vanilla}}{4 \text{ eggs}}$$

Cross multiply to obtain:

$$\frac{1}{2}x = 3 \times 4, \text{ so } x = 2 \times 3 \times 4 = 24$$

7. **(B)** We have $\frac{1}{3} + \frac{1}{5} = \frac{8}{15}$. Therefore he didn't read $1 - \frac{8}{15} = \frac{7}{15}$. The ratio of the part he read to the part he didn't read is therefore $8 : 7$.

8. **(E)** The amount still owed on the house is $\$400,000 - \$50,000 = \$350,000$. The ratio of paid to unpaid amount is $\frac{50,000}{350,000} = \frac{1}{7}$, which is $1 : 7$.

9. **(A)** The amount that the car depreciated is $\$42,000 - \$14,000 = \$28,000$. So we have the ratio of the amount sold to depreciated as $\frac{14,000}{28,000} = \frac{1}{2}$. The ratio is therefore $1:2$.

10. **(B)** If he paid off a third of his credit card debt, he still owes two-thirds. The ratio he owes to the paid off amount is:

$$\frac{\frac{2}{3}}{\frac{1}{3}} = \frac{2}{\cancel{3}} \times \frac{\cancel{3}}{1} = 2$$

The ratio therefore is $2 : 1$. We can see here that we don't need to know how much money he owes to find the ratio.

Chapter 10: Rates, Ratios, and Proportions

11. **(D)** If the team lost 3 in 5 games, that means they won 2 in 5 games. We have $90 = \frac{2}{5}X$, where X is the total number of games played. To understand this equation, notice that the equation states that 90 games won is two-fifths of the total number of games played. What is X? That is the total number of games. So we multiply both sides of the equation by $\frac{5}{2}$ to obtain $X = \frac{5}{2} \times 90 = 225$. They already played 5 games, so they have 220 more games to go.

12. **(C)** If 1 in 8 were accepted, then 7 in 8 were rejected. Therefore, simply multiply 7/8 by 6480 to obtain: $\frac{7}{8} \times 6480 = 5670$.

13. **(E)** We have a total of $3 \times 6 + 1 = 19$ winners. If 3686 screenplays were entered and there were 19 winners, that means that there are $3686 - 19 = 3667$ non-winners. Therefore, the ratio of winners to non-winners is $\frac{19}{3667} = \frac{1}{193}$, which is 1 : 193.

14. **(B)** We call blue balloons, B, and red balloons, R. So we have

$$B = 5R, \text{ and } B + R = 18$$

In the first equation, we plug $5R$ into the second equation to obtain:

$$5R + R = 18$$
$$6R = 18$$
$$R = 3$$

15. **(C)** Since the ratio of boys to girls is 5 : 6, this means that 5/11 of the total number of students, 4,400, are boys. Simply multiply 5/11 by 4400 to get:

$$\frac{5}{11} \times 4400 = 2000 \text{ boys}$$

Chapter 11
Percentages

What Is Percentage?

The Latin word cent means 100. So percent means per hundred, or divided by 100.

Percentages are represented by the symbol %, and can easily be translated into fractions or decimals by dividing by 100. For example, 50% translates to $\frac{50}{100}$, which reduces to $\frac{1}{2}$. Likewise, you can make a percent from a decimal by multiplying by 100 and adding the percent sign. For example, 0.2 translates to
$$0.2 \times 100 = 20\%$$

Rule 1: To <u>m</u>ake a percentage, you <u>m</u>ultiply by 100 and add the percent sign.

Rule 2: To <u>d</u>rop a percentage, you <u>d</u>ivide by 100 and drop the percent sign.

To illustrate:

Example 1. Convert 0.4 to percent.

Answer: 40%. We calculate this from **Rule 1**:
$$0.4 \times 100 = 40\%$$

Example 2. Convert 35% to a fraction.

Answer: $\frac{7}{20}$. By **Rule 2**, we drop a percentage by dividing by 100:
$$35\% = \frac{35}{100} = \frac{7}{20}$$
Here, we see that the percent sign disappeared.

To understand percentage intuitively, let us consider a family of four sharing a pizza with 8 slices. The four members each eat one slice — the family finished exactly half of the total pizza. What percentage of the pizza did they finish? We know that one half is the same as 50% (recall the expression, fifty-fifty, which literally means half-half). But how did we get from one half to 50%?

We apply **Rule 1**:
$$\frac{1}{2} \times 100 = 50\%$$

If the family were to collectively finish two more slices, only two would remain — which is one quarter of the pizza, or 25% of the pizza. We get from "one quarter" to "25%" as follows:
$$\frac{1}{4} \times 100 = 25\%$$

Chapter 11: Percentages

Let's try going backwards, to find the fraction equivalent of a percentage. If George eats 30% of a sandwich, what fraction of the sandwich does he eat? Using **Rule 2**, we calculate:

$$\frac{30\%}{100} = \frac{3}{10}$$

In decimal form, we have $\frac{3}{10} = 0.3$.

Table 1 on the right provides some percentages and their fraction and decimal equivalents. The fractions and percentages in Table 1 are some of the most common, and we recommend they be memorized to save time while taking the test.

Taking a Percentage

Example 3. What is 15% of 340?

- (A) 5.1
- (B) 17
- (C) 34
- (D) 51
- (E) 54

Answer: D. Translate the percent into a fraction to solve a problem. Also, keep in mind that "of" means "times." 15% of 340 translates to

$$\frac{15}{100} \times 340$$

The result is 51.

The solution to example 3 is found by reducing the fraction in stages:

$$\frac{15}{100} \times 340 = \frac{15 \times 340}{100} = \frac{15 \times 34}{10}$$

$$= \frac{3 \times 34}{2} = 3 \times 17 = 51$$

Table 1

Fraction	Decimal	Percent
$\frac{0}{2} = \frac{0}{3} = \frac{0}{4} = \cdots$	0	0%
$\frac{1}{10}$	0.1	10%
$\frac{1}{8}$	0.125	12.5%
$\frac{1}{5} = \frac{2}{10}$	0.2	20%
$\frac{1}{4} = \frac{2}{8}$	0.25	25%
$\frac{3}{10}$	0.3	30%
$\frac{1}{3}$	0.333...	33.3%
$\frac{3}{8}$	0.375	37.5%
$\frac{2}{5} = \frac{4}{10}$	0.4	40%
$\frac{1}{2} = \frac{2}{4} = \frac{4}{8} = \frac{5}{10}$	0.5	50%
$\frac{3}{5} = \frac{6}{10}$	0.6	60%
$\frac{5}{8}$	0.625	62.5%
$\frac{2}{3}$	0.666...	66.7%
$\frac{7}{10}$	0.7	70%
$\frac{3}{4} = \frac{6}{8}$	0.75	75%
$\frac{4}{5} = \frac{8}{10}$	0.8	80%
$\frac{7}{8}$	0.875	87.5%
$\frac{9}{10}$	0.9	90%
$\frac{2}{2} = \frac{3}{3} = \frac{4}{4} = \cdots$	1	100%
$\frac{2}{1} = \frac{4}{2} = \frac{6}{3} = \cdots$	2	200%

Fractions, ratios, and proportions can be converted into percentages by determining the decimal equivalent. This can require a bit of work — the fraction may need to be divided out.

$$\frac{2}{5} = 0.4 = 40\%$$
$$\frac{21}{60} = \frac{7}{20} = 0.35 = 35\%$$
$$\frac{8}{13} \approx 0.615 = 61.5\%$$

Finding a Percentage

Example 4. If, in a group of 84 people, 36 are men, approximately what percentage of the group is men?

- Ⓐ 30%
- Ⓑ 43%
- Ⓒ 48%
- Ⓓ 54%
- Ⓔ 57%

Answer: B. There are 36 men out of a total of 84 people. This is represented by the fraction: $\frac{36}{84}$.

$$\frac{36}{84} \approx 0.4286$$

which is closest to 43%.
($\approx$ means "approximately equal to").

Practice translating between fractions and percentages below by filling in the empty cells in the following table.

Fraction	Percent
$\frac{3}{4}$	75%
a	80%
$\frac{12}{15}$	b
c	42%
$\frac{1}{3}$	d

Fraction	Percent
$\frac{15}{5}$	e
f	165%
$\frac{27}{73}$	g
h	0.4%
$\frac{6}{900}$	i

Answers:

a. $80\% = \frac{80}{100} = \frac{8}{10} = \frac{4}{5}$

b. $\frac{12}{15} = \frac{4}{5} = 0.8 = 0.8 \times 100\% = 80\%$

c. $42\% = \frac{42}{100} = \frac{21}{50}$

d. $\frac{1}{3} = 0.333... \times 100\% = 33.3\%$

e. $\frac{15}{5} = 3 \times 100\% = 300\%$

f. $165\% = \frac{165}{100} = \frac{33}{20}$

g. $\frac{27}{73} = 0.36986... \approx 37\%$

h. $0.4\% = \frac{0.4}{100} = \frac{4}{1000} = \frac{1}{250}$

i. $\frac{6}{900} \approx 0.67\%$

In the calculations above for item *h*, 0.4% is converted to $\frac{1}{250}$. How do we know this? We have $\frac{0.4}{100}$. Multiplying both the numerator and denominator by 10 we obtain $\frac{4}{1000}$. Then, dividing both the numerator and denominator by 4 we obtain $\frac{1}{250}$.

Similarly, to convert $\frac{6}{900}$ to a percent we have $\frac{6}{900} \times 100 = \frac{6}{9}\% = \frac{2}{3}\% = 0.666...\% \approx 0.67\%$.

Interpreting Tables

Understanding percentages is necessary to obtaining a good score on the GED Math exam. A few questions, like the first two in this chapter, will focus solely on calculating percentages. But percentages will be incorporated into several other question types as well. Take the following, for example:

Grade	Number of Students
A	14
B	13
C	8
D	5
E	2

Example 5. The table above represents the grades received by a class of students on a test. Approximately what percentage of the students did not receive an A on the test?

- (A) 33%
- (B) 50%
- (C) 67%
- (D) 83%
- (E) 95%

Answer: C. From the table, we can calculate the total number of students in the class, and how many students did not receive an A. The class has a total of $14 + 13 + 8 + 5 + 2 = 42$ students. Of these, $13 + 8 + 5 + 2 = 28$ students did not receive an A.

$$\frac{28}{42} = \frac{2}{3} = 0.666...$$

which is closest to **C**, 67%.

Three Types of Word Problems with Percentages

There are only a few limited ways in which a percentage word problem may be phrased. Almost all percentage problems can be reduced to one of the questions below. If we understand how to translate these problems into math, we can solve practically any percent problem on the GED Math test.

Use the table below to help you translate the English word into symbolic form.

English Word	Symbolic Form
is	=
of	×
what	x variable
what percent	$x/100$

Example 6. What is 40% of 60?

Translation: What (x) is (=) 40% (which converts to 0.4) of (×) 60:

$$x = 0.4 \times 60 = 24$$

Example 7. What percentage of 60 is 40?

Translation: What percentage ($x/100$) of (×) 60 is (=) 40:

$$\frac{x}{100} \times 60 = 40$$

Multiply both sides of the equation by $\frac{100}{60}$ to obtain

$$x = 4\cancel{0} \times \frac{100}{6\cancel{0}} = \frac{400}{6} = \frac{200}{3} = 66.7\,\%$$

Example 8. 30 is what percentage of 90?

Answer: We write $30 = \frac{x}{100} \times 90$. Multiply both sides of the equation by $\frac{100}{90}$ to obtain

$$x = 30 \times \frac{100}{90} = \frac{100}{3} = 33.3\,\%.$$

Percent Change

Percent change is the difference between the new value and the original value, divided by the original value. The result of this operation is a fraction, which is converted to a percentage by multiplying by 100.

$$\text{Percent Change} = \frac{\text{New Value} - \text{Original Value}}{\text{Original Value}} \times 100$$

A negative value indicates a Percent Decrease, and a positive value a Percent Increase.

Example 9. A store owner changes the price of a product from $25 to $29. Which of the following represents the percent increase in the cost?

- (A) 4%
- (B) 16%
- (C) 20%
- (D) 54%
- (E) 86%

Answer: B. The original price is $25. The new price is $29. The difference is $4. The percent increase, therefore, is

$$\frac{29 - 25}{25} = \frac{4}{25} = 0.16$$

which translates to 16% increase.

Example 10. 32 inches is removed from a length of a rope. If the rope is now 96 inches long, what is the percent decrease in the length of the rope?

- (A) 25%
- (B) 28%
- (C) 32%
- (D) 64%
- (E) 84%

Answer: A. The original length of the rope must be calculated from the information. If the rope is 96 inches long after 32 inches were removed, then the original length of the rope was $96 + 32 = 128$. The percent decrease is the fraction of the difference over the original amount. Therefore, the percent decrease is

$$\frac{32}{128} = \frac{1}{4} = 0.25$$

which translates to a 25% decrease.

Combining Percentages and Amounts

The GED Math test may contain a word problem or two that combines percentages and fixed amounts.

Example 11. Sports Today normally sells a pair of running shoes for $69, but the shoes are marked $20 off today. Sports Today is giving another 15% off all merchandise if the customer opens a store credit card. How much do the shoes cost after both discounts, before any tax is added?

- (A) $34.58
- (B) $38.65
- (C) $41.65
- (D) $42.95
- (E) $45.40

Chapter 11: Percentages

Answer: C. The cost of the shoes after the $20 markdown is

$$\$69 - \$20 = \$49$$

Now subtract 15% of $49:

$$\$49 - (0.15) \times \$49 = \$49 - \$7.35$$
$$= \$41.65$$

You can also take 85% of $49 and get the same number, as 100% − 15% = 85%. If you answered **B**, you took 15% off the normal price of the shoes and then took $20 off, which is the wrong order of operations.

Problems Where Answers Are in Terms of a Variable

Sometimes a word problem may involve taking percentages without a specific amount, and then asking for the final answer in terms of the variable.

Example 12. A clothing store discounts a dress that costs D dollars by 60%. The next week, the store marks down the dress by another 60% on a clearance sale. Which expression below represents the price of the dress in terms of D after the clearance sale?

- (A) $D - 60 - 60$
- (B) $D \times 60 \times 60$
- (C) $D \times 0.6 \times 0.6$
- (D) $D \times 0.4 \times 0.4$
- (E) This sale is not possible since the price of the dress will now be less than $0.

Answer: D. The first sale marks the dress with 60% off, so the customer is left paying 40% of D. Similarly with the clearance sale, the customer only has to pay 40% of what is left, which is 40% of 40% of D. Since 40% = 0.4, the answer in terms of D is

$$D \times 0.4 \times 0.4$$

To use a precise amount, choose $100 for D. After a 60% sale, the new price of the dress is $100 − $60 = $40. Now take 40% of what is left ($40) = $16. The new price of the dress, ends up being above $0, not below $0 as choice **E** states.

Long Word Problems that Include Multiple Numerical Facts

Some problems may give four or more facts that include numerical values, and thus may be confusing. It is a good idea to read the question a second time before attempting to answer it.

Example 13. A Steinway piano sells at a music store for $65,000, but is discounted by 10% on a special sale. Joseph purchases the piano and pays 10% tax. He puts down $5,000, and then finances the rest of his purchase. How much is financed?

- (A) $55,500
- (B) $56,250
- (C) $58,000
- (D) $59,350
- (E) $60,000

Answer: D. 10% discount is 10% of $65,000 = $6,500. The price after the sale is therefore

$$\$65,000 - \$6,500 = \$58,500$$

Joseph pays 10% tax which is $5,850 on top of the $58,500:

$$\$58,500 + \$5,850 = \$64,350$$

He puts down $5,000, so he finances

$$\$64,350 - \$5,000 = \$59,350$$

If you chose **E,** you thought that subtracting 10% off and then adding 10% tax didn't change the overall payment, which is untrue.

Practice Problems

1. Which of the following is equal to 25% of 736?

    (A) 73.6
    (B) 174
    (C) 184
    (D) 1,840
    (E) 18,400

2. 63 is approximately what percentage of 81?

    (A) 13%
    (B) 18%
    (C) 70%
    (D) 78%
    (E) 144%

3. The price of a toy is increased by 20%. The resulting price is later decreased by $40. If the original price of the toy was $60, what is the final price of the toy?

    (A) $8
    (B) $16
    (C) $24
    (D) $32
    (E) $40

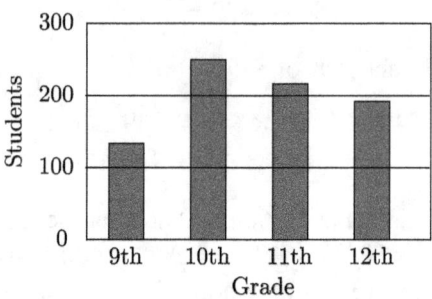

4. The chart above shows the distribution of students across each grade for a given high school. Approximately what percentage of the students are not in the 12th grade?

    (A) 18%
    (B) 26%
    (C) 30%
    (D) 75%
    (E) 82%

5. A number is decreased by 50%, and the result is increased by 50% to yield 99. What is the original number?

    (A) 25
    (B) 50
    (C) 74
    (D) 99
    (E) 132

Chapter 11: Percentages

6. 40% of $\frac{1}{4}$ =

   (A) $\frac{1}{10}$

   (B) $\frac{1}{2}$

   (C) 1

   (D) 4

   (E) 10

7. The area of square A is 40 ft^2. The area of square B is 250% of that of square A. What is the length of one side of square B?

   (A) 2 ft
   (B) 5 ft
   (C) 10 ft
   (D) 12 ft
   (E) 100 ft

8. Which of the following values is the greatest?

   (A) 15% of 480
   (B) 20% of 480
   (C) 30% of 320
   (D) 35% of 320
   (E) 40% of 120

Color	Percent
Red	35%
Blue	22%
White	16%
Black	15%
Green	12%

9. 1,100 dresses at a store come in 5 colors, as shown by the distribution in the table above. How many dresses in the store are white?

   (A) 160
   (B) 176
   (C) 220
   (D) 242
   (E) 924

10. If $T \div 3 = R$, then 60% of R is ?

    (A) $T \div 5$

    (B) $T \div 2$

    (C) $T \times \frac{6}{5}$

    (D) $T \times 20$

    (E) $T \times 180$

11. Ninety percent of X is 198. What is X?

    (A) 178.2
    (B) 217.8
    (C) 220
    (D) 222
    (E) 376.2

12. A glass container contains 22 blue marbles and 18 green marbles. If 5 marbles are removed from the container, what is the percentage decrease in the total number of marbles?

    (A) 12.5%
    (B) 14.3%
    (C) 22.7%
    (D) 27.8%
    (E) 29.4%

13. 90 is what percentage of 150?

    (A) 16.7%
    (B) 40%
    (C) 60%
    (D) 66.6%
    (E) 90%

Group	Men	Women	Total
A	8	5	13
B	7	5	12
C	9	6	15
D	7	7	14
Total	31	23	54

14. A medical study is conducted with 54 people. The individuals are assigned to 4 different groups as shown in the table above. Approximately what percentage of Group B are women?

    (A) 5%
    (B) 12%
    (C) 23%
    (D) 42%
    (E) 54%

15. What is 37.5% of the fraction $\frac{4}{9}$?

    (A) $\frac{1}{7}$
    (B) $\frac{1}{6}$
    (C) $\frac{2}{9}$
    (D) $\frac{5}{9}$
    (E) $\frac{4}{3}$

16. Tonya purchases a sweater for *D* dollars. She gets a discount of 30%, and then gets another 40% off. She then pays 6% tax. What is the final amount Tonya pays for the shirt in terms of *D*?

    (A) $D \times 0.36$
    (B) $D \times 0.76$
    (C) $D \times 0.4 \times 0.3 \times 0.06$
    (D) $D \times 0.4 \times 0.3 \times 1.06$
    (E) $D \times 0.6 \times 0.7 \times 1.06$

17. Bob loans Eric $25,000, but charges him 2% a month simple interest for 6 months. Eric has not repaid any of the debt when, a year later, he defaults on his loan and must pay Bob an additional 35% attorney fees on the new amount he owes Bob. Eric manages to pay Bob $16,500. How much does Eric still owe Bob?

    (A) $9,800
    (B) $14,560
    (C) $21,300
    (D) $22,578
    (E) $23,460

18. A 50% sale off sneakers is followed by a 50% off clearance sale. The total discount is:

    (A) 25%
    (B) 75%
    (C) 87.5%
    (D) 92.5%
    (E) 100%

Population of Country Y

Year	Population
1980	5,000,000
1990	5,200,050
2000	5,678,900
2010	6,250,000

19. The population of Country Y is shown in the table above for four years from 1980 to 2010. By what percentage did the population grow from 1980 to 2010?

    (A) 10%
    (B) 15%
    (C) 20%
    (D) 25%
    (E) 30%

20. Company stock ABC increased by 40% in 2016, increased 10% more in 2017, and then went down 10% in 2018. What is the net change in percent between 2016 and 2018, in terms of the original price, *O*?

    (A) $O \times 1.4 \times 1.1 \times 0.9$
    (B) $O \times 0.6 \times 1.1 \times 0.9$
    (C) $O \times 0.4 \times 0.9 \times 0.9$
    (D) $O \times 0.6 \times 0.9 \times 0.9$
    (E) $O \times 0.4 \times 0.1 \times 0.1$

Answers to Practice Problems

1. **(C)** 25% of 736 can be written as $\frac{25}{100} \times 736$ which is equal to $\frac{1}{4} \times 736 = 184$.

2. **(D)** The problem is asking for the percentage equivalent of the fraction 63/81. First, reduce the fraction to 7/9. Divide through to obtain the decimal equivalent: 0.777… Finally, multiply by 100 to get 77.7%. The closest answer is 78%, **D**.

3. **(D)** The initial price is $60. 20% of $60 is
$$\frac{20}{100} \times 60 = \frac{60}{5} = \$12$$
Therefore the price of the toy is $60 + $12 = $72 after the increase. If we subtract $40 from this price, we get $32.

4. **(D)** Solving this problem requires reading a chart. The number of students in each grade must be estimated from reading the chart so that a total may be calculated to derive the percentage of students not in the 12th grade. The number of students in the 9th grade looks close to 140. The 10th grade population looks close to 230. The average of the 11th and 12th grades appear to have about 200 students. The total number of students is about
$$140 + 230 + 200 + 200 = 770$$
and those that are not in the 12th grade is about $140 + 230 + 210 = 580$. The percentage is
$$\frac{580}{770} = \frac{58}{77} \approx 0.75 = 75\%$$

5. **(E)** A number is decreased by 50% and then increased by 50%. If x is the original number, this can be expressed mathematically by
$$(x \times 0.5) \times 1.5 = 99$$
$$0.75x = 99$$
So, $x = \frac{99}{0.75} = 132$.

6. **(A)** To solve this problem, just convert the percentage into a fraction and multiply through:
$$40\% \times \frac{1}{4} = \frac{40}{100} \times \frac{1}{4} = \frac{40}{400} = \frac{1}{10}$$

7. **(C)** The area of square B is 250% that of square A. So, the area of square B is
$$\frac{250}{100} \times 40 = 2.5 \times 40 = 100 \text{ ft}^2$$
The length of one side of a square is equal to the square root of the area (see chapter 16). So, the length of each side of the square B is $\sqrt{100} = 10$, so, the length of each side of square B is 10 ft.

8. **(D)** Just from looking at the answer choices, before doing any calculations, we should be able to eliminate **A**. (15% of 480) because it is obviously less than **B**. (20% of 480). Similarly, we can eliminate **C**. (30% of 320) because it is obviously less than **D**. (35% of 320). We calculate each of the remaining answer choices:

   B. $\frac{20}{100} \times 480 = \frac{480}{5} = 96$

   D. $\frac{35}{100} \times 320 = \frac{7}{20} \times 320 = 7 \times 16 = 112$

   E. $\frac{40}{100} \times 120 = \frac{2}{5} \times 120 = 2 \times 24 = 48$

   The largest value is **D** 112.

9. **(B)** According to the table, 16% of the dresses are white. There are a total of 1,100 dresses in the store. Therefore, the number of white dresses is
$$16\% \times 1100 = \frac{16}{100} \times 1100 = 16 \times 11 = 176$$

10. **(A)** We are trying to find 60% of R. The value 60% is equal to $\frac{60}{100} = \frac{3}{5}$. We can substitute R in the equation $\frac{3}{5} \times R$ with $R = \frac{T}{3}$. This gives $\frac{3}{5} \times \frac{T}{3} = \frac{T}{5}$.

11. **(C)** The percentage can be first translated into a fraction in the problem:

    $$\frac{90}{100} X = 198$$

    From this, we can see that

    $$X = 198 \times \frac{100}{90} = \frac{1980}{9} = 220$$

12. **(A)** Percentage change is given by the difference divided by the original total. The original total is $18 + 22 = 40$ marbles. The decrease is 5 marbles. The percentage change is then

    $$\frac{5}{40} = \frac{1}{8} = 12.5\%$$

13. **(C)** The percentage is found by just dividing

    $$\frac{90}{150} = \frac{9}{15} = \frac{3}{5} = 0.6 = 60\%$$

    Alternatively, we can translate the question into a math equation:

    $$90 = \frac{x}{100} \times 150$$

    Then, multiply both sides by $\frac{100}{150}$ to get

    $$x = 90 \times \frac{100}{150} = \frac{900}{15} = 60\%$$

14. **(D)** The table provides more information than is necessary to solve this problem. The total number of people in Group B (12) and the number of women in Group B (5) are the only two numbers needed from the table. The percent of women in Group B can be calculated from these two numbers:

    $$\frac{5}{12} = 41.666... \approx 42\%$$

15. **(B)** 37.5% is equivalent to the fraction 3/8. Multiply through to find the answer:

    $$\frac{3}{8} \times \frac{4}{9} = \frac{3 \times 4}{8 \times 9} = \frac{1 \times 1}{2 \times 3} = \frac{1}{6}$$

16. **(E)** Tanya first got 40% off, leaving her with 60% (0.6). She then got another 30 percent off, leaving her with 70% of the new amount. Therefore, we have $D \times 0.6 \times 0.7$. Now, she must pay 6% tax, so adding 6% to the newest amount we obtain

    $$1.06 \times (D \times 0.6 \times 0.7) = D \times 0.6 \times 0.7 \times 1.06$$

17. **(C)** Eric starts with borrowing $25,000 plus 2% × 6 of $25,000:

    $$\$25{,}000 + (12\% \times \$25{,}000) = \$28{,}000$$

    Now Eric must pay Bob 35% of $28,000 = $9,800. So in total Eric owes Bob $37,800.

    Eric manages to pay Bob $16,500, so he still owes Bob $37,800 − $16,500 = $21,300.

18. **(B)** Choose $100 for the initial price of the pair of sneakers. Now subtract 50% (half) off $100 to obtain $50. Now take half of $50 off from 50 to obtain $25. The sneakers were discounted in total $50 + $25 = $75 off $100, which is 75% of the starting amount.

19. **(D)** Use the formula for percent change:

    $$\frac{\text{New Value} - \text{Original Value}}{\text{Original Value}} \times 100$$

    $$\frac{6{,}250{,}000 - 5{,}000{,}000}{5{,}000{,}000} \times 100 = 25\%$$

20. **(A)** O is the beginning stock price. The value of O after the first increase of 40% is:

    $$O \times 1.4$$

    After the 10% increase it is:

    $$O \times 1.4 \times 1.1$$

    After the decrease of 10% it is:

    $$O \times 1.4 \times 1.1 \times 0.9$$

Chapter 12
Simple Interest

What Is Simple Interest?

Simple interest is either the interest charge on a loan or the interest received on an investment. Annual interest is calculated by multiplying the annual interest rate times the principal (the outstanding balance) times the number of years that elapsed between payments.

For example, if you receive 2% annual simple interest in a money market account, that will provide you with $2 for every $100 invested, every year. The second year, you will receive another $2, and so forth.

The calculation of simple interest doesn't consider the effect of compounding. It is calculated as follows:

Simple Interest Formula

$$I = P \times R \times T$$

Where:
- P = Principal Amount (The initial investment or loan)
- R = Interest Rate (in decimal form)
- T = The number of times the money is accrued

The period, T, must be expressed for the same time span as the interest rate. For example, if the interest is expressed as a yearly rate, such as a 2% annual interest rate loan, then the number of periods the interest is charged must also be expressed in years.

Example 1. Ms. Higgins invests $10,000 at a 3% annual interest rate. She would like to calculate how much interest she will earn in 10 years.

Write the formula: $I = P \times R \times T$.
I = ($10,000) $\times$ (3% a year) $\times$ (10 years)
= 10,000 $\times$ 0.03 $\times$ 10 = $3,000.

Example 2. Jon borrows money from his sister, who is willing to give him a four-year, non-compounding loan of $6,500, with a 1.5% annual interest rate. If Jon pays his sister back the principal amount plus interest at the end of the four-year period, how much will he pay her?

- (A) $390
- (B) $3,900
- (C) $6,890
- (D) $10,400
- (E) $39,000

Answer: C. Write the formula $I = P \times R \times T$. Plug in the values for P, R, and T like so:

$$I = 6500 \times 0.015 \times 4 = \$390.$$

He will have to pay her back $6,500 + $390 = $6,890

Example 3. Jimmy invests $1250 in a CD that pays 1.15% simple interest. How much will he receive after 7 years, rounded to the nearest cent?

- (A) $100.63
- (B) $131.25
- (C) $1,350.63
- (D) $1,381.25
- (E) $10,062.50

Answer: C. Write the formula $I = P \times R \times T$. Plug in the values for P, R, and T like so:

$$I = 1250 \times 0.0115 \times 7 = \$100.63.$$

Add $100.63 + $1,250 = $1,350.63.

Practice Problems

1. Martha loans Cecilia $240 and asks for 3.5% annual simple interest. If Martha collects the money from Cecilia after 3 years, how much would she collect?

    (A) $25.20
    (B) $252
    (C) $265.20
    (D) $745.20
    (E) $2,760

2. Jason invests $500 in a savings account that pays .78% annual simple interest for 15 years. How much interest in total will he earn during that time?

    (A) $5.85
    (B) $58.50
    (C) $580.50
    (D) $585
    (E) $5,850

3. Mike invests $7,500 in a 5-year CD that pays annual 1.62% interest. How much will Mike collect after the CD matures?

    (A) $121.50
    (B) $607.50
    (C) $7,621.50
    (D) $8,107.50
    (E) $1,2150.00

4. Sarah owes Bart $42.50 in interest for a simple interest loan he gave her. If she pays him 2% simple annual interest for 3 years, how much did she borrow to the nearest cent?

    (A) $708.03
    (B) $708.33
    (C) $1,202.70
    (D) $2,125
    (E) $7,080.33

Chapter 12: Simple Interest

5. David places $1,200 in a savings account that pays .45% annual simple interest. How much does he have after 6 months?

    (A) $1,202.70
    (B) $1,205.40
    (C) $1,227
    (D) $1,470
    (E) $1,740

6. Clara owes Sally $1,500 after one year for a one-year simple annual interest loan. If she borrowed $1,400, what interest rate is Clara paying?

    (A) 3.45%
    (B) 6.67%
    (C) 7.14%
    (D) 8.91%
    (E) 9.98%

7. Tom borrows $5000 from the bank to pay for a used car. If he pays 9.9% simple interest, how much interest did he incur after 8 months?

    (A) $330
    (B) $371.25
    (C) $495
    (D) $3,300
    (E) $4,950

8. Gus invests $15,000 in a money market account that pays 2.6% annual simple interest for 20 years. How much money will he have in the account after 20 years?

    (A) $22,800
    (B) $23,800
    (C) $122,950
    (D) $780,000
    (E) $795,000

Answers to Practice Problems

1. **(C)** $I = P \times R \times T = 240 \times 0.035 \times 3 = 25.2$. Martha will collect $240 + $25.2 = $265.2

2. **(B)** $I = P \times R \times T = 500 \times 0.0078 \times 15 = $58.5

3. **(D)** $I = P \times R \times T = 7500 \times 0.0162 \times 5 = $607.5. Add $7,500 to $607.5 to get $8107.50.

4. **(B)** $I = P \times R \times T$.

    $42.5 = P \times 0.02 \times 3 = 0.06P$.

    Divide both sides of the equation by 0.06:

    $$P = \frac{42.50}{0.06} = \$708.33.$$

5. **(A)** $I = 1200 \times 0.0045 \times 6/12 = \$2.70$. Add $2.70 + $1,200 = $1202.70. The reason you divide 6 by 12 is because the interest accumulates for 6 out of 12 months.

6. **(C)** Clara paid $100 in interest since $1,500 − $1,400 = $100. Write $I = P \times R \times T$. Plug in $100 for I, $1400 for P and 1 for T.

    $100 = 1400 \times R \times 1 = 1400R$

    Divide both sides of the equation by 1400 to get $R = \dfrac{100}{1400} = 0.0714$. That is a 7.14% interest rate.

7. **(A)** $I = P \times R \times T = 5000 \times 0.099 \times 8/12 = \$330$. You divide 8 by 12 because the interest is for 8 out of 12 months.

8. **(A)** $I = P \times R \times T = 15000 \times 0.026 \times 20 = 7800$. Add $7,800 to $15,000 to get $22,800.

Chapter 13

Speed, Distance, and Time Word Problems

On the GED Math test, one or two problems about distance, speed, and time may appear. In case you have difficulty tackling these types of problem, an entire chapter on these word problems follows.

Problems involving speed, distance, and time are solved using one basic formula:

$$\text{Speed (rate)} = \frac{\text{Distance}}{\text{Time}} \quad (1)$$

This formula can be manipulated to have two other forms:

$$\text{Distance} = \text{Speed} \times \text{Time} \quad (2)$$

$$\text{Time} = \frac{\text{Distance}}{\text{Speed}} \quad (3)$$

All three equations describe the same relationship between the three variables.

In order to solve word problems on speed, distance, and time on the GED Math test, all you need is to know the formulas above and to have an understanding of how to manipulate the equations to match the units of the final answer.

The units for distance on the GED Math test will usually be feet, meters, kilometers, and miles.

The units for time will usually be seconds, minutes, and hours.

The units for speed are miles/hour, kilometers/hour, meters/second, etc.

Why is the equation (1) equivalent to the equation (2)? If you use the equation (1) and multiply both sides of the equation by Time, you obtain:

$$\frac{\text{Distance}}{\cancel{\text{Time}}} \times \cancel{\text{Time}} = \text{Speed} \times \text{Time}$$

The time unit on the left-hand side cancels out to obtain

$$\text{Distance} = \text{Speed} \times \text{Time}$$

Similarly, to solve for time, you perform the following operation: multiply both sides of the equation (1) by Time/Speed.

$$\frac{\cancel{\text{Time}}}{\text{Speed}} \times \frac{\text{Distance}}{\cancel{\text{Time}}} = \cancel{\text{Speed}} \times \frac{\text{Time}}{\cancel{\text{Speed}}}$$

$$\frac{\text{Distance}}{\text{Speeed}} = \text{Time}$$

Now let's look at some simple examples before dealing with more difficult problems.

Example 1. Stephen drives his car from Washington, D.C., to Philadelphia in 150 minutes. The distance from Washington, D.C., to Philadelphia is 140 miles. What was Stephen's average speed in mph?

- (A) 48 miles / hour
- (B) 52 miles / hour
- (C) 56 miles / hour
- (D) 58 miles / hour
- (E) 63 miles / hour

Answer: C. We use the equation (1)
$$\text{Speed} = \frac{\text{Distance}}{\text{Time}}$$
and plug in 140 minutes for distance and 150 miles for time to obtain:
$$\text{Speed} = \frac{140 \text{ miles}}{150 \text{ minutes}} = \frac{14 \text{ miles}}{15 \text{ minutes}}$$
To convert the answer into mph, we perform the following calculation:
$$\frac{14 \text{ miles}}{15 \text{ minutes}} \times \frac{60 \text{ minutes}}{1 \text{ hour}} = 56 \text{ miles/hour}$$

Example 2. Jason flew from Boston to New York City at an average speed of 400 miles/hour. The flight covered a distance of 250 miles. How long did the plane take to travel in minutes?

- (A) 25 minutes
- (B) 28 minutes
- (C) 35 minutes
- (D) 37.5 minutes
- (E) 42.5 minutes

Answer: D. We use the equation (3)
$$\text{Time} = \frac{\text{Distance}}{\text{Speed}}$$
and plug in the numbers:
$$\text{Time} = \frac{250 \text{ miles}}{400 \text{ miles/hour}} = \frac{250 \text{ hours}}{400} = \frac{5}{8} \text{ hour}$$
To convert to minutes, we perform the following calculation:
$$\frac{5 \text{ hours}}{8} \times \frac{60 \text{ minutes}}{\text{hour}} = 37.5 \text{ minutes}$$

Example 3. A train travels from Chicago to Detroit for 2.5 hours at a speed of 120 miles/hour. How far did the train travel?

- (A) 180 miles
- (B) 240 miles
- (C) 300 miles
- (D) 350 miles
- (E) 360 miles

Answer: C. We use the formula
$$\text{Distance} = \text{Speed} \times \text{Time}$$
and plug in the numbers.
$$2.5 \text{ hours} \times \frac{120 \text{ miles}}{\text{hour}} = 300 \text{ miles}$$

Now that you know the basics, let us now practice some slightly more difficult problems that will still make use of our three formulas.

Chapter 13: Speed, Distance, and Time

Example 4. A train travels at an average speed of 110 mph while a truck travels at an average speed of 55 mph. If the train and truck both leave the same spot at 1 PM, and travel at those average speeds, how far are they apart at 6 PM?

(A) 25 miles
(B) 75 miles
(C) 175 miles
(D) 225 miles
(E) 275 miles

Answer: E. Let's find the distance each travels in the 5-hour period from 1 PM to 6 PM. We use the equation Distance = Speed × Time.

For the train the distance is 110 miles/hour × 5 hours = 550 miles. The truck travels a distance of 55 miles/hour × 5 hours = 275 miles. Therefore, the distance between the train and the truck is 550 − 275 miles = 275 miles.

A quicker calculation is to take the difference in speed, which is 110 mph − 55 mph = 55 mph, and then multiply 55 mph × 5 hours = 275 miles.

Example 5. A car travels from City A to City B at a constant speed, traveling 120 miles in 2.5 hours. How fast is the car traveling in miles per hour?

(A) 4.8 miles/hour
(B) 30 miles/hour
(C) 48 miles/hour
(D) 60 miles/hour
(E) 65 miles/hour

Answer: C. Speed = Distance/Time. Plug in 120 miles for distance and 2.5 hours for time to obtain:

$$\text{Speed} = \frac{120 \text{ miles}}{2.5 \text{ hours}} = 48 \text{ miles/hour}$$

Practice Problems

1. Jake drives at a speed of 60 mph for 5 hours. How many miles does he cover?

    (A) 225 miles
    (B) 300 miles
    (C) 325 miles
    (D) 340 miles
    (E) 400 miles

2. Nancy drives without stops from Chicago to New York City. It takes her 12 hours to reach New York. Chicago is about 800 miles from New York City. How fast was she traveling in miles/hour to the nearest mph?

    (A) 50 miles/hour
    (B) 55 miles/hour
    (C) 60 miles/hour
    (D) 63 miles/hour
    (E) 67 miles/hour

3. Darcy bikes at a speed of 15 mph and covered a distance of 3 miles. How long did she bike for?

    (A) 5 minutes
    (B) 10 minutes
    (C) 12 minutes
    (D) 15 minutes
    (E) 45 minutes

4. A bus travels at an average speed of 60 mph while a truck travels at an average speed of 50 mph. If the bus and truck both leave the same spot at 4 PM, and travel at those average speeds along the same road, how far are they apart at 10 PM?

    (A) 60 miles
    (B) 70 miles
    (C) 75 miles
    (D) 80 miles
    (E) 110 miles

5. If a dog runs at 12 miles per hour, traveling 1/2 mile, how many minutes did the dog run to the nearest hundredth?

    (A) 0.042 minutes
    (B) 2.50 minutes
    (C) 4.20 minutes
    (D) 6.00 minutes
    (E) 24.00 minutes

6. A bus travels from Seattle to Portland, Oregon at 43 miles per hour and reaches Portland in 4 hours. How far are the cities apart?

    (A) 162 miles
    (B) 172 miles
    (C) 182 miles
    (D) 190 miles
    (E) 210 miles

7. Two cars travel toward each other. Car A and Car B are 1.5 mile apart at 12:00 noon, and .3 miles apart at 12:01 pm. If they are both traveling at the same speed, how fast is each car moving?

    (A) 0.6 miles per hour
    (B) 1.2 miles per hour
    (C) 18 miles per hour
    (D) 36 miles per hour
    (E) 72 miles per hour

8. A plane flies from City A to City B at 500 miles per hour. If the two cities are 300 miles apart, how long in minutes will it take the plane to reach City B from City A?

    (A) 36 minutes
    (B) 42 minutes
    (C) 48 minutes
    (D) 60 minutes
    (E) 72 minutes

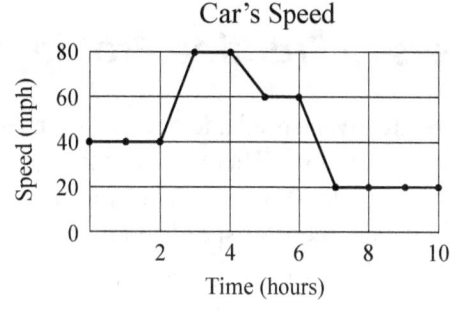

9. The graph above shows a car's speed in mph and the time it spent driving on a highway in hours. During which time period did the car travel the greatest number of miles?

    (A) During the first 2 hours
    (B) Between 2 and 3 hours
    (C) Between 3 and 4 hours
    (D) Between 4 and 5 hours
    (E) Between 5 and 7 hours

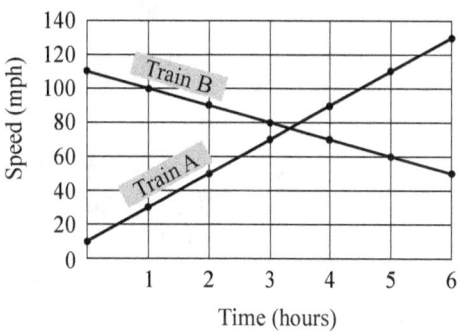

10. The graph above shows the speed and travel time of two trains. The upward sloping line shows train A and the downward sloping line shows train B. Which train covers more miles and by how much?

    (A) Train A traveled 40 miles more than train B.
    (B) Train A traveled 60 miles more than train B.
    (C) Train B traveled 60 miles more than train A.
    (D) Train B traveled 120 miles more than train A.
    (E) Train A and train B traveled an equal number of miles.

Answers to Practice Problems

1. **(B)** We are given speed and time, so we need to solve for distance. Therefore, use the distance formula, Distance = Speed × Time. Plug in the numbers for speed and time:

   60 mph × 5 hours = 300 miles

2. **(E)** We know the distance and time, so we need to solve for speed.

   $$\text{Speed} = \frac{\text{Distance}}{\text{Time}} = \frac{800 \text{ miles}}{12 \text{ hours}}$$
   $$= 66.7 \text{ miles/hour}$$

3. **(C)** We know speed and distance, so we use the formula for Time:

   $$\text{Time} = \frac{\text{Distance}}{\text{Speed}} = \frac{3 \text{ miles}}{15 \text{ miles/hour}}$$
   $$= \frac{1}{5} \text{ hours}$$
   $$= 12 \text{ minutes}$$

4. **(A)** The difference in speed between the bus and truck is 60 − 50 = 10 miles/hour. We want to find the distance between the bus and truck after 6 hours (10 PM − 4 PM). Use the formula Distance = Speed × Time and plug in the numbers for Speed and Time to get

   Distance = 10 mph × 6 hours = 60 miles

5. **(B)** We use the equation (3)

   $$\text{Time} = \frac{\text{Distance}}{\text{Speed}}$$

   and plug in the numbers:

   $$\text{Time} = \frac{0.5 \text{ miles}}{12 \text{ miles/hours}} = 0.042 \text{ hours}$$

   Converting to minutes: 0.042 × 60 = 2.50 hours

6. **(B)** We use the formula

   Distance = Speed × Time

   and plug in the numbers.

   $$4 \text{ hours} \times 43 \frac{\text{miles}}{\text{hours}} = 172 \text{ miles.}$$

7. **(D)** Write the equation

   $$\text{Speed} = \frac{\text{Distance}}{\text{Time}}.$$

   Plug in $\frac{1.5 - 0.3 \text{ miles}}{1 \text{ minute}} = 1.2$ miles/minute.

   Therefore, each travels at half that speed or 0.6 miles/minute. Converting to miles per hour, multiply by 60 to get 36 miles per hour.

8. **(A)** Write the equation

   $$\text{Time} = \frac{\text{Distance}}{\text{Speed}}.$$

   So, Time = $\frac{300 \text{ miles}}{500 \text{ miles/hour}} = 0.6$ hours or 36 minutes.

9. **(E)** We want to solve for distance, so we use the formula Distance = Speed × Time. Go through each of the 5 choices. In choice **A**, time = 2 hours, and the speed = 40 mph, and therefore the distance is 2 × 40 = 80 miles. In choice **B**, the average speed was (80 + 40)/2 = 60 mph and the time is 1 hour, so the distance is 60 × 1 = 60 miles. In choice **C**, the average speed is 80 mph and the time is 1 hour, so the distance is 80 × 1 = 80 miles. In choice **D**, the speed is 60 mph and the time is 1 hour, so the distance is 60 × 1 = 60 miles. In choice **E**, the distance is

   $$(60 \times 1) + \left(\frac{60 + 20}{2} \times 1\right) = 60 + 40$$
   $$= 100 \text{ miles}$$

   Therefore, choice **E** is correct.

10. **(C)** Use Distance = Speed × Time. The average speed of train A is $\frac{130 + 10}{2}$ = 70 mph. The travel time is 6 hours, so the distance is 70 mph × 6 hours = 420 miles. The average speed train B travels is $\frac{110 + 50}{2}$ = 80 mph. Therefore, the distance traveled by train B is 80 × 6 = 480 miles. The difference is 480 − 420 = 60 miles that train B traveled farther than train A.

Chapter 14
Units and Measurements

There are two major systems of measurement: the U.S. Customary System of Measurement and the Metric System of Measurement. These two systems are made up of units that are used to describe some amount of time or an object's length, weight, or volume.

Time
60 seconds (sec) = 1 minute (min)
60 minutes (min) = 1 hour (hr)
24 hours (hr) = 1 day
365 days = 1 non-leap year

Length
1 foot (ft) = 12 inches (in)
1 yard (yd) = 3 feet (ft)
1 mile (mi) = 5,280 feet (ft)
1,000 meters (m) = 1 kilometer (km)
100 centimeters (cm) = 1 meter (m)
10 millimeters (mm) = 1 centimeter (cm)
1 mile = 1.6 km (approximately)
1 inch = 2.54 cm

Weight
1 pound (lb) = 16 ounces (oz)
1 ton (t) = 2,000 pounds (lb)
1,000 grams (g) = 1 kilogram (kg)
1 kg = 2.2 lbs

Volume
1 cup (c) = 8 fluid ounces (fl oz)
1 pint (pt) = 2 cups (c)
1 quart (qt) = 2 pints (pt)
1 gallon (gal) = 4 quarts (qt)
1 gallon (gal) = 8 pints (pt)
1 gallon (gal) = 16 cups (c)
1 liter (L) = 1,000 milliliters (ml)

Most GED Math problems involving measurement will ask you to turn a larger unit of measurement into a smaller unit or vice versa. As a result, the ability to convert between units is an essential skill to master.

Example 1. A book weighs 80 ounces. How many pounds does the book weigh?

- (A) 1.2 lb
- (B) 2.7 lb
- (C) 5 lb
- (D) 7.1 lb
- (E) 8.3 lb

Answer: C. This problem requires a knowledge of the U.S. Customary System of Measurement, specifically the unit pound (lb) and ounce (oz). In order to complete the problem, we must convert the book's weight in ounces to pounds. To accomplish this, we take the weight of the book in ounces, 80 ounces, and divide that number by the total number of ounces in one pound. When a term is found to be in both the numerator and the denominator of a fraction, it can be canceled. The following illustrates this:

$$80 \text{ oz} \times \frac{1 \text{ lb}}{16 \text{ oz}} = 5 \text{ lb}$$

Example 2. John travels 3,600 m to school each day. How many kilometers does John travel?

- (A) 2.1 km
- (B) 3.0 km
- (C) 3.2 km
- (D) 3.6 km
- (E) 4.2 km

Answer: D. This problem requires a knowledge of the Metric System of Measurement, specifically the unit meters and the prefix kilo-. First, it is important to know that there are 1,000 meters in a single kilometer. Thus, in order to solve the problem, we must take the total number of meters, in this case 3,600, and divide by 1,000 in order to get the total number of kilometers. The following illustrates this:

$$3,600 \text{ m} \times \frac{1 \text{ km}}{1000 \text{ m}} = 3.6 \text{ km}$$

Example 3. Thomas has 7 pieces of rope, each piece measuring 144 in. What is the total length of all 7 pieces of rope in yards?

- (A) 16 yd
- (B) 28 yd
- (C) 84 yd
- (D) 108 yd
- (E) 1008 yd

Answer: B. In order to solve this problem, two operations must be completed. First, we must calculate the total length of each piece of rope when combined. If each piece of rope is 144 inches long, and there are 7 pieces of rope, the total length in rope can be determined through the expression, 7 pieces × 144 inches, which equals 1,008 inches total. This number must then be divided by the number of inches in a single foot in order to determine the length of rope in feet, then divided by 3 to determine the number of yards. The following illustrates this:

$$7 \text{ pieces} \times \frac{144 \text{ in}}{1 \text{ piece}} \times \frac{1 \text{ ft}}{12 \text{ in}} \times \frac{1 \text{ yd}}{3 \text{ ft}} = 28 \text{ yd}$$

Example 4. A swimming pool holds 9,000 liters of water. How many milliliters of water are in the pool?

- (A) 90 ml
- (B) 90,000 ml
- (C) 900,000 ml
- (D) 9,000,000 ml
- (E) 90,000,000 ml

Answer: D. In order to solve this problem, it is important to understand the relationship between liters and milliliters. The prefix milli- tells us that there are 1,000 milliliters in 1 liter.

Thus, solving this problem requires the multiplication of 9,000 liters by 1,000 since there are 1,000 milliliters in a liter. The following illustrates this:

$$9,000 \text{ L} \times \frac{1,000 \text{ ml}}{1 \text{ L}} = 9,000,000 \text{ ml}$$

Example 5. Vincent ran a 2-mile dash on Sunday. About how many millimeters did Vincent run?

- (A) 3,200 mm
- (B) 64,000 mm
- (C) 320,000 mm
- (D) 3,200,000 mm
- (E) 6,400,000,000 mm

Answer: D. As previously mentioned in this chapter, there are about 1.6 km in a mile, 1,000 meters in a km, 100 centimeters in a meter, and 10 millimeters in a centimeter (cm). Thus, to complete this problem, we must multiply the number of meters by 100 in order to determine the number of centimeters. The following illustrates this calculation:

$$2 \text{ miles} \times \frac{1.6 \text{ km}}{1 \text{ mile}} \times \frac{1,000 \text{ m}}{1 \text{ km}} \times \frac{100 \text{ cm}}{1 \text{ m}} \times \frac{10 \text{ mm}}{1 \text{ cm}}$$

$$= 3,200,000 \text{ mm}$$

Example 6. Which of the following represents 10 feet in centimeters?

- (A) 0.864 cm
- (B) 120 cm
- (C) 304.8 cm
- (D) 3,650 cm
- (E) 864,000 cm

Answer: C. This problem requires knowing the relationship between feet and inches and inches and centimeters. There are 12 inches in one foot and 2.54 centimeters in an inch. Therefore, in order to solve this problem, you must multiply the number of feet represented in the problem by the number of inches in one foot and then the number of centimeters in an inch. The following illustrates this calculation:

$$10 \text{ ft} \times \frac{12 \text{ in}}{1 \text{ ft}} \times \frac{2.54 \text{ cm}}{1 \text{ in}} = 304.8 \text{ cm}$$

Example 7. Which of the following represents 2 gallons in fluid ounces?

- (A) 1.6 ounces
- (B) 16 ounces
- (C) 17.2 ounces
- (D) 196 ounces
- (E) 256 ounces

Answer: E. This problem requires the completion of multiple conversions. First, you must convert from gallons to quarts, then from quarts to pints to cups to ounces. The following represents this calculation:

$$2 \text{ gal} \times \frac{4 \text{ qt}}{1 \text{ gal}} \times \frac{2 \text{ pt}}{1 \text{ qt}} \times \frac{2 \text{ c}}{1 \text{ pt}} \times \frac{8 \text{ oz}}{1 \text{ c}} = 256 \text{ oz}$$

Problems Involving Converting Rates of Change

A problem might involve converting miles per hour to meters per second, or some other rate.

Example 8. If a car travels 16 miles per hour on a highway, how many meters per second is it traveling?

- (A) 2.8 m/s
- (B) 10 m/s
- (C) 16 m/s
- (D) 28 m/s
- (E) 120 m/s

Answer: A. You must convert miles to meters and hours to seconds as shown below:

$$\frac{16 \text{ mi}}{\text{hr}} \times \frac{\text{km}}{1.6 \text{ mi}} \times \frac{1000 \text{ m}}{1 \text{ km}} \times \frac{\text{hr}}{60 \text{ min}} \times \frac{\text{min}}{60 \text{ sec}}$$

$$= 2.8 \text{ m/sec}$$

Chapter 14: Units and Measurements

Example 9. A water fountain pours out 100 gallons of water per hour. About how many cups per minute does it pour out?

- (A) 2 cups per minute
- (B) 10 cups per minute
- (C) 27 cups per minute
- (D) 112 cups per minute
- (E) 1500 cups per minute

Answer: C. Here you must convert gallons to cups and hours to minutes as follows:

$$\frac{100 \text{ gal}}{\text{hr}} \times \frac{\text{hr}}{60 \text{ min}} \times \frac{16 \text{ cups}}{\text{gal}} = 26.7 \text{ cups/min}$$

Example 10. Brian lost 120 pounds in a year. How many ounces did Brian lose every week?

- (A) 5
- (B) 12
- (C) 37
- (D) 98
- (E) 324

Answer: C. Perform the operations as follows, converting pounds to ounces and years to weeks, knowing that there are 52 weeks in a year and 16 ounces in a pound:

$$\frac{120 \text{ lb}}{\text{yr}} \times \frac{\text{yr}}{52 \text{ wk}} \times \frac{16 \text{ oz}}{\text{lb}} = 37 \text{ oz/wk}$$

Practice Problems

1. John runs for 3.5 hours. Which of the following represents John's run, in minutes?

    A) 2.10 min
    B) 21.0 min
    C) 210 min
    D) 2,100 min
    E) 21,000 min

2. A golf ball has a mass of 0.045 kg. How many grams is the golf ball?

    A) 45 g
    B) 450 g
    C) 4,500 g
    D) 45,000 g
    E) 450,000 g

3. Tyler walked 7.2 km. How many millimeters (mm) did Tyler walk?

    A) 3,600 mm
    B) 72,000 mm
    C) 120,000 mm
    D) 144,000 mm
    E) 7,200,000 mm

4. A length of rope measures 15.7 feet. How many inches long is the same piece of rope?

    A) 188.4 in
    B) 1,884 in
    C) 18,840 in
    D) 188,400 in
    E) 1,884,000 in

5. Raúl drives a car across the United States in 6 days. How many minutes does it take Raúl to drive across the United States?

    A) 3,600 minutes
    B) 8,640 minutes
    C) 19,600 minutes
    D) 240,000 minutes
    E) 296,540 minutes

6. Chris needs 18 ounces of vanilla extract to bake cakes for a party. How many cups of vanilla extract does Chris need?

    A) 0.75 cups
    B) 1.5 cups
    C) 2.25 cups
    D) 3.75 cups
    E) 22.5 cups

7. A large truck weighs 3 tons. How many ounces does the truck weigh?

    (A) 6,000 oz.
    (B) 6,600 oz.
    (C) 60,000 oz.
    (D) 96,000 oz.
    (E) 960,000 oz

8. Kevin needs 100 ounces of water to make a large batch of oatmeal. About how many quarts of water does Kevin require?

    (A) 1.1 quarts
    (B) 1.7 quarts
    (C) 2.1 quarts
    (D) 2.7 quarts
    (E) 3.1 quarts

9. Taylor drove a car approximately 1,000,000 millimeters (mm). How many miles did Taylor drive?

    (A) 0.05 miles
    (B) 0.625 miles
    (C) 6.25 miles
    (D) 13.5 miles
    (E) 135 miles

10. Jill invests $1,000 in her IRA every month. How many cents does she invest every day?

    (A) 252
    (B) 856
    (C) 1,205
    (D) 1,825
    (E) 3,333

11. A plane travels from Washington, D.C., to Boston at 500 miles per hour. How many kilometers does it travel per minute?

    (A) 9
    (B) 13
    (C) 22
    (D) 56
    (E) 105

12. The circumference of the Earth is 24,901 miles. How fast does it rotate in kilometers per hour?

    (A) 440
    (B) 590
    (C) 1,660
    (D) 15,700
    (E) 29,800

13. A blizzard causes snow to accumulate at 4 inches per hour. How many centimeters accumulate in one minute?

    A) 0.17
    B) 3.5
    C) 19.8
    D) 29.2
    E) 108.9

14. If the population of Earth were to increase by 81,330,639 in 2050, a non-leap year, how fast would the population have grown per hour?

    A) 36
    B) 156
    C) 1,560
    D) 9,284
    E) 24,560

15. Your son grew 2 inches this year. How fast did he grow in millimeters per day?

    A) 0.02
    B) 0.14
    C) 1.45
    D) 3.49
    E) 14.6

Chapter 14: Units and Measurements

Answers to Practice Problems

1. **(C)** To solve this problem you must convert between hours and minutes. The following represents this calculation:

$$3.5 \, \text{hr} \times \frac{60 \, \text{min}}{\text{hr}} = 210 \, \text{min}$$

2. **(A)** In order to solve this problem, you must remember that there are 1,000 grams in one kilogram. The following represents the calculation required:

$$0.045 \, \text{kg} \times \frac{1,000 \, \text{g}}{\text{kg}} = 45 \, \text{g}$$

3. **(E)** In order to complete the problem, you must convert kilometers to millimeters. Thus, it is important to remember that there are 1,000 meters in one kilometer. The following represents the necessary calculation:

$$7.2 \, \text{km} \times \frac{1,000 \, \text{m}}{\text{km}} \times \frac{100 \, \text{cm}}{\text{m}} \times \frac{10 \, \text{mm}}{\text{cm}}$$

$$= 7,200,000 \, \text{mm}$$

4. **(A)** In order to solve the problem, you must convert feet to inches. Thus, it is important to remember that there are 12 inches in one foot. The following represents the necessary calculation:

$$15.7 \, \text{ft} \times \frac{12 \, \text{in}}{\text{ft}} = 188.4 \, \text{in}$$

5. **(B)** There are 24 hours in one day and 60 minutes in an hour. Using this information, it is possible to convert days to minutes. The following represents this calculation:

$$6 \, \text{days} \times \frac{24 \, \text{hr}}{\text{day}} \times \frac{60 \, \text{min}}{\text{hr}} = 8,640 \, \text{min}$$

6. **(C)** In order to solve this problem, you must have a working knowledge of the Standard System of Measurement, specifically the ounce and the cup. Therefore, it is important to remember that there are 8 fluid ounces in one cup. The following represents the necessary calculation:

$$18 \, \text{oz} \times \frac{1 \, \text{cup}}{8 \, \text{oz}} = 2.25 \, \text{cups}$$

7. **(D)** In order to solve this problem, you must have a knowledge of the U.S. Customary System of Measurement, specifically the ton, pound, and ounce. Further, the problem requires a two-step conversion. First, you must convert from tons to pounds, and then pounds to ounces. To accomplish these conversions, it is important to remember there are 2,000 pounds in one ton, and 16 ounces in one pound. The following represents this conversion:

$$3 \, \text{tons} \times \frac{2,000 \, \text{lb}}{\text{ton}} \times \frac{16 \, \text{oz}}{\text{lb}} = 96,000 \, \text{oz}$$

8. **(E)** This problem requires a knowledge of the U.S. Customary System of Measurement. To solve this problem, you must convert between ounces, cups, pints, and quarts. The following represents this calculation:

$$100 \, \text{oz} \times \frac{\text{cup}}{8 \, \text{oz}} \times \frac{\text{pint}}{2 \, \text{cups}} \times \frac{\text{quart}}{2 \, \text{pints}}$$

$$= 3.125 \, \text{quarts}$$

9. **(B)** To solve this problem, you must make 4 conversions, between millimeters to centimeters, then centimeters to meters, then meters to kilometers, and then finally from kilometers to miles. The following represents this calculation:

$$1,000,000 \, \text{mm} \times \frac{\text{cm}}{10 \, \text{mm}} \times \frac{\text{m}}{100 \, \text{cm}}$$

$$\times \frac{\text{km}}{1,000 \, \text{m}} \times \frac{\text{mile}}{1.6 \, \text{km}} = 0.625 \, \text{miles}$$

10. **(E)** Perform the calculation as follows, converting dollars to cents, then a month to days:

$$\frac{1{,}000 \text{ dollars}}{\text{month}} \times \frac{\text{month}}{30 \text{ days}} \times \frac{100 \text{ cents}}{\text{dollar}}$$

$$= 3{,}333 \text{ cents/day}$$

Make an estimate by dividing 30 into 100 to obtain roughly three. Three multiplied by 1,000 is 3,000. The only answer choice that makes sense therefore is choice **E**.

11. **(B)** Convert miles to kilometers by multiplying miles by 1.6, then convert hours to minutes by dividing by 60:

$$\frac{500 \text{ mi}}{\text{hr}} \times \frac{1.6 \text{ km}}{\text{mi}} \times \frac{\text{hr}}{60 \text{ min}}$$

$$= 13.3 \text{ km/min}$$

To make the calculation, multiply 500 by 1.6 to obtain 800. Now $\frac{800}{6} = \frac{80}{6} = \frac{40}{3} \approx 13$.

12. **(C)** The Earth rotates 24,901 miles (the circumference of the Earth) in 24 hours. We must convert miles to kilometers as follows:

$$\frac{24{,}901 \text{ mi}}{24 \text{ hr}} \times \frac{1.6 \text{ km}}{\text{mi}} = 1{,}660 \text{ km/hr}$$

13. **(A)** First convert inches to centimeters, knowing that there are 2.54 cm in an inch, and then convert hours to minutes as shown below:

$$\frac{4 \text{ in}}{\text{hr}} \times \frac{2.54 \text{ cm}}{\text{in}} \times \frac{\text{hr}}{60 \text{ min}} = 0.17 \text{ cm/min}$$

14. **(D)** The setup is simple: divide the number of people by 365 to convert years to days, and then convert days to hours by dividing by 24 as follows:

$$\frac{81{,}330{,}000 \text{ people}}{\text{yr}} \times \frac{\text{yr}}{365 \text{ days}} \times \frac{\text{day}}{24 \text{ hr}}$$

$$= 9{,}284 \text{ people/hr}$$

This means that every hour, the population of planet Earth increases by 9,284 people.

15. **(B)** You need to convert inches into centimeters, then centimeters into millimeters. You must also convert years to days by dividing by 365 as follows:

$$\frac{2 \text{ in}}{\text{yr}} \times \frac{2.54 \text{ cm}}{\text{in}} \times \frac{10 \text{ mm}}{\text{cm}} \times \frac{\text{yr}}{365 \text{ days}}$$

$$= 0.14 \text{ mm/day}$$

Chapter 15
Lines

In order to understand anything about geometry, one must first understand and become familiar with lines. This may seem simple enough, and for the most part, it is, but without a solid understanding of lines, learning geometry would be impossible. Everything complex in the physical and mathematical world depends on understanding fundamental concepts, and lines are highly fundamental.

However, before understanding lines, we must first understand "points". A **point** is just that–a point in space, or a plane, or on a graph. It does not have a direction or any dimension. A point is precisely ZERO dimensions.

Figure 1. Point A and Point B

Observe Point A and Point B in the figure above. At this point (pardon the pun), they have nothing to do with one another. And this is where lines become relevant.

A **line** connects two points, and continues on in both directions, indefinitely. A line is one-dimensional, and a straight line is the shortest distance between two points. Figure 2 depicts a line that passes through both Point A and Point B, and, as stated, continues on in both directions. Now, A and B are part of the same line, which is denoted as $\overleftrightarrow{AB}$.

Figure 2. A line passing through Point A and Point B

In addition, there are also rays and line segments, which also fall under the general umbrella of "lines." A **ray** begins at one point, passes through another, and continues on in that same direction, as seen in Figure 3, which begins at B and continues on through A, denoted as $\overleftarrow{AB}$. A ray beginning at A and continuing on through B would be denoted as $\overrightarrow{AB}$.

Figure 3. A ray beginning at Point B, and continuing in that direction

Similarly, a **line segment** begins at one point, reaches the second point, and stops. Oftentimes, outside of strict geometry lessons, you will see this also referred to as a "line," but specifically, and for the sake of this chapter, it is a line *segment*. A line segment from *A* to *B*, such as the one in the following figure, is denoted as $\overline{AB}$.

Figure 4. Line segment between Point A and Point B

Example 1. Which of the following images depicts a ray?

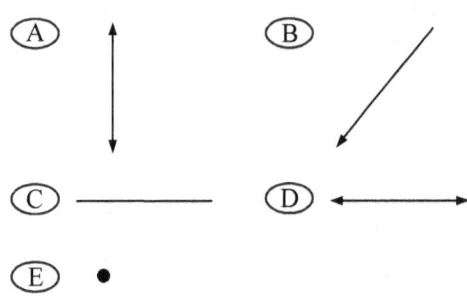

Answer: B. A ray only continues in ONE direction.

When two lines intersect, they form two pairs of the same angle, sometimes referred to as **congruent angles**, or **vertical angles**.

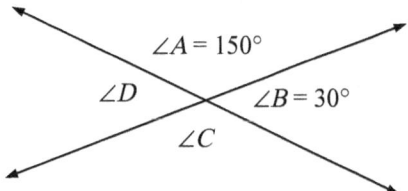

Figure 5. Two intersection lines form four angles

Due to the intersection of two lines in the above image (Fig. 5), four angles are created: *A*, *B*, *C*, and *D*. ∠*A* and ∠*B* form a full 180°, as is the case with angles that form a straight line (see chapter 14). These are referred to as **adjacent angles**. Additionally, ∠*A* and ∠*C* are the same in value (in this case both 150°), and ∠*B* and ∠*D* are the same (30°). These pairs of angles ∠*A* and ∠*C*, and ∠*B* and ∠*D* are referred to as **vertical angles**. The degree values of vertical angles are the same, and therefore vertical angles are **congruent**. Congruent angles are two or more angles that are equal in value. With the knowledge of adjacent and congruent angles, one can figure out all the necessary information for this image even if only ONE angle value was given.

Examples 2-4 pertain to the following figure.

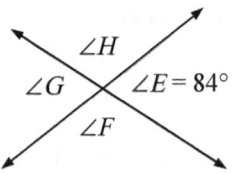

Example 2. In the above image, what is the value of ∠*F* ?

Ⓐ 6°
Ⓑ 84°
Ⓒ 96°
Ⓓ 102°
Ⓔ 140°

Answer: C. Angles *E* and *F* are adjacent angles, so their values add up to 180°. If *E* is 84°, then *F* is 180° − 84° = 96°.

Example 3. What is the value of ∠*G*?

Ⓐ 84°
Ⓑ 90°
Ⓒ 96°
Ⓓ 100°
Ⓔ 120°

Chapter 15: Lines

Answer: A. Angles *E* and *G* are vertical angles (or "congruent" angles) and are therefore equal to each other. So, the value of ∠*G* is 84°.

Example 4. What is the sum of angles *F* and *H*?

    (A) 132°
    (B) 150°
    (C) 168°
    (D) 180°
    (E) 192°

Answer: E. Angles *F* and *H* are congruent angles. Because *E* and *F* together equal 180°, we know that *F* is 180°−84° = 96°. Therefore, *H* is also 96°, and 96°+96° = 192°.

It should be evident that not all lines will intersect. Lines that never, or WILL never intersect are known as **parallel lines**. Lines that intersect at a 90° angle are **perpendicular lines**, and are often denoted by a square at the intersection of these two lines, as seen in the right-hand pair of lines in Figure 6. A 90° angle is known as a **right angle**.

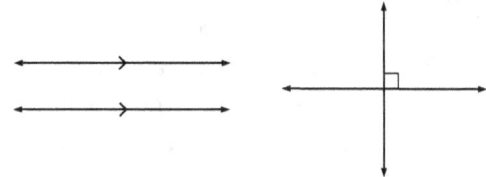

Figure 6. On the left, a pair of parallel lines that never intersect, indicated by the arrow marks; on the right, a pair of perpendicular lines that form right angles at the point of intersection, denoted by a square.

Examples 5-7 pertain to the following figures.

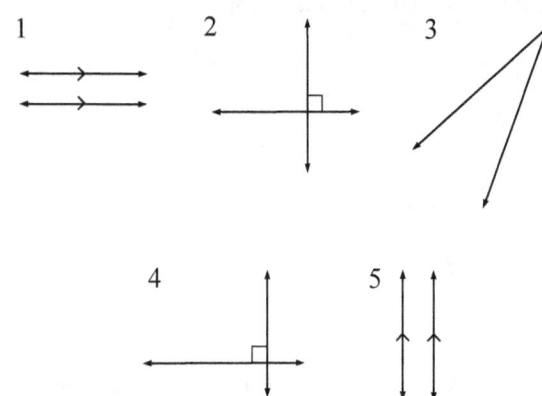

Example 5. In the above image, which pair or pairs of lines, if any, are parallel?

    (A) 1 only
    (B) 2 and 4
    (C) 1 and 5
    (D) 3 only
    (E) None

Answer: C. 1 and 5 are the only parallel lines, as they never intersect.

Example 6. Which pair or pairs of lines, if any, are perpendicular?

    (A) 1 only
    (B) They are all perpendicular.
    (C) 3 only
    (D) 2 and 4
    (E) None of them are perpendicular.

Answer: D. Only pairs 2 and 4 form right angles.

Example 7. Which of the following can describe the angle formed by the lines in pair 1?

Choose all answers that apply.

[A] 0°

[B] 45°

[C] 90°

[D] 180°

[E] 270°

Answer: A, D. The lines in the first image are parallel, meaning they never intersect and both 0° and 180° can represent the angle formed by parallel lines.

When one line (a **transversal** line) crosses two others, a third angle type become relevant: **corresponding angles**. Corresponding angles are angles that occupy the same relative position at the intersection. If the first two lines are parallel, the corresponding angles will be equal. If they are not parallel, the corresponding angles won't be equal. This can be seen in Figure 7.

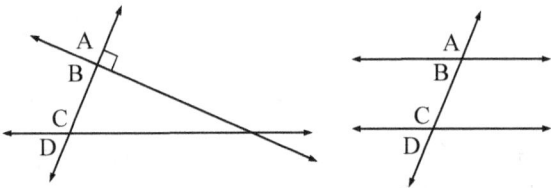

Figure 7. Examples of corresponding angles where, A. there are no parallel lines (left) B. there are parallel lines (right).

A lot of information can be derived from the above image, such as:

(1) In both situations, *A and C* and *B and D* are corresponding angle pairs.

(2) In the left-hand image, *A and C* and *B and D* are NOT equal, even though they are corresponding angles.

(3) In the right-hand image, *A and C* and *B and D* ARE equal, because they arise from parallel lines being intersected by the transversal.

(4) In both situations, *A and B* and *C and D* are adjacent angles, and all of these pairs add up to 180°.

In the case of two lines being intersected by a transversal, the **alternate interior angles** are angles that lie *inside* the pair of lines on opposite sides of the transversal line.

Similarly, **alternate exterior angles** also exist. They lie *outside* the pair of lines on opposite sides of the transversal. If the lines being intersected by the transversal are parallel, then there will be two pairs of alternate interior angles that are equal, and two pairs of alternate exterior angles that have the same angle values.

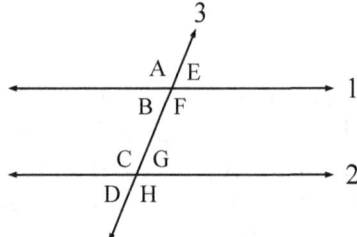

Figure 8. Transversal line intersecting parallel lines, creating alternate interior angles and alternate exterior angles.

In the image above (Fig. 8), lines 1 and 2 are parallel, and are being intersected by the transversal line, 3. This means that *C and F*, and *B and G* are *alternate interior angles*, with C and F having the same value, and B and G having the same value. Additionally, it means that *A and H* and *E and D* are *alternate exterior angles*, with A and H having the same value, and E and D having the same value. **If lines 1 and 2 were not parallel, these angle pairings would not be equal in value, although they would still be classified as alternate interior/exterior angles.**

Examples 8-10 pertain to the following images.

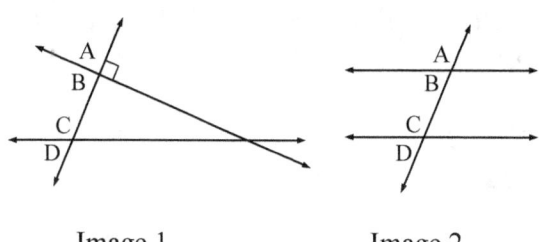

Image 1   Image 2

Example 8. In image 1 above, what are the values of angles A and B?

- (A) Both are 0°.
- (B) Both are 45°.
- (C) Both are 90°.
- (D) Angle A is 180° and B is unknown.
- (E) They do not form an angle.

Answer: C. ∠A and ∠B are the result of two perpendicular lines, as seen by the square to the right of ∠A. Therefore, both ∠A and ∠B must each be 90°.

Example 9. What is the value of ∠A in image 2?

- (A) 90°
- (B) 100°
- (C) 120°
- (D) 180°
- (E) Not enough information to know.

Answer: E. There is no information on any values of any of the denoted angles OR adjacent angles; therefore, we cannot know the value of ∠A in image 2.

Example 10. What are the values for ∠A + ∠B in image 1 and ∠C + ∠D in image 2?

- (A) 90°
- (B) 180°
- (C) 270°
- (D) 360°
- (E) Not enough information to know.

Answer: B. Despite the fact that we do not know the values of any angles apart from A and B in image 1, we still know that all adjacent angles add up to 180°, and that is all the information we need to answer this question.

Practice Problems

Questions 1-8 pertain to the image below, where lines *a* and *b* are parallel, and are intersected by transversal lines *c* and *d* (which do not intersect in the segment shown).

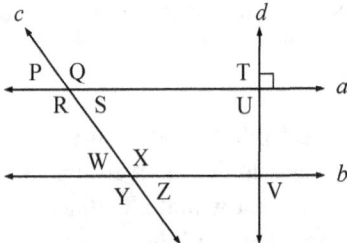

1. In the above image, which of the following pairs are classified as alternate *interior* angles?

   (A) P and S; W and Z
   (B) R and X; S and W
   (C) R and Q; X and Y
   (D) P and R; W and Y
   (E) Q and S; T and U

2. In the above image, which of the following pairs are classified as alternate *exterior* angles?

   (A) Q and Z; P and Y
   (B) R and Z; U and V
   (C) P and Z; Q and Y; T and V
   (D) T and V only
   (E) There are no alternate exterior angle pairs in the image.

3. If ∠Q is equal to 123°, what is the value of ∠R?

   (A) 33°
   (B) 57°
   (C) 123°
   (D) 180°
   (E) 237°

4. Which, if any, of the angles are 90°?

   (A) T, U
   (B) T only
   (C) None
   (D) T, U, V
   (E) U only

5. If ∠Z is 76°, what is the value of ∠Y?

   (A) 14°
   (B) 76°
   (C) 90°
   (D) 100°
   (E) 104°

Chapter 15: Lines   171

6. ∠V has two adjacent angles and one congruent angle. What are their values?

   Ⓐ 90°
   Ⓑ 180°
   Ⓒ 360°
   Ⓓ Whatever the value of angle Z is.
   Ⓔ Not enough information to know.

7. If ∠P is equal to 61°, what is the value of ∠P + ∠W?

   Ⓐ 90°
   Ⓑ 122°
   Ⓒ 180°
   Ⓓ 200°
   Ⓔ 241°

8. What is the value of all the labeled and unlabeled angles in the image added together?

   Ⓐ 360°
   Ⓑ 720°
   Ⓒ 1080°
   Ⓓ 1440°
   Ⓔ 1620°

Questions 9-15 are related to the image below. Let's say the previous image is rotated 90°, like so, where lines *a* and *b* are now the transversal lines:

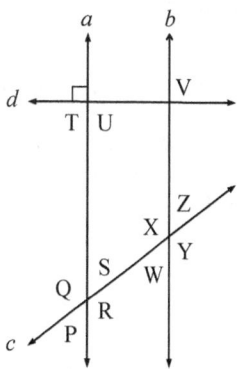

9. What can be said about angles T and P?

   Ⓐ They are equal in value.
   Ⓑ They are alternate interior angles.
   Ⓒ They are corresponding angles.
   Ⓓ They are alternate exterior angles.
   Ⓔ There is not enough information to know.

10. Which pairs of angles are alternate interior angles?

    Ⓐ T and R only
    Ⓑ T and S; U and Q
    Ⓒ S and X; R and W
    Ⓓ U and P; T and R
    Ⓔ There are no alternate interior angles.

11. Which of the following statements about ∠W is FALSE?

    (A) It is equal in value to ∠X.
    (B) It is equal in value to ∠Z.
    (C) It is an alternate exterior angle along with ∠V.
    (D) It is an adjacent angle to both ∠X and ∠Y.
    (E) When ∠W is added to either ∠X or ∠Y, the result is 180°.

12. Which pairs, if any, can be categorized as alternate exterior angles?

    (A) V and Y
    (B) X and Y
    (C) T and R
    (D) V and W
    (E) None of the above.

13. What is the value of angles P, Q, R, S added together?

    (A) 90°
    (B) 180°
    (C) 360°
    (D) 540°
    (E) 720°

14. Which of the following pairs of angles are NOT congruent angles?

    (A) Q and P
    (B) Q and R
    (C) P and S
    (D) X and Y
    (E) W and Z

15. The value of angle Q is also equal to the value of:

    (A) P and S
    (B) U and R
    (C) T and P
    (D) R and X only
    (E) R, X, and Y

Answers to Practice Problems

1. **(B)** Alternate interior angles are defined as being inside parallel lines on opposite sides of the transversal. Only angle pairs <u>R and X</u> and <u>S and W</u> fall into this category.

2. **(C)** Alternate exterior angles are defined as being outside parallel lines and on opposite sides of the transversal. This includes <u>P and Z</u>, <u>Q and Y</u>, and <u>T and V</u>.

3. **(C)** Angles <u>Q and R</u> are vertical angles, meaning that they are equal in value. So, if Q is 123°, so is R.

4. **(D)** Angle T is adjacent to the 90° angle (right angle), which means it must also be 90°. Additionally, angle T and U are also adjacent angles, and therefore also add up to 180°. So, if T is 90°, U must also be 90°. Finally, T and V are alternate exterior angles and are EQUAL due to the fact that they arise from *parallel* lines with a transversal. So, angle V is also 90°.

5. **(E)** Angles Y and Z are adjacent angles, meaning they add up to 180°. 180° − 76° = 104°.

6. **(A)** Angle V is an alternate exterior angle to angle T due to *parallel* lines being intersected by a transversal, so it must be 90°. Therefore, its adjacent angles must also be 90°, as well as its congruent angle.

7. **(B)** Angle W and angle S are alternate interior angles for *parallel* lines intersected by a transversal, so they are equal in value. Additionally, angle S and angle P are congruent, so they are also equal. Therefore, angle W and P are equal, and are each 61°. Added together, they yield 122°.

8. **(D)** There are 8 individual pairs of adjacent angles, which add up to 180° each. 180° × 8 = 1440°.

9. **(C)** These angles are corresponding angles: occupying the same relative position at an intersection where a straight transversal line crosses two others. However, since lines c and d are *not parallel*, these corresponding angles are not equal in value.

10. **(B)** Although lines c and d are *not parallel*, this does not mean there cannot still be alternate interior/exterior angles due to a transversal line. However, you cannot mix and match angles created from two different transversal lines. <u>T and S</u> and <u>U and Q</u> are inside the lines c and d and on opposite sides of the transversal line a, making them the only alternate interior angles from the choices listed.

11. **(A)** Angle V is 90°, because it is the result of two perpendicular lines intersecting. We know this because there is a right-angle symbol (square) where lines a and d intersect, and since a and b are parallel, we know that b and d are perpendicular. So, angle V is a right angle. However, lines c and d are NOT parallel, so angle W cannot have the same value as angle X.

12. **(D)** <u>V and W</u> are the only pair of angles that fit the description of alternate exterior angles: outside the pair of lines, on opposite sides of the transversal.

13. **(C)** There are four angles, which can be combined as two pairs of adjacent angles, which always equal 180°. So, 180° × 2 = 360°.

14. **(A)** Q and P are not equal in value to each other, and therefore cannot be categorized as congruent angles.

15. **(E)** Angle R is the congruent vertical angle to angle Q, and is therefore equal in value. Angle X is the corresponding angle to Q due to the parallel lines, and angle Y is angle X's congruent angle. Therefore, all four of these angles are equal in value.

Chapter 16
Angles and Triangles

One of the most central aspects of Euclidean geometry is understanding angles and triangles. It is important to be able to distinguish the different types of each, as questions about both will appear on the GED Math exam. Knowledge about angles and triangles is also important outside of pure geometry, in subjects like physics, chemistry, engineering, and even art.

An angle is formed when two rays share an endpoint; the angle is measured in degrees, which is demonstrated with the symbol °. Let us begin with how angles are denoted.

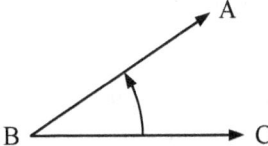

Figure 1. How to denote an angle–this one is referred to as ∠ABC.

In Figure 1, an angle is formed between three points, A, B, and C, and the angle is therefore referred to as *angle A BC*, with point B as the vertex. If the angle itself is labeled, it will appear as:

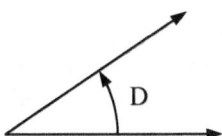

Figure 2. Another way to denote an angle, referred to as ∠D.

Here, the angle shown in Figure 2 is referred to simply as ∠D. In each of the instances, the angles are measured in either degrees, denoted with a ° symbol, or in radians. Radians can be converted into degrees, or vice versa. Radians will be covered later in the chapter on circles. In the *x-y* coordinate plane, the number of degrees beginning at the positive *x* axis and ending, again, at the positive *x* axis (making a circle) is 360°.

There are a few types of angles that one should be comfortable identifying:

Acute angles are angles that have a value between 0° and 90°. They can often look like this:

Chapter 16: Angles and Triangles

Right angles are angles that are exactly 90° and are denoted with a square symbol in the corner, like so:

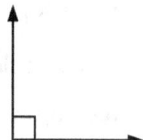

Obtuse angles are angles that have a value over 90° but less than 180°, like the one below:

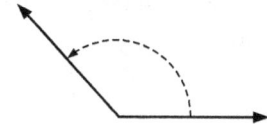

A **straight angle** is one that measures exactly 180°, which is essentially a straight line.

A **reflex angle** is one that extends beyond 180° but is still less than 360°.

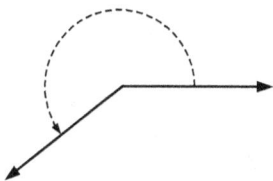

Complementary angles are two angles that add up to 90°.

Supplementary angles are two angles that add up to 180°.

Examples 1-2 pertain to the figure below.

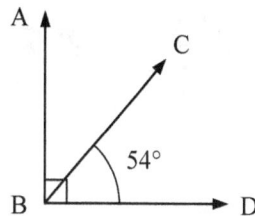

Example 1. How many acute angles are there in the image?

(A) 1
(B) 2
(C) 3
(D) 4
(E) None

Answer: B. The value of ∠ABD is 90°, denoted by the square, making it a right angle. From this image, we also know that ∠ABC and ∠CBD are complementary angles, and they add up to 90°, meaning that each of them must be less than 90°. So, there are two acute angles in the above image.

Example 2. What is the value of ∠ABC ?

(A) 36°
(B) 54°
(C) 60°
(D) 90°
(E) 126°

Answer: A. The value of the two angles, ∠ABC and ∠CBD add up to 90°. ∠CBD is 54°, so this means that ∠ABC is 90° − 54° = 36°.

Example 3. Which of the following choices is an obtuse angle?

- Ⓐ 30°
- Ⓑ 45°
- Ⓒ 89°
- Ⓓ 132°
- Ⓔ 251°

Answer: D. An obtuse angle is defined as an angle over 90° but less than 180°. Only choice **D**, 132°, qualifies.

Examples 4-5 pertain to the figure below.

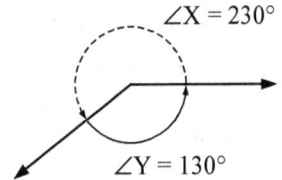

Example 4. Which angle category does ∠X qualify as?

- Ⓐ Obtuse angle
- Ⓑ Reflex angle
- Ⓒ Acute angle
- Ⓓ Straight angle
- Ⓔ None of the above

Answer: B. ∠X is greater than 180° but less than 360°, so it is a reflex angle.

Example 5. Which of the following is TRUE about the above image?

- Ⓐ ∠Y is an obtuse angle.
- Ⓑ ∠X and ∠Y are complementary angles.
- Ⓒ ∠X and ∠Y are supplementary angles.
- Ⓓ ∠Y is an acute angle.
- Ⓔ None of the above is true.

Answer: A. Angle Y is greater than 90° but less than 180°, making it an obtuse angle. X and Y do not fit the definition of either complementary or supplementary angles.

Triangles

Now that we are a little more familiar with angles, we can move on to triangles. A triangle is a geometrical shape with three vertices. Its angles add up to 180°, and is often referred to by its vertices:

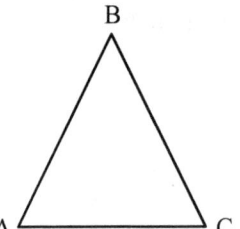

Figure 3. The above triangle would be referred to as "triangle ABC"

There are different types of triangles to familiarize yourself with. They are as follows:

Chapter 16: Angles and Triangles

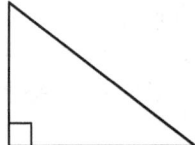

A **right triangle** has a right angle and two acute angles which are complimentary.

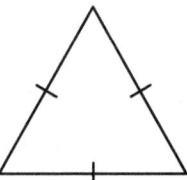

Equilateral triangles are triangles where all three sides are equal in length, denoted by lines through the sides. All the angles are equal, each being 60°.

Isosceles triangles have two equal-length sides (and, therefore, angles). When a triangle has two sides that are EQUAL in length, the angles directly opposite to each of those sides will be the same value in degrees.

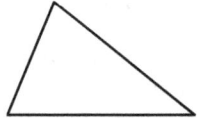

Scalene triangles are triangles where none of the sides and angles are equal. If a triangle has all different length sides, making it scalene, all of its angles will also be different values.

Triangles can also fall into multiple classifications. For example: An **obtuse triangle** is one where one of the angles is greater than 90°, and an **acute triangle** is one where all three angles are less than 90 degrees.

Examples 6-7 pertain to the figure below.

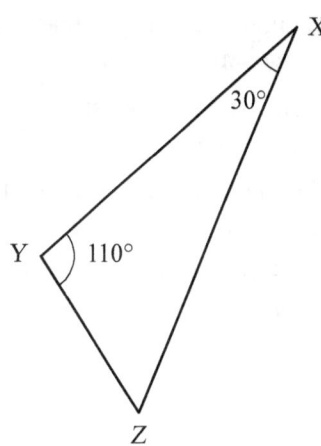

Example 6. In the figure above, what is the value of ∠Z?

Ⓐ 10°
Ⓑ 30°
Ⓒ 40°
Ⓓ 60°
Ⓔ Not enough information to know

Answer: C. We know that the angles of a triangle must add up to 180°. So, 180° − 110° − 30° = 40°.

Example 7. The triangle XYZ can be classified in which ways?

Choose all answers that apply.

[A] Obtuse triangle
[B] Acute triangle
[C] Scalene triangle
[D] Right triangle
[E] Equilateral triangle

Answer: A, C. Because of the obtuse angle in the triangle, the triangle is obtuse. It is also scalene because none of the sides are of equal length.

Congruent Triangles

Congruent triangles are triangles that have one of the following in common:

- **Side-Side-Side (SSS)** – The sides of both triangles are the same
- **Angle-Side-Angle (ASA)** – Two angles and the side between them are the same
- **Side-Angle-Side (SAS)** – Two sides and the angle between them are the same

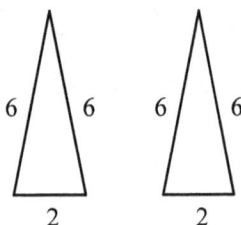

Example 8. How can these two triangles be classified?

- A) They are congruent triangles
- B) They are isosceles triangles
- C) They are scalene triangles
- D) A and B
- E) None of the above

Answer: D. These triangles are congruent due to the SSS theorem, but they are also isosceles triangles, as they have two sides equal in length.

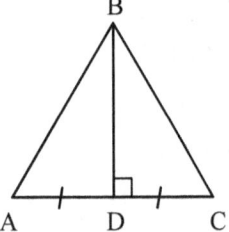

Example 9. True or False? In the figure above, the triangles ABD and CBD, are congruent.

Answer: True. They share the side BD, and AD and DC are denoted to be equal in length. The right angle between these sides completes the SAS theorem.

Similar Triangles

Similar triangles are a little different than congruent triangles. Similar triangles are those where either:

- All corresponding sides are in the same ratio.
- All angles in the first triangle are equal to all angles in the second triangle.

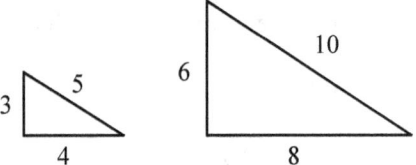

Example 10. Are the above triangles similar?

Answer: Yes. Because the ratios between the sides are the same, the triangles are similar. Notice that the lengths of the sides of the triangle on the right are just double the value of the lengths of the triangle on the left.

Pythagorean Theorem

The Pythagorean theorem, named after the Greek mathematician Pythagoras, states that for any right triangle, the square of the two shorter sides added together gives the square of the hypotenuse. The **hypotenuse** is the side opposite to the right angle. In the triangle below, side c is the hypotenuse.

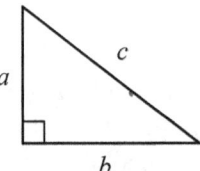

The equation for this right triangle, and all right triangles, is: $a^2 + b^2 = c^2$

Chapter 16: Angles and Triangles

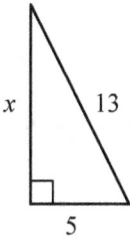

Example 11. What is the value of x in the figure above?

- (A) 11
- (B) 12
- (C) 13
- (D) 15
- (E) 17

Answer: B. According to the Pythagorean theorem, we know that $5^2 + x^2 = 13^2$. Solving for x gives us 12:

$$x^2 = 13^2 - 5^2$$
$$= 169 - 25$$
$$= 144$$

So, we obtain $x^2 = 144$. Taking the square root of both sides, we obtain:

$$x = \sqrt{x^2} = \sqrt{144} = 12$$

Special Triangles

There are two special triangles that you should memorize, which are: A. a 3-4-5 right triangle, and B. a 5-12-13 triangles shown in example 10 and 11. Most triangles have sides that do not all have integer values. There are a few other special triangles with all integer values, but it is useful to memorize these two special right triangles to save time on calculations with the Pythagorean theorem as they might pop up on the test. Also note that triangles with any multiple of these values such as 6-8-10 (each side of 3-4-5 is multiplied by 2) or 10-24-26 (each side of 5-12-13 is multiplied by 2) are also triangles that have three sides with all integer values.

Sum of Angles in Quadrilaterals

One last topic in this chapter is the sum of the angles in a quadrilateral, which is 360°. A square for example has 4 right angles, which you know are all 90°. Summing up the angles we get $4 \times 90° = 360°$. The same applies to rectangles, parallelograms, trapezoids, rhombuses, and irregular quadrilaterals.

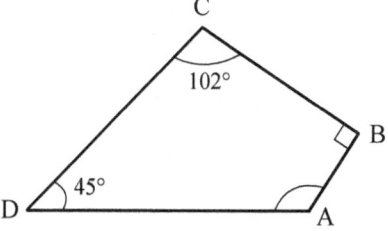

Example 12. In quadrilateral ABCD above, what does angle A equal to:

- (A) 111°
- (B) 113°
- (C) 117°
- (D) 121°
- (E) 123°

Answer: E. Call angle A, x. Therefore, we have:

$$x + 90° + 102° + 45° = 360°$$

So we get $x = 360° - 90° - 102° - 45° = 123°$.

Practice Problems

Problems 1-8 pertain to the figure below.

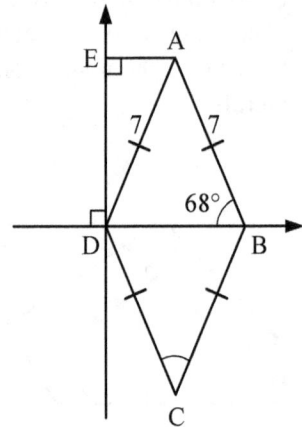

1. How can triangles ABD and BCD be described?

   (A) They are congruent triangles
   (B) They are isosceles triangles
   (C) Both A and B
   (D) They are equilateral triangles
   (E) Both A and D

2. What is the value of ∠ADB?

   (A) 22°
   (B) 54°
   (C) 60°
   (D) 68°
   (E) 90°

3. What is the value of ∠DAB?

   (A) 22°
   (B) 44°
   (C) 60°
   (D) 68°
   (E) 83°

4. What is the value of ∠C?

   (A) 22°
   (B) 30°
   (C) 44°
   (D) 45°
   (E) 68°

5. How can triangle AED be categorized?

   (A) It is a similar triangle to triangle ADB
   (B) It is congruent to ADB
   (C) It is a right triangle
   (D) It is a scalene triangle
   (E) Both C and D

Chapter 16: Angles and Triangles

6. What is the value of ∠EAB?

   (A) 22°
   (B) 44°
   (C) 90°
   (D) 112°
   (E) 136°

7. Which of the following statements about the image is FALSE?

   (A) ∠ABD is an obtuse angle
   (B) ∠BDA is an acute angle
   (C) ∠DEA is a right angle
   (D) ∠EAB is obtuse
   (E) All of the above are true.

8. What is the length of side BC?

   (A) 3.6
   (B) 4
   (C) 5.5
   (D) 6
   (E) 7

Problems 9-15 pertain to the figure below.

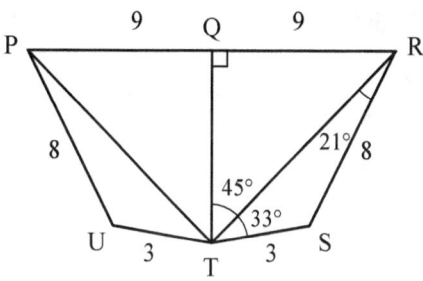

9. What is the length of QT?

   (A) 8
   (B) 9
   (C) 10
   (D) 11
   (E) 12

10. What can be said about triangles PQT and RQT?

   (A) They are congruent triangles
   (B) They are right triangles
   (C) They are isosceles triangles
   (D) All the above
   (E) None of the above

11. What is the value of ∠QPT?

    (A) 45°
    (B) 60°
    (C) 66°
    (D) 75°
    (E) 87°

12. Which of the following is FALSE?

    (A) Triangles PUT and RST are similar triangles
    (B) ∠PTU is 33°
    (C) The length of RT is greater than 9
    (D) Triangle PQT is scalene
    (E) Triangle PTR is isosceles

13. What is the value of ∠U?

    (A) 102°
    (B) 114°
    (C) 126°
    (D) 147°
    (E) 159°

14. What is the length of TR?

    (A) $\sqrt{70}$
    (B) 9
    (C) $\sqrt{130}$
    (D) 12
    (E) $\sqrt{162}$

15. What is angle TSR equal to?

    (A) 54
    (B) 96
    (C) 126
    (D) 132
    (E) 144

Answers to Practice Problems

1. **(C)** Triangle ABD and BCD share a side BD and have their other two congruent sides equal, as denoted by lines. According to the SSS theorem, they are congruent triangles. Furthermore, because they have two sides that are equal in length, they are isosceles triangles as well.

2. **(D)** We know that AD and AB are the same length (7), which means that the angles across from these sides must be equal. So, if ∠B is 68°, that means that ∠ADB is also 68°.

3. **(B)** The value of all the angles of a triangle added together is always 180°. We know that both angles ADB and ABD measure 68°. So, 180° − 68° − 68° = 44°.

4. **(C)** ∠C = ∠A because the angles are congruent. Therefore, angle C = 44°.

5. **(E)** We know that triangle AED is a right triangle because of the square in the corner. We also know that all three sides are a different length, making it also a scalene triangle.

6. **(D)** From problem 2, we know ∠ADB is 68°, and therefore ∠EAD = 68° because ∠EAD and ∠ADB are alternate interior angles. From problem 3, we know that ∠DAB is 44°. Adding these two angles together, we get 44° + 68° = 112°.

7. **(A)** ∠ABD is 68°, which is less than 90°, making it an acute angle. So, statement A is false. Answer choices B, C, and D are true.

8. **(E)** Because triangles ABD and BDC are congruent triangles, we know that the length of BC is the same as AB (also denoted by the lines), which is 7.

9. **(B)** We know that ∠QRT is

    180° − 90° − 45° = 45°

    and because it has the same value as ∠QTR, the opposite sides must be equal. So, if QR has a value of 9, so does QT.

10. **(D)** Triangles PQT and RQT are congruent by the SAS theorem (they have two same-length sides, and the angle between these two sides are the same–in this case, 90°, making them right triangles), and because we know that QT is also 9 (and RT cannot be 9 due to the Pythagorean theorem), they must be isosceles triangles as well.

11. **(A)** Because triangles PQT and RQT are the same, we know that ∠QPT is the same as ∠QRT, which is 45°.

12. **(D)** Triangle PQT has two sides that are equal in length, so, by definition, it cannot be scalene.

13. **(C)** Since $\overline{PU} = \overline{RS}$, $\overline{UT} = \overline{ST}$, and $\overline{PT} = \overline{RT}$, triangles PUT and RST are congruent to each other. So we know that the value of ∠U is the same as ∠S. To find this value, we simply do 180° − 33° − 21° = 126°.

14. **(E)** To find TR, we simply use the Pythagorean theorem:

    $$(TR)^2 = 9^2 + 9^2$$
    $$= 162$$
    $$TR = \sqrt{162}$$

15. **(C)** The sum of the three angles in triangle TSR is 180 degrees, so angle TSR = 180 − 33 − 21 = 126°.

Chapter 17

Circles

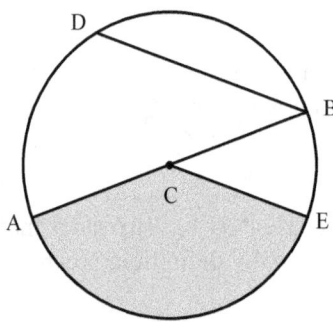

A circle is the set of all points in a plane that are equidistant from a given point, C, called the center of the circle. A circle has 360°. That is, there are 360 degrees in one complete rotation of the circle. A few important facts about circles include:

- The **radius**, $\overline{CE}$, is a segment whose endpoints are the center of the circle and any point on the edge of the circle. It is usually represented by r and $r = \frac{1}{2}d$, where d is the diameter. The plural of radius is radii

- The **diameter**, $\overline{AB}$, is any straight line segment that passes through the center of the circle, whose endpoints lie on the circle. It can also be defined as the longest chord of the circle. The diameter, represented by d, is twice the length of the radius, or $d = 2r$.

- A **chord**, $\overline{DB}$, is a straight line segment whose endpoints lie on the circle.

- $\angle BCE$, is a **central angle** whose vertex is at the center of the circle.

- The **arc**, $\widehat{AD}$, is a curve whose endpoints are A and D on the circle. An arc is a portion of the circumference of a circle.

- The **semicircle** is an arc that has the same endpoints as a diameter. The semicircle is half of a circle, and the arc of the semicircle measures 180 degrees.

- A **sector** is the area between an arc and two radii of the circle. For example, the shaded area of ACE is referred to as sector ACE, shown above.

Example 1. Victoria bought a circular picture frame. The radius of the frame is 2 feet. How does the size of the diameter of the frame compare to its radius?

(A) The radius of the frame is twice its diameter.

(B) The radius of the frame is twice its circumference.

(C) The diameter of the frame is twice its radius.

(D) The diameter of the frame is half its radius.

(E) The diameter of the frame is half its circumference.

Answer: C. From the definition of the diameter, we know that the diameter is twice as long as the radius, where $d = 2r$.

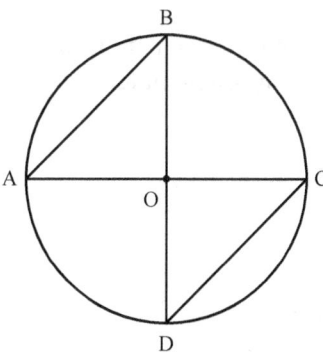

Note: Figure not drawn to scale.

Example 2. The figure above shows a circle with center, O. Which of the following must be true?

- (A) $\overline{DB}$ is perpendicular to $\overline{AC}$
- (B) $\overline{DC}$ is perpendicular to $\overline{AC}$
- (C) AOB and COD are equilateral triangles.
- (D) $\overline{DB} = \overline{AC}$
- (E) $\overline{AB} = \overline{OD}$

Solution D. Since O is the center of the circle, $\overline{DB}$ and $\overline{AC}$ are both diameters of the circle, and all diameters of a circle are equal. Choice **A** is incorrect because there is no indication that the lines are perpendicular (if there was, there would be a little square perpendicular sign at the center of the circle).

Circumference of a Circle

The circumference of a circle is the distance around the circle. It is usually represented by the capital letter, C. The circumference, C, can be calculated by using the radius or the diameter:

- Using the radius r, $C = 2\pi r$
- Using the diameter d, $C = \pi d$

The value of π is approximately 3.14 and is equal to the circumference of the circle divided by the diameter.

π is an irrational number that is equal to approximately 3.14. As an irrational number, the digits after the decimal point are infinite. On the GED Math test, you can estimate it by using 3.14. π is also equivalent to 180°. For example, $2\pi = 360°$ because $2 \times 180° = 360°$. You know there are 360 degrees in a circle, and therefore there are 2π degrees in a circle. If this is confusing to you, we will do some exercises that will clarify these statements.

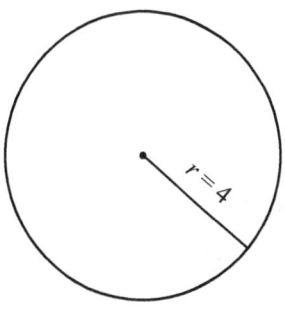

Example 3. What is the circumference of a circle with a radius of 4 cm?

- (A) 22.15 cm
- (B) 25.12 cm
- (C) 28.34 cm
- (D) 31.23 cm
- (E) 33.12 cm

Answer: B. We know that the radius of the circle equals 4 cm. Therefore, by substituting 4 cm into the circumference formula, we get

$$C = 2\pi r = 2\pi(4) = 8\pi = 8(3.14) = 25.12 \text{ cm}$$

Example 4. What is the diameter of a circle equal to in inches with a circumference of 14π inches?

- (A) 7 inches
- (B) 10 inches
- (C) 12 inches
- (D) 14 inches
- (E) 15 inches

Answer: D. We know that the formula of the circumference of a circle is $C = \pi d$. Dividing both sides of the equation by π, we get:

$$d = \frac{C}{\pi} = \frac{14\pi}{\pi} = 14 \text{ inches}$$

Example 5. A circular bicycle trail has a diameter of length 2 miles. Michael biked around the trail 5 times. Approximately how many miles did Michael travel?

- (A) 6.28 miles
- (B) 21.4 miles
- (C) 26.2 miles
- (D) 29.6 miles
- (E) 31.4 miles

Answer: E. In order to find out the total distance Michael biked, we need to calculate the circumference of the bicycle trail,

$$C = \pi d = \pi(2) = 2\pi$$

and then multiply the distance by 5. Since Mike biked around the trail 5 times, the total number of miles he traveled is

$$5C = 5(2\pi) = 10\pi = 10(3.14) = 31.4 \text{ miles}$$

Area of a Circle

The area of a circle is usually represented by the capital letter, A. The area of a circle is equal to $A = \pi r^2$, where $r =$ the radius of the circle.

Example 6. The area of a circle is 314 ft². What is the radius of the circle in feet?

- (A) 10 ft
- (B) 11 ft
- (C) 12 ft
- (D) 13 ft
- (E) 14 ft

Answer: A. Since the area of the circle is given, we can use the formula for the area of a circle, $A = \pi r^2 = 314$. Isolate r^2 by dividing by π.

$$r^2 = \frac{314}{\pi} = \frac{314}{3.14} = 100$$

Take the square root of both sides to get:
$r = \sqrt{100} = 10$ ft.

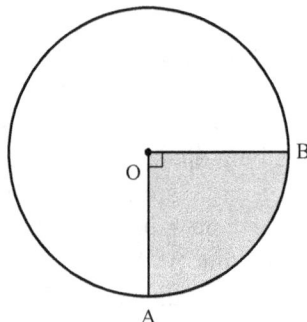

Example 7. The figure above shows a circle, with center O, and a radius of 6 inches. What is the area of the shaded sector?

- (A) 3π in²
- (B) 9π in²
- (C) 12π in²
- (D) 18π in²
- (E) 36π in²

Answer: B. To get the area of the shaded sector, we must calculate the area of the whole circle, and then divide by 4, because one fourth of the circle is shaded. We know the shaded area is one-fourth of the circle because line segment OA and OB are perpendicular (shown by perpendicular sign), and therefore are 90 degrees apart. Since a circle has 360 degrees, we have $\frac{90}{360} = \frac{1}{4}$. The area of the circle is $A = \pi r^2 = \pi(6)^2 = 36\pi$. So, $\frac{1}{4}$ of 36π is 9π in^2.

Example 8. What is the area of a circle with a circumference of 6π cm?

- (A) 6π cm²
- (B) 7π cm²
- (C) 9π cm²
- (D) 12π cm²
- (E) 36π cm²

Answer: C. To find the area of a circle, write $A = \pi r^2$. Since r is not given, we need to calculate it first. Given that $C = 6\pi$ centimeters, and $C = 2\pi r$, we write the following equation: $2\pi r = 6\pi$. Then $r = \frac{6\pi}{2\pi} = 3$ cm. Therefore, the area of the circle is $A = \pi r^2 = \pi(3)^2 = 9\pi$ cm².

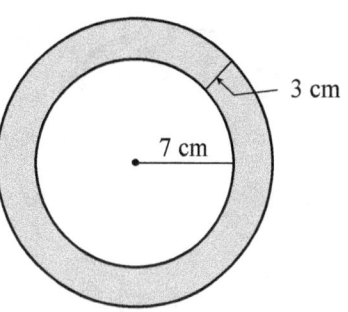

Example 9. The figure above shows a donut. The radius of the inner circle is 7 cm, and the distance between the edges of the two circles is 3 cm. What is the area of the shaded region?

- (A) 9π cm²
- (B) 16π cm²
- (C) 51π cm²
- (D) 58π cm²
- (E) 100π cm²

Answer: C. The area of the shaded region is the difference between the area of the outer and inner circles. The area of the outer circle is

$$A_{Outer} = \pi(10)^2 = 100\pi \text{ cm}^2$$

where $r = 10$ because the radius of the outer circle is equal to the distance between the edge of the outer circle and the center of the circles, which is $7 + 3 = 10$. The area of the inner circle is

$$A_{Inner} = \pi(7)^2 = 49\pi \text{ cm}^2$$

Therefore, the area of the shaded region is

$$A_{Outer} - A_{Inner} = 100\pi - 49\pi = 51\pi \text{ cm}^2$$

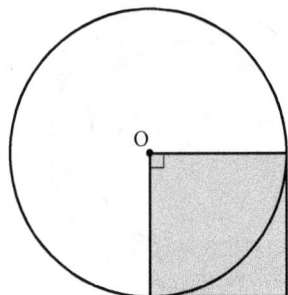

Example 10. The area of the circle shown below is 36π m². A portion of the shaded square overlaps with the circle, and each side of the square is equal in length to the radius of the circle. Given that the area of a square is the length of one side × the length of the other side, what is the area of the shaded square?

Ⓐ 16 m²
Ⓑ 24 m²
Ⓒ 25 m²
Ⓓ 36 m²
Ⓔ 144 m²

Answer: D. The area of the circle is $A = \pi r^2 = 36\pi$. We can cancel π from both sides of the equation, to get $r^2 = 36$, so $r = 6$ m. Since the sides of the square are equal to the radius of the circle, each side of the square is also equal to 6 m, and therefore the area of the shaded square is $6 \times 6 = 36$ m².

Practice Problems

1. Which of the following terms is the longest chord in a circle?

   (A) Radius
   (B) Diameter
   (C) Circumference
   (D) Arc
   (E) Sector

2. James is decorating a circular birthday cake for his brother's birthday. How does the cake's circumference compare to the cake's diameter?

   (A) The circumference of the cake is approximately 1/3 the length of the diameter.
   (B) The circumference of the cake is approximately 1/2 the length of the diameter.
   (C) The circumference of the cake is approximately 2/3 the length of the diameter.
   (D) The circumference of the cake is approximately twice the length of the diameter.
   (E) The circumference of the cake is approximately three times the length of the diameter.

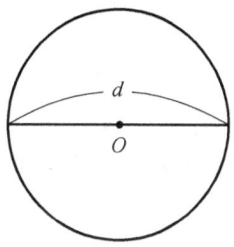

3. What is the length of the diameter of the circle above if its circumference is 2π inches?

   (A) 1 inch
   (B) 2 inches
   (C) 4 inches
   (D) 6 inches
   (E) 8 inches

4. Frank drives 2,200 ft to a bookstore. The tires on his car have a circumference of 5 ft. How many rotations does each tire make during Frank's trip?

   (A) 110
   (B) 205
   (C) 220
   (D) 440
   (E) 660

5. A bicycle tire has a radius of 10 inches. Approximately how far will the bicycle travel in 20 rotations?

   (A) 20π inches
   (B) 400π inches
   (C) 420π inches
   (D) 488π inches
   (E) 640π inches

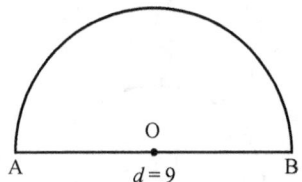

6. In the figure above, find the arc length $\widehat{AB}$ of the semicircle.

    (A) 1.5π
    (B) 2.5π
    (C) 3.5π
    (D) 4.5π
    (E) 5.5π

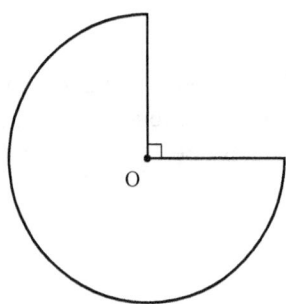

7. In the figure above, the radius of the circle is 4 units. Find the arc length of the partial circle.

    (A) 2π
    (B) 4π
    (C) 6π
    (D) 8π
    (E) 12π

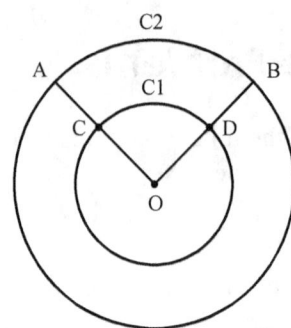

8. The figure above shows two circles that have the same center, O. C1 and C2 represent arc length of CD and AB, respectively. Which of the following is true?

    (A) $\angle COD > \angle AOB$
    (B) $\angle COD < \angle AOB$
    (C) $\angle COD = \angle AOB$
    (D) $C2 < C1$
    (E) $C2 = C1$

9. Jack has a circular garden in his backyard that has a radius of 9 feet. If he uses 5 ounces of fertilizer for every square foot, how many ounces of fertilizer does Jack need to cover his garden?

    (A) 405π ounces
    (B) 420π ounces
    (C) 440π ounces
    (D) 464π ounces
    (E) 488π ounces

Chapter 17: Circles

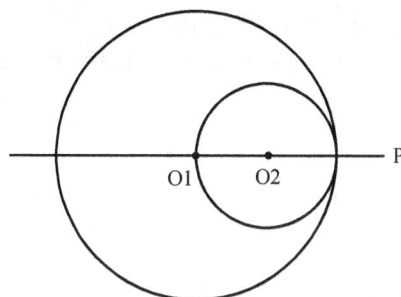

10. Circles O1 and O2 have their centers and diameters on line P, as shown above. If the diameter of the smaller circle is 8 units long, what is the ratio of the area of the larger circle to the area of the smaller circle?

   (A) 2.5 : 1
   (B) 2.75 : 1
   (C) 3 : 1
   (D) 3.33 : 1
   (E) 4 : 1

11. How many degrees are there in two-thirds of a circle?

   (A) 180°
   (B) 210°
   (C) 240°
   (D) 270°
   (E) 300°

12. What is the area of a circle with a diameter of 14 inches?

   (A) 14π in²
   (B) 28π in²
   (C) 49π in²
   (D) 98π in²
   (E) 196π in²

13. A circle that has radius of 6 meters is divided into 6 equal sectors. What is the area of each sector?

   (A) π m²
   (B) 2π m²
   (C) 4π m²
   (D) 6π m²
   (E) 8π m²

14. Two circles have radii, 2 cm and 4 cm, respectively. What is the ratio between the areas of these two circles?

   (A) 1 : 2
   (B) 1 : 3
   (C) 1 : 4
   (D) 1 : 6
   (E) 1 : 8

15. Which of the following statements is true?

   Choose all answers that apply.

   [A] There are infinitely many equally long radii in a circle.

   [B] The diameter of a circle is always twice as long as its radius.

   [C] The circumference of a circle is equal to its area when $r = 2$ inches.

   [D] The circumference of a circle is the same as its diameter when $r = 1$ inch.

   [E] The radius of a circle is always smaller than its circumference.

16. If the diameter of a circle is doubled, by how many times will the circle's area increase?

    (A) 2
    (B) 4
    (C) 6
    (D) 8
    (E) 16

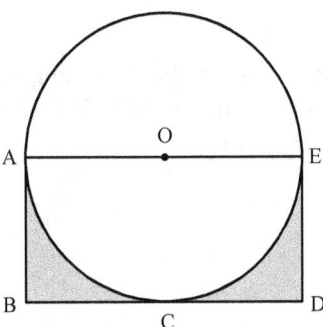

17. In the figure above, the radius of circle O is 6 cm. Diameter AE is parallel to BD, and segments AB and ED are parallel to each other. Given that the area of a rectangle is length × width (see next chapter for more on this topic), what is the area of the shaded region?

    (A) $36 - 18\pi$ cm²
    (B) $42 - 9\pi$ cm²
    (C) $42 - 18\pi$ cm²
    (D) $72 - 9\pi$ cm²
    (E) $72 - 18\pi$ cm²

18. If the ratio of the diameters of two circles is 2 : 3, what is the ratio of the circumference of these circles?

    (A) 2 : 3
    (B) 2 : 4
    (C) 2 : 9
    (D) 1 : 2
    (E) 4 : 9

Answers to Practice Problems

1. **(B)** A chord is a segment and its endpoints are on the circle. Choices **C**, **D**, and **E** are not segments. Choice **A** is incorrect because the diameter is twice the length of the radius.

2. **(E)** The formula for the circumference of the circle is $C = \pi d$. Since $\pi = 3.14 \approx 3$, the circumference, C, is just a little larger than $3 \times d$.

3. **(B)** Since the circumference, $C = \pi d = 2\pi$,
$$d = \frac{2\pi}{\pi} = 2 \text{ inches.}$$

4. **(D)** We can use the formula, distance (d) = number of rotations (n) × the circumference of the tire (C) or $d = nC$. Given that Frank drives 2200 ft, and the circumference is 5 ft,
$$n = \frac{d}{C} = \frac{2200 \text{ ft}}{5 \text{ ft}} = 440$$

5. **(B)** Use the formula, distance (d) = number of rotations (n) × the circumference of the tire (C) or $d = nC$. The circumference of the bicycle tire is $C = 2\pi r = 2\pi(10) = 20\pi$ inches. Hence, the bicycle travels a distance
$$d = nC = (20)(20\pi) = 400\pi \text{ inches}$$

6. **(D)** The arc length of the semicircle is half the circumference of the circle, which is
$$\frac{C}{2} = \frac{\pi d}{2} = \frac{9\pi}{2} = 4.5\pi$$

7. **(C)** The arc length of the partial circle is 3/4 the size of the full circumference of the circle. We know this because the central angle is 90° and the portion of the missing arc length is $\frac{90°}{360°} = \frac{1}{4}$. The total circumference, $C = 2\pi r = 2\pi(4) = 8\pi$. Therefore, the arc length of the partial circle is $\frac{3}{4} \times 8\pi = 6\pi$.

8. **(C)** The central angle is always the same regardless of how large the arc length is between the rays of any given angle.

9. **(A)** First, calculate the area of the circular garden, $A = \pi r^2 = \pi(9)^2 = 81\pi$ ft². Since he uses 5 ounces of fertilizer for every square foot, the number of ounces of fertilizer used is
$$81\pi \text{ ft}^2 \times \frac{5 \text{ oz}}{\text{ft}^2} = 405\pi \text{ ounces.}$$

10. **(E)** Since the diameters of the two circles are on the same line, we know that the diameter of the smaller circle is 8 units long, which is also the radius of the larger circle.

    - Area of small circle:
    $A_S = \pi r^2 = \pi(4)^2 = 16\pi$,
    where $r = d/2 = 8/2 = 4$ units.

    - Area of large circle:
    $A_L = \pi r^2 = \pi(8)^2 = 64\pi$

    Therefore, the ratio of the area of the larger circle to the area of the smaller circle is:
    $$A_L : A_S = 64\pi : 16\pi = 4 : 1$$

11. **(C)** $\frac{2}{3} \times 360° = 240°$

12. **(C)** The area of a circle is $A = \pi r^2$. Given that $d = 14$, we get $r = 14/2 = 7$. Therefore, the area of the circle is
$$A = \pi r^2 = \pi(7)^2 = 49\pi \text{ in}^2$$

13. **(D)** Since $r = 6$ m, the area of the circle is $A = \pi r^2 = \pi(6)^2 = 36\pi$. The area of each sector is $\frac{1}{6} \times 36\pi = 6\pi$.

14. **(C)** To find the areas of these two circles, plug the value of the radius, r into the formula for the area of a circle:

    - Area of the smaller circle:
      $A_S = \pi r^2 = \pi(2)^2 = 4\pi$

    - Area of the larger circle:
      $A_L = \pi r^2 = \pi(4)^2 = 16\pi$

    Therefore, the ratio of the area of the smaller circle to the area of the larger circle is:

    $A_S : A_L = 4\pi : 16\pi = 1 : 4$

15. **(A), (B), (E)** By the property of the circle, **A** and **B** are true. In **C**, the unit of the circumference and the area are different, so **C** is incorrect. The diameter is never the same length as the circumference. The diameter is always $\dfrac{C}{\pi}$. **E** is correct because $C = 2\pi r$. In order for this statement to be false 2π would have to be smaller than or equal to 1, which is false.

16. **(B)** Since the length of the diameter has doubled, the new diameter will be $2d$, and the radius will be $2 \times 2r = 4r$. The new area of the circle will be

    $A = \pi r^2 = \pi(4r)^2 = 16\pi r^2$

    Since the old area is

    $A = \pi r^2 = \pi(2r)^2 = 4\pi r^2$

    the area increases by a factor of 4 when the diameter is doubled.

17. **(E)** The semicircle and a portion of the rectangle ABDE overlap. The area of the shaded region is the area of the rectangle minus the area of the semicircle.

    - Area of semicircle:

      $A = \dfrac{\pi r^2}{2} = \dfrac{\pi(6)^2}{2} = 18\pi$ cm²

    - Area of rectangle ABDE:

      $A = l \times w = 12 \times 6 = 72$ cm², where $l =$ the length of the diameter of the circle, and $w =$ width of rectangle = the radius of the circle.

    Therefore, the shaded region is the area of the rectangle ABDE − area of the semicircle =

    $72 - 18\pi$ cm²

18. **(A)** Since the ratio of the circles' diameters is $2 : 3$, the ratio of the radii is also $2 : 3$.

    Let the radii of the two circles be 2 and 3, respectively. Then the circumference of the smaller circle will be $2\pi r = 2\pi(2) = 4\pi$ and the circumference of the larger circle will be $2\pi r = 2\pi(3) = 6\pi$. Therefore, the ratio of the circumferences of the circles is $4\pi : 6\pi = 2 : 3$.

Chapter 18
Perimeter, Area, Volume, and Surface Area

1. Perimeter

The **perimeter** of an object is a measurement of distance around it. For example, the perimeter of a city block is the total distance you would have to walk to go around the block. The perimeter of a city block can be measured by simply adding up the length of its sides, assuming you had a large enough measuring tape. A perimeter is a measurement of *distance* or *length* and is one-dimensional (or 1-D). The possible units of distance include inches, feet, meters, kilometers, or miles, to name a few.

A circumference is a special case of a perimeter when the object in question is something curved, like a circle or ellipse. This is just a naming convention, and for practical purposes a circumference and perimeter are the same thing. The circumference of a circle is $2\pi r$, where r is the circle's radius.

Example 1. What is the perimeter of a rectangular object that measures 10 meters in length and 5 meters in width?

- (A) 5 meters
- (B) 10 meters
- (C) 30 meters
- (D) 50 meters
- (E) 100 meters

Answer: C. The rectangle has two 10-meter sides and two 5-meter sides, so when you add up the length of each side, you get:

$$10 + 10 + 5 + 5 = 30$$

Example 2. Which of the following statements are true?

Choose all answers that apply.

- [A] The perimeter of a rectangle is $2l + 2w$, where l is its length and w is its width.
- [B] The perimeter of a square is $2l$, where l is its length.
- [C] The perimeter of an octagon is $8l$, where l is the length of one of its sides.
- [D] The circumference of a circle is πd, where d is the diameter of the circle.
- [E] The perimeter of a square is l^2.

Answer: A, C, D. We know that Statement **A** is true based on the previous example problem. Statement **B** is wrong because a square has four sides of length l, so its perimeter should be $4l$, not $2l$. Statement **C** is true, because an octagon as 8 sides, so its perimeter should be $8l$. Statement **D** is also true. It was stated that the circumference of a circle is $2\pi r$, and a circle's diameter is twice its radius, so this is equivalent to πd. Statement **E** is wrong because $l^2 = l \times l \neq 4l$.

2. Area

The area of an object is the amount of two-dimensional (2-D) space on a flat surface. For example, the area of a piece of paper is the amount of space that you have to write on. Some common expressions for area are listed below:

- Area of a square $= l^2$
  ($l =$ length of one side)

- Area of a rectangle $= l \times w$
  ($l =$ length, and $w =$ width)

- Area of a triangle $= \dfrac{1}{2}(b \times h)$
  ($b =$ length of the base, $h =$ height)

- Area of a circle $= \pi r^2$
  ($r =$ radius of the circle)

- Area of a parallelogram $= bh$
  ($b =$ base, $h =$ height)

- Area of a trapezoid $= \dfrac{1}{2}(b_1 + b_2)h$
  ($b_1 =$ first base, $b_2 =$ second base, $h =$ height)

Notice that the formula for area always consists of two measures of length or distance multiplied with each other. This is because area is a **two-dimensional measurement**, so it has units of two one-dimensional measurements. For example, let's say the length of a square is 10 cm. Then the area of a square would be $10^2 = 100\,\text{cm}^2$ (notice the units are centimeters squared or cm^2 because we multiplied two measurements in centimeters by each other). It is important that all dimensions must be **in the same units** when we calculate an area.

A three-dimensional (3-D) shape such as a sphere or cube has an area measurement called "surface area." This is simply the total area contained on the outer surface of the object, as the name implies. For example, the surface area of a cube is just the sum of the areas of each of its faces. So, a cube would have a surface area of $6l^2$ because the area of each face is l^2 and a cube has 6 faces.

Example 3. Which of the following statements is true?

- (A) A triangle with base of 1 m and height of 2 m has an area of 1 m.
- (B) A square with sides of length 10 cm has an area of 40 cm².
- (C) The area of a square with side length x is always greater than the area of a circle with a diameter of x.
- (D) Doubling the length of a rectangle and halving its width will increase its area.
- (E) Increasing the circumference of a circle will decrease its area.

Answer: C. It can be helpful to draw a diagram like the one below. Both the square and the circle have the same length, but it is clear the square covers a large area.

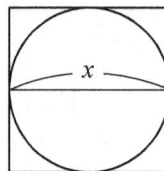

We can rule out the other options based on the following reasoning.

A: Although it has the right *number* for the area of the triangle, it has the wrong *units*. The correct answer would be 1 m².

B: 40 cm is the *perimeter* of a square with sides of length 10 cm. The *area* of the square would be $10^2 = 100\,\text{cm}^2$.

D: The area of a rectangle is the length times the width. If we make the length twice as long but make the width half as long, we will end up with the exact same area after multiplying the new side lengths together!

E: If we increase the circumference of a circle, that means we are making it larger, which means that its area must also be *increasing*, not decreasing.

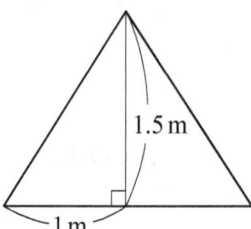

Example 4. Calculate half of the area of the triangle in the figure above.

- (A) 0.375 m²
- (B) 0.75 m²
- (C) 1.5 m²
- (D) 3 m²
- (E) 6 m²

Answer: B. Keep in mind that the total base length is 2 m. Using the formula $A = \frac{1}{2}(b \times h)$, we get $A = \frac{1}{2}(2 \times 1.5) = 1.5$ m². But the question asked for *half* of the triangle's area, so we arrive at our final answer of 0.75 m².

Example 5. Find the area of the following trapezoid:

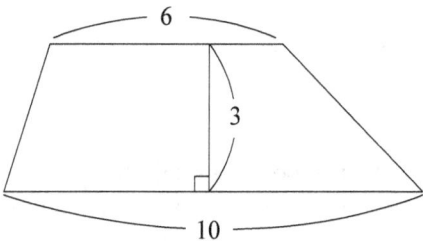

Answer: 24. Write the formula for the area of a trapezoid: $A = \frac{1}{2}(b_1 + b_2)h$. Plug in 3 into h and 6 for b_1 and 10 for b_2 (or 10 for b_1 and 6 for b_2) to obtain:

$$A = \frac{1}{2}(6 + 10) \cdot 3 = 24.$$

Example 6. Find the area of the following parallelogram:

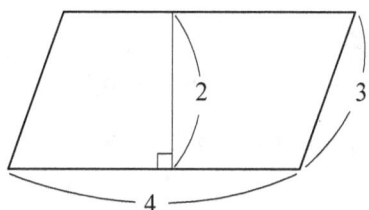

Answer: 8. Write the formula for the area of a parallelogram: $A = bh$. Insert 4 for the base and 2 for the height to get $A = 4 \cdot 2 = 8$.

Example 7. You are building a garden and want the total area to be 48 ft². Based on the size of your yard, you decide to make one side of the garden 8 ft long. How long must the other side be in order to have the correct desired area?

- (A) 4 ft
- (B) 6 ft
- (C) 8 ft
- (D) 32 ft
- (E) 40 ft

Answer: B. If the area must be 48 ft² and one side is 8 ft, then the other side must be 6 ft, because $6 \times 8 = 48$.

Example 8. Now that you have calculated the two dimensions of the garden (length = 8 ft, width = 6 ft), in example 6, you need to go to the hardware store for lumber to make the perimeter of the garden box. How much lumber, in total length, do you need to buy?

- (A) 14 ft
- (B) 28 ft
- (C) 36 ft
- (D) 48 ft
- (E) 64 ft

Answer: B. You would need enough lumber to cover the perimeter, which is 28 ft.

$$\text{Perimeter} = 2 \times 8 + 2 \times 6 = 28$$

3. Volume

We have seen that perimeter is a 1-D measurement and area is a 2-D measurement. Volume is an analogous quantity that measures the total three-dimensional space that an object takes up. For example, the amount of water that fits into a water bottle is a volume. Just like area (a 2-D measurement) has units of length squared, volume has units of length cubed. Some examples of units for volume include cm^3, m^3, in^3, etc. There are also volume-specific units like liters or gallons, so the units for volume are not *always* cubed.

For the GED Math exam, you need to know the formulas for the volume of a cube and the volume of a rectangular solid, which are the following:

- Volume of a cube $= l^3$
  (l = length of a side)
- Volume of a rectangular solid $= l \cdot w \cdot h$
  (l = length, w = width, h = height)
- Volume of a pyramid $= \frac{1}{3}Bh$
  (B = area of the base, h = height)

- Volume of a cone $= \frac{1}{3}\pi r^2 h$
  (r = radius, h = height)
- Volume of a sphere $= \frac{4}{3}\pi r^3$
  (r = radius)
- Volume of a cylinder $= \pi r^2 h$
  (r = radius, h = height)

Example 9. What is the side length of a cube with a volume of 1 m³?

- (A) 1/10 m
- (B) 1/3 m
- (C) 1 m
- (D) 2 m
- (E) 3 m

Answer: C. The volume of a cube is l^3 and the only option that gives a volume of 1 m³ is if the side is 1 m because $1^3 = 1$.

Example 10. You have assembled a garden box. It is 8 ft in length, 6 ft in width, and 3 ft in height. How much soil do you need in order to fill the box to a depth of 2 ft?

- (A) 48 ft³
- (B) 96 ft³
- (C) 108 ft³
- (D) 44 ft³
- (E) 512 ft³

Answer: B. The box is 3 ft tall, but you only want to fill it with 2 ft of soil. The volume in soil would then be $V = 8 \times 6 \times 2 = 96$ ft³.

Example 11. Find the volume of the following figures. Use the formulas above:

A.
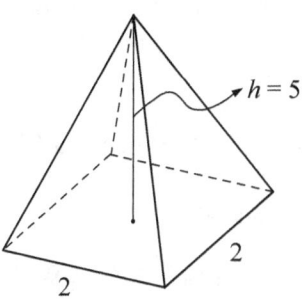

B.
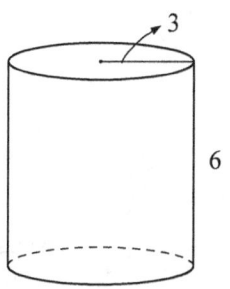

C.
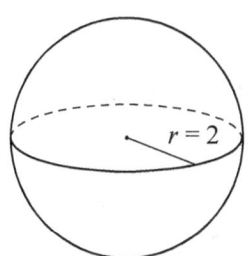

D.
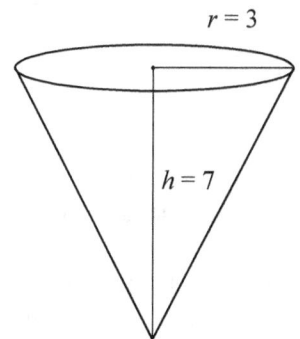

Answers:

A. **20/3.** For the volume of a pyramid write:
$$V = \frac{1}{3}Bh = \frac{1}{3}(2 \times 2)(5) = \frac{20}{3}.$$

B. **169.56.** For the volume of a cylinder, write:
$$V = \pi r^2 h = (3.14)(3^2)(6) = 169.56.$$

C. **33.49.** For the volume of a sphere, write:
$$V = \frac{4}{3}\pi r^3 = \frac{4}{3}(3.14)(2^3) = 33.49.$$

D. **65.94.** For the volume of a cone, write:
$$V = \frac{1}{3}\pi r^2 h = \frac{1}{3}(3.14)(3^2)(7) = 65.94.$$

Example 12. A cone with a height of 5 cm and a radius of 2 cm is being filled with water at the rate of 10 cm³ per second. How many seconds will it take to fill it up to the top to the nearest second?

- (A) 1
- (B) 2
- (C) 3
- (D) 4
- (E) 5

Answer: B. First find the volume of the cone:
$$V = \frac{1}{3}\pi r^2 h = \frac{1}{3}(3.14)(2^2)(5) = 20.93 \text{ cm}^3.$$

Divide the volume by the rate:
$$V = \frac{20.93 \text{ cm}^3}{10 \text{ cm}^3/\text{sec}} = 2.09 \text{ sec.}$$

Alternatively, you can make a proportion:
$\frac{1}{10} = \frac{x}{20.93}$, then multiply both sides of the equation by 20.93 to get $x = \frac{20.93}{10} = 2.09.$

Example 13. A cup with a radius of 3 cm and a height of 9 cm contains water. If 20 cm³ of salt is added to the water, what is the ratio of salt to water to the nearest tenth?

- (A) 0.078
- (B) 0.12
- (C) 0.24
- (D) 0.35
- (E) 0.36

Answer: A. First find the volume of the cup, which is a cylinder, by using the formula $V = \pi r^2 h$, which in this case is equal to: $(3.14)(3^2)(9) = 254.34$ cm³. If one adds 20 cm³ of salt, the ratio is $\dfrac{20}{256.34} = 0.078$.

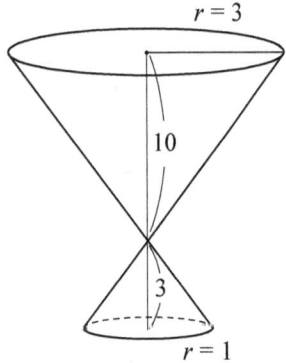

Example 14. Calculate the volume of the figure above to the nearest tenth of a unit.

- (A) 94.2
- (B) 97.3
- (C) 188.4
- (D) 194.7
- (E) 282.6

Answer: B. Both parts of the figure are cones, with the smaller one having a radius of 1 and the larger one having a radius of 3. The height of the bottom cone is 3 and the height of the top cone is 10. Add the two volumes together. The volumes of the bottom cone is

$$\frac{1}{3}\pi r^2 h = \frac{1}{3}(3.14)(1^2)(3) = 3.14$$

The volumes of the top cone is

$$\frac{1}{3}\pi r^2 h = \frac{1}{3}(3.14)(3^2)(10) = 94.2$$

In total, the volume is $3.14 + 94.2 = 97.3$.

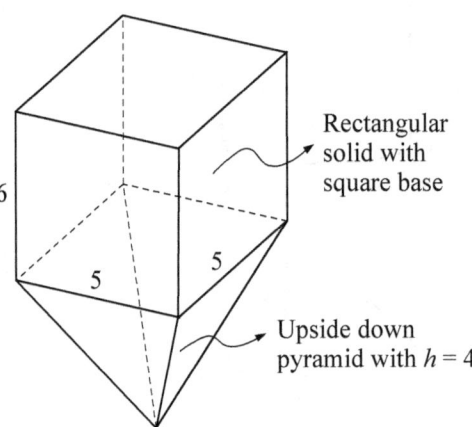

Example 15. Calculate the volume of the figure above to the nearest tenth.

- (A) 159
- (B) 166
- (C) 177
- (D) 180
- (E) 183

Answer: E. The figure is a rectangular solid with a square base of sides 5 and a height of 6. The bottom part of the figure is an upside down pyramid with the same base as the rectangular solid and height of 4. To find the total volume of the figure, add the volume of the rectangular solid

Chapter 18: Perimeter, Area, Volume, and Surface Area

and the volume of the pyramid. The volume of the retangular solid is

$$5 \times 5 \times 6 = 150.$$

The volume of the pyramid is

$$\frac{1}{3}Bh = \frac{1}{3}(5 \times 5)(4) = 33.33.$$

The total volume is $150 + 33.33 = 183.33 \approx 183$.

4. Surface Area

The surface area is a 2-dimentional number, which is equal to the sum of the areas of each of the outside faces of a 3-dimentional figure. Unlike the volume which has a dimension of three, as in m³ or cm³, inches³, the surface area is 2D, with units such as m², cm², inches², etc. This is because the surface area is 2-dimensional even though the figure is 3-dimensional.

Here is a summary of the surface areas of various solids:

- Rectangular solid/right prism

    $$SA = ph + 2B$$

    (h = height, p = perimeter of base with area B)

    or

    $$SA = 2lw + 2wh + 2hl$$

    (l = length of the base, w = width of the base, h = height)

- Pyramid

    $$SA = \frac{1}{2}ps + B$$

    (s = slant height, p = perimeter of base with area B)

- Cone $SA = \pi rs + \pi r^2$ (s = slant height)
- Cylinder $SA = 2\pi rh + 2\pi r^2$
- Sphere $SA = 4\pi r^2$

Example 16. Find the surface areas of the following figures to the nearest unit:

A.

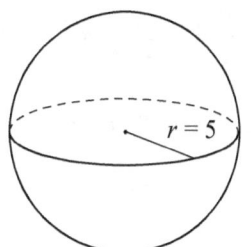

B.

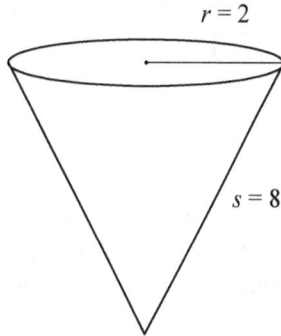

C.

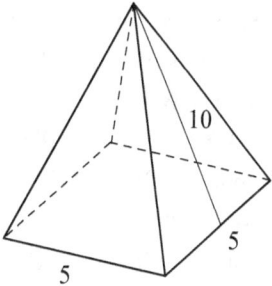

D.

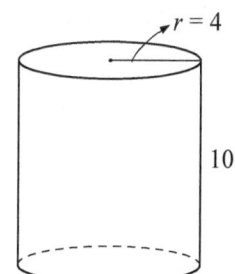

Answer:

A. **314.** The surface area of a sphere is
$$4\pi r^2 = 4(3.14)(5^2) = 314.$$

B. **63.** The surface area of a cone is
$$\pi rs + \pi r^2 = (3.14)(2)(8) + (3.14)(2^2)$$
$$= 62.8.$$

C. **125.** The surface area of a pyramid is
$$\frac{1}{2}ps + B = \frac{1}{2}(5 \times 4)(10) + 5^2 = 125.$$

D. **352.** The surface area of a cylinder is
$$2\pi rh + 2\pi r^2 = 2(3.14)(4)(10) + 2(3.14)(4^2)$$
$$= 351.68.$$

Example 17. A sphere has a radius of r_1. If the sphere were to be expanded so that the new radius is twice the old radius, which of the following is true?

- (A) The new spere will have twice the surface area of the old sphere
- (B) The new sphere will have triple the surface area of the old sphere
- (C) The new sphere will have four times the surface area of the old sphere
- (D) The new sphere will have six times the surface area of the old sphere
- (E) The new sphere will have eight times the surface area of the old sphere.

Answer: C. The ratio of the new sphere to the old sphere will be
$$\frac{4\pi r_2^2}{4\pi r_1^2} = \left(\frac{r_2}{r_1}\right)^2 = \left(\frac{2}{1}\right)^2 = 4.$$

Chapter 18: Perimeter, Area, Volume, and Surface Area

Practice Problems

1. What is the perimeter of a square that has an area of 64 in²?

    A) 8 in
    B) 16 in
    C) 32 in
    D) 64 in
    E) 256 in

2. What is the ratio of a circle's area to its circumference, where r is the circle's radius?

    A) $2\pi r$
    B) $\dfrac{r}{2}$
    C) πr^2
    D) $\dfrac{r^2}{2}$
    E) $\dfrac{2}{r}$

3. Which of the following units is a unit of volume?

    A) kg³
    B) in
    C) acres
    D) cm²
    E) m³

4. What is the volume of a cube with sides of length 10 cm?

    A) 0.0001 m³
    B) 0.001 m³
    C) 0.01 m³
    D) 0.1 m³
    E) 1 m³

5. You place a square rug with 6 ft sides in a rectangular room of 10 ft in width and 12 ft in length. What percentage of the room is not covered by the rug?

    A) 30%
    B) 36%
    C) 64%
    D) 70%
    E) 120%

6. How many 1 ft³ cube blocks would fit inside a rectangular solid with length = 10 ft, width = 4 ft, and height = 2 ft?

    A) 1 block
    B) 8 blocks
    C) 40 blocks
    D) 80 blocks
    E) 800 blocks

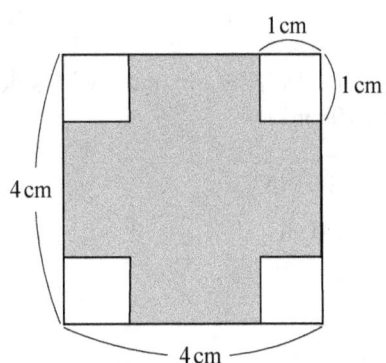

7. In the figure above, four small squares of side lengths of 1cm are removed from the corners of a square with side lengths of 4cm. What is the perimeter of the resulting shape (shaded)?

  Ⓐ 2 cm
  Ⓑ 8 cm
  Ⓒ 12 cm
  Ⓓ 16 cm
  Ⓔ 18 cm

8. Calculate the area of a semicircle with a radius of half a meter.

  Ⓐ $\frac{\pi}{8}$ m^2
  Ⓑ $\frac{\pi}{4}$ m^2
  Ⓒ $\frac{\pi}{2}$ m^2
  Ⓓ π m^2
  Ⓔ 2π m^2

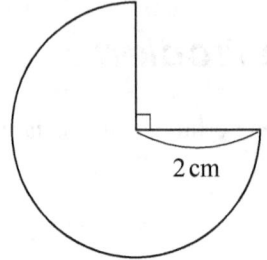

9. Calculate the area of the missing part of the circle in the figure above.

  Ⓐ π cm^2
  Ⓑ 2 cm^2
  Ⓒ 2π cm^2
  Ⓓ 3π cm^2
  Ⓔ 4π cm^2

Problems 10-11 pertains to the figure below.

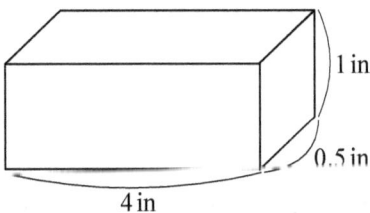

10. What is the volume of the object in the figure above?

  Ⓐ 2 in^2
  Ⓑ 2 in^3
  Ⓒ 4 in^3
  Ⓓ 4 in^2
  Ⓔ 13 in^2

11. What is the surface area of the object in the figure above?

    (A) 2 in²
    (B) 6.5 in²
    (C) 12 in²
    (D) 13 in²
    (E) 14 in²

Problems 12-13 pertains to the figure below.

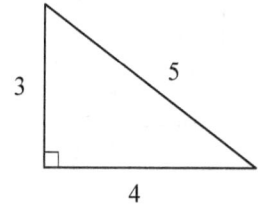

12. If each length of each side of the above triangle were doubled, how many times larger would the area be?

    (A) 2
    (B) 4
    (C) 8
    (D) 12
    (E) 24

13. What is the ratio of the above right triangle's area to its perimeter?

    (A) $\frac{1}{2}$
    (B) $\frac{5}{8}$
    (C) $\frac{5}{6}$
    (D) $\frac{8}{5}$
    (E) 2

14. If you double the length of the sides of a square, how much will the perimeter and area increase?

    (A) The perimeter will double, and the area will also double.
    (B) The perimeter will double, and the area will quadruple.
    (C) The perimeter will quadruple, and the area will double.
    (D) The perimeter will quadruple, and the area will also quadruple.
    (E) The perimeter will quadruple, and the area will increase eight fold.

15. You need to calculate how much paint you need to cover a wall in your house. The wall measures 15 ft × 8 ft and has two windows, each measuring 3 ft × 3 ft. What square footage worth of paint do you need?

    (A) 18 ft²
    (B) 102 ft²
    (C) 111 ft²
    (D) 120 ft²
    (E) 138 ft²

17. What is the ratio of the outer circle's circumference to the inner circle's circumference?

    (A) 1/2
    (B) 1
    (C) 2
    (D) 4
    (E) 8

Problems 16-17 pertains to the figure below.

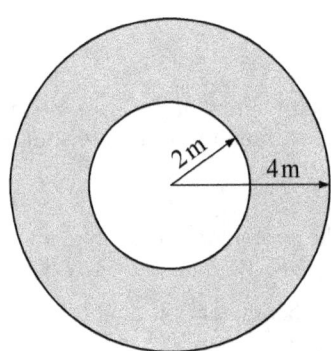

16. Calculate the area of the shaded region in the above figure.

    (A) 4π m²
    (B) 8π m²
    (C) 12π m²
    (D) 16π m²
    (E) 20π m²

18. What is the surface area and volume of the cylinder below?

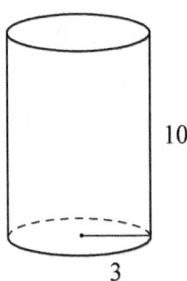

19. What is the volume of the cone below?

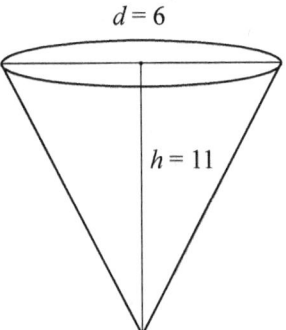

20. What is the surface area and volume of the sphere below?

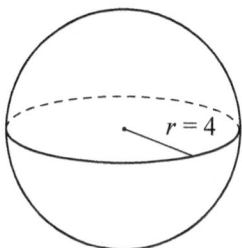

21. What is the surface area of the pyramid below?

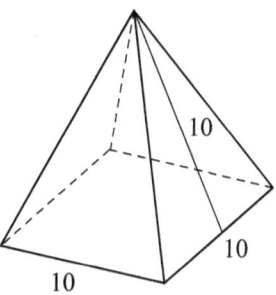

22. A swimming pool below is being filled with water. The swimming pool has a radius of 2 units and a height of 6 units. If 50 units of water can be filled per hour, how many hours will it take to fill the entire swimming pool to the nearest tenth of an hour?

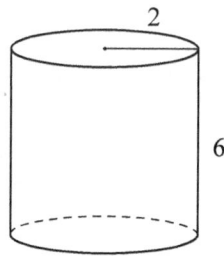

23. A ball has a diameter of 1 meter. What is its surface area?

24. What is the volume of the figure below?

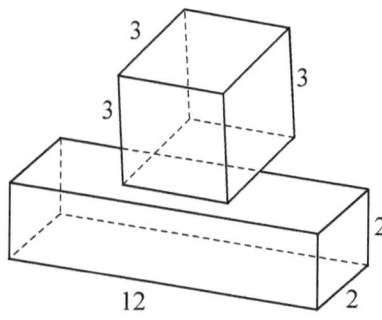

25. The volume of the box below is 120 cubic inches. What is the height of the box?

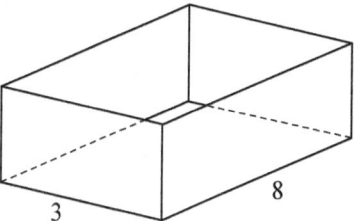

26. What is the volume of the figure below?

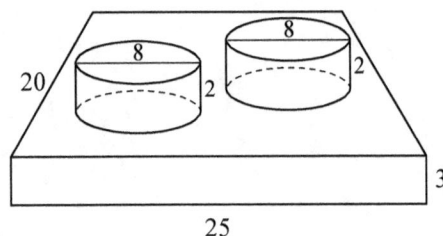

27. What is the volume of the dumbbell below?

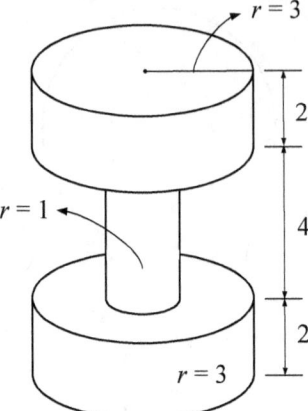

Answers to Practice Problems

1. **(C)** The square has sides of length 8 inches if its area is 64 in². And since it has four equal sides, its perimeter would then be $4 \times 8 = 32$.

2. **(B)** The area of a circle is πr^2 and the perimeter is $2\pi r$, so if we take the ratio of these two, we get: $\dfrac{\pi r^2}{2\pi r} = \dfrac{r}{2}$.

3. **(E)** m³ is the only option with units of (length)³. In choice **A**, kg is not a unit of length, it is a unit of mass.

4. **(B)** All the answers are in m³, so its easiest for first convert the side length to meters and then calculate the volume. 10 cm = 0.1 m, so the volume is then
$$V = 0.1 \times 0.1 \times 0.1 = 0.001 \text{ m}^3$$

5. **(D)** The area of the rug is $6 \times 6 = 36$ ft² and the area of the rooms is $10 \times 12 = 120$ ft². So $\dfrac{36}{120} \times 100 = 30\%$ of the room is covered by the rug, meaning that 70% is not covered.

6. **(D)** The volume of the rectangular solid is $V = 10 \times 4 \times 2 = 80$ ft³. We are filling it with cubes, each having one cubic foot of volume, meaning that 80 blocks will fit.

7. **(D)** We have to add up the lengths of all the sides. There are 4 sides with length 2 cm and 8 sides with length 1 cm, so the perimeter is:
$$4(2) + 8(1) = 16 \text{ cm}$$

8. **(A)** A semicircle is half of a circle, so its area will simply be half of πr^2. When we plug numbers in, we get:
$$A = \dfrac{1}{2}\pi \left(\dfrac{1}{2}\right)^2 = \dfrac{\pi}{8}$$

9. **(A)** The area of the full circle would be $\pi r^2 = \pi \cdot 2^2 = 4\pi$ cm². But we want the area of the missing part. The missing part is $\dfrac{1}{4}$ of the circle, so its area would be $\dfrac{1}{4}$ of the area, so the answer is π cm².

10. **(B)** This is a rectangular solid, so its volume will be:
$$V = lwh = 4 \cdot \dfrac{1}{2} \cdot 1 = 2 \text{ in}^3$$

11. **(D)** To calculate the surface area, we need to add up the areas of each face. There are two 4×1 in² faces, two $4 \times \dfrac{1}{2}$ in² faces, and two $1 \times \dfrac{1}{2}$ in² faces. So we get:

    Surface Area
    $$= 2(4 \times 1) + 2\left(4 \times \dfrac{1}{2}\right) + 2\left(1 \times \dfrac{1}{2}\right)$$
    $$= 13 \text{ in}^2$$

12. **(B)** The area of the original triangle was $\dfrac{1}{2} \times 3 \times 4 = 6$. The sides of the new triangle are 6, 8 and 10, so the area of the new triangle is $\dfrac{1}{2} \times 6 \times 8 = 24$, which is 4 times larger than the original area.

13. **(A)** There are no units supplied in this problem so we can ignore them. The area of the triangle is $\dfrac{1}{2}bh = \dfrac{1}{2} \cdot 4 \cdot 3 = 6$. And the perimeter is $3 + 4 + 5 = 12$. So, the ratio of the area to the perimeter is $\dfrac{6}{12} = \dfrac{1}{2}$.

14. **(B)** A square has four equal sides, so the perimeter is just $P = 4l$ where l is the length of the sides. So, if l is twice as large, then the perimeter will be twice (2×) as large. The area

of a square is $A = l^2$, so if l is twice as large then the area will be 4 times as large, since $2^2 = 4$. To better understand this concept, it is helpful to calculate the perimeter and area of two example squares and check your answer. You could try with squares with sides of length 2 and 4 centimeters, for example. You will find that the perimeter of the larger square is twice as large, and its area is four times as large.

15. **(B)** The area of the wall is $15 \times 8 = 120$ ft^2. But we have to subtract off the square footage of the two windows, so the final answer is:

$$120 - 2(3 \times 3) = 102 \text{ ft}^2$$

16. **(C)** To get the area of the outer shaded region, we can calculate the area of the larger circle ($r = 4$ m) and subtract the area of the inner circle ($r = 2$ m). So, we get:

$$A = \pi \cdot 4^2 - \pi \cdot 2^2 = 16\pi - 4\pi = 12\pi \text{ m}^2$$

17. **(C)** The outer radius is twice as large as the inner radius. Therefore, the perimeter will be twice as large. We can confirm this by using the equation for circumference. The outer circumference is $2\pi(4) = 8\pi$ m. The inner circumference is $2\pi(2) = 4\pi$ m. So if we take the ratio of the two, we get: $\dfrac{8\pi}{4\pi} = 2$.

18. **242.58, 94.2.** The surface area is
$2\pi r^2 + 2\pi rh = 2(3.14)(3)^2 + 2(3.14)(3)(10)$
$= 242.58$. The volume is $\pi r^2 h =$
$(3.14)(3)(10) = 94.2$.

19. **9.42.** Volume of cone $= \dfrac{1}{3}\pi r^2 h =$
$= \dfrac{1}{3}(3.14)(6/2)^2(11) = 9.42.$

20. **267.95, 200.96.** Volume of sphere
$= \dfrac{4}{3}\pi r^3 = \dfrac{4}{3}(3.14)(4)^3 = 267.95$. The
surface area is $4\pi r^2 = 4(3.14)(4^2) = 200.96$.

21. **300.** Surface area of a pyramid $= \dfrac{1}{2}ps + B$. The perimeter is $10 \times 4 = 40$, the base area is $10 \times 10 = 100$. So we have

$$\dfrac{1}{2}(40)(10) + 100 = 300.$$

22. **1.51.** The volume of a cylinder is $\pi r^2 h = (3.14)(2^2)(6) = 75.36$. If 50 units can be filled per hour, the total pool can be filled in $75.36/50 = 1.51$ hours.

23. **3.14 m².** The surface area of a sphere is $4\pi r^2$. Since the diameter is 1 m, the radius is $\dfrac{1}{2}$ meter. Therefore, the surface area is

$$4(3.14)\left(\dfrac{1}{2}\right)^2 = 3.14 \text{ m}^2.$$

24. **75.** The total volume of the figure is the volume of the bottom rectangular prism plus the volume of the cube above. This is equal to $(2 \times 2 \times 12) + (3 \times 3 \times 3) = 75$.

25. **5.** The volume is base × height. The base is $3 \times 8 = 24$, and the volume is given as 120. Therefore we write $120 = 24h$. Dividing both sides of the equation by 24 we get
$h = \dfrac{120}{24} = 5.$

26. **1700.96.** The volume of the rectangular prism on the bottom is $25 \times 20 \times 3 = 1500$. The volume of one cylinder is $\pi r^2 h$, and we have two of them, so the volume of both cylinders is $2 \times (3.14)(4^2)(2) = 200.96$, where the radius is 8/2 (half the length of the diameter. Adding them together, we get $1500 + 200.96 = 1700.96$.

27. **125.6.** The volume of the dumbbell is the volume of the cylinder on top plus the volume of the cylinder on the bottom (which are equal to each other) plus the volume of the cylinder on the middle:

$$2\pi r_1^2 h_1 + \pi r_2^2 h_2 = 2(3.14)(3^2)(2) + (3.14)(1^2)(4)$$
$$= 125.6.$$

Chapter 19
Probability and Statistics

The GED Math exam will include many questions on probability and statistics. We start with probability, then examine Venn diagrams, central tendencies, correlation, and statistical studies.

What is Probability?

In statistics, **probability** indicates the likelihood of an event's occurrence.

- The probability is a number between 0 and 1, inclusively.
- The probability is expressed as a decimal or percentage.
- The probability that event E will happen is denoted as $P(E)$.

  If $P(E) = 0$, event E will not occur.

  If $P(E) = 1$, event E will occur.

  If $P(E) = \frac{1}{2}$, event E has a 50-50 chance of occurring.

Mathematically, we define the probability of event E as:

$$P(E) = \frac{\text{Number of favorable possible outcomes}}{\text{Total number of possible outcomes}}$$

Example 1. If all 8 sections in the circle above have the same area, what is the probability that the hand on the spinner lands on "$100?"

- (A) $\frac{1}{8}$
- (B) $\frac{1}{6}$
- (C) $\frac{1}{4}$
- (D) $\frac{1}{3}$
- (E) $\frac{1}{2}$

Answer: C. The event in question is that the spinner's hand lands on $100. Notice that there are a total of 8 possible outcomes on the spinner, and 2 favorable outcomes, "$100." So the probability of spinning "$100" is $2/8 = 1/4$.

Example 2. A basket contains 3 yellow, 4 blue, and 5 black balls. If a ball is randomly pulled out of the basket, what is the probability that the ball will be blue?

(A) $\frac{1}{4}$

(B) $\frac{1}{3}$

(C) $\frac{2}{5}$

(D) $\frac{1}{2}$

(E) $\frac{2}{3}$

Answer: B. In this problem, there are 4 blue balls that constitute favorable outcomes, out of a total of 12 possible outcomes. So the probability of picking a blue ball is $\frac{4}{12} = \frac{1}{3}$.

Probability of Independent and Dependent Events

Event A and event B are **independent** if the occurrence of event A has no effect on the occurrence of event B, and vice versa. The probability of two independent events is

$$P(A \text{ and } B) = P(A) \times P(B)$$

Event A and event B are **dependent** if the occurrence of event A affects the occurrence of the event B, and vice versa. The probability that event B will happen *given that* event A has occurred, is called **conditional probability** and denoted as $P(B|A)$. The probability of the two dependent events is

$$P(A \text{ and } B) = P(A) \times P(B|A)$$

Let's use the following examples to understand the difference between the two.

Example 3. Seven slips of paper numbered 1 to 7 are placed in a hat. Jason randomly selects a paper slip, places it back into the hat, and then selects a second slip. What is the probability that the first number is even and the second number is odd?

(A) $\frac{12}{49}$

(B) $\frac{16}{49}$

(C) $\frac{7}{49}$

(D) $\frac{2}{7}$

(E) 1

Answer: A. Since Jason places the first paper slip back into the hat before selecting the second slip, his action is termed **with replacement**. The occurrence of selecting the first slip and the second slip are independent events, so

$$P(\text{even and odd}) = P(\text{even}) \times P(\text{odd})$$
$$= \frac{3}{7} \times \frac{4}{7} = \frac{12}{49}$$

because there are 3 even numbers and 4 odd numbers included in the numbers 1 through 7, inclusively.

Example 4. A hat holds 7 slips of paper numbered 1 to 7. Jason randomly selects a slip, then selects a second slip without replacing the first one. What is the probability that Jason picks an even number, then an odd number?

(A) $\frac{12}{49}$

(B) $\frac{7}{49}$

(C) $\frac{1}{7}$

(D) $\frac{2}{7}$

(E) $\frac{1}{2}$

Answer: D. Since Jason doesn't place the first paper slip back into the hat before he selects the second one, the action is termed **without replacement**. The occurrences of selecting the first slip and the second slip are dependent events, so

$$P(\text{even and odd}) = P(\text{even}) \times P(\text{odd}|\text{even})$$
$$= \frac{3}{7} \times \frac{4}{6} = \frac{2}{7}$$

where $P(\text{even} \mid \text{odd}) = \frac{4}{6}$ because there is one slip fewer in the hat after his first pick.

Mean, Median and Mode

In descriptive statistics, there are three measures of central tendency to quantify the centrality of data points.

- **Mean.** Mean is most commonly known as "average." It is the arithmetic mean or average of a data set.

  $$\text{Mean or Average} = \frac{\text{The sum of the data points}}{\text{The number of data points}}$$

- **Median.** Median is the middle value after the data are ordered from least to greatest. The median splits the data in half, and is calculated in two ways, based on whether there is an even or odd number of data points.

  Odd number of data points:

  Data = {1, 2, 3, 4, 5}
  Median = the middle value of the data set, which is 3.

  Even number of data points:

  Data = {1, 2, 3, 4, 5, 6}
  Median = $\frac{3+4}{2}$ = 3.5, which is obtained by averaging the two middle values of the data points.

- **Mode.** Mode is the most frequently found number in a dataset. Note that there may be more than one mode in a data set.

Data = {1, 2, 3, 3, 4, 4, 4, 5, 5}
Mode = the most frequently found value is 4

Data = {1, 2, 3, 3, 4, 4, 4, 5, 5, 5}
Mode = 4 and 5

- **Outlier.** An outlier is an observed value in a dataset that is much higher or lower than the rest of the numbers. Outliers can affect the mean of the dataset, but they don't affect the median or mode.

  A dataset without an outlier:

  Data = {1, 2, 3, 4, 5}
  Mean = 3; Median = 3; Mode = None

  A dataset with an outlier:

  Data = {1, 2, 3, 4, 50}
  Mean = 12; Median = 3; Mode = None

  "50" is a value that is significantly higher than the other numbers in the dataset. Therefore, 50 is an outlier.

After removing an outlier from the dataset, the mean will change, the median may or may not change, and the mode remains the same. You may ask how is it that the median may not change. Let's say you have the following list of numbers: 1, 5, 5, 5, 60. The median is clearly 5. Now, if you take the outlier, 60, out of the list, the list becomes 1,5,5,5, and the median is still 5! There is no change in the median because the median, 5, repeats several times.

{9, 10, 13, 18, 20, 20}

Example 7. Given the dataset above, find the measure of central tendency that has the least value among mean, median, and mode.

(A) Mean of 13
(B) Median of 15.5
(C) Mean of 15
(D) Median of 18
(E) Mode of 20

Answer: C. The sum of the data points is $9 + 10 + 13 + 18 + 20 + 20 = 90$, and the number of data points is 6. Therefore:

$$\text{Mean} = \frac{90}{6} = 15$$

Since the dataset has an even number of data points, the **median** is the average of the middle values 13 and 18, which equals 15.5. The **mode** is the most frequently found value, which is 20. Therefore, the least value among the mean, median, and mode is the mean, 15.

Example 8. The grade received in a statistics course is determined by the score on four unit exams. Tom scored the following grades on his first 3 exams: 85%, 84%, and 92%. If Tom would like an "A" for this course, achieved only if his average score on his 4 unit exams is 90% or higher, what must he score on his fourth exam, in percent?

- (A) 92%
- (B) 95%
- (C) 97%
- (D) 99%
- (E) 100%

Answer: D. To solve this problem, we use x to represent his 4th unit exam score, so we can write that the mean on the four exams equals:

$$\frac{85 + 84 + 92 + x}{4} = 90$$

To solve for x, multiply both sides of the equation by 4:

$$85 + 84 + 92 + x = 360$$
$$261 + x = 360$$
$$x = 360 - 261$$
$$= 99$$

Permutations

An ordering of n objects is a permutation of the objects. For example, there are six permutations of the letters A, N, and P: ANP, APN, NPA, NAP, PAN, and PNA. While dealing with permutations one should be concerned about the selection as well as arrangement. This counting principal can be employed to find the number of permutations of n objects.

Representation of Permutation

We can represent permutation in many ways, such as:

$$P_{n,r} \quad P(n, r) \quad {}_nP_r$$

One important explanation necessary in the calculation of permutations (and combinations) is the symbol ! in math, following a number such as 3! or 11!. $x!$ means

$$x \times (x - 1) \times (x - 2) \times (x - 3) \ldots 1.$$

For example 3! means $3 \times 2 \times 1$. 8! means $8 \times 7 \times 6 \times 5 \times 4 \times 3 \times 2 \times 1$, etc.

Let's look at an example that employs that rule:

A. Eight skiers are competing in the semifinals of the Olympic skiing competition. In how many different ways can the skiers finish the competition, assuming there are no ties?

Solution: There are 8! Different ways that the skiers can finish the competition:

$$8 \times 7 \times 6 \times 5 \times 4 \times 3 \times 2 \times 1 = 40{,}320 \text{ ways.}$$

B. In how many different ways can 3 of the skiers finish first, second, and third to win the gold, silver, and bronze medals?

Solution: Eight skiers can finish first, then the remaining 7 skiers can win the silver medal, and any of the remaining 6 skiers can finish third to win the bronze medal. So the number of ways that the skiers can win the medals is:

$$8 \times 7 \times 6 = 336.$$

Chapter 19: Probability and Statistics

Formula

The formula for permutation of n objects for r selection of objects is given by:

$$P(n,r) = \frac{n!}{(n-r)!}$$

Using the example above, $n = 8$. In part **A**, we use the formula $P(n,r) = \frac{8!}{(8-8)!} = \frac{8 \times 7 \times 6 \times 5 \times 4 \times 3 \times 2 \times 1}{(8-8)!} = 40{,}320$. This is because $0! = 1$ by definition. As you can see, we obtain the same number.

For part **B**, we use $n = 8$ and $r = 3$ to get

$$P(8,3) = \frac{8!}{(8-3)!} = \frac{8!}{5!}$$
$$= \frac{8 \times 7 \times 6 \times 5 \times 4 \times 3 \times 2 \times 1}{5 \times 4 \times 3 \times 2 \times 1}$$
$$= 8 \times 7 \times 6 = 336.$$

This is because $\frac{5 \times 4 \times 3 \times 2 \times 1}{5 \times 4 \times 3 \times 2 \times 1} = 1$.

Example 9. How many 5 letter words can be formed out of 10 letters, if none of the letters repeat, and the words may be fictitious words?

(A) 50
(B) 500
(C) 1,024
(D) 9,046
(E) 30,240

Answer: E. We write

$$P(10,5) = \frac{10!}{(10-5)!} = \frac{10!}{5!}$$
$$= \frac{10 \times 9 \times 8 \times 7 \times 6 \times 5 \times 4 \times 3 \times 2 \times 1}{5 \times 4 \times 3 \times 2 \times 1}$$
$$= 10 \times 9 \times 8 \times 7 \times 6$$
$$= 30{,}240.$$

Example 10. A license plate is created with the letters A,B,C and 1,2,3. How many different license plates can be formed if a license plate is comprised of 4 letters and numbers and none of the letters or numbers can be repeated?

(A) 6
(B) 12
(C) 48
(D) 360
(E) 1,024

Answer: D. We use the formula

$$P(n,r) = \frac{n!}{(n-r)!} = \frac{6!}{(6-4)!} = \frac{6!}{2!}$$
$$= \frac{6 \times 5 \times 4 \times 3 \times 2 \times 1}{2 \times 1}$$
$$= 6 \times 5 \times 4 \times 3 = 360.$$

Combinations

A combination is a selection of r objects from a group of n objects where the order is not important. For example:

Christine eats a Thanksgiving meal. She has 10 dishes to choose from and she wants 6 dishes. How many combinations of dishes can she eat?

In this case we do not use a permutation because the order makes no difference. Instead, we use a combination formula to solve the problem.

The combination formula is

$$C(n,r) = \frac{n!}{(n-r)!r!}.$$

For the above problem we use $n = 10$ and $r = 6$.

Write

$$C(n,r) = \frac{10!}{(10-6)!6!} = \frac{10!}{4!6!}$$
$$= \frac{10 \times 9 \times 8 \times 7 \times 6 \times 5 \times 4 \times 3 \times 2 \times 1}{(4 \times 3 \times 2 \times 1)(6 \times 5 \times 4 \times 3 \times 2 \times 1)}$$
$$= \frac{10 \times 9 \times 8 \times 7}{4 \times 3 \times 2 \times 1}$$
$$= 210.$$

Example 11. You want to purchase a used car. There are 8 different types of optional equipment you can buy. You can afford to buy 3 of the options. How many combinations are there for you to choose from?

(A) 24
(B) 56
(C) 81
(D) 108
(E) 144

Answer: B. Use the formula

$$C(n,r) = \frac{n!}{(n-r)!r!}, n = 8, \text{ and } r = 3.$$

Therefore

$$C(8,3) = \frac{8!}{(8-3)!3!} = \frac{8!}{5!3!}$$
$$= \frac{8 \times 7 \times 6 \times 5 \times 4 \times 3 \times 2 \times 1}{(5 \times 4 \times 3 \times 2 \times 1)(3 \times 2 \times 1)}$$
$$= 56.$$

Example 12. A summer concert series has 10 different performing artists. You decide to attend 7 concerts. How many different combinations of concerts can you attend?

(A) 70
(B) 74
(C) 80
(D) 120
(E) 144

Answer: D. $n = 10$, and $r = 7$, so

$$C(10,7) = \frac{10!}{(10-7)!7!} = \frac{10!}{3!7!}$$
$$= \frac{10 \times 9 \times 8}{3 \times 2 \times 1}$$
$$= 120.$$

Line Plot

A line plot is used to represent data similarly to a frequency table. A line plot displays the frequency of data along a number line. It normally uses small dots or ×'s. Like so:

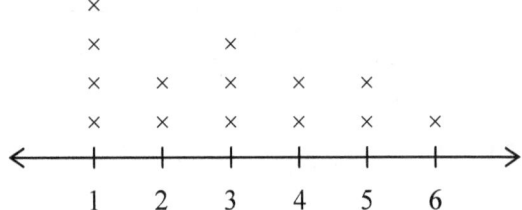

The bar graph shows the number of presents children received on Christmas. 4 children received 1 present, 2 children received 2 presents, 3 children received 3 presents, 2 children received 4 presents, 2 children received 5 presents and 1 child received 6 presents.

The most frequent number of presents received by the 14 children was 1.

Example 1. Fifteen bags of lollipops are opened. In each one, a certain number of purple lollipops are found, as shown on the line plot below. How many bags had more than 3 purple lollipops?

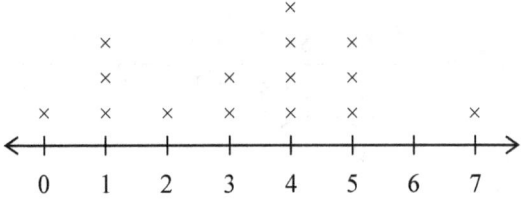

Chapter 19: Probability and Statistics

Answer: 8. Count the number of x's above the numbers 4,5,6, and 7.: $4 + 3 + 0 + 1 = 8$.

Example 13. Questions 1 and 2 are based on the following information: A study conducted on a drug showed that side effects varied in number per person, as shown on the line plot below:

```
            x
  x         x
  x    x    x              x
  x    x    x    x    x    x    x
<-+----+----+----+----+----+----+----+->
  0    1    2    3    4    5    6    7
```

1. How many people were in the study?

Answer: 14. Add up the number of x's:
$3 + 2 + 4 + 1 + 1 + 2 + 1 = 14$.

2. Which value (number of side effects) has the highest frequency in the data?

Answer: 2. There are 4 data points over the number 2, which is higher than any other number.

Example 14. The following frequency table shows the number of movies seen by people in January:

Number of Movies	Number of People
1	3
2	2
3	1
4	4
5	3
6	2
7	2

Which line plot represents this data?

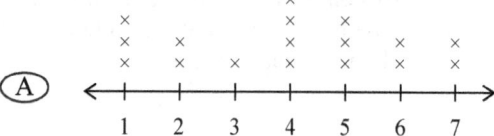

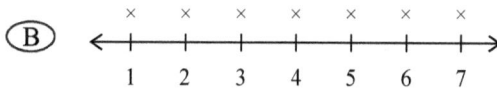

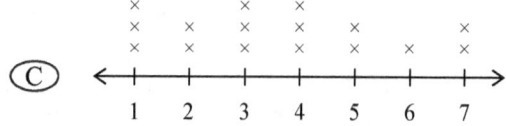

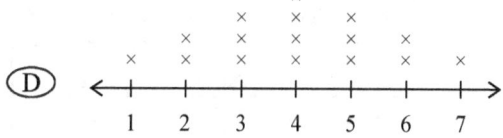

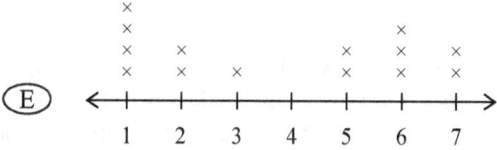

Answer: A. The line graph shows 3 people saw 1 movie, 2 people saw 2 movies, one person saw 3 movies, 4 people saw 4 movies, 3 people saw 5 movies, 2 people saw 6 movies and 2 people saw 7 movies.

Practice Problems

1. A spinner contains 15 integers, 1 through 15. What is the probability that the spinner's hand will land on a prime number?

   (A) $\frac{1}{15}$
   (B) $\frac{1}{12}$
   (C) $\frac{2}{15}$
   (D) $\frac{2}{5}$
   (E) $\frac{3}{5}$

Blood Type	Number of People
O	65
A	31
B	34
AB	20

2. The table above shows the distribution of blood types among a group of 150 people. If a person is selected randomly from this group, what is the probability that he or she will have blood type AB?

   (A) $\frac{1}{20}$
   (B) $\frac{2}{17}$
   (C) $\frac{2}{15}$
   (D) $\frac{1}{6}$
   (E) $\frac{2}{7}$

3. A basket contains 4 yellow, 6 blue, and 8 black balls. If a ball is randomly selected from the basket, what is the probability that it will be blue?

   (A) $\frac{1}{4}$
   (B) $\frac{1}{3}$
   (C) $\frac{1}{2}$
   (D) $\frac{2}{3}$
   (E) $\frac{3}{4}$

4. A quarter and a dime are tossed simultaneously. What is the probability of getting 1 head and 1 tail?

   (A) 25%
   (B) 50%
   (C) 70%
   (D) 75%
   (E) 100%

5. There are 2 purple, 3 blue, 3 red, and 4 white marbles in a jar. Two marbles are drawn out of the jar in succession, with replacement. What is the probability that both draws are red?

   (A) $\frac{1}{20}$
   (B) $\frac{1}{19}$
   (C) $\frac{1}{18}$
   (D) $\frac{1}{17}$
   (E) $\frac{1}{16}$

6. There are 2 purple, 3 blue, 3 red, and 4 white marbles in a jar. Two marbles are drawn out of the jar, in succession without replacement. What is the probability that both draws will be red?

   (A) $\dfrac{1}{24}$

   (B) $\dfrac{1}{23}$

   (C) $\dfrac{1}{22}$

   (D) $\dfrac{1}{16}$

   (E) $\dfrac{1}{8}$

7. There are 2 purple, 3 blue, 3 red, and 4 white marbles in a jar. Three marbles are drawn out of the jar, in succession without replacement. What is the probability that the first draw will be a white marble, the second draw a blue marble, and the third draw a purple marble?

   (A) $\dfrac{3}{216}$

   (B) $\dfrac{1}{57}$

   (C) $\dfrac{1}{56}$

   (D) $\dfrac{1}{55}$

   (E) $\dfrac{2}{3}$

{5.0, 3.8, 4.5, 3.5, 5.2, 4.0}

8. Find the mean of the data set above.

   (A) 4.25

   (B) 4.33

   (C) 5.25

   (D) 5.5

   (E) 5.75

9. Which of the following set has the same median as the set, {2, 4, 10, 20, 35, 76}?

   (A) {8, 9, 15, 22, 42, 55}

   (B) {8, 10, 11, 20, 35, 42}

   (C) {8, 8, 11, 22, 26, 40}

   (D) {5, 7, 25, 31, 46, 76}

   (E) {5, 7, 9, 21, 46, 54}

{2, 2, 2, 5, 8, 14, 16, 16, 18, 18, 18}

10. Find the mode(s) of the data seta above.

    (A) {2}

    (B) {16}

    (C) {2, 18}

    (D) {16, 18}

    (E) {2, 16, 18}

11. In a math class at Tilden Middle School, students took 6 quizzes during a semester. Tracy averaged 78% on her first 3 quizzes and 88% on her last 3. What is her average score on the 6 quizzes combined?

    (A) 83
    (B) 85
    (C) 87
    (D) 88
    (E) 89

                25, 27, 31, 33, 39, 41, 44

12. The set above is a list of 7 test scores received by Mr. Jenkins' history students. One of the scores was accidentally typed as 39 instead of 99. Which measure(s) of central tendency is/are unaffected by the incorrect score?

    I. Mean
    II. Median
    III. Mode

    (A) I only
    (B) I and II only
    (C) I and III only
    (D) II and III only
    (E) I, II, and III

13. In how many ways can the vowels (a, e, i, o, u) be arranged if none of the letters repeat?

    (A) 24
    (B) 25
    (C) 60
    (D) 120
    (E) 240

14. How many phone numbers can be formed if there are 10 numbers and each phone number consists of 7 numbers that don't repeat?

    (A) 70
    (B) 720
    (C) 14,920
    (D) 604,800
    (E) 1,200,564

15. Darlene orders a pizza from a restaurant. She has a choice of 12 toppings and can afford 3 toppings. How many types of pizzas can she order?

    (A) 42
    (B) 144
    (C) 220
    (D) 1,320
    (E) 1,440

16. 8 students stand in line. How many ways can the students stand in line?

    (A) 64
    (B) 5,040
    (C) 40,320
    (D) 168,540
    (E) 16,777,216

Chapter 19: Probability and Statistics 221

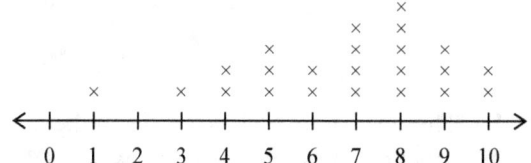

17. The line plot above shows the distribution of grades on a quiz worth 10 points. How many students passed the test if a passing score is 6 out of 10?

  Ⓐ 2
  Ⓑ 9
  Ⓒ 14
  Ⓓ 16
  Ⓔ 19

18. A study of 10 consumers showed that 9 in 10 people prefer to shop more than once a week than just once a week. Which of the following line plots could represent the data if 1 data point represents once a week, 2 data points represent twice per week, etc.?

Ⓐ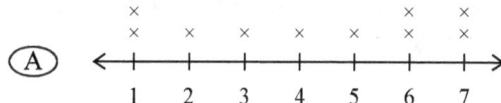

Ⓑ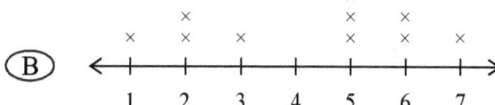

Ⓒ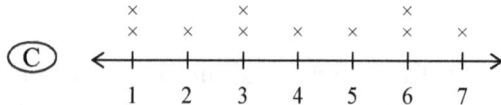

Ⓓ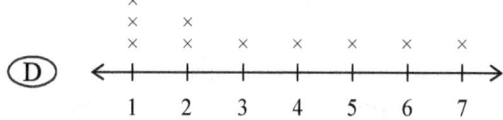

Ⓔ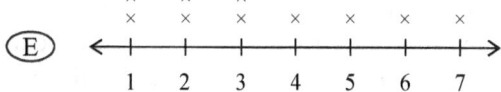

Answers to Practice Problems

1. **(D)** We know that a prime number has exactly two factors, 1 and itself. There are 6 prime numbers from 1 to 15 and they are {2, 3, 5, 7, 11, 13}. Therefore, the probability of spinning a prime number is 6/15, which equals 2/5.

2. **(C)** A total of 150 people participated in the study group, yielding 150 possible outcomes. There are 20 favorable outcomes for blood type AB. Therefore, the probability that blood type AB is selected is:

$$P(AB) = \frac{20}{150} = \frac{2}{15}$$

3. **(B)** The favorable outcome is blue, and there are 6 of them. The total number of possible outcomes is 18. So the probability of picking a blue ball is $6/18 = 1/3$.

4. **(B)** We know that the possible combinations from tossing a dime and a quarter are

$$\{HH, HT, TH, TT\}$$

where H = head and T = tail. The favorable event is one head and one tail. Because there are 2 combinations for one head and one tail, the probability is 2/4 =50%.

5. **(E)** There is a total of 12 marbles in the jar. Since two marbles will be drawn with replacement, the event of selecting first a red marble and then another red marble, is independent, so

$$P(\text{red and red}) = \frac{3}{12} \times \frac{3}{12} = \frac{1}{4} \times \frac{1}{4} = \frac{1}{16}$$

6. **(C)** There is a total of 12 marbles in the jar. Since two marbles will be drawn without replacement, the event of selecting first a red marble and then a second red marble is dependent, so

$$P(\text{red and red}) = P(\text{red}) \times P(\text{red}|\text{red})$$
$$= \frac{3}{12} \times \frac{2}{11} = \frac{1}{22}$$

7. **(D)** There is a total of 12 marbles in the jar. Since two marbles will be drawn without replacement, the selection of the three marbles are dependent events. Therefore,

$$P(w \text{ and } b \text{ and } p) = P(w) \times P(b|w) \times P(p|w,b),$$

where w = white, b = blue *and* p = purple. $P(p|w,b)$ is a conditional probability and necessitates finding the probability of drawing a purple marble given that the first draw is a white marble and the second draw is a blue marble. Therefore,

$$P(w \text{ and } b \text{ and } p) = P(w) \times P(b|w) \times P(p|w,b)$$
$$= \frac{4}{12} \times \frac{3}{11} \times \frac{2}{10} = \frac{1}{55}$$

8. **(B)** Using the formula for the mean, we obtain:

$$\text{Mean} = \frac{\text{The sum of the data points}}{\text{The number of data points}}$$
$$= \frac{5.0 + 3.8 + 4.5 + 3.5 + 5.2 + 4.0}{6}$$
$$= 4.33$$

9. **(E)** From the given data set, {2, 4, 10, 20, 35, 76}, we can calculate that the median = $(10 + 20)/2 = 15$. Then we calculate the median for the five answer choices:

   A. {5, 9, <u>15, 22</u>, 42, 55}:
   Median = $(15 + 22)/2 = 18.5$.

   B. {8, 10, 11, 20, 35, 42}:
   Median = $(11 + 20)/2 = 15.5$.

   C. {8, 8, 11, 22, 26, 40}:
   Median = $(11 + 22)/2 = 16.5$.

   D. {5, 7, 25, 31, 46, 75}:
   Median = $(25 + 31)/2 = 28$.

   E. {5, 7, 9, 21, 46, 54}:
   Median = $(9 + 21)/2 = 15$.

Chapter 19: Probability and Statistics

10. **(C)** The mode is the most frequently found number in a dataset. There are three 2's and 18's. Therefore, the mode has elements {2, 18}.

11. **(A)** To get the average of the 6 quizzes combined, we could compute the sum of the first 3 quizzes and the sum of the next 3 quizzes, and then divide by 6.

    Sum of the first 3 quizzes = average × number of the quizzes = 78 × 3 = 234

    Sum of the last 3 quizzes = average × number of the quizzes = 88 × 3 = 264

    Finally, The average of all 6 quizzes = Total sum of all 6 quizzes divided by the total number of quizzes:

    $$\frac{234 + 264}{6} = 83$$

    However, you'd be well advised for time consideration to perform the calculation by taking the average of her first 3 and last 3 quizzes $= \dfrac{78 + 88}{2} = 83$.

12. **(D)** The mean depends on the sum of the values, so its value will change if one of the numbers in the set is different. The median is 33 and unchanged because both 39 and 99 are greater than 33. There is no mode in either case. Therefore, the median and the mode are unaffected.

13. **(D)** This is a permutation problem since the order matters. Use the formula

    $$P(5,5) = \frac{5!}{(5-5)!} = \frac{5!}{0!}$$
    $$= 5 \times 4 \times 3 \times 2 \times 1$$
    $$= 120.$$

14. **(D)** This is a permutation problem since the order of numbers matters. Use the formula

    $$P(10,7) = \frac{10!}{(10-7)!} = \frac{10!}{3!}$$
    $$= 10 \times 9 \times 8 \times \ldots \times 4$$
    $$= 604,800.$$

15. **(C)** This is a combination problem since the order of toppings does not matter. Use the formula

    $$C(12,3) = \frac{12!}{(12-3)!3!} = \frac{12!}{9!3!}$$
    $$= \frac{12 \times 11 \times 10}{3 \times 2 \times 1} = 220.$$

16. **(C)** This is a permutation problem since order matters. Use the formula

    $$P(8,8) = \frac{8!}{(8-8)!} = \frac{8!}{0!} = \frac{8!}{1} = 8!$$
    $$= 8 \times 7 \times 6 \times 5 \times 4 \times 3 \times 2 \times 1$$
    $$= 40,320.$$

17. **(D)** The number of students who passed the test equals the number of students who scored a 6 plus the number of students who scored above a 6, which is $2 + 4 + 5 + 3 + 2 = 16$.

18. **(B)** Only choice B shows one data point over the 1, indicated that all other nine data points are greater than 1

Chapter 20
Inequalities

Given two different real numbers, one of them must be smaller than the other. The "less than" symbol " $<$ " means that the number to the left of the symbol is smaller than the number to the right of the symbol. For example, $5 < 7$ means in math, 5 is less than 7. The "greater than" symbol, " $>$ " means that the number to the left is greater than the number to the right. Think of a hungry crocodile's jaws opening toward the larger quantity. This mental imagery can help you decide whether the statement $11 > 8$ is true or false. This statement means 11 is greater than 8, which is a true statement.

Other true statements would be:
- $4 < 5$
- $6.5 > 6.45$
- $4 + 3 < 1 + 7$
- $-5 < -2$

Inequality symbols also include $\leq$, which means smaller than or equal to, and $\geq$, which means greater than or equal to.

Inequality symbols can be used to compare variables as well.

For example, the statement $x < 6$, would be true for $x = 2$, since $2 < 6$, but it would be false if we choose $x = 7$, since $7 < 6$ is a false statement.

Example 1. Given that $x \geq -3$, which of the following values of x would make the statement false?

Choose all answers that apply.

[A] 0
[B] -1
[C] -3
[D] -4
[E] -5

Answer: D, E. -4 and -5 are smaller than -3, and therefore the statement $-4 \geq -3$ is false and $-5 \geq -3$ is also false. In **C**, $-3 \geq -3$, so the statement would hold true for -3.

Number Lines

Let us refresh our memory on number lines. A **number line** can be defined as a straight line with numbers placed at equal intervals along its length. A number line can be extended infinitely in any direction and is usually represented horizontally.

Numbers increase from left to right. For example, the number 6 is to the right of the number 5 on the number line below, because 6 is greater than 5. Negative numbers are smaller than positive numbers, so they are located to the left of zero on the number line, while positive numbers are located to the right of zero, as shown below.

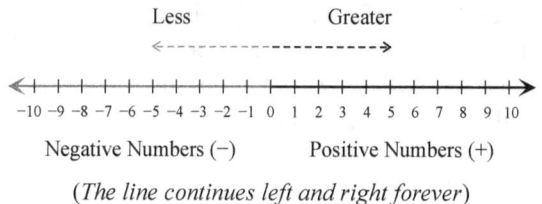

Negative Numbers (−)   Positive Numbers (+)

(*The line continues left and right forever*)

An inequality can be drawn on a number line.

- An empty dot on a number line means that the number at the dot is not included in the inequality statement.
- A closed dot means that the number on the dot is included in the inequality statement. An arrow on the drawing means that the numbers continue infinitely in the direction of the arrow.

Example 2. Draw a number line that states that $x \geq -3$.

Solution:

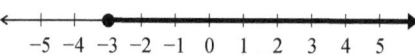

Here we see that the number -3 is included with a filled in dot, and a line with an arrow extends to the right of it, which means that all real numbers greater than -3 satisfy the inequality.

Example 3. Draw a number line that states that $x > -3$.

Solution:

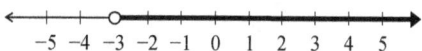

This time we see the same graph except that -3 has a hole on it. This means that -3 is not a point on the graph, and that is because if $x = -3$, the inequality would be false.

Example 4. Draw a number line that states that $x \neq 4$.

Solution:

This time we see all real numbers are on the graph except 4, because the statement states that x is not equal to 4.

Example 5. Draw a number line that states that $-1 < x \leq 4$.

Solution:

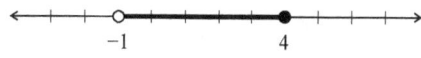

The statement asks for values that are greater than -1 and smaller than or equal to 4. The number line shown above shows the values of x that satisfy the inequality. Notice that the values of x are larger than -1 AND smaller than or equal to 4 at the same time. When two conditions are true at once, a line is drawn between two points.

Example 6. Draw a number line that states that $x < -3$ or $x \geq 4$.

Solution:

The question asks for values of x that are smaller than -3 OR greater than or equal to 4. Notice that a number smaller than -3 cannot be greater than 4 at the same time. The statement that includes OR means that the arrows point in opposite directions, away from each other.

Solving an Inequality Algebraically

We can also solve an inequality algebraically. For example, if $3x < 6$, divide both sides of the inequality by 2 to get $x < 2$.

$$2x - 3 < 8$$

Example 7. Which of the following values of x satisfies the inequality above?

(A) 5
(B) 6
(C) 7
(D) 8
(E) 9

Answer: A. Add 3 to both sides of the inequality to get $2x < 11$, then divide by 2 to get $x < \frac{11}{2}$ or $x < 5.5$. Of all answer choices, choice **A**, 5, is the only number less than 5.5.

Multiplying an Inequality by a Negative Number

When multiplying or dividing an inequality by a negative number, the inequality sign flips.

For example, if $-x < 3$, then $x > -3$. Here we multiplied both sides of the inequality by -1, and then flipped the sign.

Why does the sign flip? Look at our example $-x < 3$. What values can we plug into x? If we were to transform the inequality to $x < -3$, then that would imply that -4, which is smaller than -3 would satisfy the initial condition. Is $-(-4) < 3$? $-(-4) = 4$ which is greater than 3, not smaller than 3. So not flipping the sign will yield a false statement. Therefore, remember to flip the inequality sign when multiplying or dividing by a negative number.

$$-3x + 5 \geq 7$$

Example 8. Which of the following numbers would satisfy the given inequality above?

(A) -0.72
(B) -0.56
(C) -0.14
(D) 0
(E) 0.03

Answer: A. Solve as follows: Subtract 5 from both sides of the inequality to obtain $-3x \geq 2$. Then divide both sides of the inequality by -3 to obtain $x \leq -\frac{2}{3}$. Of all answer choices, choice **A**, -0.72 is the only number that is smaller than $-\frac{2}{3}$ (or -0.667).

Chapter 20: Inequalities

Inequality Problems Involving Logical Reasoning

Some problems on the GED Math test may involve inequalities but also test logical reasoning, as the following two problems demonstrate.

Example 9. A student claimed that if $x + y \geq 8$, then $\frac{2x}{y} < 4$. Which of the following sets of numbers for x and y disprove his claim?

- (A) $x = 4$, $y = 4$
- (B) $x = -4$, $y = 20$
- (C) $x = 5$, $y = 3$
- (D) $x = 9$, $y = 1$
- (E) $x = -5$, $y = -2$

Answer: D. We want numbers for x and y that satisfy the first inequality but don't satisfy the second inequality. The best way to solve this problem is to plug in numbers.

For choice **A**, we have $4 + 4 = 8$, which satisfies the first inequality, while $\frac{2 \cdot 4}{4} = 2 < 4$, and therefore also satisfies the second inequality. Therefore, choice **A** is incorrect.

For choice **B**, $-4 + 20 = 16 > 8$, and therefore satisfy the first inequality. $\frac{2 \cdot (-4)}{20} = -\frac{2}{5} < 4$, so those values also satisfy the second inequality, and therefore choice **B** is incorrect. For choice **C**, $5 + 3 = 8 \geq 8$, and $\frac{2 \cdot 5}{3} = \frac{10}{3} < 4$, and therefore these values also satisfy the second inequality. Therefore, choice **C** is incorrect.

In choice **D**, $9 + 1 = 10 \geq 8$, and therefore these values satisfy the first inequality. $\frac{2 \cdot 9}{1} = 18$, which is not smaller than 4, and therefore the second inequality is not satisfied. Choice **D** is thus correct.

In choice **E** $-5 + (-2) = -7$ is not greater than 8, and therefore does not satisfy the first inequality. The statement said that if $x + y \geq 8$, a second condition would result, but since the numbers for x and y don't satisfy the first condition, the statement does not contradict the student's claim.

Example 10. John claimed that if $x^2 \geq y$, then it is possible that $x < y$. Which of the following set of numbers for x and y proves his claim?

- (A) $x = -2$, $y = -1$
- (B) $x = -2$, $y = 5$
- (C) $x = -1$, $y = 2$
- (D) $x = -3$, $y = 18$
- (E) John is wrong for all values of x and y.

Answer: A. Plug in the values of x and y in each answer choice. Notice that all choices satisfy the second inequality ($x < y$), so we only need to make sure that one of the statements in an answer choice satisfies the first inequality, $x^2 \geq y$. Remember that when a negative number is squared, a positive number is obtained because a negative times a negative is a positive.

For choice **A**, we have $(-2)^2 = 4$, while $y = -1$. 4 is greater than -1, which satisfies the first inequality, and so choice **A** is correct.

In choice **B**, $(-2)^2 = 4$, but 4 is smaller than 5, so this does not satisfy the first inequality.

In choice **C**, $(-1)^2 = 1$, which is not greater to or equal to 2, so choice **C** is incorrect as well.

In choice **D**. $(-3)^2 = 9$, which is not greater than 18, so choice **D** is incorrect.

Quadratic Inequalities

There may be a problem on your test that involves a quadratic inequality such as the following two examples.

Example 11: Solve the following inequality for x: $3x^2 - 26 \geq 22$.

- (A) $-4 \leq x \leq 4$
- (B) $x \leq 4$
- (C) $x \geq 4$ or $x \leq -4$
- (D) $x \geq -4$
- (E) $x \geq 4$

Answer: C. First add 26 to both sides of the inequality to obtain $3x^2 \geq 48$. Divide both sides of the inequality by 3 to obtain $x^2 \geq 16$. This means that $x \geq 4$ or $x \leq -4$. The line graph below shows the solution set for x.

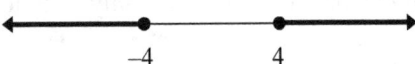

You can check this by plugging in numbers. Try plugging in a -5, which is smaller than -4, into x^2. You have $(-5)^2 = 25 > 16$.

Example 12. Solve the following inequality for x: $3x^2 - 1 \leq 74$.

- (A) $-4 \leq x \leq 4$
- (B) $-5 \leq x \leq 5$
- (C) $x \leq 5$
- (D) $x \geq 5$ or $x \leq -5$
- (E) $x \geq -5$

Answer: B. Add 1 to both sides, then divide by 3 to get, $x^2 \leq 25$. Therefore $-5 \leq x \leq 5$. The line graph below show the solution set for x.

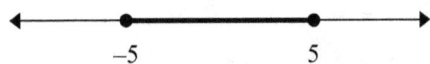

Try plugging in a value smaller than -5 into x^2, like -6. -6 squared is positive 36, which violates the inequality, and therefore $x = -6$ is not included in the solution. Try -4. $(-4)^2 = 16$, which does satisfy the inequality because $16 < 25$.

Chapter 20: Inequalities

Practice Problems

1. Which of the following number lines shows that $-4 < x < 3$?

   (A)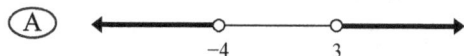

   (B)

   (C)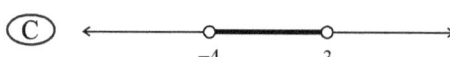

   (D)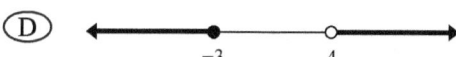

   (E)

3. Which of the following number lines shows that $x > 4$ or $x < 0$?

   (A)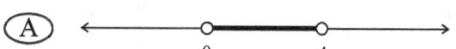

   (B)

   (C)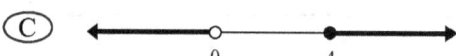

   (D)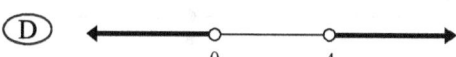

   (E)

2. Which of the following number lines shows that $-1 \leq x < 5$?

   (A)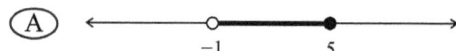

   (B)

   (C)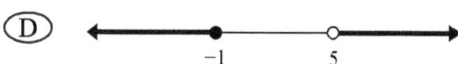

   (D)

   (E)

4. Which of the following number lines shows that $x \neq 0$?

   (A)

   (B)

   (C)

   (D)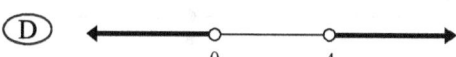

   (E)

5. Which of the following number lines shows that $x > 4$, $x \neq 6$?

   A

   B

   C

   D

   E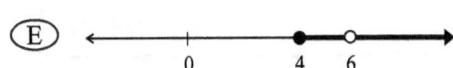

7. Which of the following values of x does not satisfy the inequality below:

   $$2 < 3x - 1 \leq 5$$

   A) 1.25
   B) 1.66
   C) 1.75
   D) 2
   E) 2.25

6. Which of the following number lines shows that $2x - 1 > 3$?

   A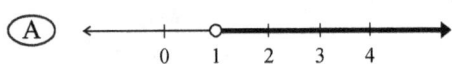

   B

   C

   D

   E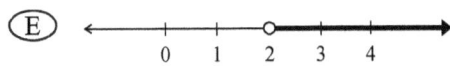

8. Which of the following expressions is equivalent to:

   $$-5 \leq 3x + 4 < 7$$

   A) $-\dfrac{1}{3} \leq 3x < 3$
   B) $-3 \leq x < 11$
   C) $-3 \leq x < 1$
   D) $-3 \leq x < 3$
   E) $x < -3$ or $x > 1$

Chapter 20: Inequalities

9. If $\dfrac{x}{y} > 2$ and $x > -2$, which of the following sets of values for x and y satisfy both inequalities?

   (A) $x = -3, y = \dfrac{1}{4}$

   (B) $x = -6, y = -2$

   (C) $x = -1, y = -1$

   (D) $x = -1, y = -\dfrac{1}{3}$

   (E) $x = 4, y = 6$

10. Solve for x: $6x^2 - 34 \geq 20$

    (A) $x \geq 3$ or $x \leq -3$

    (B) $-3 \leq x \leq 3$

    (C) $x \geq 3$

    (D) $x \geq \dfrac{7}{3}$

    (E) $x \leq -\dfrac{7}{3}$ or $x \geq \dfrac{7}{3}$

11. Which of the following values of x satisfies the inequality below?

    $$x^2 + 5x + 6 \leq 0$$

    (A) -4

    (B) -2

    (C) -1

    (D) 0

    (E) 1

12. Darlene claims that if $\dfrac{3x}{y} > 6$, then $-3x > -6y$. Which of the following sets of values for x and y satisfy both inequalities?

    (A) $x = -3, y = 1$

    (B) $x = 3, y = 1$

    (C) $x = \dfrac{1}{2}, y = -\dfrac{1}{2}$

    (D) All of the above

    (E) None of the above

13. Solve for x: $-\dfrac{3}{2}x - 5 \geq 7$

    (A) $x \geq -8$

    (B) $x \leq -8$

    (C) $-\dfrac{4}{3} \leq x \leq \dfrac{4}{3}$

    (D) $-8 \leq x \leq 8$

    (E) $x \leq -18$

14. Solve for x: $3x^2 + 14 < 62$

    (A) $x < -4$ or $x > 4$

    (B) $-4 < x < 4$

    (C) $x < 4$

    (D) $x > -4$

    (E) $x < 16$

15. Solve the following inequality for x: $x^2 > -1$

    (A) $x > -1$

    (B) $-1 < x < 1$

    (C) $x > -1$ or $x < 1$

    (D) $x < -1$ or $x > 1$

    (E) All real numbers

16. Solve the following inequality for x: $2x^2 - 4 < -36$

    (A) $x > -4$

    (B) $x < -4$

    (C) $-4 < x < 4$

    (D) $x > 4$ or $x < -4$

    (E) There is no real solution.

Answers to Practice Problems

1. **(C)** The solution shows numbers between -4 and 3. The points -4 and 3 are empty holes because they are not included in the solution.

2. **(E)** The number line shows points between -1 and 5, including -1 (with a dark point shown) but not including 5 (with an empty hole shown).

3. **(D)** The line number shows the solution for numbers that are smaller than 0, not including 0, and numbers greater than 4, not including 4.

4. **(A)** The number line shows all numbers are included in the solution except 0, shown by an empty hole.

5. **(B)** The solution shows all numbers greater than 4, except 6.

6. **(E)** $2x - 1 > 3$, therefore $2x > 4$ and $x > 2$. The solution shows all numbers greater than 2.

7. **(E)** Add 1 to all sides of the given inequality to obtain $3 < 3x \leq 6$. Then divide by 3 to obtain $1 < x \leq 2$. So x includes all numbers greater than 1 and smaller or equal to 2. The only answer choice that is outside that range is choice **E**, 2.25.

8. **(C)** Subtract 4 from both sides of the inequality to obtain $-9 \leq 3x < 3$. Then divide by 3 to obtain $-3 \leq x < 1$.

9. **(D)** Plug in the values for x and y given in the answer choices and see whether the inequality holds. Start with the first inequality. **A** is not true according to the first inequality, **B** is true, **C** is false, **D** is true, and **E** is false. Therefore, we need to test inequality 2 for only choices **B** and **D**. For the second inequality, **B** is false, and **D** is true. Therefore, choice **D** is the only choice that satisfies both conditions.

10. **(A)** $6x^2 - 34 \geq 20$, add 34 to both sides to obtain: $6x^2 \geq 54$. Then divide by 6: $x^2 \geq 9$. Therefore, $x \geq 3$ or $x \leq -3$.

11. **(B)** Plug in the five answer choices:
    For Choice **A**, you have
    $(-4)^2 + 5(-4) + 6 = 16 - 20 + 6 = 2 > 0$.
    False. In choice **B**, you get
    $(-2)^2 + 5(-2) + 6 = 4 - 10 + 6 = 0$. True.
    For **C**, $(-1)^2 + 5(-1) + 6 > 0$. False.
    For **D**, $(0)^2 + 5(0) + 6 > 0$. False.
    For **E**, $(1)^2 + 5(1) + 6 > 0$. False.

12. **(E)** You can plug in the numbers for x and y from each of the first three answer choices, and then see that none satisfies both inequalities, so the answer is **E**. Notice that Darlene forgot to flip the inequality sign, and that is why the first 3 answer choices are incorrect.

13. **(B)** $-\frac{3}{2}x - 5 \geq 7$. Add 5 to both sides to get $-\frac{3}{2}x \geq 12$. Multiply each side of the inequality by $\frac{2}{3}$ to get $-x \geq 12 \cdot \frac{2}{3} = 8$. Multiply both sides of the inequality by -1 and flip the sign to get: $x \leq -8$.

14. **(B)** Subtract 14 from both sides of the inequality to obtain $3x^2 < 48$. Divide by 3 to obtain $x^2 < 16$. Taking the square root of both sides we get $-4 < x < 4$.

15. **(E)** When any real number is squared, the result is always either zero or positive, and certainly larger than -1. Therefore, we can plug in any number into x to make x^2 larger than -1. And so the answer is **E**, all real numbers.

16. **(E)** Add 4 to both sides to obtain: $2x^2 < -32$. Divide both sides to obtain $x^2 < -16$. Since the smallest number x^2 can be is zero, the inequality has no real solution.

Chapter 21
Geometry in the Coordinate Plane

The **Coordinate Plane**, also known as the **Cartesian Plane**, is a space that denotes each precise point uniquely (a point being a zero dimensional "shape," as defined in chapter 13 on lines), along two axes. You have probably seen an example of coordinate geometry in algebra, where points on an *x-y* graph form a line. In the case of real numbers and the Cartesian plane, each point must be assigned an independent variable (often "*x*") and a dependent variable (often "*y*"), although any letter would be fine to use, as often is the case in physical sciences. Exactly one ordered pair of numbers (*x*, *y*) names a given point in the plane. We will use *x* and *y* for the rest of the chapter. All points on the plane are centered around the origin, with the coordinates (0, 0), and sometimes called "*O*," for "origin".

In coordinate geometry, the *y*-axis runs vertically, while the *x*-axis runs horizontally. Through these two axes, the plane is divided into four quadrants, I, II, III, and IV. We see what the coordinate plane looks like above, with two points, A and B, with coordinates (6, 3) and (−3, 1), respectively. Also note the standard is that "up" and "right" are positive directions and "down" and "left" are negative.

Let's do some examples to familiarize ourselves with the coordinate plane:

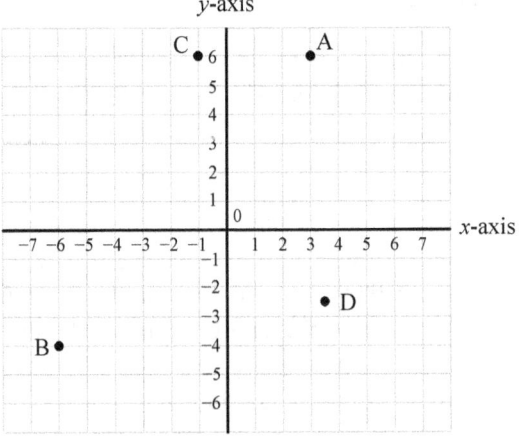

Figure 2. Four points A, B, C, D in the coordinate plane.

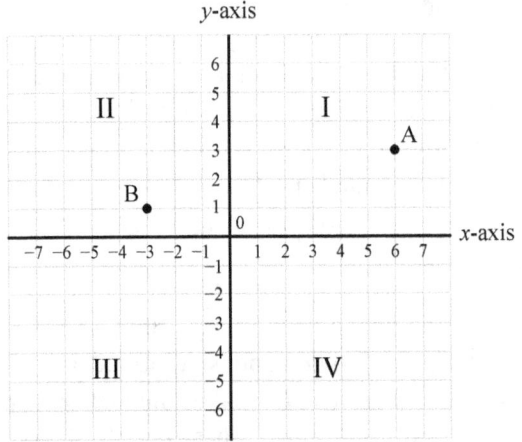

Figure 1. Cartesian plane showing all four quadrants, and both the y-axis and x-axis, and points A and B.

Chapter 21: Geometry in the Coordinate Plane

Example 1. In Figure 2, in which quadrant does point C lie?

- (A) I
- (B) II
- (C) III
- (D) IV
- (E) V

Answer: B. According to the labeling in Figure 1, we can see that point C lies in quadrant II.

Example 2. In Figure 2, what are the coordinates for point A?

- (A) (3, 7)
- (B) (6, 3)
- (C) (3, 6)
- (D) (−1, 6)
- (E) (2, 6)

Answer: C. Remember that the x coordinate is always named first. Point A lies at 3 on the x-axis and 6 on the y-axis, making its coordinate (3, 6).

Example 3. What are the coordinates of point D?

- (A) (3, −2)
- (B) (3, −3)
- (C) (4, −2)
- (D) (4, −3)
- (E) None of the above

Answer: E. Point D is found in the middle of one of the graph's squares, as opposed to on the corner. This means that the coordinates for D on both the x- and y-axes are not whole numbers, which is okay because coordinates do not have to be integers. Therefore, the correct answer is "None of the above."

Points on a coordinate plane can be connected together to form line segments.

Slope of a Line

When dealing with lines in the coordinate plane, one must become familiar with the **slope** of the line, which is a term that you are probably familiar with from algebra. The **slope** of a line corresponds to the **rate of change of the y-axis over the rate of change of the x-axis**. It can also be considered the "steepness" of a line. A flat, horizontal line has a slope of zero, because there is no steepness. A vertical line has no slope, an "undefined" slope, or sometimes, a slope of "infinity," because it is "infinitely steep." All other lines will have some numerical value to their slope and can be either positive or negative.

As an example, if there are two points on the coordinate plane, we can calculate the slope as $\frac{y_2 - y_1}{x_2 - x_1}$, where (x_1, y_1) and (x_2, y_2) are two points on the line. Using points (6, 5) and (1, 2), the slope is: $\frac{5 - 2}{6 - 1}$, which gives a slope of $\frac{3}{5}$. We can also do this subtraction the opposite way, with $\frac{2 - 5}{1 - 6} = \frac{-3}{-5}$, which also yields $\frac{3}{5}$. Either way, the slope of this line is $\frac{3}{5}$ and is positive. A line whose y-coordinate increases when going from the left side of the line to the right side has a positive slope. A line whose y-coordinate decreases when going from the left side of the line to the right side has a negative slope. The types of slopes are shown below, in Figure 3.

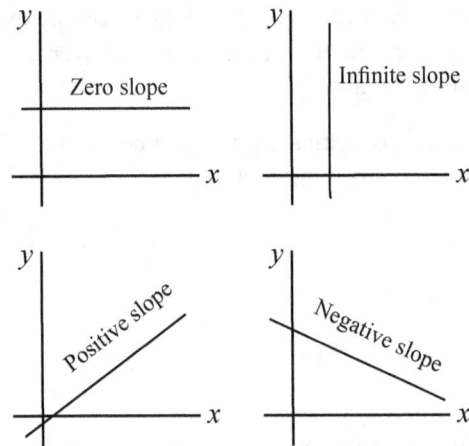

Figure 3. Types of slopes in the coordinate plane.

Examples 4-7 pertain to Figure 4 below.

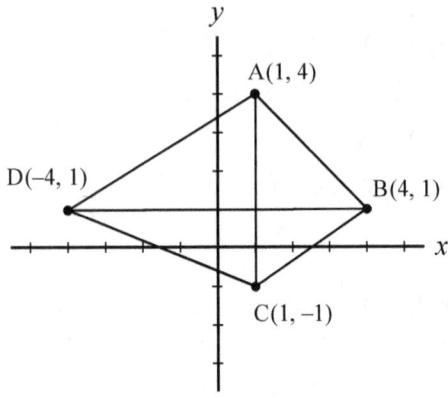

Figure 4. Lines in a coordinate plane between four points, A, B, C, D.

Distance Between Two Points

In order to find the **distance between two points**, one must employ the use of the Pythagorean theorem, first introduced in chapter 14 on angles and triangles. One can think of the distance between two lines as the hypotenuse of a triangle, like so:

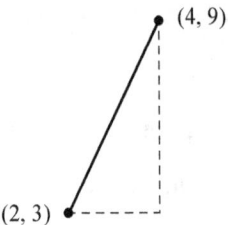

Let's say that two points, (4, 9) and (2, 3), exist on the coordinate plane. To find the distance between the two, we want to find the hypotenuse, which would mean finding the square root of the sum of the change in x, squared, and the change in y, squared, where the symbol Δ, pronounced "delta," signifies a "change in." More simply, in this instance it would be:

$$d = \sqrt{(\Delta x)^2 + (\Delta y)^2}, \text{ or } \sqrt{(4-2)^2 + (9-3)^2}$$

This yields a distance of $\sqrt{2^2 + 6^2} = \sqrt{40}$, or approximately 6.32.

Example 4. In the above image, what is the slope of $\overline{AC}$?

(A) −1
(B) 0
(C) 0.5
(D) 1
(E) Undefined

Answer: E. In the above figure, $\overline{AC}$ is a vertical line, which means that the slope is infinite, or "undefined."

Example 5. What is the slope of $\overline{AB}$?

(A) −1
(B) 0
(C) 1
(D) 2
(E) Undefined

Answer: A. By using the "change in *y* over change in *x*" method, we see that the slope of this line is $\frac{4-1}{1-4}$, which simplifies to $\frac{3}{-3}$, or -1.

Example 6. Which of the following statements is true?

Choose all answers that apply:

[A] The slope of $\overline{BD}$ is undefined.

[B] The slope of $\overline{AD}$ is negative.

[C] The distance between *B* and *D* is 8.

[D] The slope of $\overline{AB}$ is negative.

[E] The slope of $\overline{CB}$ is positive.

Answer: C, D, E. In choice **A**, the slope of BD is zero. In choice **B**, the slope of AD is positive. In choice **C**, we can see that the difference between the *x*-coordinates is 8 because $4 - (-4) = 8$. In this case the change in *y* values is zero. We can use the Pythagorean theorem to calculate the distance between these points, with $\Delta x = 8$ and $\Delta y = 0$: $\sqrt{8^2 + 0^2} = \sqrt{64} = 8$. We can tell from looking at the image that $\overline{AD}$ has a positive slope. We can even calculate it: $\frac{4-1}{1-(-4)} = \frac{3}{5}$, which is positive.

Example 7. What is the distance between points A and B?

(A) 3
(B) 3.5
(C) 4
(D) 4.2
(E) 5

Answer: D. Using the equation for the length of a line (or distance between two points), we see that the distance equals:

$$\sqrt{(1-4)^2 + (4-1)^2} = \sqrt{(-3)^2 + 3^2} = \sqrt{18}$$

or approximately 4.2.

Midpoint of Two Points on a Line

The **midpoint** is as it sounds–it is the "middle" of the line segment. The midpoint is quite simple to calculate, by using the equation

$$M = \left(\frac{x_1 + x_2}{2}, \frac{y_1 + y_2}{2}\right)$$

For line segment $\overline{BC}$ in Figure 5 where point B has the coordinates (2, −5) and point C has the coordinates (4, 2), the midpoint for the *x*-coordinate is: $\frac{2+4}{2} = 3$, and the midpoint for the *y*-coordinate is: $\frac{-5+2}{2} = -1.5$. Therefore, the midpoint is (3, −1.5).

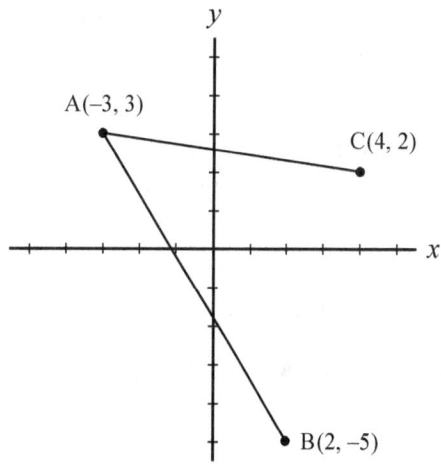

Figure 5. Points A, B, and C on a coordinate plane

Example 8. What is the midpoint of the line that connects points A and B?

- (A) $(-1, -2)$
- (B) $(-2, -2)$
- (C) $(-1, -3)$
- (D) $(-0.5, -1)$
- (E) $(0, 0)$

Answer: D. By using the equation to calculate the midpoint of a line, we see that the x-coordinate is $\dfrac{-3+2}{2} = -0.5$, and that the y-coordinate is $\dfrac{3-5}{2} = -1$.

Y-intercept

Calculating the *y*-intercept of a line is an important part of coordinate geometry as well, and is usually first taught in 7th grade math or pre-algebra. The *y*-intercept is the point where the line crosses the *y*-axis. This can be calculated in one of two ways: looking at the graph and seeing where the line crosses the *y*-axis, or if there is no graph shown, by using the equation

$$y = mx + b$$

where x and y are the coordinates of some point on the line, m is the slope and b is the *y*-intercept (m and b are used by universal convention).

For example, to calculate the *y*-intercept for a line that contains the point $(2, 3)$ with a slope of 1, use the equation $y = mx + b$. We know that the slope, m is 1, so we have

$$y = (1)x + b = x + b$$

Now we plug in the point $(2, 3)$ to get

$$3 = 2 + b$$

Subtracting 2 from both sides of the equation, we get $b = 1$, and therefore the *y*-intercept is 1.

Example 9. In Figure 5, what is the *y*-intercept of $\overline{AB}$?

- (A) -2
- (B) $-\dfrac{9}{5}$
- (C) $-\dfrac{8}{5}$
- (D) $-\dfrac{7}{6}$
- (E) $-\dfrac{6}{5}$

Answer: B. First, we must calculate the slope of this line. Based on the equation previously mentioned, we know that the slope can be calculated by using the coordinates of points A and B. The slope is

$$m = \frac{3-(-5)}{-3-2} = \frac{8}{-5} = -\frac{8}{5}$$

We can then plug either point A or B into the equation $y = mx + b$ to calculate b. Let's use the point A:

$$y = -\frac{8}{5}x + b$$

$$3 = -\frac{8}{5}(-3) + b$$

$$3 = \frac{24}{5} + b$$

$$b = 3 - \frac{24}{5} = \frac{15}{5} - \frac{24}{5} = -\frac{9}{5}$$

Example 10. In Figure 5, what is the *y*-intercept of $\overline{AC}$?

- (A) $\dfrac{10}{7}$
- (B) 2
- (C) $\dfrac{15}{7}$
- (D) 2.5
- (E) $\dfrac{18}{7}$

Answer: E. In the same way that we calculated the slope in the previous problem, we divide the change in y by the change in x. This becomes:

$$m = \frac{3-2}{-3-4} = -\frac{1}{7}$$

We can now use the equation $y = mx + b$, and plug in either point A or C. Let's use C, which has the coordinates (4, 2). Now, we have:

$$y = -\frac{1}{7}x + b$$
$$2 = -\frac{1}{7}(4) + b$$
$$2 = -\frac{4}{7} + b$$
$$b = 2 + \frac{4}{7}$$
$$b = \frac{14}{7} + \frac{4}{7} = \frac{18}{7}$$

Graphing a Line

A question on the GED Math exam may ask you to choose a graph that matches an equation or choose an equation that matches a graph. For example, if the equation $y = 3x - 2$ is given, you should be able to graph it. Remember the y-intercept occurs when x is 0, in this case, −2, and then use the slope, in this case, +3, to draw another point. Once you have two points, you can connect the points with a line. The line is the graph of the equation.

Let's look at an example and graph the equation $y = 3x - 2$. We start with the y-intercept, −2, and plot a point at (0, −2). We look at the slope, 3. $3 = \frac{3}{1}$, which means you go up 3 units, then go right one unit, like so:

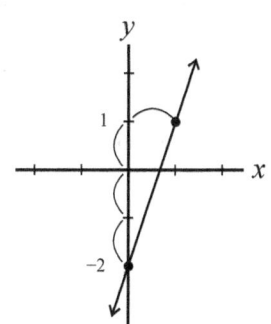

Example 11. Which of the following is the graph of $y = -\frac{1}{3}x + 4$?

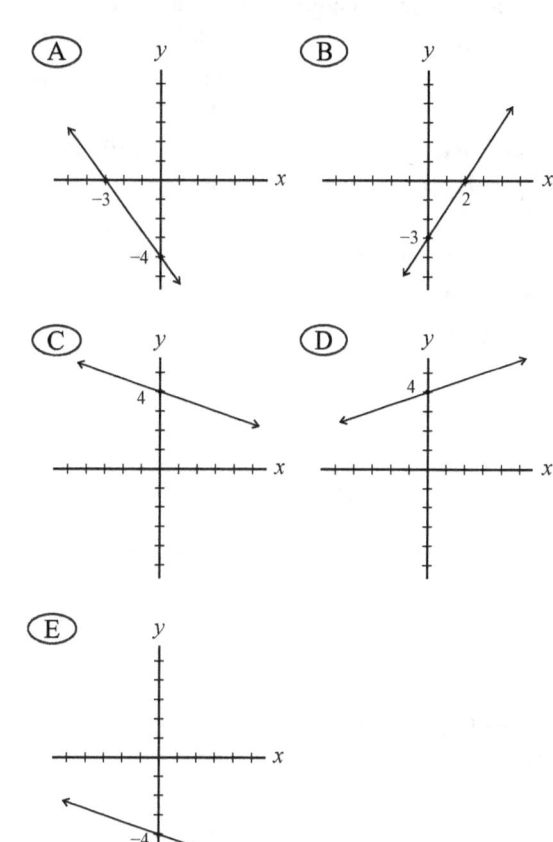

Answer: C. Start with the y-intercept of 4 at (0, 4). Go down one unit and across 3 units to the right as shown below.

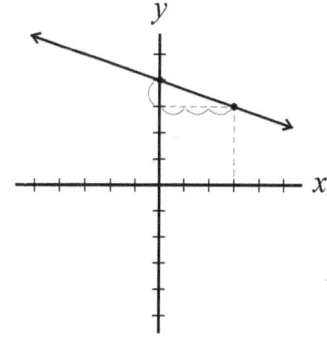

Example 12. Graph the equation: $3x + 4y = 12$

Solution: There is a neat trick you can do to graph a graph in the form $ax + by = c$ as in this example. Here $a = 3$, $b = 4$ and $c = 12$. If you plug in a zero for x, you get $3(0) + 4y = 12$, which means $y = 3$, so you have point $(0, 3)$ on the graph. If you plug a zero into y, you get $3x + 4(0) = 12$, so $x = 4$, giving you the point $(4, 0)$. You can now connect points $(0, 3)$ and $(4, 0)$ with a line, which will give you the graph of the equation of the line.

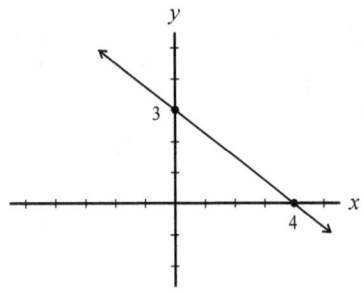

Example 13: Which of the following is the graph of the equation $-2x + 5y = 10$?

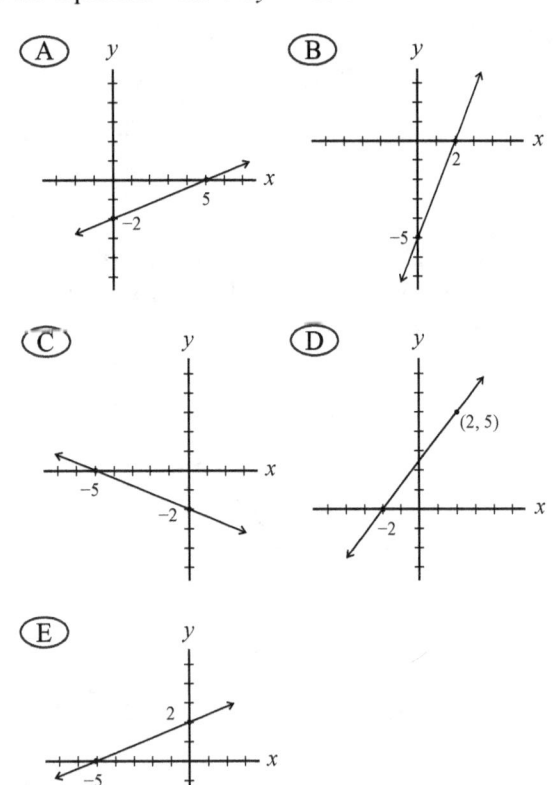

Answer: E. Plug in a 0 into x to get $-2(0) + 5y = 10$, so $y = 2$, to give you point $(0, 2)$. Now plug in a 0 into y to get $-2x + 5(0) = 10$, so $x = -5$ to give you the point $(-5, 0)$. Now connect the two points with a line.

Graphing Inequalities

As you now see, equations can be graphed in two dimensions. Inequalities can also be graphed in 2 dimensions, as long as there are two variables. Take for example the inequality, $y \geq 2x - 3$. The graph is shown below:

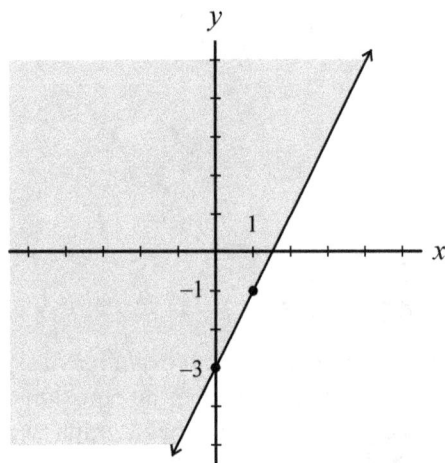

You can see that a solid line is drawn, which is the graph of $y = 2x - 3$, but unlike with an equation, here shading is inserted above the line. The shaded area indicates a region where $y > 2x - 3$. If you are not sure whether to shade above the line or below the line, plug the point $(0, 0)$ into the inequality and see if the inequality holds true. In this case check whether $0 > 2(0) - 3$. This is a true statement, and therefore the point $(0, 0)$ is in the shaded region.

Chapter 21: Geometry in the Coordinate Plane

Example 14. Which of the following is the graph of $y \leq -3x + 4$?

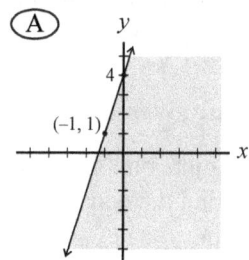

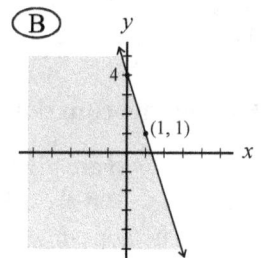

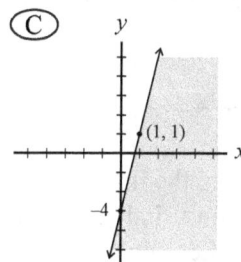

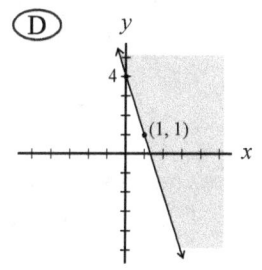

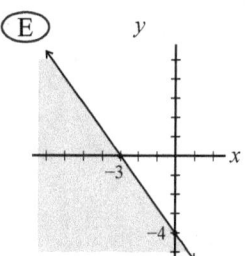

Answer: B. First draw the graph of the equation $y = -3x + 4$. Start with the y-intercept of 4 and plot the point $(0, 4)$. Then from this point, go down 3 units and across right one unit, then connect the points with a line. Choose point $(0, 0)$. Ask yourself, is $0 < -3(0) + 4$. The answer is yes, so shade the area that includes the origin below the line.

If the inequality does not include the $=$ sign, the solid line is replaced with a dashed line.

The following is the graph of $y > 2x - 3$:

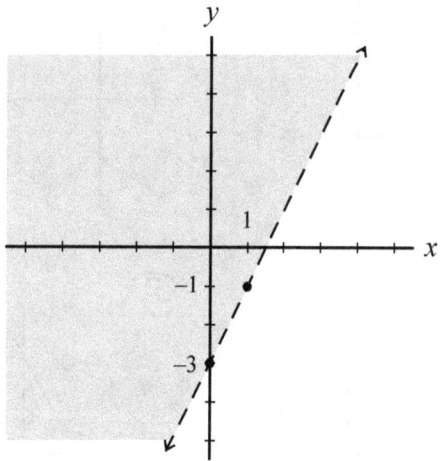

The inequality may be shown with both variables on the same side. For example, the inequality $2x - 3y > 6$ can be graphed. First, start with the equation, $2x - 3y = 6$, by drawing its graph, except draw a dashed line instead of a solid line since it is really an inequality, not an equation. Plug in $x = 0$, so that $2(0) - 3y = 6$, or $y = -2$, then plug in $y = 0$ so that $2x - 3(0) = 6$ or $x = 3$. Plot the points $(0, -2)$ and $(3, 0)$ and then connect them with a dashed line. Then test the point $(0,0)$ and see if it is included in the shaded region. Is $2(0) - 3(0) > 6$? No, so the origin is not included in the shaded region, and you should shade the opposite side of the dashed line:

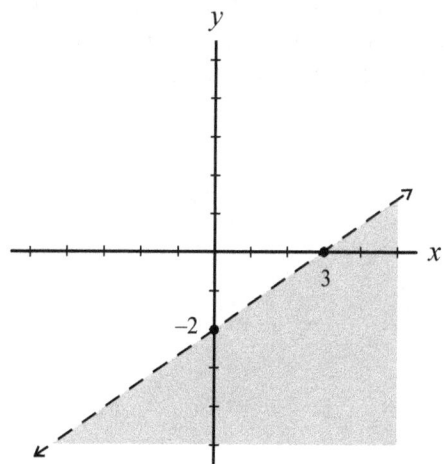

Example 15. Which of the following is the graph of $-5x + 3y \leq 15$?

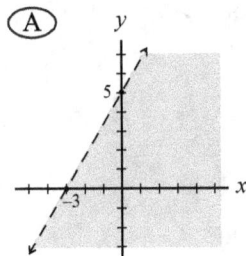
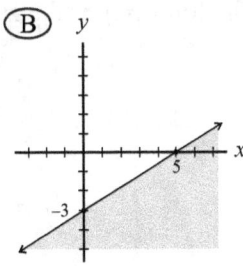
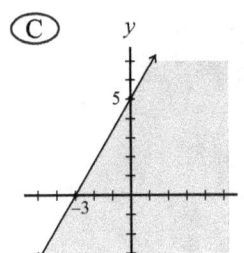
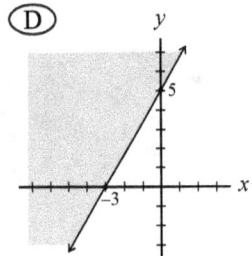
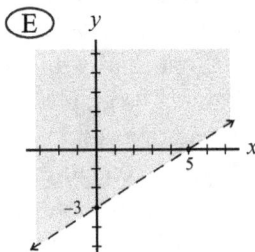

Answer: C. Plug in $x = 0$, so that $y = 5$, so we have point $(0, 5)$. Plug in $y = 0$ to get point $(-3, 0)$. Connect the points with a solid line. Plug in $(0, 0)$ to find that it is included in the shaded region. We find that choice **C** is the correct response. Choice **A** is incorrect because it has a dashed line rather than a solid line.

Finding an Equation of a Line

We can find an equation of a line given: a. two points on the line, b. one point on the line and the slope of a line. Let's see how we can accomplish that.

Finding the equation of a line given two points

Let's say you are given two points on a line, $(3, 4)$ and $(4, 2)$. You are asked to find the equation of the line in slope-intercept form, $y = mx + b$, passing through the two points, where m is the slope and b is the y-intercept. To do so, first find the slope of the line, in this case

$$m = \frac{2-4}{4-3} = \frac{-2}{1} = -2.$$

Now you know the equation of the line is $y = -2x + b$, and we now must find b. Plug in any one of the points given. Let's choose $(3, 4)$. Plug 4 into y and 3 into x to obtain $4 = -2(3) + b, 4 = -6 + b$. Add 6 to both sides of the equation to obtain $b = 10$. Now you know that the equation of the line is $y = -2x + 10$. Done!

Example 16. Find the equation of the line passing through $(3, -4), (5, 3)$.

Ⓐ $y = \frac{2}{7}x + \frac{11}{7}$

Ⓑ $y = \frac{2}{7}x + \frac{103}{2}$

Ⓒ $y = \frac{7}{2}x - \frac{29}{2}$

Ⓓ $y = \frac{7}{2}x + \frac{41}{2}$

Ⓔ $y = -\frac{1}{2}x + \frac{11}{2}$

Chapter 21: Geometry in the Coordinate Plane 243

Answer: C. Find the slope: $\dfrac{3-(-4)}{5-3} = \dfrac{7}{2}$.

Write: $y = \dfrac{7}{2}x + b$. Plug in one of the points, let's choose (5, 3) to get $3 = \dfrac{7}{2}(5) + b$, so $3 = \dfrac{35}{2} + b$. Subtract $\dfrac{35}{2}$ from both sides to get

$$b = 3 - \dfrac{35}{2} = \dfrac{6}{2} - \dfrac{35}{2} = -\dfrac{29}{2}.$$

So we get the equation $y = \dfrac{7}{2}x - \dfrac{29}{2}$.

Example 17. Find the equation of a line passing through (4, 3) and (6, 3)

- (A) $y = -x + 1$
- (B) $y = -1$
- (C) $y = 3$
- (D) $y = -x + 3$
- (E) $y = 4$

Answer: C. Calculate the slope: $\dfrac{3-3}{6-4} = 0$. Then the equation of the line is $y = 0x + b$, so $y = b$. Plug in one point (4, 3) to get $3 = 0 \cdot 4 + b$, so $b = 3$. Therefore, the equation is $y = 3$. This is a horizontal line with a y-intercept of 3.

Finding the equation of a line given a slope and a point.

Example 18. Find the equation of the line with a slope of -4, passing through the point (3, −2).

- (A) $y = -4x + 10$
- (B) $y = -4x + 14$
- (C) $y = -4x - 14$
- (D) $y = -4x - 5$
- (E) $y = -4x + 11$

Answer: A. In this case, part of the work in example 13 is already done for you: Instead of having to first find the slope of the line, the slope is already provided. Therefore, we write $y = -4x + b$. Plug in the point (3, −2), $-2 = -4(3) + b$, so $b = 10$. The equation is $y = -4x + 10$.

Practice Problems

Problems 1-5 pertain to Figure 6 below.

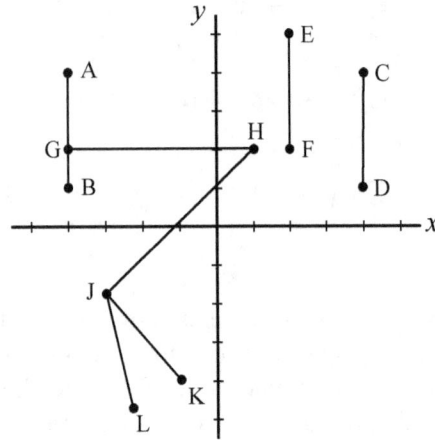

Figure 6. Several lines in the coordinate plane

1. What are the coordinates for point E in the above figure?

   (A) (2, 3)
   (B) (2, 4)
   (C) (2, 5)
   (D) (3, 3)
   (E) (3, 4)

2. Which of the following lines is completely located in the second quadrant of the coordinate plane?

   (A) $\overline{CD}$ and $\overline{EF}$
   (B) $\overline{AB}$ only
   (C) $\overline{JK}$ only
   (D) $\overline{AB}$ and $\overline{GH}$
   (E) None of the lines is in quadrant II.

3. What is the slope of $\overline{GH}$?

   (A) –1
   (B) 0
   (C) 1
   (D) 2
   (E) Undefined

4. Which line segment or segments are completely located in quadrant IV?

   (A) $\overline{AB}$
   (B) $\overline{CD}$ and $\overline{EF}$
   (C) $\overline{JK}$
   (D) $\overline{GB}$
   (E) None of the line segments is in quadrant IV.

5. Which of the following statements about $\overline{HJ}$ is FALSE?

   (A) It travels through the point (–2, –2).
   (B) It travels through the point (0, 1).
   (C) It has a positive slope.
   (D) It travels through the point (–1, 0).
   (E) It travels through quadrants I, II, and

Questions 6-13 pertain to Figure 7 below.

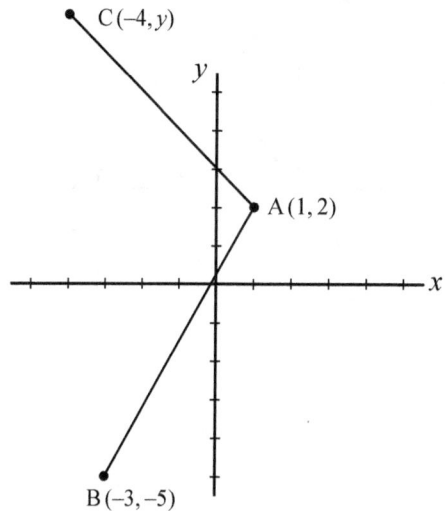

Figure 7. Line segments $\overline{AB}$ and $\overline{AC}$ in the coordinate plane

6. What is the slope of $\overline{AB}$?

    (A) $-\dfrac{7}{4}$

    (B) -1

    (C) 1

    (D) $\dfrac{7}{4}$

    (E) Undefined

7. What is the y-intercept of $\overline{AB}$?

    (A) 0

    (B) $\dfrac{1}{16}$

    (C) $\dfrac{1}{8}$

    (D) $\dfrac{1}{4}$

    (E) $\dfrac{1}{2}$

8. Without doing any calculations, determine the y-intercept of $\overline{AC}$.

    (A) -3

    (B) -2

    (C) 1

    (D) 3

    (E) 5

9. What is the slope of $\overline{AC}$?

    (A) -2

    (B) -1

    (C) 0

    (D) 1

    (E) 2

10. What is the value of y in coordinate point C?

    (A) -8

    (B) -7

    (C) 5

    (D) 6

    (E) 7

11. What is midpoint of $\overline{AB}$?

    A) (1, −1.5)
    B) (−1, −2)
    C) (−1, −1.5)
    D) (−1, −3)
    E) (−1.5, −1)

12. What is the distance between points B and C?

    A) $\sqrt{5}$
    B) $\sqrt{65}$
    C) $\sqrt{143}$
    D) $\sqrt{145}$
    E) $\sqrt{175}$

13. If a line were to be drawn between points B and C, what could be said of its slope?

    A) It would be negative.
    B) It would be 0.
    C) It would be positive.
    D) It would be undefined.
    E) Not enough information to know.

14. Which of the following is the graph of $3x - 6y = 18$?

    A)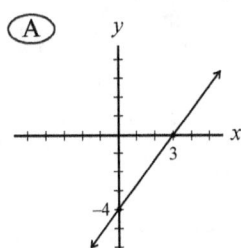
    B)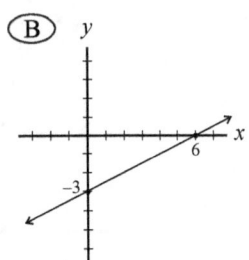
    C)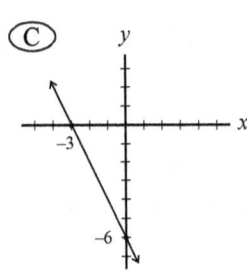
    D)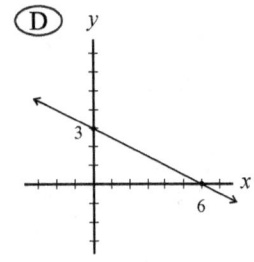
    E)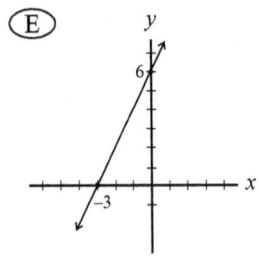

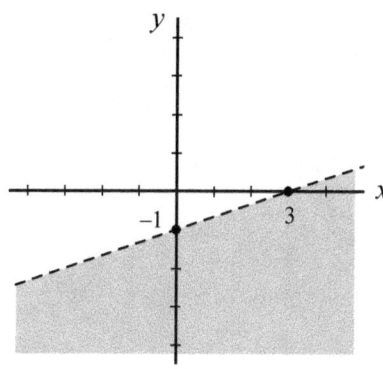

15. The graph shown above shows which of the following inequalities?

    (A) $y \leq \frac{1}{3}x - 1$

    (B) $y \geq \frac{1}{3}x - 1$

    (C) $y < \frac{1}{3}x - 1$

    (D) $y < -\frac{1}{3}x + 1$

    (E) $y < 3x - 1$

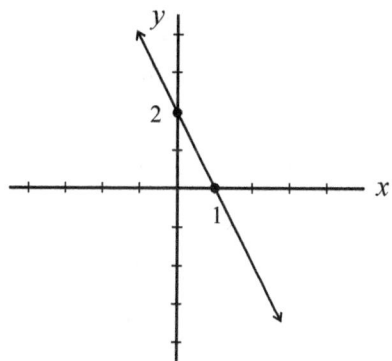

16. What is the equation of the line in the graph below?

    (A) $y = 2x + 2$
    (B) $y = -x + 1$
    (C) $y = -2x + 1$
    (D) $y = x + 2$
    (E) $y = -2x + 2$

17. Find the equation of a line passing through $(-1, 0)$ and $(4, 3)$.

    (A) $y = \frac{3}{5}x + \frac{3}{5}$

    (B) $y = \frac{3}{5}x + \frac{5}{3}$

    (C) $y = \frac{5}{3}x + \frac{3}{5}$

    (D) $y = \frac{5}{3}x + \frac{1}{5}$

    (E) $y = \frac{3}{5}x - \frac{1}{5}$

18. Find the equation of a line passing through $(3, -6)$, and $(-3, 6)$

    (A) $y = -2x$

    (B) $y = -2x - 12$

    (C) $y = -\frac{1}{2}x$

    (D) $y = -\frac{1}{2}x - 3$

    (E) $y = -\frac{1}{2}x + 3$

19. Find the equation of a line passing through the point $(-2, -1)$ with a slope of -1.

    (A) $y = -x + 3$
    (B) $y = -x - 3$
    (C) $y = -x - 1$
    (D) $y = -x - 3$
    (E) $y = -x + 1$

20. Find the equation of a line passing through $(-3, 4)$ with a slope of 0.

   (A) $y = -4$
   (B) $y = -3$
   (C) $y = 4$
   (D) $x = -3$
   (E) $x = 4$

Answers to Practice Problems

1. **(C)** By counting the markings on the *x*- and *y*-axis, we see that point E is 2 units over on the *x*-axis, and 5 units up on the *y*-axis.

2. **(B)** The quadrants start from the positive *x* and positive *y* quadrant, known as quadrant I, and continue in a counterclockwise order, making the top left quadrant the second quadrant, where $\overline{AB}$ lies completely.

3. **(B)** $\overline{GH}$ is a flat line, which means that it has zero slope (no steepness). Therefore, the correct answer is choice **B**.

4. **(E)** Quadrant IV is the bottom right quadrant. There are no line segments that pass through this quadrant.

5. **(A)** $\overline{HJ}$ increases in *y*-value from left to right, meaning that it has a positive slope. Looking at the image, it clearly travels through the points (0, 1) and (−1, 0), as well as through quadrants I, II, and III, so choice **A** is the only false statement.

6. **(D)** The slope of $\overline{AB}$ can be calculated by using the values given for both point A and point B. To find the slope, we first find the change in *y*, which happens to be (2 − (−5)), which equals 7, and divide it by the change in *x*, which is (1 − (−3)), which equals 4. So, the slope for this line is 7/4.

7. **(D)** Using the value of the slope found in the previous problem, 7/4, we can use either point A or point B to plug into the equation of a line, $y = mx + b$ in order to find the value of the *y*-intercept. Let us use point A, which is (1, 2). Plugging these values into the equation, along with the slope, we get:

$$2 = \frac{7}{4}(1) + b$$

Solving for *b*, we get

$$b = 2 - \frac{7}{4}(1) = \frac{8}{4} - \frac{7}{4} = \frac{1}{4}$$

8. **(D)** We can see from the figure that $\overline{AC}$ goes right through the *y*-axis at a value of 3.

9. **(B)** Since we know the *y*-intercept for $\overline{AC}$, (0, 3) and we also have the value for point A, (1, 2) we can use these two points to find the slope, which becomes $\frac{3-2}{0-1} = -1$.

10. **(E)** Now that we know the slope of $\overline{AC}$, we can use it to find the *y*-coordinate of point C. we know that $\frac{\Delta y}{\Delta x} = -1$. We use points (−4, *y*) and (1, 2). Plugging in our values, we get:

$$\frac{2-y}{1-(-4)} = \frac{2-y}{5} = -1$$

Solving for *y* gives, $2 - y = -1 \times 5 = -5$. Therefore, $y = 7$.

11. **(C)** We can calculate the coordinates of the midpoint by adding up the values of *x* and *y* separately, and dividing each by 2. This gives us:

$$x = \frac{1+(-3)}{2} = -1$$

$$\text{and } y = \frac{2+(-5)}{2} = -1.5$$

So, the coordinates for the midpoint of $\overline{AB}$ are (−1, −1.5).

12. **(D)** To calculate the distance, we must think of $\overline{BC}$ as the hypotenuse of a right triangle. Note: this "triangle" does not include the lines $\overline{AB}$ and $\overline{AC}$. Rather, we must use the coordinates for both B and C to calculate this value. From problem 10, we know that the coordinates of point C are $(-4, 7)$, and we already have the point $(-3, -5)$. So, the difference in x coordinates is $-4 - (-3)$, which is equal to -1. The difference in the y-coordinates is $7 - (-5) = 12$. Plugging these into the Pythagorean equation, we get that the distance between the two points (or the length between points B and C) is

$$\sqrt{(-1)^2 + 12^2} = \sqrt{145}$$

13. **(A)** Now that we know the value of the coordinates of C, we can use this to calculate the slope for a line $\overline{BC}$. We have our Δy value as $7 - (-5) = 12$, and our Δx value as $-4 - (-3) = -1$. So, the slope is $\frac{12}{-1} = -12$. Therefore, the slope is negative.

14. **(B)** If $3x - 6y = 18$, then when $x = 0$, $3(0) - 6y = 18$ and $y = -3$. When $y = 0$, $3x - 6(0) = 18$ and $x = 6$. Therefore, the graph goes through $(0, -3)$ and $(6, 0)$.

15. **(C)** The inequality does not include an equal sign since a dashed line is drawn rather than a solid line, and therefore, choices **A** and **B** can be eliminated. The y-intercept is -1, and so choice **D** can be eliminated. You can tell that the slope is 1/3 because going from the point $(0, -1)$ to the point $(3, 0)$, the y-value increases by one unit while the x-value goes across 3 units.

16. **(E)** We can see that the graph goes through $(0, 2)$ and therefore the y-intercept is 2. If you pick points $(0, 2)$ and $(1, 0)$, the slope can be calculated as: $\frac{0-2}{1-0} = -2$. The equation of any line is $y = mx + b$, and here $m = -2$ and $b = 2$, so we have $y = -2x + 2$.

17. **(A)** Calculate the slope: $\frac{3-0}{4-(-1)} = \frac{3}{5}$. Write $y = \frac{3}{5}x + b$, so choosing point $(4, 3)$, we get $3 = \frac{3}{5} \cdot 4 + b$, $3 = \frac{12}{5} + b$, $b = \frac{15}{5} - \frac{12}{5} = \frac{3}{5}$. Therefore $y = \frac{3}{5}x + \frac{3}{5}$.

18. **(A)** Calculate the slope $\frac{6-(-6)}{-3-3} = \frac{12}{-6} = -2$. Write $y = -2x + b$. Use point $(3, -6)$ to get $-6 = -2(3) + b$. Add 6 to both sides to get $b = 0$. Therefore, the equation of the line is: $y = -2x$.

19. **(B)** Write $y = -x + b$, plug in the value -1 for y and -2 for x to get $-2 = -(-1) + b$, $b = -3$.

20. **(C)** This is a horizontal line, so the equation has the form $y = b$, in this case $b = 4$ since the horizontal line passes through the point $(0, 4)$, which is the y-intercept, so $y = 4$.

Chapter 22
Interpretation of Graphs

The GED Math exam is sure to include at least a few questions on various types of graphs. The graph questions will likely cover the following types of graphs: bar graphs, circle graphs, line graphs, and scatterplots.

Questions may involve reading information off a graph, determining the relationship between variables, solving a word problem based on the graph, or making a prediction based on the trend in the graph. All techniques will be covered in this chapter.

Bar Graphs

There are a few different types of bar graphs that may appear on the exam, but they are all bar graphs. This means that there are two axis lines, one for the number of bars, and one for the "height" of the bars. Compare the two examples below. Both are bar graphs, even though they are oriented in different directions. Each one shows the numbers of cars sold by month. Each month is represented by a bar, and the number of cars is represented by the height of the bar.

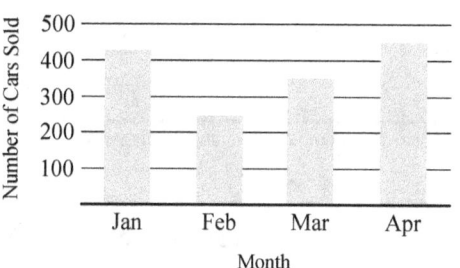

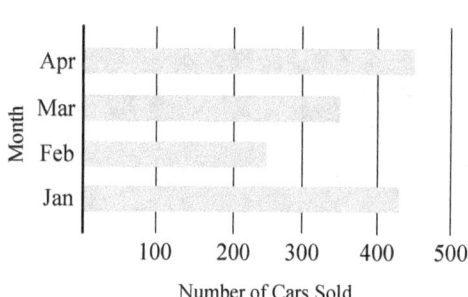

When you encounter a bar graph, always start by reading the labels. Next, you might benefit from writing down what each bar represents. For the graphs above, you could write "Jan: 425 cars, Feb: 250 cars, Mar: 350 cars, Apr: 450 cars." Then, you have all the information you need to solve the question plainly written out. If the question asks you "How many more cars were sold in January than in February?" you can look at your data and perform the operation 425 − 250 to get 175 cars.

Sometimes it can be hard to read exact values from the graph, so it's okay to estimate and then pick the answer that's closest. But if your answer is far off the multiple-choice options, or is close to more than one answer, then go back to the graph and make sure you read the numbers correctly.

Test yourself with the following questions, and then go through the explanations.

Examples 1-2 pertain to the following graph.

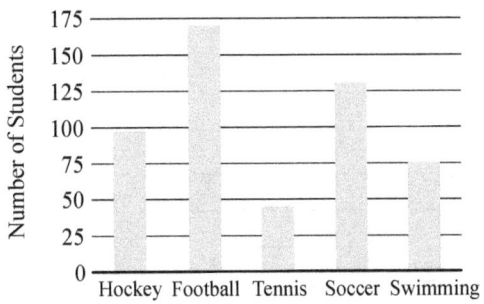

Example 1. How many students are there in tennis and swimming combined?

- (A) Around 50
- (B) Around 75
- (C) Around 120
- (D) Around 340
- (E) Around 500

Answer: C. There are around 40 students who play tennis (note that the bar is a little below the 50 mark) and around 75 students who do swimming. 40 + 75 = 115, and the closest answer to that is 120. You could also approximate tennis as having 50 students, or 45 students, which means you would get 125 or 120. All these estimates are closest to answer **C**, making **C** a good choice.

Example 2. How many more students play football compared to soccer?

- (A) Around 40
- (B) Around 80
- (C) Around 100
- (D) Around 130
- (E) Around 170

Answer: A. About 170 students play football while 130 play soccer. 170 − 130 = 40. If the question asks, "how many more," we subtract the smaller quantity from the larger quantity.

Circle Graphs

Circle graphs are also called pie charts, which you may be familiar with already. Although they look very different, circle graphs are actually pretty similar to bar graphs, except they're easier to work with because the value of each "slice of pie" is usually written out. See the graph below for an example.

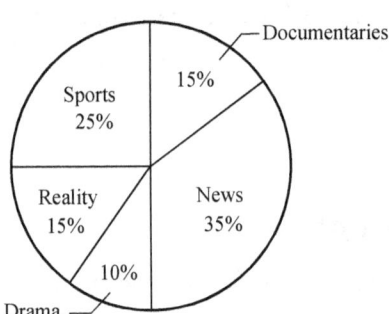

Favorite type of show of U.S. TV viewers

The size of each slice of pie corresponds to the percentage written. So, if a slice were 50%, it would take up half the pie.

Questions on circle graphs will usually be interpretation questions. For example, in the graph above, 35% of the people surveyed said their favorite TV genre was news. If 300 people were surveyed, then how many people said their favorite genre was news? Or how many said their favorite was drama? To answer this question, take the total number of people (300) and multiply by the percentage indicated on the graph. For news programs, 35% of people said it was their favorite genre, so that's $300 \times 0.35 = 105$. For drama, 10% of people said it was their favorite, so $300 \times 0.1 = 30$.

Test yourself with the following questions, then go through the explanations.

Examples 3-4 pertain to the the graph below.

American students' favorite subjects

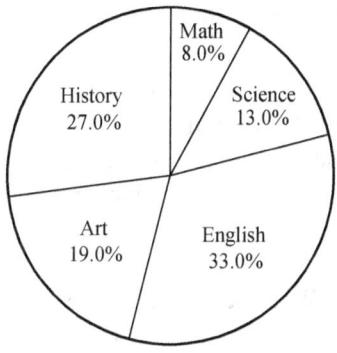

Example 3. If 1,000 students were surveyed, how many chose art as their favorite subject?

(A) 120
(B) 190
(C) 270
(D) 330
(E) 450

Answer: B. If 19% of people chose art, then the number of people who chose art is $1000 \times 0.19 = 190$. Remember, to convert a percent into a decimal, divide by 100. So $19\% = 19/100 = 0.19$.

Example 4. If 2,000 people were surveyed, how many people chose math or science as their favorite subject?

(A) 80
(B) 130
(C) 210
(D) 420
(E) 660

Answer: D. The percent of people who chose math or science is $8\% + 13\% = 21\%$. Then, $21\% = 21/100 = 0.21$. So, if there were 2,000 people total, then $2000 \times 0.21 = 420$.

Line Graphs

Line graphs typically show how some value changes over time, as in the example below. Line graphs may or may not have dots on the line (as pictured). Questions about line graphs will be similar to questions about bar graphs. Generally, the strategy is to figure out the value of each time period and then use that data to answer the question, just like with a bar graph.

To better understand this process, take a look at the example questions below.

Examples 5-8 pertain to the graph below.

The graph shows the sales data for a company between 2015 and 2019.

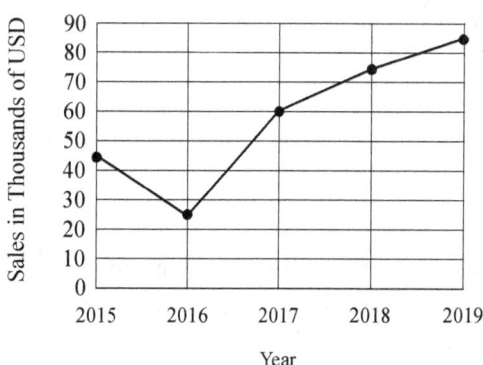

Example 5. What was the total value of sales in 2016 and 2017?

- (A) $25,000
- (B) $60,000
- (C) $70,000
- (D) $75,000
- (E) $85,000

Answer: E. This example is sneaky because the values don't match the numbers on the graph. Instead, each number represents a thousand. The value of $25 on the vertical axis is actually $25,000 because on the vertical axis, we see sales *in thousands*. Always look carefully at the graph before answering the question. For this question, look at the amount of sales in 2016 and 2017. 2016 had $25,000 in sales, and 2017 had $60,000 in sales. The total amount of sales for the two years was $25,000 + $60,000 = $85,000.

Often, the answer choices will give you a clue about what to look for on the graph. If you're expecting the answer to be 30 and the lowest possible answer is 10 million, take another look at the units on the graph!

Now try the following example question, about the same graph.

Example 6. By what percent did sales improve in 2018 compared to 2017?

- (A) 10%
- (B) 25%
- (C) 40%
- (D) 60%
- (E) 125%

Answer: B. This question is asking about the *percent increase*. The formula for finding a percent change is the following:

$$\frac{\text{Final Value} - \text{Original Value}}{\text{Original Value}} \times 100 \, (\%).$$

You can have a percent increase or a percent decrease. For the question above, the sales for 2018 were $75,000 and the sales for 2017 were $60,000. If we subtract the value for 2017 from 2018 we obtain, $75,000 − $60,000 = $15,000. Then $15,000/$60,000 = 25%. Therefore, the *percent increase* was 25%.

Keep in mind that percent increases can be greater than 100%. For example, if the percent increase was 100%, that means the value doubled. Here's a mathematical example: if the original value is $15 and the final value is $30, then ($30 − $15) / $15 = $15 / $15 = 1.00 = 100%. $30 is twice of $15. If the percent increase is 200%, that means the value tripled. For example, if the original value is $15 and the final value is $45, then ($45 − $15) / $15 = $30 / $15 = 2.00 = 200%.

Now try the following questions about percent changes, based on the above graph, then compare your answers to the explanations below.

Example 7. What year had the greatest percent increase in sales compared to the previous year?

- (A) 2016
- (B) 2017
- (C) 2018
- (D) 2019
- (E) There was no increase in sales in any year

Answer: B. The fastest way to solve this problem is to pick the year in which the steepness of the graph is largest. We can see immediately that the curve is steepest between 2016 and 2017. Because the question asks for a comparison between the year in question and the previous year, the right answer is 2017.

Example 8. How much greater were the sales in 2018 and 2019 combined compared to the sales in 2016 and 2017 combined?

- (A) $75,000
- (B) $85,000
- (C) $100,000
- (D) $120,000
- (E) $150,000

Answer: A. The sales in 2018 were $75,000 and the sales in 2019 were $85,000. Combined, that sums to $160,000. The sales in 2016 were $25,000 and the sales in 2017 were $60,000. Combined, these come to $85,000. The difference is $160,000 − $85,000 = $75,000.

Scatterplots

The final type of graph we will talk about is the scatterplot. The scatterplot is very different from the previous types of graphs because you will not be trying to find exact values. Instead, you will be looking at the general trend of the graph and make predictions.

Let's take a look at the following graph, which shows the number of people who visit the ocean as a function of outdoor temperature.

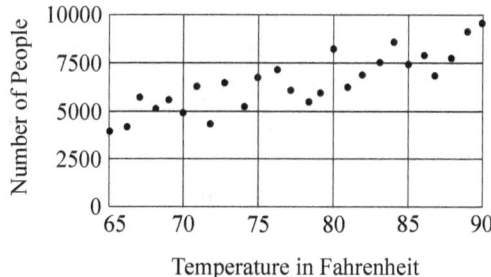

When you see a graph like this, in your mind draw a line through the center of the points. Your line should look something like this:

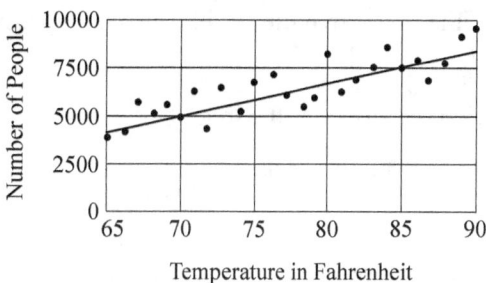

This is called the trendline and represents the relationship between the *x* variable (the outdoor temperature) and the *y* variable (the number of people).

Now let's look at the original chart again.

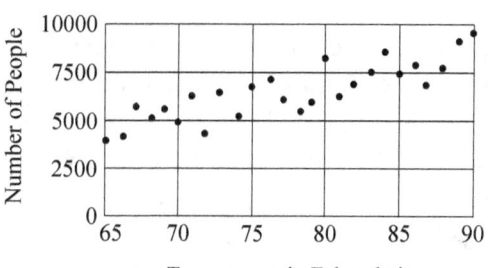

Do more people visit the ocean when the temperature is 65°F or when the temperature is 90°F? In general, the points are higher around 90°F than around 65°F, so we would say that more people visit the ocean when the temperature is around 90°F.

Questions about scatterplots will often involve estimating the trendline. A precise trendline uses a complicated equation that you won't be asked about on the test, but it's a lot simpler to estimate a trendline from a scatterplot. Using the techniques discussed in chapter 19 on geometry in the coordinate plane, imagine in your mind two points that lie on your imaginary trendline. This is harder if you're taking the test on a computer instead of on paper, because you can't just draw it in. Try to make your points near the gridlines on the graph.

For example, for the graph above, convenient points are (70°F, 5,000 people) and (85°F, 7,500 people). Note that these points seem to lie nicely on the imaginary trendline, while also being easy to read.

Now find the slope for the trendline:

$$\frac{7500 - 5000}{85 - 75} = \frac{2500}{15} = 166.66 \text{ people/°F}$$

If you're confused about how to find the slope, look back at chapter 19 on geometry in the coordinate plane.

If you are asked to find the equation of the line, look at the y-intercept first. In this graph, the y-intercept is about 4000, so the equation is near to $y = 167x + 4000$. To find the exact y-intercept, in order to find the exact equation, follow the content of chapter 19.

Another type of question might ask for an estimate in the increase in the number of people for each 1°F increase. This question is actually asking about the slope of the trendline. The slope for our trendline is around 167, so for each 1°F increase in temperature, an additional 167 are estimated to go to the ocean. The slope describes the change in y as a function of the change in x. So, if a question asks about how the y-value might change compared to x, then it is asking about the slope.

Keep in mind that you can also have a downward pointing trendline! In which case, the question might ask for an estimate in the *decrease* in the number of people for each 1°F increase.

Test yourself with the following questions, then go through the explanations.

Examples 9-10 pertain to the graph below.

The graph compares the number of home sales to the number of apartment residents in a residential area over a certain time frame.

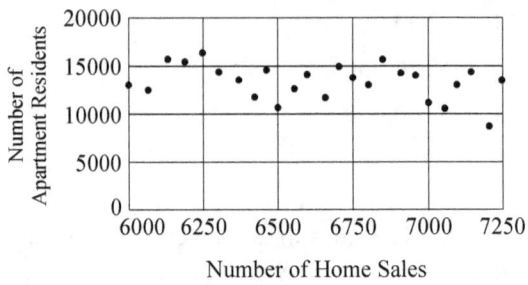

Example 9. If the number of home sales increases to 10,000, how do you expect the number of apartment residents to change based on the graph above?

- (A) It will decrease significantly.
- (B) It will decrease slightly.
- (C) It will increase slightly.
- (D) It will increase significantly.
- (E) It will increase slightly, then decrease slightly.

Answer: B. Looking at the graph, draw an imaginary trendline in your mind. If you extend the line to the right all the way to 10,000, then following the line of the graph, the number of apartment residents will be slightly less. Note that choice **E** is not possible for a linear trend. For a scatterplot with a linear trend, you should never assume that the graph will change direction suddenly.

Chapter 22: Interpretation of Graphs

Example 10. If the number of home sales drops to 5,000, then how do you expect the number of apartment residents to change based on the graph above?

    Ⓐ It will decrease significantly.
    Ⓑ It will decrease slightly.
    Ⓒ It will increase slightly.
    Ⓓ It will increase significantly.
    Ⓔ It will increase significantly and then decrease.

Answer C. For this question, we are following the imaginary graph line to the left, so the number of apartment residents will be a little higher. If we were following the line out very far, then we might expect the increase to be significant, but because the trendline is pretty close to flat, we can assume that the increases or decreases of the trendline will be small.

Practice Problems

Problems 1-3 refer to the graph below.

The graph shows the number of apartment units sold between September and December.

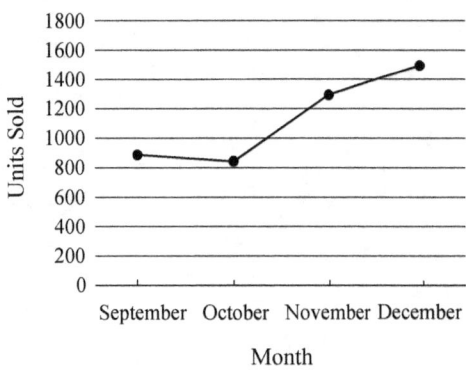

1. What was the percent increase of units sold from October to November?

   (A) 26%
   (B) 37%
   (C) 53%
   (D) 67%
   (E) 121%

2. Which two months had the greatest combined number of sales?

   (A) September and October
   (B) October and November
   (C) September and December
   (D) October and December
   (E) November and December

3. Which month had the greatest increase in sales compared to the previous month?

   (A) September
   (B) October
   (C) November
   (D) December
   (E) None

Problems 4-7 pertain to the graph below.

The graph shows the percentage of students in a history class who received each grade A-F.

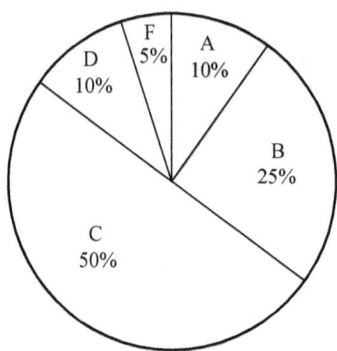

4. If there were 200 students in the class, how many students received an A?

   (A) 11
   (B) 14
   (C) 20
   (D) 24
   (E) 28

Chapter 22: Interpretation of Graphs   259

5. If there were 200 students in the class, how many students received a D or an F grade?

    (A) 14
    (B) 24
    (C) 30
    (D) 38
    (E) 44

6. If there were 1,400 students in the class, how many students got a C or better?

    (A) 892
    (B) 913
    (C) 1,012
    (D) 1,134
    (E) 1,190

7. If there were 1,400 students in the class, how many more students received an A than an F?

    (A) 42
    (B) 70
    (C) 98
    (D) 140
    (E) 192

Problems 8-10 pertain to the following graph.

The graph shows the number of applicants to a university's math program.

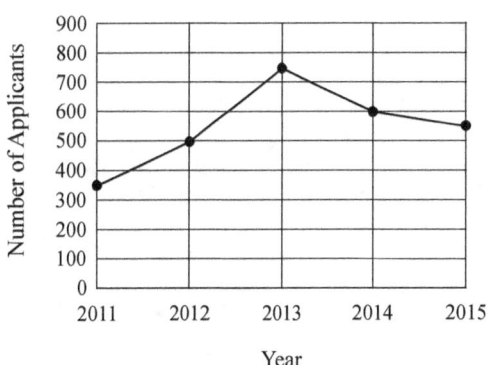

8. For the given period from 2011–2015, how many years did the university's math program receive less than 700 applications?

    (A) 1
    (B) 2
    (C) 3
    (D) 4
    (E) 5

9. How many more applications did the math program receive in the best year than in the worst year?

    (A) 150
    (B) 200
    (C) 250
    (D) 350
    (E) 400

10. How many total applications did the math program receive from 2011 to 2015?

    A) 1,250
    B) 2,500
    C) 2,750
    D) 3,050
    E) 3,200

12. What was the total value of sales for the two worst years?

    A) $700,000
    B) $775,000
    C) $850,000
    D) $925,000
    E) $1,000,000

Problems 11-14 pertain to the following graph.

The graph shows the amount of sales per year for a large store.

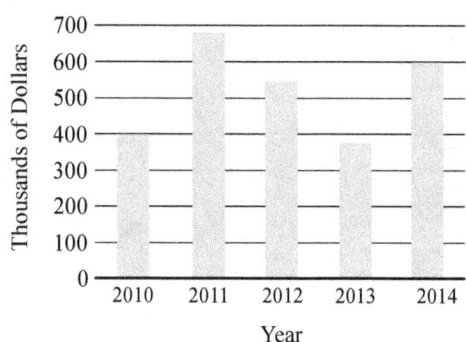

13. What was the total for combined sales for the two best years?

    A) $775,000
    B) $925,000
    C) $1,275,000
    D) $1,450,000
    E) $1,625,000

11. What was the percent increase in the value of sales between 2010 and 2014?

    A) 20%
    B) 25%
    C) 35%
    D) 50%
    E) 60%

14. How much greater were the sales in the best year compared to the sales in the worst year?

    A) $100,000
    B) $200,000
    C) $300,000
    D) $400,000
    E) $500,000

Chapter 22: Interpretation of Graphs

Problems 15-20 pertain to the following graph.

The graph shows the survey results when people were asked about their favorite holiday.

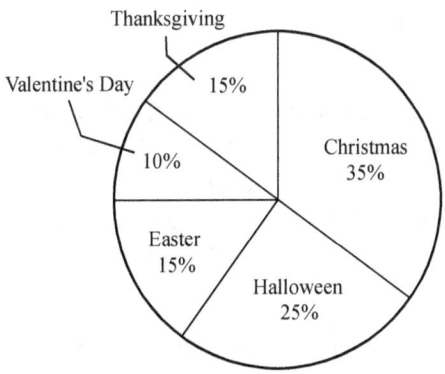

15. If 1,500 people were surveyed, how many more people said Christmas was their favorite holiday than said Halloween was their favorite holiday?

   (A) 150
   (B) 215
   (C) 280
   (D) 325
   (E) 355

16. If 100 people said that Valentine's Day was their favorite holiday, how many people in total were surveyed?

   (A) 100
   (B) 500
   (C) 750
   (D) 1,000
   (E) 1,250

17. If 960 people said either Christmas or Thanksgiving were their favorite holiday, how many people in total were surveyed?

   (A) 960
   (B) 1,140
   (C) 1,920
   (D) 2,450
   (E) 3,300

18. If 405 people said either Valentine's Day or Easter were their favorite holiday, how many people in total were surveyed?

   (A) 1,620
   (B) 1,700
   (C) 1,840
   (D) 1,920
   (E) 2,000

19. Suppose that 1,500 people in total were surveyed. Which holiday was the favorite of 375 people?

   (A) Christmas
   (B) Easter
   (C) Halloween
   (D) Thanksgiving
   (E) Valentine's Day

20. Suppose that 1,700 people in total were surveyed. Which holiday was the favorite of 170 people?

   (A) Christmas
   (B) Easter
   (C) Halloween
   (D) Thanksgiving
   (E) Valentine's Day

Answers to Practice Problems

1. **(C)** There were about 1,300 units sold in November and about 850 sold in October. So
$$\frac{1300 - 850}{850} = \frac{450}{850} = 0.53 = 53\%$$

2. **(E)** November and December were the two months with the highest sales, so combined, those two months also had more sales than any other two-month period.

3. **(C)** The simplest way to solve the problem is to find the steepest line between the months shown, and that line extends from October to November.

4. **(C)** There are 200 students, so multiply
$$200 \times 10\% = 200 \times 0.1 = 20$$

5. **(C)** $200 \times (5\% + 10\%) = 200 \times 0.15 = 30$

6. **(E)** First add up the percentages of all the students who got a C or better: 50% + 25% + 10% = 85%. 85% of 1,400 = 1,400 × 0.85 = 1,190.

7. **(B)** 10% of 1,400 students received an A and 5% received an F. The difference between the two is 10% − 5% = 5%. Take 5% of 1,400 = 70 students.

8. **(D)** 2013 was the only year when the university received more than 700 applicants. In 2011, 2012, 2014, and 2015, the university received less than 700 applicants.

9. **(E)** The best year was 2013 with around 750 applicants, and the worst year was 2011 with around 350 applicants. 750 − 350 = 400.

10. **(C)** Add up the number of applicants for each year. 350 + 500 + 750 + 600 + 550 = 2,750.

11. **(D)** The percent change (increase) is
$$\frac{600 - 400}{400} = \frac{200}{400} = 0.5 = 50\%$$

12. **(B)** The number of sales was $400,000 + $375,000 = $775,000. Notice that the graph shows the value of sales *in thousands*. That is why all the answers are in the hundreds of thousands rather than in the hundreds.

13. **(C)** This is very similar to the previous question, except worded slightly differently and it asks about the two best years instead of the two worst years. The two best years were 2011 and 2014, so the value of sales was $675,000 + $600,000 = $1,275,000.

14. **(C)** The best year was 2011 and the worst year was 2013. Notice that sales for 2013 were slightly less than for 2010. The difference in sales is $675,000 − $375,000 = $300,000

15. **(A)** The difference in percentage between Christmas and Halloween is 35% − 25% = 10%. Take 10% of 1,500 = 150 more people said Christmas was their favorite holiday than said Halloween was their favorite holiday.

16. **(D)** This question is a little tricky because it's asking the opposite question from the previous ones. Ten percent of people said Valentine's Day is their favorite holiday, so 100% of people is exactly 10 times the number of people who love Valentine's Day the most. Therefore, all we need to do is multiply the number of people who said they loved Valentine's Day the most by 10. In this case, we perform the following calculation: 100 × 10 = 1,000 people.

Another method that could be useful for more complex numbers, is to call the number of people surveyed, X. Then 10% of X equals 100. Write the equation $0.1 \times X = 100$. Here we use 0.1 because $0.1 = 10\%$. Divide both sides of the equation by 0.1 to get

$$X = \frac{100}{0.1} = 1000$$

17. **(C)** This is similar to the previous question, with an added twist. Now we have to add up the percentages for Christmas and Thanksgiving. In total, that's 50%. So Total × 0.50 = 960. Then 960/0.50 = 1,920 total people.

18. **(A)** This is the same as the question above, but with Valentine's Day and Easter. The added percentage is $10\% + 15\% = 25\%$. So Total × 0.25 = 405, so then 405/0.25 = 1,620 total people.

19. **(C)** This question adds another twist. Now, the thing we don't know is the percentage. We know that Total × Percentage gives us the number of people who liked a specific holiday. This question can be rephrased as "375 is what percentage of 1500?" So now we can rearrange this equation, to get

$$\frac{375}{1500} = \text{percentage} = 0.25 = 25\%$$

So, looking back at the chart, the correct answer is Halloween.

20. **(E)** This is the same as the previous question, but with different numbers. This question can be rephrased as "170 is what percentage of 1700?" Rearranging our formula, we get

$$\frac{170}{1700} = \text{percentage} = 0.1 = 10\%$$

So, looking back at the chart, the correct answer is Valentine's Day.

Chapter 23
Scientific Notation

Scientific notation is used to format numbers, but not change their values. Although it can be used to represent any number, it is most often used for very large and very small numbers, such as ones that would not fit on a calculator screen. Earth's circumference or the mass of an electron are measurements that are typically represented in scientific notation. Please review chapter 5 on powers before reading this chapter.

Review of Exponents

Before we understand scientific notation, we must understand exponents. If we wanted to express $10 \times 10 \times 10 \times 10 \times 10 \times 10$ using exponents, we count the number of times 10 appears, which is 6 in this case, and simply write: 1,000,000. But what if you are an astrophysicist and want to represent the number 1,000,000,000,000,000,000? It is inconvenient to count zeros. Instead we can represent the number more simply in scientific notation as 1×10^{18}. The exponent, 18, is the number of zeros after 1. As in the case with this number, if the decimal point is not seen, the decimal is located at the end of the number. What if we wanted to express instead of a huge number, a tiny number, such as the weight of a proton? The mass of the proton is $1.67262171 \times 10^{-27}$ kilograms. The negative exponent indicates that the number is less than 1 (or if the number is negative, between zero and negative one). In fact, the mass of a proton is

0.00000000000000000000000000167262171

kilograms. Now you know why we need exponents! Examples of powers of 10:

$$10^3 = 1,000$$
$$10^2 = 100$$
$$10^1 = 10$$
$$10^0 = 1$$
$$10^{-1} = \frac{1}{10^1} = 0.1$$
$$10^{-2} = \frac{1}{10^2} = 0.01$$

Format of Scientific Notation

The form of scientific notation is $n \times 10^m$, where n is the coefficient, and $1 \leq n < 10$ or $-10 < n \leq -1$, and m is the exponent, which can be any integer.

Examples:

0.00456 is written as 4.56×10^{-3} in scientific notation. Here, $n = 4.56$ and $m = -3$.

−910,000 is written as -9.1×10^5 in scientific notation. Here $n = -9.1$ and $m = 5$.

Chapter 23: Scientific Notation

To change a number to scientific notation, move the decimal point so that it is right after the first non-zero digit. For example, take the number 13.4. We want to change it so that it is in scientific notation. 1.34 would be in scientific notation. But changing 13.4 to 1.34 moves the decimal point to the left once. Therefore, we need to multiply by 10 raised to the first power to obtain 1.34×10^1. Here the exponent above the 10 is positive one. It's positive because we moved the decimal to the left, and one because we moved the decimal once.

Now take the number 0.0134. Again, we want to change it so that the number is 1.34×10^m. We move the decimal place two units to the right this time. Therefore, we multiply by 10 raised to the negative two power, to get 1.34×10^{-2}. It's negative because we moved the decimal to the right, and two because we moved the decimal two places.

To sum up, when we take a number that is not in scientific notation and convert it into scientific notation, if we move the decimal place to the right the exponent, m, will be negative, as in the number 0.0134. Similarly, if we move the decimal place to the left, the exponent, m, will be positive, as in the case with the number 13.4.

We can form four rules:

Rule 1: In converting scientific notation to standard decimal form, a positive exponent moves the decimal point to the right.

Rule 2: In converting scientific notation to standard decimal form, a negative exponent moves the decimal point to the left.

Rule 3: In converting a number in standard form to scientific notation, if you move the decimal to the left, the exponent will be positive.

Rule 4: In converting a number in standard form to scientific notation, if you move the decimal to the right, the exponent will be negative.

Example 1. Write 3,200 in scientific notation.

- (A) 0.32×10^{-3}
- (B) 3.20×10^1
- (C) 0.32×10^2
- (D) 3.20×10^2
- (E) 3.2×10^3

Answer: E. We start with a number greater than 1. Therefore, we must move the decimal point to the left, which will make the exponent, m, positive (see Rule 3). In order to have $1 \leq n < 10$, we move the decimal 3 places to the left (remember if the decimal is not seen, it is always at the far right of 3,200). Therefore,

$$3,200 = 3.2 \times 10^3$$

Example 2. Write −910,000 in scientific notation.

- (A) -9.1×10^5
- (B) 9.1×10^{-5}
- (C) -9.1×10^{-3}
- (D) 0.91×10^{-1}
- (E) 91.0×10^5

Answer: A. Even though the number is negative, we will still move the decimal point to the left. Therefore, m will be positive (Rule 3). In order to have $-10 < n \leq -1$, we must move the decimal place 5 places to the left. Thus,

$$-910,000 = -9.1 \times 10^5$$

Example 3. Express 0.345 in scientific notation.

- (A) 34.50×10^3
- (B) 3.45×10^{-1}
- (C) 0.0345×10^1
- (D) 3.45×10^1
- (E) -3.45×10^{-1}

Answer: B. Since the number is less than 1, we know that we must move the decimal point to the right in order for $1 \leq n < 10$. Since we are moving the decimal point right, the exponent m will be negative (Rule 4). Thus,

$$0.345 = 3.45 \times 10^{-1}$$

Converting Scientific Notation to Standard Form

To go from scientific notation to a number in standard form, we simply do the opposite of converting from standard form to scientific notation. For the next two examples, follow Rules 1 and 2.

Example 4. Write 4.56×10^{-3} in standard form.

- (A) 0.0456
- (B) 0.456
- (C) −0.00456
- (D) 0.00456
- (E) −456

Answer: D. Since the exponent m is negative, we must move the decimal point 3 spaces to the left (Rule 2).

Remember: The decimal point for an integer is after the number. For example, 980 and 980.0 are the same number. The decimal is not required after integers, but can be helpful when manipulating numbers into scientific notation.

Example 5. Write 98763.21 in scientific notation.

- (A) 987.6321×10^{-4}
- (B) 9.876321×10^{-4}
- (C) 9.876321×10^{3}
- (D) 9.876321×10^{4}
- (E) 9.876321×10^{6}

Answer: D. Since the number is larger than one, move the decimal point to the left, making the exponent positive (Rule 3). Count the number of times you moved the decimal to the left, which in this case is 4. Therefore, the exponent is 4.

Example 6. Write −0.0081 in scientific notation.

- (A) -8.1×10^{-4}
- (B) 8.1×10^{-3}
- (C) -8.1×10^{-3}
- (D) 8.1×10^{4}
- (E) 0.0081×10^{4}

Answer: C. Move the decimal so that it is after the 8. Because it had to be moved 3 places to the right, the exponent must be −3. The sign in front of the number is still negative.

Example 7. 0.048042 can be written as 4.8042×10^{x}. What is the value of x?

- (A) −4
- (B) −2
- (C) 1
- (D) 2
- (E) 4

Answer: B. The decimal point is moved 2 places to the right, so the exponent must be −2.

Example 8. Write 0.8020 in scientific notation.

- (A) -0.8020×10^{-1}
- (B) 8.02×10^{-2}
- (C) 8.02×10^{-1}
- (D) 0.802×10^{1}
- (E) 80.2×10^{-2}

Chapter 23: Scientific Notation   267

Answer: C. The decimal point is moved one space to the right, and therefore the exponent is negative.

Example 9. Convert 3.334×10^5 to decimal form.

- (A) 0.3334
- (B) 0.000334
- (C) 3334
- (D) 33,340
- (E) 333,400

Answer: E. Move the decimal point 5 places to the right since the exponent is positive 5.

Example 10. $(4 \times 10^3) \times (2 \times 10^3)$ can also be written in which way?

- (A) 6×10^6
- (B) 6×10^9
- (C) 8×10^3
- (D) 8×10^6
- (E) 4.2×10^6

Answer: D. The Associative Property of Multiplication allows us to change the order of multiplication. Then multiply $10^3 \times 10^3$ to get $10 \times 10 \times 10 \times 10 \times 10 \times 10 = 10^6$ by adding the exponents when the bases are the same. We also multiply 4 by 2 to get 8, and then put it in scientific notation to obtain 8×10^6.

Example 11. 2.5×100 is <u>greater</u> than which number?

- (A) 0.25×10^5
- (B) 2.5×10^4
- (C) 2500×10^{-1}
- (D) 2.5×10^2
- (E) 2500×10^{-2}

Answer: E. The numbers can be written in decimal form to be compared to $2.5 \times 100 = 250$. Choice **A** is equal to 2,500. Choice **B** is equal to 25,000, Choice **C** is equal to 250 which is equal to the number in question, not greater or smaller than it: choice **D** is also equal to 250. Choice **E** is equal to 25, and therefore is smaller than 250, leading to choice **E** being correct.

Example 12. Compute $(5 \times 10^6) + (2 \times 10^4)$.

- (A) 2.5×10^{10}
- (B) 10×10^{10}
- (C) 5.2×10^{10}
- (D) 10×10^{24}
- (E) 5.02×10^6

Answer: E. The coefficients can only be added if they have the same base and exponent. Change the numbers so that they have the same power of 10. $2 \times 10^4 = 0.02 \times 10^6$. Use the Distributive Property to add the coefficients and keep the same power of 10.

$(5 \times 10^6) + (2 \times 10^4) = (5 \times 10^6) + (0.02 \times 10^6)$
$= (5 + 0.02) \times 10^6 = 5.02 \times 10^6$

Practice Problems

1. Write 802,000,000 in scientific notation.

2. Write 0.00091 in scientific notation.

3. Convert −34,000,100.01 to scientific notation.

4. Write 9.0630×10^{-3} in decimal form.

5. 500,900,700 can be written as 5.009007×10^c. What is the value of c?

    A) −8
    B) −6
    C) 3
    D) 6
    E) 8

6. Which choice represents 5×300 in scientific notation?

    A) 1.5×10^2
    B) 1.5×10^3
    C) 15.0×10^{-2}
    D) 15.0×10^2
    E) 1500

7. Which of the following numbers is equal to 580,000 and expressed in scientific notation?

    A) 0.580000×10^4
    B) 0.58×10^6
    C) 5.8×10^7
    D) 58×10^4
    E) 5.8×10^5

8. How is 6 represented in scientific notation?

    A) 6
    B) 6.0
    C) 6×10^0
    D) 6×10^1
    E) 6.00×10^{-2}

9. Express 0.01071977 in scientific notation.

    A) 0.1071977×10^{-1}
    B) 1.071977×10^{-2}
    C) 1.071977×10^2
    D) 10.71977×10^{-5}
    E) 10.71977×10^3

10. $\dfrac{5}{100{,}000}$ is equal to which number?

- (A) 0.0005
- (B) 0.5×10^4
- (C) 5×10^{-5}
- (D) 5×10^{-4}
- (E) 5×10^4

11. 8.9898×10^3 has the same value as which of the following?

Choose all answers that apply.

- [A] 8989.8
- [B] 89.898×10^2
- [C] 89898×10^{-1}
- [D] 898.98
- [E] 8989.8×10^{-2}

12. $(12 \times 10^8) \times (3 \times 10^2)$ is equal to:

- (A) 3.6×10^{10}
- (B) 15×10^{16}
- (C) 36×10^{16}
- (D) 15×10^{10}
- (E) 3.6×10^{11}

13. Which statements are true?

Choose all answers that apply.

- [A] $5.8 \times 10^3 < 5.8 \times 10^4$
- [B] $5.8 \times 10^{-3} < 5.8 \times 10^{-4}$
- [C] $5.8 \times 10^{-4} < 5.8 \times 10^{-3}$
- [D] $5.8 \times 10^{-3} < 5.8 \times 10^{-2}$
- [E] $-5.8 \times 10^{-3} < -5.8 \times 10^{-2}$

14. 9.82×10^{-5} is <u>less</u> than which of following numbers?

- (A) -9.82×10^{-4}
- (B) -9.82×10^5
- (C) 9.82×10^{-6}
- (D) 9.82×10^0
- (E) 982×10^{-8}

15. Which number is <u>not</u> equivalent to 2.468×10^8?

- (A) 0.2468×10^9
- (B) 246.8×10^{-4}
- (C) 24.68×10^7
- (D) 246,800,000
- (E) $246{,}800{,}000 \times 10^0$

Answers to Practice Problems

1. 8.02×10^8. Since we must move the decimal toward the left, the exponent will be positive. We move the decimal place 8 places to the left so that the exponent will be between 1 and 10. Therefore, we get 8.02×10^8.

2. 9.1×10^{-4}. Move the decimal to the right 4 places so that it is after the first non-zero digit, 9. Because you moved the decimal 4 places to the right, the exponent will be −4.

3. -3.400010001×10^7. Move the decimal to the left 7 places, so that it is after the first non-zero digit. Since you moved the decimal 7 places to the left, the exponent is positive 7.

4. 0.009063. Since the exponent is −3, move the decimal 3 places to the left.

5. **(E)** The decimal must be moved from the end of the number 8 places to the left. The exponent is positive since we moved the decimal to the left.

6. **(B)** First compute $5 \times 300 = 1500$. Then move the decimal from the end of the number to the left so that it is after the 1. Because this required a movement of three spaces, and $1500 > 10$, the exponent is positive 3.

7. **(E)** Start from evaluating the answer choices. In choice **E**, the decimal place is moved 5 spaces to the right to make the number equal to 580,000.

8. **(C)** The decimal is after the 6 in the original number and does not move anywhere, so the exponent is 0. Remember that when the exponent is zero, and the base is non-zero, the expression is equal to one.

9. **(B)** Place the decimal after the first 1. To get it there, it must be moved 2 places to the right. Since we moved the decimal to the right, the exponent must be negative.

10. **(C)** $\frac{5}{100.000} = \frac{5}{10^5} = 5 \times 10^{-5}$. Note that when we divide by 100,000, that is the same as moving the decimal to the left 5 spaces.

11. **(A), (B), (C)** 8.9898×10^3 can be rewritten as 8989.8 in decimal form. Choice **B**, 89.898×10^3, can be written as 8989.8, because the decimal is moved to the right two places. Choice **C**, 89898×10^{-1}, can also be written as 8989.8 because the decimal is moved one place to the left. In **E**, $8989.8 \times 10^{-2} = 89.898$ because the decimal is moved two places to the left. Therefore, only **A**, **B**, and **C** are equal to the original expression.

12. **(E)** $(12 \times 10^8) \times (3 \times 10^2) = (12 \times 3) \times (10^8 \times 10^2) = 36 \times 10^{10}$. Remember to add the exponents, not multiply when the bases are equal. This expression is equal 3.6×10^{11} because $36 = 3.6 \times 10^1$, and $36 \times 10^{10} = 3.6 \times 10^1 \times 10^{10} = 3.6 \times 10^{11}$.

13. **(A), (C), (D)** Statement **A** can be written as $5{,}800 < 58{,}000$, which is true. Statement **B** can be written as $0.0058 < 0.00058$, which is false. Statement **C** can be written as $0.00058 < 0.0058$, which is true. Statement **D** can be written as $0.0058 < 0.058$, which is true. Statement **E** can be written as $-0.0058 < -0.058$, which is false.

14. **(D)** $9.82 \times 10^{-5} = 0.0000982$. This is less than $9.82 \times 10^0 = 9.82 \times 1 = 9.82$.

15. **(B)** Rewrite 2.468×10^8 as 246,800,000 by moving the decimal 8 places to the right. Rewrite each of the answers to see that $246.8 \times 10^{-4} = 0.02468$, which is the only expression not equivalent to the original number.

Chapter 24

Quadratic Expressions and Functions

A binomial is an algebraic expression of the sum or the difference of two terms, such as $x + 3$ or $2x - 4$, for example.

In algebra, there is often a need to multiply two binomials together, as well as in many application problems in math, science, and engineering.

The FOIL method allows you to multiply two binomials. The letters in FOIL stand for two terms (one from each of two binomials) multiplied together in a certain order: First, Outer, Inner, and Last.

Example 1. Multiply $(3x - 2)$ by $(2x + 1)$.

The following steps show you how to implement FOIL on this problem.

(1) Multiply the first term of each binomial together.
$$(3x)(2x) = 6x^2$$

(2) Multiply the outer terms together.
$$(3x)(+1) = +3x$$

(3) Multiply the inner terms together.
$$(-2)(2x) = -4x$$

(4) Multiply the last term of each expression together.
$$(-2)(+1) = -2$$

(5) Now add the four terms together:
$$6x^2 + 3x - 4x - 2$$

(6) Combine like terms to obtain:
$$6x^2 - x - 2$$

Therefore $(3x - 2)(2x + 1) = 6x^2 - x - 2$.

Example 2. Simplify $(2x + 1)(4x - 3)$.

- (A) $8x - 3$
- (B) $6x^2 + 4x - 3$
- (C) $8x^2 - 2x - 3$
- (D) $8x^2 - 6x - 3$
- (E) $6x^2 - 2x + 3$

Answer: C. Perform the following steps, following the method of FOIL.
$$(2x + 1)(4x - 3) = 8x^2 - 6x + 4x - 3$$
$$= 8x^2 - 2x - 3$$

Chapter 24: Quadratic Expressions and Functions

Example 3. Multiply the following two binomials: $(5x + 1)(5x - 1)$

- (A) $25x^2 - 1$
- (B) $5x^2 - 1$
- (C) $10x - 1$
- (D) $10x$
- (E) $25x^2 + 1$

Answer: A.

$$(5x + 1)(5x - 1) = 25x^2 - 5x + 5x - 1$$
$$= 25x^2 - 1$$

Notice in the final simplification, the expression doesn't contain a multiple of x, only a multiple of x^2 plus a constant. This is because the $5x$ and $-5x$ cancel each other out. The expression, $25x^2 - 1$, is the difference between two perfect squares, $25x^2$ and 1. The square root of $25x^2$ is $5x$ and the square root of 1 is 1.

Now that you understand the method of FOIL, you need to know how to go backwards from a standard binomial or trinomial expression to its factors.

Factoring

Look at example 1 above. If the problem stated to factor $6x^2 - x - 2$, the answer would be $(3x - 2)(2x + 1)$. Therefore, you need to have a method of factoring quickly. First, you need to know the multiplication table. You also have to go backwards and know how to factor a number. For example, if you are given the number 24, you need to know that $24 = 1 \times 24$, 2×12, 3×8, and 4×6. It also equals -1×-24, -2×-12, -3×-8, and -4×-6. If you don't know the multiplication table by now, memorize it today!

"Reverse FOIL" is a method of factoring a quadratic trinomial by trial-and-error. A quadratic expression is any algebraic expression whose power or degree is two. This means that it is an expression that uses variables in which the highest exponent is two. A quadratic trinomial is a quadratic expression with three terms, such as, $x^2 - 3x + 4$ or $2x^2 + 3x - 5$. The strategy is to determine the **First** and **Last** terms of each binomial in the factored product, so that the **Outer** and **Inner** products add up to the middle term.

The best way to understand the method is to jump right into a problem.

Example 4. Factor $x^2 + 5x + 6$.

First, we concentrate on x^2 and $+6$. x^2 is the product of x and x, so we place these **First** terms of the factors:

$$x^2 + 5x + 6 = (x \quad\quad)(x \quad\quad)$$

Now the product $+6$ could result in 4 ways. It could be 1×6, 2×3, -1×-6, or -2×-3.

To make it easier, we ignore the negative factors for now, and try the two positive products of 6, and then ask ourselves if it is possible to get the middle term, $5x$, by adding the **Outer** and **Inner** products:

$$x^2 + 5x + 6 = (x + 1)(x + 6)$$

Outer $= 6x$, **I**nner $= 1x$

Now add the two to obtain: $6x + 1x = 7x$. This doesn't work because we want $5x$, not $7x$.

Let's try $x^2 + 5x + 6 = (x + 3)(x + 2)$

Outer $= 2x$, **I**nner $= 3x$

This works because $2x + 3x = 5x$, which is what is shown in the original expression.

Therefore, the factorization is:

$$x^2 + 5x + 6 = (x + 3)(x + 2)$$

If in the problem the answer appears as $(x + 2)(x + 3)$, this is an identical expression because of the commutative law of multiplication. Either answer might appear as one of the choices and both are equally correct.

Example 5. Factor $2x^2 + 10x + 12$.

- (A) $2(x^2 + 10x + 12)$
- (B) $2x(10x + 6)$
- (C) $(x + 3)(2x + 4)$
- (D) $2(x^2 + 5x + 6)$
- (E) Both C and D

Answer: E.

Step 1: Take a 2 out of the three terms, to rewrite as $2(x^2 + 5x + 6)$.

Step 2: Follow the example 4 above to get $2(x + 3)(x + 2)$.

Step 3: Rewrite $2(x + 3)(x + 2)$ as $(2x + 6)(x + 2)$ or $(x + 3)(2x + 4)$. You did that by distributing the 2 outside the parentheses into the first or second parentheses. Any of the three expressions may appear as an answer choice.

Example 6. Factor $3x^2 + 13x + 12$.

- (A) $(3x + 6)(2x + 2)$
- (B) $(3x + 4)(x + 3)$
- (C) $(3x + 1)(x + 12)$
- (D) $(3x - 1)(3x - 12)$
- (E) $(3x + 3)(x + 4)$

Answer: B. This time, there is a coefficient not equal to 1 in front of the first term, x^2, but 3 doesn't go into 13, the second coefficient. So, this problem is a bit more difficult.

First, we look at $3x^2$ and 12. $3x^2$ is the product of $3x$ and x, so we place these first terms of the factors:

$$3x^2 + 13x + 12 = (3x\quad)(x\quad)$$

Now $+12$ could result in various ways. It could be 1×12, 2×6, 3×4, -1×-12, -2×-6, and -3×-4. Because 13, the second coefficient, is positive, we only want to try the positive factors of 12, and then check if it is possible to get the middle term, $13x$, by adding the inner and outer terms.

$$3x^2 + 13x + 12 = (3x + 2)(x + 6)$$
$$\text{Outer} = 18x, \text{ Inner} = 2x$$

$18x + 2x = 20x$, so this doesn't work since we want to obtain $13x$, not $20x$.

Let's try reversing the order:

$$3x^2 + 13x + 12 = (3x + 6)(x + 2)$$
$$\text{Outer} = 6x, \text{ Inner} = 6x$$

$6x + 6x = 12x$, so this also doesn't work.

$$3x^2 + 13x + 12 = (3x + 3)(x + 4)$$
$$\text{Outer} = 12x, \text{ Inner} = 3x$$

$12x + 3x = 15x$, so this doesn't work either.

$$3x^2 + 13x + 12 = (3x + 4)(x + 3)$$
$$\text{Outer} = 9x, \text{ Inner} = 4x$$

This does work because $4x + 9x = 13x$. Therefore, we get:

$$3x^2 + 13x + 12 = (3x + 4)(x + 3)$$

Example 7. Factor $2x^2 - x - 6$.

- (A) $(2x - 1)(x + 6)$
- (B) $(2x - 6)(x + 1)$
- (C) $(2x + 3)(x - 2)$
- (D) $(2x - 2)(x + 3)$
- (E) $(2x + 6)(x - 1)$

Answer: C. First, we look at $2x^2$ and -6. $2x^2$ is the product of $2x$ and x, so we place these first terms of the factors:

$$2x^2 - x - 6 = (2x\quad)(x\quad)$$

Now -6 could result by multiplying 1×-6, -1×6, 3×-2, or -3×2. Let's try each possibility. We want to obtain $-x$ as the sum of the outer and inner terms:

$2x^2 - x - 6 = (2x - 1)(x + 6)$

$\quad$ Outer $= 12x$, Inner $= -x$

$12x - x = 11x$, so this doesn't work since we want to obtain $-x$.

Let's try reversing the order:

$2x^2 - x - 6 = (2x + 6)(x - 1)$

$\quad$ Outer $= -2x$, Inner $= 6x$

$-2x + 6x = 4x$, so this also doesn't work.

$2x^2 - x - 6 = (2x + 1)(x - 6)$

$\quad$ Outer $= -12x$, Inner $= x$

$-12x + x = -11x$, so this doesn't work.

$2x^2 - x - 6 = (2x - 6)(x + 1)$

$\quad$ Outer $= 2x$, Inner $= -6x$

This doesn't work because $2x - 6x = -4x$.

Let's try $(2x + 2)(x - 3)$. Outer term $= -6x$, Inner term $= 2x$, and $-6x + 2x = -4x$. No.

Let's try $(2x + 3)(x - 2)$. Outer term $= -4x$, Inner term $= 3x$, and $-4x + 3x = -x$. Yes, this is what we want. Therefore,

$2x^2 - x - 6 = (2x + 3)(x - 2)$

You might get lucky and find that the first or second try works out. You need to do many problems to solve factoring problems quickly. Because this is a timed test, work through many problems like these. Eventually, you will be able to solve a problem like this in 15 seconds or less.

Example 8. Factor $x^2 - 11x + 24$.

Ⓐ $(x - 24)(x - 1)$
Ⓑ $(x + 24)(x + 1)$
Ⓒ $(x - 6)(x - 4)$
Ⓓ $(x - 4)(x + 6)$
Ⓔ $(x - 3)(x - 8)$

Answer: E. Notice the constant is positive ($+24$), but the middle term has a negative coefficient. When this happens, the outer and inner terms are both negative, since a negative times a negative is a positive (we want $+24$), and two negatives added together add up to a negative number (we want -11).

The negative factors of 24 are: -1×-24, -2×-12, -3×-8, and -4×-6. Among these pairs of factors, only -3 and -8 will work because $(x - 3)(x - 8) = x^2 - 8x - 3x - 24 = x^2 - 11x - 24$. Therefore,

$x^2 - 11x + 24 = (x - 3)(x - 8)$

To help you solve the problem more quickly, put the factors of 24 in a column like so:

$\quad -1 \quad\quad -24$
$\quad -2 \quad\quad -12$
$\quad -3 \quad\quad -8$
$\quad -4 \quad\quad -6$

Now see which two numbers add up to -11. Obviously -3 and -8 do, so these must be the factors. This method, though, works only if the leading coefficient of the expression is 1.

Example 9. Factor $2x^2 - 7x + 6$.

Ⓐ $(2x - 6)(x - 1)$
Ⓑ $(2x - 3)(x - 2)$
Ⓒ $(2x + 7)(x - 1)$
Ⓓ $(2x - 1)(x + 6)$
Ⓔ $(2x - 1)(x + 7)$

Answer: B. The last coefficient is positive, and the second coefficient is negative, so both the outer term and inner term must be negative (because the product 6 is positive, and the sum of the factors -7, is negative).

The negative factors of 6 are

$\quad -1 \times -6$ and -2×-3.

Let's try $(2x - 2)(x - 3)$. Outer term $= -6x$, Inner term $= -2x$, and $-6x - 2x = -8x$. No.

Let's try $(2x - 3)(x - 2)$. Outer term $= -4x$, Inner term $= -3x$, and $-4x - 3x = -7x$. Yes. Therefore, $2x^2 - 7x + 6 = (2x - 3)(x - 2)$.

Example 10. Factor $3x^2 + x - 2$.

- (A) $(3x - 2)(x + 1)$
- (B) $(3x + 2)(x - 1)$
- (C) $(3x + 1)(x - 2)$
- (D) $(3x - 1)(x + 2)$
- (E) $(3x - 1)(x + 2)$

Answer: A. This time, the constant, -2, is negative, so one factor must be positive, and one factor must be negative, since a positive number times a negative number is a negative number, which is what we are looking for. The only way to get a product of -2 is: -1×2, or -2×1.

We want the inner and outer terms to add up to $+x$.

So, let's try $(3x + 1)(x - 2)$. Outer term $= -6x$, Inner term $= x$, and $-6x + x = -5x$. No.

Try $(3x - 2)(x + 1)$. Outer term $= 3x$, Inner term $= -2x$, and $3x - 2x = x$. Yes! Therefore $3x^2 + x - 2 = (3x - 2)(x + 1)$.

Example 11. If $(x + 1)(x - 2) = 0$, which of the following values of x would satisfy the equation?

- (A) -1 and -2
- (B) 1 and -2
- (C) -1 and 2
- (D) Only 1
- (E) Only -2

Answer: C. If $(x + 1)(x - 2) = 0$, then either $(x + 1) = 0$ or $(x - 2) = 0$. This is because any number multiplied by zero equals 0, which is the value we want on the right side. If $x + 1 = 0$, then $x = -1$. If $x - 2 = 0$, then $x = 2$. Therefore, the only values of x that satisfy the equation are -1 and 2.

$$(2x - 1)(3x + 2) = 0$$

Example 12. Which of the following values of x would satisfy the equation above?

- (A) $\frac{1}{2}, -\frac{2}{3}$
- (B) $-\frac{1}{2}, \frac{2}{3}$
- (C) $1, -2$
- (D) $-1, 2$
- (E) $0, -\frac{2}{3}$

Answer: A. $2x - 1 = 0$ or $3x + 2 = 0$. Solving for the first equation, $x = \frac{1}{2}$ and for the second equation, $x = -\frac{2}{3}$.

$$x^2 + 5x + 6 = 0$$

Example 13. Which of the following values of x satisfy the equation above?

- (A) 5
- (B) 6
- (C) $-3, -2$
- (D) $3, 2$
- (E) $5, 6$

Answer: C. From example 4, we find that
$$x^2 + 5x + 6 = (x+3)(x+2)$$
Therefore
$$(x+3)(x+2) = 0$$
from which we determine that
$$x = -3 \text{ or } x = -2$$

$$4x^2 - 25 = 0$$

Example 14. Which of the following values of x satisfy the equation above?

(A) 4, 25
(B) 4, −25
(C) 2, 5
(D) $\frac{5}{2}, -\frac{5}{2}$
(E) $\frac{2}{5}, -\frac{2}{5}$

Answer: D. There are two ways to solve the equation.

Method 1: Add 25 to both sides, then divide by 4 to obtain $x^2 = \frac{25}{4}$. Now take the square root of both sides to obtain $x = \pm \frac{5}{2}$.

Method 2: Factor the equation to obtain
$$4x^2 - 25 = (2x+5)(2x-5) = 0,$$
therefore, either $2x + 5 = 0$ or $2x - 5 = 0$, so $x = \frac{5}{2}$ or $x = -\frac{5}{2}$.

$$3x^2 + x - 2 = 0$$

Example 15. Which of the following values of x satisfy the equation above?

(A) 3, −2
(B) $\frac{2}{3}, -1$
(C) $-\frac{2}{3}, 1$
(D) −2, 3
(E) $-\frac{3}{2}, -1$

Answer: B. From example 10 above we obtain
$$3x^2 + x - 2 = (3x - 2)(x + 1) = 0$$
Therefore, $3x - 2 = 0$ or $x + 1 = 0$. Solving for x, we get: $x = \frac{2}{3}$ or $x = -1$.

The Quadratic Formula

Sometimes an equation might not factor easily. Take for example the equation
$$x^2 + 3x + 1 = 0$$
This equation is not easily factorable. When this occurs, we can use the **Quadratic formula**.

The Quadratic formula can help us solve any quadratic equation. Before we use the formula, we must first write the equation in the form
$$ax^2 + bx + c = 0,$$
where a, b, and c are coefficients. Then, we plug these coefficients into the formula:
$$x = \frac{-b \pm \sqrt{b^2 - 4ac}}{2a} \qquad (1)$$

When we plug in values for a, b, and c into the formula, we get out one or two numbers that can be real or imaginary. These are called "roots." On the GED Math test, you will only deal with real roots, and so we will not discuss imaginary roots.

Let's take a look at some examples involving finding roots using the Quadratic formula. First, we will use an example of an equation that is factorable and see if we get the same values with the Quadratic formula.

Example: What is/are the possible values of x if $x^2 + 3x + 2 = 0$?

First, let's solve the equation by factoring like we learned earlier in the chapter. We get:

$$x^2 + 3x + 2 = (x + 1)(x + 2) = 0.$$

The solutions are $x = -1$ and $x = -2$ from our previous discussion.

Now let's see if we get the same answers using the Quadratic formula.

Start with finding the coefficients a, b, and c.

From the given equation we have $a = 1$, $b = 3$, and $c = 2$.

Now plugging in these values into the Quadratic formula (1) we obtain:

$$x = \frac{-b \pm \sqrt{b^2 - 4ac}}{2a}$$

$$= \frac{-3 \pm \sqrt{3^2 - 4(1)(2)}}{2(1)}$$

$$= \frac{-3 \pm \sqrt{9 - 8}}{2}$$

$$= \frac{-3 \pm \sqrt{1}}{2} = \frac{-3 \pm 1}{2}$$

This gets us two answers:

$$\frac{-3 + 1}{2} = \frac{-2}{2} = -1 \text{ or } \frac{-3 - 1}{2} = \frac{-4}{2} = -2$$

We get $x = -1$ and $x = -2$ as the complete solution set, which is the answer we got using simple factoring.

Example 16. Find the complete solution set for the equation $x^2 + 3x + 1 = 0$.

Ⓐ $\left\{\dfrac{-3 + \sqrt{3}}{2}, \dfrac{-3 - \sqrt{3}}{2}\right\}$

Ⓑ $\left\{\dfrac{-2 + \sqrt{3}}{2}, \dfrac{-2 - \sqrt{3}}{2}\right\}$

Ⓒ $\left\{\dfrac{-3 + \sqrt{5}}{5}, \dfrac{-3 - \sqrt{5}}{5}\right\}$

Ⓓ $\left\{\dfrac{-3 + \sqrt{5}}{3}, \dfrac{-3 - \sqrt{5}}{3}\right\}$

Ⓔ $\left\{\dfrac{-3 + \sqrt{5}}{2}, \dfrac{-3 - \sqrt{5}}{2}\right\}$

Answer: E. Here $a = 1$, $b = 3$, and $c = 1$.

Plugging in these coefficients into the Quadratic formula, we get:

$$x = \frac{-b \pm \sqrt{b^2 - 4ac}}{2a}$$

$$= \frac{-3 \pm \sqrt{3^2 - 4(1)(1)}}{2(1)}$$

$$= \frac{-3 \pm \sqrt{5}}{2}$$

So, we have two roots:

$$\frac{-3 + \sqrt{5}}{2} \text{ and } \frac{-3 - \sqrt{5}}{2}$$

No wonder we couldn't factor it easily!

Chapter 24: Quadratic Expressions and Functions

Example 17. What are the solutions of the equation $3x^2 + 6x + 2 = 0$?

(A) $x = -\dfrac{1}{4} - \dfrac{\sqrt{12}}{3}$ or $x = -\dfrac{1}{4} + \dfrac{\sqrt{12}}{3}$

(B) $x = -\dfrac{1}{2} - \dfrac{\sqrt{6}}{6}$ or $x = -\dfrac{1}{2} + \dfrac{\sqrt{6}}{6}$

(C) $x = -\dfrac{1}{4} - \dfrac{\sqrt{12}}{4}$ or $x = -\dfrac{1}{4} + \dfrac{\sqrt{12}}{4}$

(D) $x = -1 - \dfrac{\sqrt{12}}{6}$ or $x = -1 + \dfrac{\sqrt{12}}{6}$

(E) $x = -6 - \dfrac{\sqrt{6}}{3}$ or $x = -6 + \dfrac{\sqrt{6}}{3}$

Answer: D. We have $a = 3$, $b = 6$, and $c = 2$. Plugging in these values into the Quadratic formula we get:

$$\dfrac{-6 \pm \sqrt{6^2 - 4(3)(2)}}{2(3)} = \dfrac{-6 \pm \sqrt{12}}{6}$$

Therefore, $x = -1 - \dfrac{\sqrt{12}}{6}$ or $x = -1 + \dfrac{\sqrt{12}}{6}$.

Example 18. Find the values of x that satisfy the equation $x^2 + 4x + 4 = 0$ using the Quadratic formula.

(A) $\left\{\dfrac{1}{4}, -\dfrac{1}{2}\right\}$

(B) $\left\{\dfrac{1}{2}, -\dfrac{1}{4}\right\}$

(C) $\left\{-\dfrac{1}{2}\right\}$

(D) $\left\{\dfrac{2}{3}, -\dfrac{2}{3}\right\}$

(E) $\left\{-2\right\}$

Answer: E. We have $a = 1$, $b = 4$, and $c = 4$. Plugging in these values into the Quadratic formula, we get:

$$\dfrac{-4 \pm \sqrt{4^2 - 4(1)(4)}}{2(1)} = \dfrac{-4 \pm \sqrt{0}}{2} = \dfrac{-4 \pm 0}{2}$$

The root is $\dfrac{-4}{2} = -2$. Here we get only one root.

Solving Radical Equations - continued

In chapter 5 on exponents and roots, we learned how to solve a basic radical equation. We continue with this topic here because there is a type of radical equation that will necessitate using factoring or sometimes the Quadratic formula.

Example 19. What is the value of x if $x = \sqrt{x+3} + 3$?

(A) 1
(B) 6
(C) 8
(D) 1 and 6
(E) 6 and 8

Answer: B. Subtract 3 from both sides:

$$x - 3 = \sqrt{x+3}.$$

Square both sides to get:

$$(x - 3)^2 = \left(\sqrt{x+3}\right)^2$$
$$(x - 3)(x - 3) = x + 3$$
$$x^2 - 6x + 9 = x + 3$$

Subtract $x + 3$ from both sides of the equation to get:

$$x^2 - 7x + 6 = 0$$

Now factor to get: $(x-1)(x-6) = 0$.

So $x - 1 = 0$ or $x - 6 = 0$ in which case $x = 1$ or $x = 6$.

Plug each value of x back into the original equation:
$$x - 3 = \sqrt{x+3}$$
$$(1) - 3 = \sqrt{1+3} = \sqrt{4}$$
$$-2 = 2$$

This is a false statement, and therefore 1 is an extraneous solution, meaning it is a root of the transformed equation but not of the original equation, because it is excluded from the domain of the original equation.

Plug in 6:
$$x - 3 = \sqrt{x+3}$$
$$(6) - 3 = \sqrt{6+3} = \sqrt{9}$$
$$3 = 3$$

Therefore, the solution is $x = 6$.

Example 20. What is/are the value/s of x if $x + 5 = \sqrt{2x+5} + 4$?

(A) -2
(B) 2
(C) -2 and 2
(D) -1 and 1
(E) -3 and 3

Answer: B. First subtract 4 from both sides to get:
$$x + 1 = \sqrt{2x+5}$$

Square both sides of the equation to get:
$$(x+1)(x+1) = 2x + 5$$

Now FOIL the expression to get:
$$x^2 + 2x + 1 = 2x + 5$$

Now bring all the terms to the left-hand side to get:
$$x^2 + 2x + 1 - 2x - 5 = 0$$
$$x^2 - 4 = 0$$
$$(x-2)(x+2) = 0$$

Therefore $x = 2$ or -2.

Plug these two values into the original equation:

For -2,
$$x + 5 = \sqrt{2x+5} + 4$$
$$(-2) + 5 = \sqrt{2(-2)+5} + 4$$
$$3 = \sqrt{1} + 4 = 5$$

This is not a true statement, and therefore $x = -2$ is an extraneous solution.

Let's try $x = 2$.
$$x + 5 = \sqrt{2x+5} + 4$$
$$(2) + 5 = \sqrt{2(2)+5} + 4$$
$$7 = \sqrt{9} + 4 = 7$$

Since $x = 2$ works and $x = -2$ doesn't work, the only real solution to the equation is $x = 2$.

Chapter 24: Quadratic Expressions and Functions

Practice Problems

1. What is the product of $(2x - 5)$ and $(3x - 2)$?

    Ⓐ $5x - 7$
    Ⓑ $6x + 10$
    Ⓒ $6x^2 - 19x + 10$
    Ⓓ $6x^2 + 10x + 11$
    Ⓔ $3x^2 + 12x + 5$

2. Simplify: $(6x - 5)(6x + 5)$

    Ⓐ $36x^2 - 25$
    Ⓑ $12x$
    Ⓒ $12x - 10$
    Ⓓ $12x^2 - 30x - 25$
    Ⓔ $12x^2 - 25$

3. Simplify: $(4x + 3)(7x - 5)$

    Ⓐ $11x - 2$
    Ⓑ $11x^2 - 15$
    Ⓒ $28x^2 - 2$
    Ⓓ $28x^2 - x - 15$
    Ⓔ $28x^2 + x - 15$

4. Factor: $x^2 + 8x + 15$

    Ⓐ $(x - 15)(x - 1)$
    Ⓑ $(x + 15)(x + 1)$
    Ⓒ $(x + 5)(x + 3)$
    Ⓓ $(x - 5)(x - 3)$
    Ⓔ $(x + 8)(x + 15)$

5. Factor: $16x^2 - 36$

    Ⓐ $16x(x - 36)$
    Ⓑ $(16x - 36)(x + 1)$
    Ⓒ $(4x + 6)(4x - 6)$
    Ⓓ $(8x - 18)(2x + 2)$
    Ⓔ $(8x - 2)(2x + 18)$

6. Factor completely: $8x^2 - 2x - 3$

    Ⓐ $(4x - 3)(2x + 1)$
    Ⓑ $(8x + 3)(x - 1)$
    Ⓒ $(4x - 2)(x + 1)$
    Ⓓ $(4x + 3)(2x - 1)$
    Ⓔ $(8x - 3)(x + 1)$

7. Factor completely: $45x^2 + 36x - 9$

   (A) $(45x + 3)(45x - 3)$
   (B) $9(5x - 1)(x + 1)$
   (C) $3(15x + 1)(x - 9)$
   (D) $15(x - 9)(3x + 1)$
   (E) $9(5x + 1)(x - 1)$

8. Factor completely: $2x^2 - 5x - 12$

   (A) $(2x + 3)(x - 4)$
   (B) $(2x - 12)(x + 1)$
   (C) $(2x + 12)(x - 1)$
   (D) $(2x - 6)(x + 2)$
   (E) $(2x - 3)(x + 4)$

9. Factor completely: $2x^2 + x - 15$

   (A) $(2x + 1)(x - 15)$
   (B) $(2x - 1)(x + 15)$
   (C) $(2x + 3)(x - 5)$
   (D) $(2x - 5)(x + 3)$
   (E) $(2x - 3)(x + 5)$

10. Factor: $18x^2 - 8$

    (A) $(9x - 8)(2x + 1)$
    (B) $(6x + 2)(3x - 4)$
    (C) $2(9x^2 - 4)$
    (D) $(6x + 4)(3x - 2)$
    (E) Either C or D

11. Solve for x: $(4x - 5)(x + 1/2) = 0$

    (A) $x = 5$ or $x = -1/2$
    (B) $x = 4/5$ or $x = -1/2$
    (C) $x = -5/4$ or $x = 1/2$
    (D) $x = -5$ or $x = 1/2$
    (E) $x = 5/4$ or $x = -1/2$

12. Solve for x: $36x^2 - 64 = 0$

    (A) 36 or −64
    (B) −36 or 64
    (C) 6 or 8
    (D) 4/3 or −4/3
    (E) 3/4 or −3/4

Chapter 24: Quadratic Expressions and Functions

13. Solve for x: $2x^2 - 7x + 6 = 0$

    Ⓐ -6 or 7

    Ⓑ $\dfrac{2}{3}$ or -2

    Ⓒ $-\dfrac{3}{2}$ or -2

    Ⓓ $\dfrac{3}{2}$ or 2

    Ⓔ -7 or 6

14. Solve for x: $7x^2 - 13x - 2 = 0$

    Ⓐ $-\dfrac{1}{7}$ or 2

    Ⓑ 7 or -2

    Ⓒ $-\dfrac{1}{4}$ or $\dfrac{2}{3}$

    Ⓓ $\dfrac{1}{7}$ or -2

    Ⓔ $\dfrac{1}{4}$ or $-\dfrac{2}{3}$

15. Which of the following values of x satisfy the following equation: $6x^2 - 13x + 6 = 0$?

    Ⓐ 1 or -13

    Ⓑ $\dfrac{2}{3}$ or $\dfrac{3}{2}$

    Ⓒ $-\dfrac{2}{3}$ or $-\dfrac{3}{2}$

    Ⓓ $\dfrac{6}{13}$ or -1

    Ⓔ -13 or 6

16. What can x equal if $2x^2 + 4x - 1 = 0$?

    Ⓐ $-1 + \dfrac{\sqrt{8}}{4}, \ -1 - \dfrac{\sqrt{8}}{4}$

    Ⓑ $-4 + \dfrac{\sqrt{8}}{4}, \ -4 - \dfrac{\sqrt{8}}{4}$

    Ⓒ $-1 + \dfrac{\sqrt{20}}{2}, \ -1 - \dfrac{\sqrt{20}}{2}$

    Ⓓ $-4 + \dfrac{\sqrt{24}}{4}, \ -4 - \dfrac{\sqrt{24}}{4}$

    Ⓔ $-1 + \dfrac{\sqrt{24}}{4}, \ -1 - \dfrac{\sqrt{24}}{4}$

17. What can x equal if $\sqrt{x-7} + 9 = x$?

    Ⓐ 8

    Ⓑ 9

    Ⓒ 11

    Ⓓ 8 or 11

    Ⓔ 8 or 9

18. What is the extraneous solution for the equation: $2\sqrt{x-1} + 1 = x$?

    Ⓐ 1

    Ⓑ 2

    Ⓒ 4

    Ⓓ 5

    Ⓔ There is no extraneous solution.

Answers to Practice Problems

1. **(C)** $(2x - 5)(3x - 2) = 6x^2 - 4x - 15x + 10$
   $= 6x^2 - 19x + 10$

2. **(A)** $(6x - 5)(6x + 5)$
   $= 36x^2 + 30x - 30x - 25$
   $= 36x^2 - 25$

3. **(E)** $(4x + 3)(7x - 5)$
   $= 28x^2 - 20x + 21x - 15$
   $= 28x^2 + x - 15$

4. **(C)** $x^2 + 8x + 15 = (x + 5)(x + 3)$ because $(x + 5)(x + 3) = x^2 + (3x + 5x) + 15$.

5. **(C)** $16x^2 - 36 = (4x + 6)(4x - 6)$ because $(4x + 6)(4x - 6) = 16x^2 - 24x + 24x - 36$.

6. **(A)** $8x^2 - 2x - 3 = (4x - 3)(2x + 1)$ because $(4x - 3)(2x + 1) = 8x^2 + (4x - 6x) - 3$.

7. **(B)** $45x^2 + 36x - 9 = 9(5x^2 + 4x - 1) = 9(5x - 1)(x + 1)$ because $(5x - 1)(x + 1) = 5x^2 + (5x - x) - 1$.

8. **(A)** $2x^2 - 5x - 12 = (2x + 3)(x - 4)$ because $(2x + 3)(x - 4) = 2x^2 - 8x + 3x - 12$.

9. **(D)** $2x^2 - x - 15 = (2x - 5)(x + 3)$ because $(2x - 5)(x + 3) = 2x^2 + 6x - 5x - 15$.

10. **(E)** $18x^2 - 8 = 2(9x^2 - 4)$
    $= 2(3x + 2)(3x - 2) = (6x + 4)(3x - 2)$

11. **(E)** Either $4x - 5 = 0$, in which case $4x = 5$, and $x = \frac{5}{4}$, or $x + \frac{1}{2} = 0$, in which case $x = -\frac{1}{2}$.

12. **(D)** $36x^2 - 64 = 4(9x^2 - 16) = 4(3x - 4)(3x + 4) = 0$.
    So, $3x - 4 = 0$ or $3x + 4 = 0$. Therefore $x = \pm \frac{4}{3}$.

    Another method is to add 64 to both sides of the original expression to get $36x^2 = 64$, so $x^2 = \frac{64}{36} = \frac{16}{9}$. Then take the square root of both sides to get $x = \pm \frac{4}{3}$.

13. **(D)** $2x^2 - 7x + 6 = 0$ implies that $(2x - 3)(x - 2) = 0$, in which case $2x - 3 = 0$ or $x - 2 = 0$. Therefore $x = \frac{3}{2}$ or $x = 2$.

14. **(A)** $7x^2 - 13x - 2 = 0$ implies that $(7x + 1)(x - 2) = 0$, in which case $7x + 1 = 0$ or $x - 2 = 0$. So $x = -\frac{1}{7}$ or $x = 2$.

15. **(B)** $6x^2 - 13x + 6 = 0$ implies that $(3x - 2)(2x - 3) = 0$, in which case $3x - 2 = 0$ or $2x - 3 = 0$. So $x = \frac{2}{3}$ or $x = \frac{3}{2}$.

16. **(E)** Using the Quadratic formula, we have $a = 2$, $b = 4$ and $c = -1$, so

$$x = \frac{-b \pm \sqrt{b^2 - 4ac}}{2a}$$

$$= \frac{-4 \pm \sqrt{4^2 - 4(2)(-1)}}{2(2)}$$

$$= \frac{-4 \pm \sqrt{24}}{4}$$

Therefore, the roots are

$$-1 + \frac{\sqrt{24}}{4} \text{ and } -1 - \frac{\sqrt{24}}{4}$$

17. **(C)** Subtract 9 from both sides of the equations to obtain:

$$\sqrt{x - 7} = x - 9$$

Square both sides of the equation to get

$$x - 7 = (x - 9)^2 = (x - 9)(x - 9)$$
$$x - 7 = x^2 - 18x + 81$$

Add 7 and subtract x from both sides of the equation and factor it to get:

$$x^2 - 19x + 88 = 0$$
$$(x - 11)(x - 8) = 0$$

So, $x = 11$ or $x = 8$.

Plug these values into the original equation:

$$\sqrt{11 - 7} + 9 = 11$$
$$2 + 9 = 11 \checkmark$$

So, $x = 11$ is a solution to the equation.

Plug in 8:

$$\sqrt{8 - 7} + 9 = 11$$
$$1 + 9 = 11$$

which is not true. Therefore $x = 8$ is not a solution.

18. **(E)** We have $2\sqrt{x - 1} + 1 = x$. Subtract 1 from both sides of the equation to get

$$2\sqrt{x - 1} = x - 1$$

Square both sides of the equation to get

$$(2\sqrt{x - 1})^2 = (x - 1)^2$$
$$4(x - 1) = x^2 - 2x + 1$$

(Here we distributed the exponent 2 to both 2 and $\sqrt{x - 1}$.)

Now distribute the 4:

$$4x - 4 = x^2 - 2x + 1$$

Subtract $4x$ and add 4 to both sides to get

$$x^2 - 6x + 5 = 0$$

so $(x - 1)(x - 5) = 0$. Therefore $x = 1$ or $x = 5$.

Plug in 1 into the original equation to check to see if it is a solution:

$$2\sqrt{1 - 1} + 1 = 11$$
$$2(0) + 1 = 1 \checkmark$$

Plug in 5: $\quad 2\sqrt{5 - 1} + 1 = 5$
$$2(2) + 1 = 5 \checkmark$$

Therefore, there is no extraneous solution!

Chapter 25
Functions

Definition of a Function

A **function** is a special type of mathematical transformation that takes a set of input numbers, called the **domain**, and returns a set of output numbers, known as the **range**. To be classified as a function, every input number must be matched with exactly one output number. One can think of a function as a mathematical "machine" that transforms the input numbers into the output numbers. The machine can be an algebraic equation that takes every possible input value and solves for its corresponding output value.

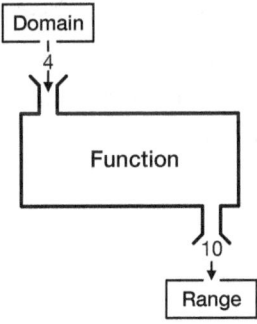

Figure 1. Conceptual schematic of a function when thought of as a machine.

Recognizing Functions in Arrow Diagrams

One way to represent a function is through use of an **arrow diagram**, where the arrows map the transformation of the input numbers to the output numbers.

Example 1. Which of the arrow diagrams below show a function?

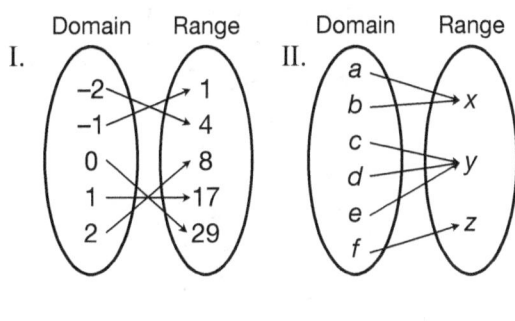

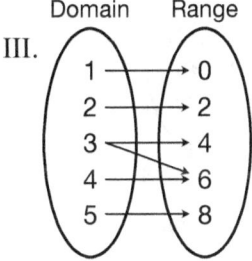

Ⓐ Diagram I
Ⓑ Diagram II
Ⓒ Diagram III
Ⓓ Diagrams I and II
Ⓔ Diagrams I, II, and III

Answer: D. Diagram **I** is a function because every input number is mapped to one and only one output number. Diagram **II** uses letters to represent numbers, where each letter stands for a different number. Notice how for Diagram **II**, multiple input numbers map to the same output number (i.e., *a* and *b* map to *x*, while *c*, *d*, and *e* map to *y*); this is allowed by the function definition. Importantly, each input number maps to only one output number, so therefore Diagram **II** is also a function. Diagram **III**, on the other hand, is not a function, because the input number 3 is transformed to two output numbers.

Let's try another example.

Example 2. Which of the following arrow diagrams show a function?

I.
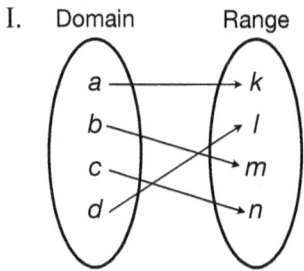

II.
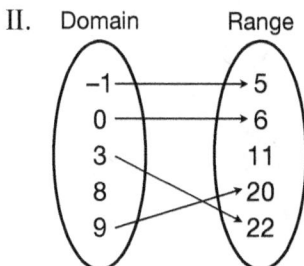

IIII.
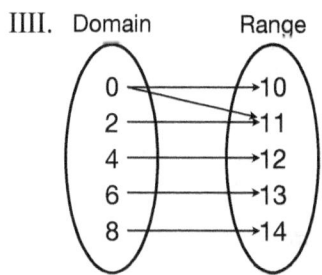

Ⓐ Diagram I
Ⓑ Diagram II
Ⓒ Diagram III
Ⓓ Diagrams I and II
Ⓔ Diagrams I, II, and III

Answer: A. Diagram **I** is a function because every input number is transformed to exactly one output number. However, Diagram **II** is not a function because the input number 8 is not mapped to any output number. Diagram **III** is also not a function because the input number 0 is transformed to two output numbers.

Function Notation

We can symbolically represent a function using the notation

$$y = f(x)$$

where the *f*-symbol denotes the transformation of an input number, represented by the independent variable *x*, into its output value, represented by the dependent variable *y*. Typically, this transformation is an algebraic equation that relates *x* to *y*.

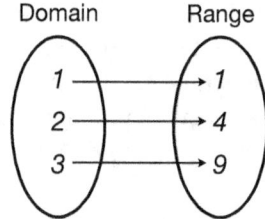

Example 3. Which of the following equations could be used to describe the function given in the arrow diagram above?

Ⓐ $y = \sqrt{x}$
Ⓑ $y = 2^x$
Ⓒ $y = x^2$
Ⓓ $y = 3x + 1$
Ⓔ $y = 3x^2 + 1$

Answer: C.

Method 1: Pattern recognition. Notice how every output number is the square of its corresponding input number. Therefore, $y = x^2$ is true for every (x, y) pair represented by an arrow.

Method 2: Plug and chug. Let's test each answer choice until we find the equation that holds for all three (x, y) pairs shown on the arrow diagram. We can eliminate answer choice **A**, $y = \sqrt{x}$, because even though $1 = \sqrt{1}$, $4 \neq \sqrt{2}$ and $9 \neq \sqrt{3}$. We can similarly eliminate answer choice **B** by plugging the three (x, y) pairs into the equation $y = 2^x$. Remember that *all three* (x, y) pairs must yield an equivalent relationship before the answer can be declared correct. For example, when we plug $(2, 4)$ into $y = 2^x$ we get $4 = 2^2$; so far so good. But when we try plugging $(3, 9)$ into $y = 2^x$ we get $9 \neq 2^3$. Plugging in all three (x, y) pairs into answer choice **C**, $y = x^2$, yields equivalent relationships for all three pairs: $1 = 1^2$, $4 = 2^2$ and $9 = 3^2$. Therefore, **C** is the correct answer. If you encounter this type of problem on the GED Math test and choose to use the plug-and-chug method, it is a good idea to test the remaining answer choices to verify that they are also incorrect, time permitting.

x	y
0	5
2	9
3	11
6	17
10	25

Example 4. Which of the equations below expresses the function $y = f(x)$ given in the table above?

    Ⓐ $y = 3x + 5$
    Ⓑ $y = -4x + 5$
    Ⓒ $y = 6x + 2$
    Ⓓ $y = 2x + 5$
    Ⓔ $y = 5x$

Answer: D.

Method 1: Constructing the equation. All answer choices represent linear equations, and therefore we can assume that the function is linear. Recall that a linear algebraic equation can be expressed by the formula $y = mx + b$, where the constants m and b are the slope and y-intercept, respectively. All answer choices fit this form, and so we know that the table represents a linear equation. The y-intercept is the value that y takes when $x = 0$, and so therefore $b = 5$, and we can eliminate answer choices **C** and **E**. To compute the slope, we select any two (x, y) pairs, and use the formula:

$$m = \frac{y_2 - y_1}{x_2 - x_1}$$

Taking $(0, 5)$ as (x_1, y_1) and $(2, 9)$ as (x_2, y_2) yields

$$m = \frac{9 - 5}{2 - 0} = \frac{4}{2} = 2$$

Note that selecting $(0, 5)$ as (x_2, y_2) and $(2, 9)$ as (x_1, y_1) yields the same answer for m, i.e.

$$m = \frac{5 - 9}{0 - 2} = \frac{-4}{-2} = 2$$

Therefore, the table fits the equation $y = 2x + 5$ and **D** is the correct answer.

Method 2: Plug and chug. Testing answer choice **A**, we plug $(x, y) = (0, 5)$ into the equation $y = 3x + 5$, and we end up with left- and right-hand sides that are equivalent: $5 = 3(0) + 5$. So far so good; however, every (x, y) pair given as a row in the table must satisfy $y = 3x + 5$. Plugging in $(x, y) = (2, 9)$ yields the inequivalent relationship $9 \neq 3(2) + 5$, and so we eliminate choice **A**. Similarly, we can eliminate choice **B** because when we test $(x, y) = (2, 9)$, we get $9 \neq -4(2) + 5$. Only answer choice **D** yields an equivalent relationship for every (x, y) pair: $5 = 2(0) + 5$ (check!); $9 = 2(2) + 5$ (check!); $11 = 2(3) + 5$ (check!); $17 = 2(6) + 5$ (check!); and $25 = 2(10) + 5$ (check!).

Example 5. Supply the missing entry in the table below.

x	y
0	0
2	4
3	
5	25
7	49

(A) 6
(B) 8
(C) 9
(D) 12
(E) 15

Answer: C. Off the bat, we can see that the functional relationship between x and y is not linear, because the choice of different (x, y) pairs yields a different $m = (y_2 - y_1)/(x_2 - x_1)$. For example, choosing rows 4 and 5 yields

$$m = (49 - 25)/(7 - 5) = 24/2 = 12$$

whereas choosing rows 1 and 2 yields

$$m = (4 - 0)/(2 - 0) = 4/2 = 2$$

Another commonly encountered type of function, known as a *power function*, has the form $y = ax^p$, where p is any real number. Inspecting the table, we see that each y-value is the square of its paired x-value. Therefore, the table describes the power function $y = x^2$, with $a = 1$ and $p = 2$. The missing value is $y = 3^2 = 9$, and choice **C** is the correct answer.

Example 6. Which of the following linear functions satisfies $f(1) = 3$ and $f(3) = -1$?

(A) $y = 3x - 1$
(B) $y = -x + 3$
(C) $y = -2x + 3$
(D) $y = 2x + 5$
(E) $y = -2x + 5$

Answer: E. We are given two (x, y) pairs: $(1, 3)$ and $(3, -1)$. We calculate the slope using

$$m = \frac{y_2 - y_1}{x_2 - x_1} = \frac{-1 - 3}{3 - 1} = \frac{-4}{2} = -2$$

Next, we find the y-intercept by solving for the point $(0, y)$ using $m = -2$ and one of the known (x, y) pairs. Here we choose $(x, y) = (1, 3)$. This gives us:

$$-2 = \frac{y_2 - y_1}{x_2 - x_1} = \frac{3 - y}{1 - 0} = 3 - y$$

Rearranging both sides, we get $y = 5$. Therefore, $y = -2x + 5$ is the correct answer.

An alternative method to solve this problem is to simply plug in 1 into x into each equation to see if $y = 3$, and then plug in 3 into x into each equation to check if $y = -1$. You will find that only choice **E** works.

Chapter 25: Functions

Recognizing Functions Graphically

On a Cartesian coordinate plane, the independent variable is plotted on the *x*-axis and the function is a curve (which can be a straight line) that maps each *x*-value to its output value on the *y*-axis. This assumes, of course, that we choose *x* and *y* to represent our independent and dependent variables, respectively, although any letter would work just as well.

Domain and Range

There are two important terms you should be familiar with:

The **domain** of a function is the complete set of possible values of the independent variable (usually *x*).

The **range** of a function is the complete set of possible values of the dependent variable (usually *y*). If the function is continuous, it includes all numbers between a minimum value and a maximum value of *y*-values.

If you are told that the domain is: $-2 < x < 3$, where *x* is our independent variable, the domain of the function consists of all numbers between -2 and 3, exclusively. On a graph, the smallest value of *x* would be the leftmost point on the graph, and the largest value of *x* would be the rightmost point on the graph.

Similarly, if we are told that $3 \leq y \leq 5$, the range is all numbers between 3 and 5, inclusively. The minimum value of *y* is 3 and the maximum value of *y* is 5. If the function is graphed, the lowest point on the graph would be 3, and the highest point on the graph would be 5.

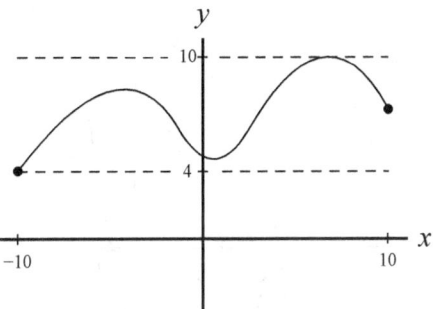

Example 7. Which of the following ordered pairs represent the domain and range, respectively, of the function plotted on the graph above?

(A) domain = $4 \leq x \leq 10$;
range = $-10 \leq y \leq 10$

(B) domain = $(-10, 10)$; range = $[4, 10)$

(C) domain = $(-\infty, +\infty)$; range = $(0, 10)$

(D) domain = $[-10, 10]$; range = $[4, 10]$

(E) domain = $-\infty < x < +\infty$;
range = $4 \leq y \leq 10$

Answer: D. The input *x*-values all come from the interval $-10 \leq x \leq 10$, while the output *y*-values are all contained within the interval $4 \leq y \leq 10$. The solid circles at the curve endpoints emphasize the fact that the curve touches the (*x*, *y*) points $(-10, 4)$ and $(10, 7)$. Remember that the bracket notation, [, or,], implies that the endpoint number/s inside the brackets are included on the graph. This is termed a "closed interval." In contrast, the parentheses imply that the endpoints (or $\pm\infty$) are not included on the graph. This is termed "an open interval." If a number were to be included in the set of parentheses, there would be a hole in the graph at that point. Therefore, $-10 \leq x \leq 10$ is equivalent to $[-10, 10]$ and $4 \leq y \leq 10$ is equivalent to $[4, 10]$.

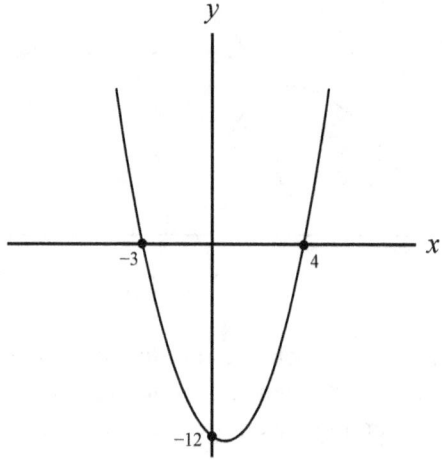

Example 8. The graph of $y = x^2 - x - 12$ is shown above. Given the graph, what is the solution set for $x^2 - x - 12 > 0$?

(A) $x > -3$

(B) $x < -3$ or $x > 4$

(C) $x < -3$

(D) $-3 < x < 4$

(E) $x > 4$

Answer: B. This question asks us to find all values of x in the domain that, when plugged into the function $f(x) = x^2 - x - 12$, yield $f(x) > 0$. The graph shows values of $x^2 - x - 12$ on the y-axis and values of x on the x-axis. We can see that when $x > 4$, $x^2 - x - 12 > 0$ because the graph is above the x-axis, where the y-values (in this case, $x^2 - x - 12$) are positive. We can see that this is also true when $x < -3$. When x is between -3 and 4, the points on the graph are below the x-axis, where the y-values are negative. Therefore, the solution is $x < -3$ or $x > 4$.

Vertical Line Test

Not every curve plotted in a Cartesian coordinate system is a function. A curve meets the function criterion only if a vertical line drawn through *any* x in the domain intersects the curve at only one point. This is known as the *vertical line test*, and it proves that each value of the independent variable transforms to only one value of the dependent variable. It is the graphical analogy to checking that each input number on an arrow diagram is mapped to only one output number.

I. 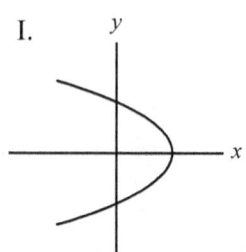   II.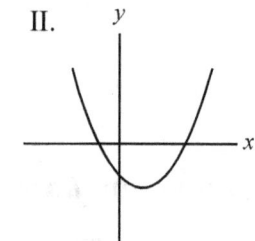

III.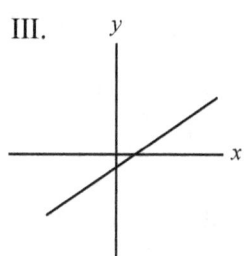

Example 9. Which of the plotted curves above are functions?

(A) I only

(B) II only

(C) III only

(D) I and II only

(E) II and III only

Answer: E. Curve **I** is not a function because a vertical line drawn through any part of it other than through its apex intersects the curve at two different points: one where y is positive, and the other where y is negative. Curves **II** and **III** are both functions because a vertical line drawn anywhere through either of them intersects the curve at only one point. Remember that all lines are considered curves.

Chapter 25: Functions

Number Sequence Patterns

Another type of question that you may encounter on the GED Math test asks you to fill in the missing value in a series of numbers. Sometimes, these number series are really functions in disguise, where the numbers themselves are the *y*-values and their corresponding input *x*-values can be related to their positions in the list. Other times, the difference between successive numbers follows a regular pattern. Either way, the pattern recognition skills that we have developed for recognizing functions described by series of (x, y) pairs can come in handy when we need to complete a sequence of numbers.

Example 10. Complete the following number sequence: 1, 2, 4, 8, __ , 32

- (A) 10
- (B) 12
- (C) 16
- (D) 24
- (E) 64

Answer: C.

Method 1: Pattern recognition. Notice how all numbers in the list are multiples of 2, except for the first number. Also, the listed numbers 2, 4, and 8 are all equal to their preceding number multiplied by 2. Therefore, the missing number is 16.

Method 2: Converting the list to a function. Recall that the exponential expression 2^x represents 2 multiplied by itself *x* times, and that $2^0 = 1$. Therefore, we can see that each number in the list satisfies *y* in the equation $y = 2^x$, where *x* is one less than its position in the list. This equation belongs to the *exponential function* family $y = b^x$ where $b > 0$ and $b \neq 1$.

Let's convert the list to a table of (x, y) values, where $y = f(x) = 2^x$.

List position	x	y
1	0	1
2	1	2
3	2	4
4	3	8
5	4	
6	5	32

The missing number in the 5th position of the list is $y = 2^4 = 2 \times 2 \times 2 \times 2 = 16$.

Practice Problems

1. Which, if any, of the following arrow diagrams are functions?

    I.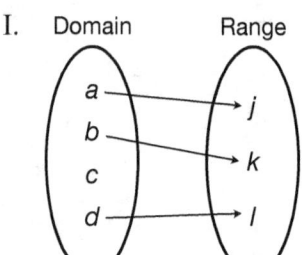

    II.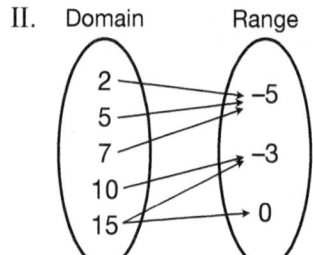

    III.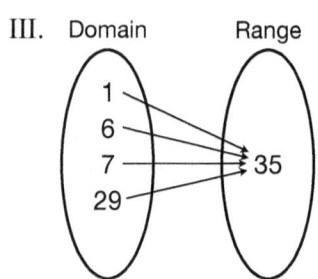

    (A) I only
    (B) II only
    (C) III only
    (D) I and II only
    (E) None

2. Which of the following arrow diagrams are functions?

    I.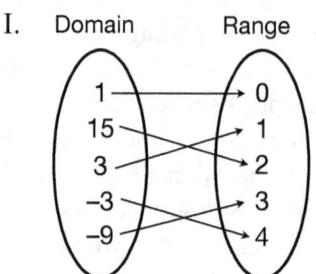

    II.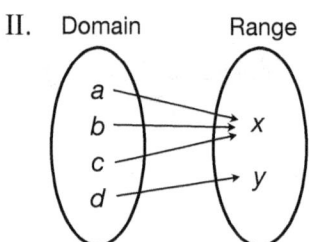

    III.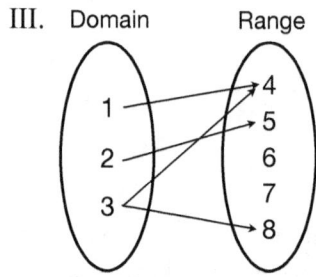

    IV.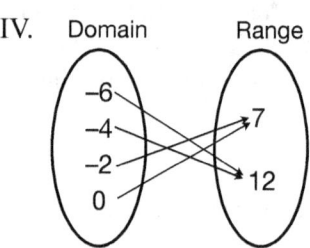

    (A) I only
    (B) I and IV only
    (C) I, II, and III only
    (D) I, II, and IV only
    (E) II, III, and IV only

3. Given that $f(n) = n^2 - 2n + 5$, what is $f(3)$?

   (A) 5
   (B) 6
   (C) 7
   (D) 8
   (E) 9

4. Which of the following tables are functions?

   Choose all answers that apply.

   [A]
x	f(x)
3	9
2	-5
-1	-5
-3	-5
2	9

   [B]
x	f(x)
-2	4
1	-5
3	3
2	3
5	4

   [C]
x	f(x)
3	4
4	5
5	6
6	7
7	8

   [D]
x	f(x)
-1	3
-1	-2
3	5
5	4
3	6

   [E]
x	f(x)
3	5
3	7
4	-2
5	-6
6	6

x	y
0	18
2	6
5	-12
8	-30
12	-54

5. Which of the following equations expresses the relationship between x and y in the table given above?

   (A) $y = -6x + 18$
   (B) $y = 3x - 18$
   (C) $y = 2x + 10$
   (D) $y = -2x + 18$
   (E) $y = x + 6$

6. Which of the following corresponds to the values of function $f(x) = -x^3 + 8$ for the series of integers $-2, -1, 0$, and 1?

   (A) 14, 11, 8, 5
   (B) 2, 9, 6, 5
   (C) 16, 9, 5, 7
   (D) 0, 7, 8, 9
   (E) 16, 9, 8, 7

7. When considering the linear function that satisfies $f(2) = -3$ and $f(8) = 0$, what is $f(4)$?

   (A) -2
   (B) -1
   (C) 1
   (D) 2
   (E) 3

8. Which of the following linear equations for $f(x)$ satisfies the condition $f(2) = -2$ and $f(5) = 7$?

   (A) $f(x) = \dfrac{5}{3}x + 3$

   (B) $f(x) = 3x - 8$

   (C) $f(x) = 4x + 3$

   (D) $f(x) = -\dfrac{5}{3}x + 8$

   (E) $f(x) = 3x - 1$

9. What are the domain and range for the function $y = x^2$?

   (A) domain = $(-\infty, +\infty)$
   range = $(0, +\infty)$

   (B) domain = $(-\infty, +\infty)$
   range = $(-\infty, 0]$

   (C) domain = $(-\infty, +\infty)$
   range = $[0, +\infty)$

   (D) domain = $(0, +\infty)$
   range = all real numbers

   (E) domain = $(-\infty, +\infty)$
   range = $(-\infty, +\infty)$

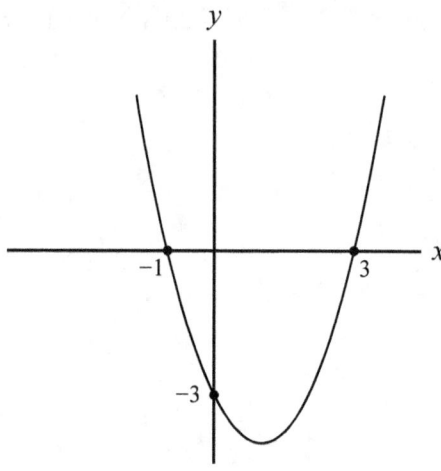

10. The graph of the function $y = x^2 - 2x - 3$ is shown above. Given this graph, what is the solution set for $x^2 - 2x - 3 < 0$?

    (A) $x > -1$

    (B) $x < 3$

    (C) $x < -1$ or $x > 3$

    (D) $-1 < x < 3$

    (E) $x > 1$

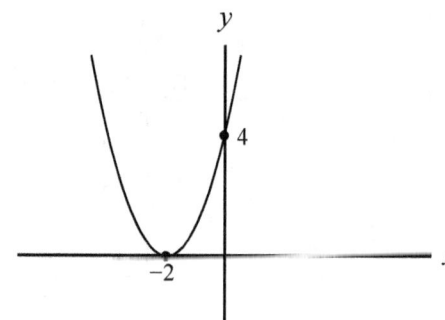

11. The graph above shows the function $y = x^2 + 4x + 4$. What is the solution set for $x^2 + 4x + 4 > 0$?

    (A) $x > 0$

    (B) $-\infty < x < +\infty$

    (C) $x > -2$

    (D) $x < -2$

    (E) $(-\infty, -2), (-2, +\infty)$

12. Which of the following plotted curves are functions?

    Choose all answers that apply.

    [A]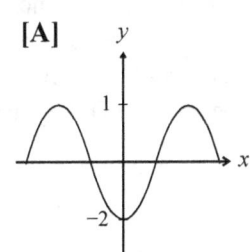
    [B]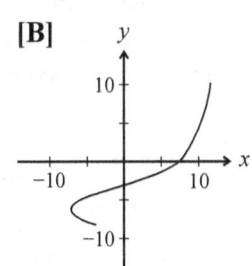

    [C]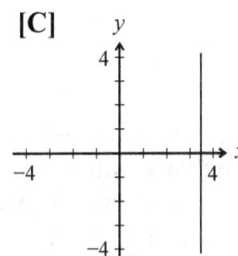
    [D]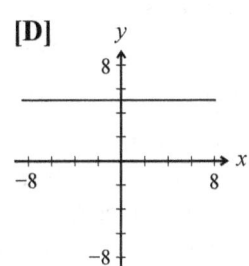

    [E]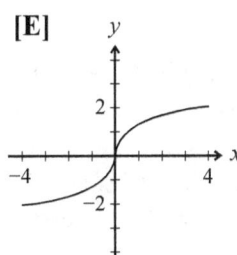

13. Complete the following number sequence:

    1, 4, 9, ___, 25, 36

    (A) 12
    (B) 14
    (C) 15
    (D) 16
    (E) 18

14. Which of the following plotted curves are functions?

    Choose all answers that apply.

    [A]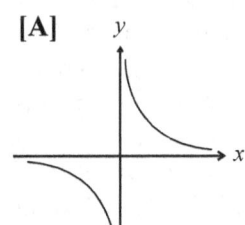
    [B]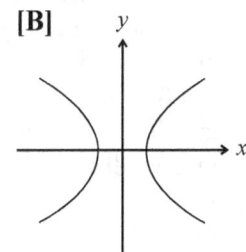

    [C]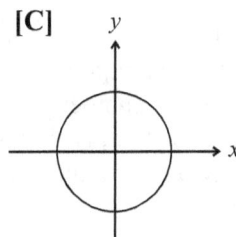
    [D]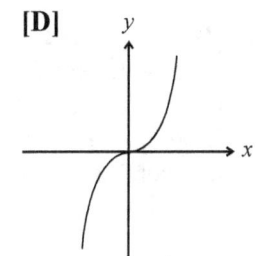

    [E]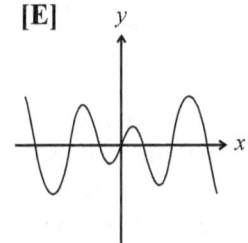

15. Complete the following number sequence:

    2, 5, 10, 17, 26, ___

    (A) 35
    (B) 37
    (C) 39
    (D) 41
    (E) 43

Answers to Practice Problems

1. **(C)** Diagram **I** is not a function because the input number represented by c is not mapped to any output number. Diagram **II** is also not a function because the input number 15 is mapped to two output numbers. Diagram **III** is a function because each input number is mapped to exactly one output number. Even though all input numbers are mapped to the same output number, this is allowed by the function definition.

2. **(D)** Diagrams **I**, **II**, and **IV** are all functions because for each one, every input number is mapped to exactly one output number. Diagram **III** is not a function because input number 3 is mapped to two output numbers.

3. **(D)** Plugging in 3 for n gives us
$$f(3) = 3^2 - 2(3) + 5 = 8$$

4. **(B), (C)** A function, $f(x)$, is a relation in which one value of x transforms to only one value of $f(x)$. A function may have two different values of x that correspond to the same value of $f(x)$, but it cannot have two different values of $f(x)$ that correspond to one value of x. Looking at our answer choices, Table **A** is not a function because $x = 2$ corresponds to both -5 and 9. Table **B** is a function because each value of x corresponds to only one value of $f(x)$. Don't be confused by the fact that $f(-2) = 4$ and $f(5) = 4$. Here the same value of $f(x)$ corresponds to two different values of x, but this is allowed in a function. Table **C** is a function because each x transforms to only one $f(x)$. However, Table **D** is not a function because it gives us $f(-1) = 3$ and also $f(-1) = -2$; furthermore, it gives us both $f(3) = 5$ and $f(3) = 6$. Table **E** is not a function because it gives us $f(3) = 5$ and also $f(3) = 7$.

5. **(A)** Since all answers have the form $y = mx + b$, we know that the functional relationship between x and y is linear. Since $y = 18$ when $x = 0$, $b = 18$. We can compute m using any two (x, y) pairs, and here let's choose $(x_1, y_1) = (0, 18)$ and $(x_2, y_2) = (2, 6)$. Therefore,
$$m = \frac{6 - 18}{2 - 0} = \frac{-12}{2} = -6$$
Therefore, the equation described by this table is
$$y = -6x + 18$$
and the correct answer is **A**.

    Alternatively, you may use the plug-and-chug method described in example 4, where you test each equation in the answer choices to see whether all (x, y) pairs given in the table satisfy the equation.

6. **(E)** Plugging -2 into $f(x)$ yields $-(-2)^3 + 8 = -(-8) + 8 = 16$. This eliminates choices **A**, **B**, and **D**. Similarly, if you plug in -1, 0, and 1 for x, you get the values 9, 8, and 7, respectively. Choice **E** shows those correct matching $f(x)$ values.

7. **(A)** Since we know that the function is linear, we can compute the slope using
$$m = \frac{y_2 - y_1}{x_2 - x_1} = \frac{0 - (-3)}{8 - 2} = \frac{3}{6} = \frac{1}{2}$$
We now know that the equation is
$$y = \frac{1}{2}x + b$$
To find b, plug in either point given, like $(2, -3)$. Set $y = -3$ and $x = 2$ in the above equation to get:
$$-3 = \frac{1}{2}(2) + b$$
$$-3 = 1 + b$$
$$b = -4$$

Therefore, we obtain the equation

$$y = \frac{1}{2}x - 4$$

To find $f(4)$, we plug 4 into the equation we just found, to get

$$y = \frac{1}{2}(4) - 4 = 2 - 4 = -2$$

which is our final answer.

8. **(B)** We are told that the function is linear and therefore the equation takes the form $y = mx + b$, where m is the slope and b is the y-intercept. You can plug 2 and 5 into x for each answer choice and see if you get the correct $f(x)$ value for both conditions, i.e., $f(x) = -2$ and $f(x) = 7$, respectively.

   Alternatively, you can find the linear equation using the two points given: $(2, -2)$ and $(5, 7)$. The slope is the change in $f(x)$ over the change in x, which in this case is

   $$m = \frac{y_2 - y_1}{x_2 - x_1} = \frac{7 - (-2)}{5 - 2} = \frac{9}{3} = 3$$

   We now know that $m = 3$, so only choices **B** and **E** are possibly correct. To find b, plug either point given into $y = 3x + b$. If we use $(5, 7)$, we get $7 = 3(5) + b$. Solving for b, we get $b = -8$, and therefore the equation is

   $$y = 3x - 8,$$

   choice **B**. Since we know that this equation is linear, and since there is only one way a line can connect two points, there is only one possible answer. You should choose the method that is quickest for you.

9. **(C)** Because you can plug any value of x into $f(x) = x^2$ and generate an output y-value that is a real number, the domain of this function is $(-\infty, +\infty)$. For all x, $f(x) \geq 0$ because the square of any positive or negative number is always positive (for example, when you square a negative number you always get a positive number as in $(-4)^2 = +16$). If you plug in a zero for x, $f(0) = 0$. Therefore, the range is $[0, +\infty)$. Note that choice **A** is incorrect because it uses an open interval surrounding $y = 0$, when in fact the value $y = 0$ is included in the range set of numbers because it is the functional output value for $x = 0$. You will note that there are parentheses beside $-\infty$ and $+\infty$ rather than brackets, because infinity is not a number, and the function never actually reaches infinity, it only approaches it.

10. **(D)** The question asks us to give the set of x-values that would make $f(x) = x^2 - 2x - 3$ smaller than zero. The graphed curve shows values of $f(x) = x^2 - 2x - 3$ on the y-axis and values of x on the x-axis. We can see that when $x > 3$, $x^2 - 2x - 3 > 0$ because the curve is above the x-axis, where the y-values (in this case, $x^2 - 2x - 3$) are positive. We can see this is also true when $x < -1$. When x is between -1 and 3, the curve is below the x-axis, where the y-values (in this case, $x^2 - 2x - 3$) are negative. Therefore, the solution is $-1 < x < 3$.

11. **(E)** The graph shows output values of the function $f(x) = x^2 + 4x + 4$ on the y-axis and the input x-values on the x-axis. We are asked to find values of x that transform to y-values (i.e., $x^2 + 4x + 4$) that are greater than zero. These points are found where the curve is above the x-axis. The only value of x that transforms to a value of $f(x) = x^2 + 4x + 4$ that is *not* greater than zero is the point $x = -2$, where the curve touches the x-axis. Therefore, the solution set is $x \neq -2$, which can also be expressed using the open interval notation $(-\infty, -2), (-2, +\infty)$.

12. **(A), (D), (E)** Curve **A** passes the vertical line test because a vertical line drawn through any part of it intersects the curve just once. However, curve **B** is not a function, because a vertical line drawn through the portion of the domain where $x < -5$ intersects the curve at two points. The vertical line shown in **C** is also not a function because $x = 3.5$ maps to an infinite number of y-values. The horizontal

line shown in **D** is a function because every x maps to one and only one y-value, even though this y-value is equivalent for all x. Choice **E** is also a function because it passes the vertical line test.

13. **(D)** All numbers in this sequence are the squares of successively larger integers:

    $1 = 1^2$; $4 = 2^2$; $9 = 3^2$; $25 = 5^2$; and $36 = 6^2$

    Therefore, the sequence numbers given to us are the y-values for the power function $y = x^2$, where $x = 1, 2, 3, \_, 5, 6$. The missing value is $y = f(4) = 4^2 = 16$.

14. **(A), (D), (E)** Curve **B**, which is a hyperbola, is not a function because a vertical line can be drawn through it that intersects two different y-values. Curve **C**, which is a circle, is also not a function for the same reason. However, curve **A**, curve **D**, and curve **E** are functions because a vertical line drawn through any portion of any of those curves intersects the curve only once.

15. **(B)** The numbers in this sequence do not form a pattern of y-values for evenly spaced x when considering either a linear function $y = mx + b$, a power function $y = ax^p$, or an exponential function $y = b^x$. However, we notice a regular pattern in the differences between successive numbers, namely:

    $5 - 2 = 3$; $10 - 5 = 5$; $17 - 10 = 7$; and $26 - 17 = 9$

    Since the difference increases by two with each successive pair, we expect the missing number to be $26 + 11 = 37$.

    Another solution method is to observe that each number is one more than a perfect square. The sequence can be written as $y = x^2 + 1$. For example, the first number in the sequence is $1^2 + 1 = 2$. The second number is $2^2 + 1 = 5$, and so forth. Therefore, the last number in the sequence will be $6^2 + 1 = 37$.

Practice Test II

Number of questions: 40

Time: 115 minutes

Directions:

There are 40 questions on this test. You have 115 minutes to complete the test. You may fill in the ovals next to the correct answers or write your answers on a separate piece of paper. You MAY use a calculator.

Below is a formula sheet that appears on the actual GED® Test. You can refer to this page on Part II of this Pretest.

Area of a:

square	$A = s^2$
rectangle	$A = hw$
parallelogram	$A = bh$
triangle	$A = \dfrac{1}{2}bh$
trapezoid	$A = \dfrac{1}{2}h(b_1 + b_2)$
circle	$A = \pi r^2$

Perimeter of a:

square	$P = 4s$
rectangle	$P = 2l + 2w$
triangle	$P = s_1 + s_2 + s_3$
Circumference of a circle	$C = 2\pi r$ or $C = \pi d$; $\pi \approx 3.14$

Surface area and volume of a:

rectangular/right prism	$SA = ph + 2B$	$V = Bh$
cylinder	$SA = 2\pi rh + 2\pi r^2$	$V = \pi r^2 h$
pyramid	$SA = \dfrac{1}{2}ps + B$	$V = \dfrac{1}{3}Bh$
cone	$SA = \pi rs + \pi r^2$	$V = \dfrac{1}{3}\pi r^2 h$
sphere	$SA = 4\pi r^2$	$V = \dfrac{4}{3}\pi r^3$

(p = perimeter of base with area B; $\pi \approx 3.14$)

Data

mean	mean is equal to the total of the values of a data set, divided by the number of elements in the data set
median	median is the middle value in an odd number of ordered value of a data set, or the mean of the two middle values in an even number of ordered values in a data set.

Algebra

slope of a line	$m = \dfrac{y_2 - y_1}{x_2 - x_1}$
slope intercept form of the equation of a line	$y = mx + b$
point-slope form of the equation of a line	$y - y_1 = m(x - x_1)$
standard form of a quadratic equation	$y = ax^2 + bx + c$
quadratic formula	$x = \dfrac{-b \pm \sqrt{b^2 - 4ac}}{2a}$
Pythagorean theorem	$a^2 + b^2 = c^2$
simple interest	$I = Prt$ (I = interest, P = principal, r = rate, t = time)
distance formula	$d = rt$
total cost	total cost = (number of units) × (price per unit)

Provided by GED® Testing Service.

$$3 - 4x^2 - 2x + 2x^2 - 7 + 4x$$

1. The expression above can also be written as:

   (A) $-6x^2 - 4x - 4$
   (B) $6x^2 + 2x + 10$
   (C) $-2x^2 + 2x - 4$
   (D) $-2x^2 + 6x + 10$

2. On a baseball team, 4 out of 12 players are left-handed. Assuming no player on the team is ambidextrous, what is the probability that two players randomly selected from the team are both right-handed?

   (A) $\frac{9}{33}$
   (B) $\frac{11}{33}$
   (C) $\frac{14}{33}$
   (D) $\frac{64}{144}$

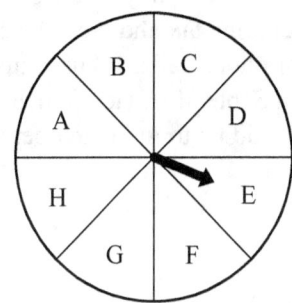

3. In the figure above, if the hand of the spinner is spun once, what is the probability that the spinner's hand will land on a vowel?

   (A) $\frac{1}{8}$
   (B) $\frac{1}{4}$
   (C) $\frac{3}{8}$
   (D) $\frac{1}{2}$

4. A box contains 3 blue, 2 red, and 4 black pens. If one pen is randomly selected from the box, what is the probability that it will be blue?

   (A) $\frac{1}{8}$
   (B) $\frac{1}{4}$
   (C) $\frac{1}{3}$
   (D) $\frac{3}{8}$

5. The telephone company charges $74 per month including tax and fees plus $0.11 a minute for phone calls. Jill used up 120 minutes in September. How much did her phone bill add up to in September?

   (A) $87.20
   (B) $92.45
   (C) $95.65
   (D) $98.40

6. Diane received her monthly water bill that totaled $32. It included a monthly fee of $12 plus a charge per gallon of water. How much did one gallon of water cost her if she used 2,000 gallons?

   (A) $0.001
   (B) $0.005
   (C) $0.01
   (D) $0.05

7. If $2x - y = 9$ and $3x + y = 11$, what is the value of y?

   (A) −2.4
   (B) −1.3
   (C) −1.0
   (D) 0.4

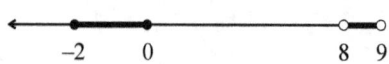

8. The number line above can be represented by which of the following expressions?

   (A) $x \neq -2, -8, x = 0, 9$
   (B) $-2 < x < 0, 8 < x \leq 9$
   (C) $-2 \leq x \leq 0, 8 < x < 9$
   (D) $x < 0, x > 8$

9. A cooler contains 3 cans of coke, 4 cans of root beer, and 6 cans of ginger ale. Two cans of ginger ale are drawn without replacement from the cooler. What is the probability that both cans are ginger ale?

   (A) $\frac{5}{26}$
   (B) $\frac{4}{13}$
   (C) $\frac{5}{12}$
   (D) $\frac{6}{13}$

10. If $2x - 3y = 5$, then what does $3y - 2x$ equal?

    (A) −10
    (B) −8
    (C) −5
    (D) 1

11. The sum of three consecutive odd numbers in a list is −15. What is the second number?

    (A) −1
    (B) −5
    (C) −7
    (D) −9

12. A number is increased by 20% and then increased again by 50%. If the resulting number is 54, what was the original number?

    (A) 25
    (B) 30
    (C) 32
    (D) 34

13. 54 inches is removed from a length of a rope. If the rope is now 66 inches long, what is the percent decrease in the length of the rope?

    (A) 33%
    (B) 45%
    (C) 60%
    (D) 72%

14. The number of children in 5 surveyed families is {3, 4, 2, 5, 1}. What is the mean number of children in these families?

    (A) 2.2
    (B) 2.7
    (C) 3.0
    (D) 3.2

15. Brittany purchases a board game for B dollars. She gets a discount of 28%, and then gets another 25% off. She then pays 8% tax. What is the final amount Brittany pays for the board game in terms of B?

    (A) $B \times 0.28 \times 0.25 \times 0.08$
    (B) $B \times 0.72 \times 0.75 \times 1.08$
    (C) $B \times 0.72 \times 0.75 \times 0.92$
    (D) $B \times 0.28 \times 0.25 \times 0.92$

16. Simplify:

    $$-2 \cdot 6^{4-2} + 5 \cdot \sqrt{49} + 3\sqrt{81} - (-3 + 5)$$

    (A) −72
    (B) −12
    (C) −8
    (D) 12

17. Simplify: $\dfrac{8}{15} - \dfrac{3}{5}$

   Ⓐ $-\dfrac{1}{3}$

   Ⓑ $-\dfrac{1}{15}$

   Ⓒ $\dfrac{1}{2}$

   Ⓓ $\dfrac{3}{5}$

18. Find the value of $4\dfrac{1}{10} - 3\dfrac{4}{5}$ to the nearest tenth.

   Ⓐ 0.1

   Ⓑ 0.2

   Ⓒ 0.3

   Ⓓ 0.4

19. A math teacher graded an exam and calculated that the mean score of eight students was 82%. She then excluded two test scores because she determined that two students had cheated. She recalculated the average score and found that the new average of the six remaining students was 78%. What was the average of the two test scores of the excluded students?

   Ⓐ 86

   Ⓑ 91

   Ⓒ 94

   Ⓓ 95

20. Which of the following statements is true?

   Ⓐ $-2^{-3} = 6$

   Ⓑ $-3^2 = -6$

   Ⓒ $\sqrt{15^2} = 15$

   Ⓓ $13^{-1} = -13$

21. Scott drove a car approximately 5,000,000 millimeters (mm). How many miles did he drive to the nearest tenth?

   Ⓐ 3.1 miles

   Ⓑ 4.1 miles

   Ⓒ 31 miles

   Ⓓ 41 miles

22. A book weighs 44 ounces. How many kilograms does it weigh? (There are 2.2 pounds in a kilogram.)

   Ⓐ 0.5 kg

   Ⓑ 1.0 kg

   Ⓒ 1.25 kg

   Ⓓ 2.4 kg

23. What is 6.022×10^{-5} in standard form?

    A) −301.1
    B) −30.11
    C) 0.00006022
    D) 0.00062

24. What is the lowest common multiple of 24, 36, and 60?

    A) 120
    B) 180
    C) 240
    D) 360

25. A toy manufacturer held a toy competition for toy, party game, and board game inventors. 5,610 toys, board games, and party games were entered. There were first, second, and third place awards in each of those three categories and one grand prize winner. What is the ratio of winners to non-winners?

    A) 1 : 496
    B) 1 : 498
    C) 1 : 499
    D) 1 : 560

26. A map of China is 7 inches long from east to west. If the scale of the map is 3 inches to 5,645 actual miles, how wide is China from east to west in miles?

    A) 2,419 miles
    B) 6,988 miles
    C) 9,880 miles
    D) 13,171 miles

27. Kim has a large credit card debt. She pays off two-fifths of the outstanding balance. What is the ratio of the amount she still owes to the amount she paid off?

    A) 1 : 2
    B) 2 : 3
    C) 3 : 2
    D) 3 : 5

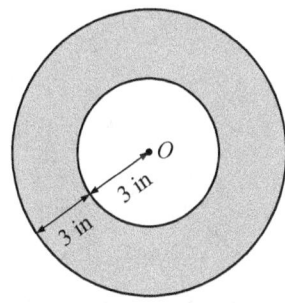

28. In the figure above, two concentric circles are shown with center, O. If the inner circle has a radius of 3 inches and the outer circle has a radius of 6 inches, what is the area of the shaded region?

    A) 9π in²
    B) 16π in²
    C) 27π in²
    D) 36π in²

29. Which of the following are complementary angles?

   (A) 70°, 110°
   (B) 20°, 80°
   (C) 35°, 55°
   (D) 45°, 90°

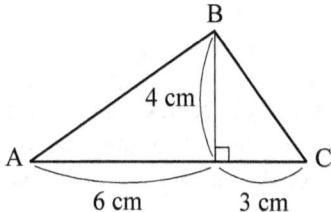

30. What is the area of triangle ABC above?

   (A) 9 cm²
   (B) 12 cm²
   (C) 18 cm²
   (D) 24 cm²

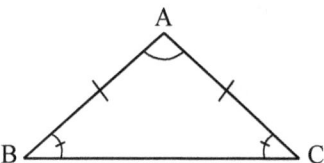

31. In the isosceles triangle above, angle B is equal to 43°, and AB = AC. What is the value of angle A?

   (A) 84°
   (B) 86°
   (C) 94°
   (D) 104°

A = {−5, 3, −1, 0, −3, −3, −3, 6, 9, 12, −4}

32. What is the mean of the set above?

   (A) −3
   (B) 0
   (C) 1
   (D) 3

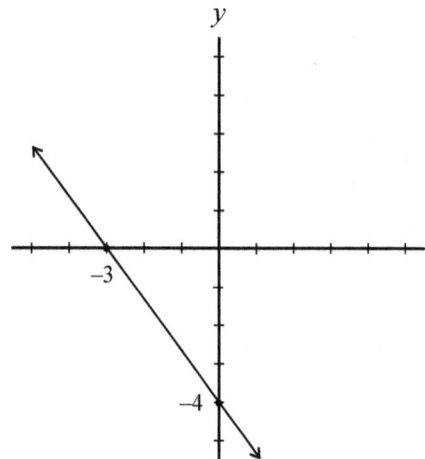

33. The graph above represents which of the following equations?

   (A) $-3x + 4y = -12$
   (B) $3x - 4y = 12$
   (C) $3x + 4y = 12$
   (D) $4x + 3y = -12$

34. What is the greatest common factor of 36, 72, and 96?

    A) 8
    B) 12
    C) 16
    D) 24

37. What is the slope of the line represented by the equation $-3x + 4y = 6$?

    A) -2
    B) $-\dfrac{3}{4}$
    C) $\dfrac{3}{4}$
    D) $\dfrac{3}{2}$

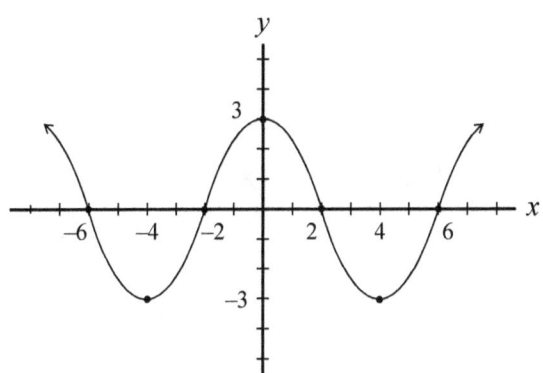

35. In the graph below, on which intervals is the function decreasing?

    A) $(-\infty, -4], [0, 4]$
    B) $(-\infty, -3], [2, +\infty)$
    C) $[-2, 2], [4, 6]$
    D) $[-2, -3], [4, +\infty)$

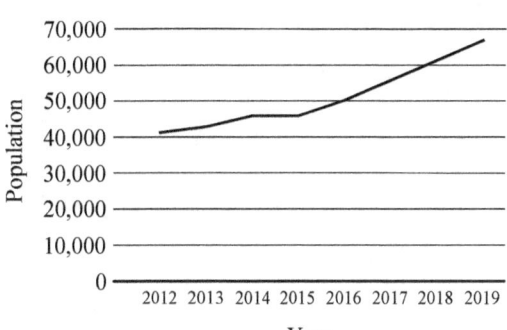

Population in City A

38. The graph above shows the population of a city during a 8-year period. By how much did the population of the city grow between 2015 and 2018?

    A) 11,000
    B) 13,000
    C) 15,000
    D) 18,000

36. Circle B has an area that is 4 times larger than that of Circle A. What is the ratio between Circle A's circumference to Circle B's circumference?

    A) 1 : 2
    B) 1 : 3
    C) 1 : 4
    D) 2 : 1

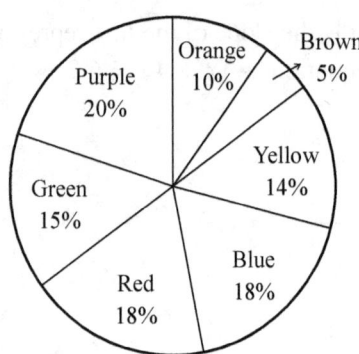

39. The figure above shows the results from a survey of children, reporting their favorite colors. If 30 more children liked red over yellow, how many children were surveyed?

    (A) 450
    (B) 520
    (C) 580
    (D) 750

40. Which of the following linear equations for $f(x)$ satisfies the condition $f(2) = -2$ and $f(5) = 7$?

    (A) $f(x) = \dfrac{5}{3}x + 3$

    (B) $f(x) = 3x - 8$

    (C) $f(x) = 4x + 3$

    (D) $f(x) = -\dfrac{5}{3}x + 8$

Answers to Practice Test II

1. **(C)** We combine like terms by combining the terms containing x^2, the terms containing x, and the constants. We can rearrange to get the following:
$$(-4x^2 + 2x^2) + (-2x + 4x) + (3 - 7)$$
$$= -2x^2 + 2x - 4$$

2. **(C)** Because 4 out of 12 players are left-handed, and no player is ambidextrous, the other 8 players are right-handed. The probability that the first player randomly selected is right-handed is $\frac{8}{12} = \frac{2}{3}$. Since there are now 11 players left to choose from, the probability that the second player is right-handed is $\frac{7}{11}$. Because the two events of selection are dependent, the probability of both players selected are right-handed is
$$\frac{2}{3} \times \frac{7}{11} = \frac{14}{33}$$

3. **(B)** Notice that there is a total of 8 possible outcomes, A through H, and 2 favorable outcomes, A and E. Therefore, there is a 2 in 8 chance that the hand will land on a vowel, which simplifies to 1 in 4, or $\frac{2}{8} = \frac{1}{4}$.

4. **(C)** In this problem, there are 3 blue pens that constitute favorable outcomes out of 9 possible outcomes. So, the probability of a blue pen being selected is $\frac{3}{9} = \frac{1}{3}$.

5. **(A)** The fixed fee is $74, and for 120 minutes Jill pays an addition $0.11 × 120. The total cost, therefore, is $74 + (0.11 × 120) = $87.20.

6. **(C)** Let G = price per gallon. Then we write $32 = $12 + (2000 × G). Subtract 12 from both sides of the equation to get $32 − $12 = $20 = 2000$G$. Divide both sides of the equation by 2000 to get G = $20/2000 = $0.01.

7. **(C)** Add the two equations together to get $5x + 0 = 20$. Therefore $x = 20/5 = 4$. Plug 4 into the second equation to get $3(4) + y = 11$, or $12 + y = 11$. (We could also use the first equation and get the same answer). Now subtract 12 from both sides of

8. **(C)** The number line shows numbers between −2 and 0, inclusive, and 8 to 9, exclusive.

9. **(A)** Since the first can isn't placed back into the cooler before the second soda is selected, the second selection is termed "without replacement." Thus, the actions of selecting the first can and then the second can are dependent events. The formula for dependent events is:

$$P(\text{ginger ale}) \times P(\text{ginger ale} \mid \text{ginger ale})$$

In words, it is the probability of the event, "A ginger ale, and then a ginger ale" is equal to the probability of "A ginger ale," and then, "A ginger ale *given* a ginger ale."

Plugging in the numbers, we get:
$$\frac{6}{13} \times \frac{5}{12} = \frac{5}{26}$$

Where $P(\text{ginger ale} \mid \text{ginger ale}) = \frac{5}{12}$ because there is one fewer ginger ales, (6 − 1) out of (13 − 1) left inside the cooler after the first pick.

10. **(C)** We see that the left-hand term in the equation differs from the expression $3y - 2x$ by a factor of −1, since $-(2x - 3y) =$

$3y - 2x$. Therefore, multiply the right side of the equation by -1 to obtain $5 \times -1 = -5$. If you did not notice this, then manipulate the equation given by subtracting $2x$ from both sides to get $-3y = 5 - 2x$. Then multiply both sides of the equation by -1 to get $3y = -5 + 2x$. Substituting $-5 + 2x$ for $3y$ into $3y - 2x$, yields $(-5 + 2x) - 2x = -5$.

11. **(B)** We call the first odd number, x. Then the next odd integer is $x + 2$, and the third number is $x + 4$. The sum of those numbers is $x + (x + 2) + (x + 4) = 3x + 6$. We are told that the sum equals -15, so we write $3x + 6 = -15$. Subtract 6 from both sides of the equation to get $3x = -21$, and therefore $x = -7$. $x + 2$ is the second number, which equals $(-7) + 2 = -5$.

12. **(B)** Let the original number be N. If N is increased by 20%, then the new value is $(1.2)N$. Then $(1.2)N$ is increased by 50%, to make the new value equal to
$$(1.5)(1.2)N = (1.8)N = 54$$
Then $N = \dfrac{54}{1.8} = 30$.

13. **(B)** If the new length of the rope is 66 inches after 54 inches is removed from it, then the original length of the rope is $66 + 54 = 120$ inches. The percent change can be calculated as
$$\dfrac{\text{Final} - \text{Initial}}{\text{Initial}} \times 100$$
$$= \dfrac{66 - 120}{120} \times 100 = -45\%$$

14. **(C)** Using the formula for the mean, we obtain:
$$\text{Mean} = \dfrac{\text{The sum of the data points}}{\text{The number of data points}}$$
$$= \dfrac{3 + 4 + 2 + 5 + 1}{5} = \dfrac{15}{5} = 3$$

15. **(B)** If Brittany gets 28% off, she is left with $100\% - 28\% = 72\% = 0.72$ of the original price. If she gets another 25% discount, she is left with $100\% - 25\% = 75\% = 0.75$ of the price after the discount. Since the tax is $8\% = 0.08$, the price after the second discount is increased by a factor of 1.08.

16. **(B)** Simplify as follows:
$$-2 \cdot 6^2 + 5 \cdot 7 + 3 \cdot 9 - 2$$
$$= -2(36) + 35 + 27 - 2$$
$$= -72 + 35 + 27 - 2 = -12$$

Make sure you can do the math on paper rather than on a calculator. It will take you less time to do it by hand and you will avoid careless errors entering numbers in your calculator. If you choose to use a calculator, make sure you follow the correct order of operations (PEMDAS).

17. **(B)** The lowest common denominator of 15 and 5 is 15, so convert the second fraction into a fraction with a denominator of 15:
$$\dfrac{8}{15} - \dfrac{9}{15} = \dfrac{-1}{15} = -\dfrac{1}{15}$$

18. **(C)** Convert the numbers into improper fractions:
$$4\dfrac{1}{10} - 3\dfrac{4}{5} = \dfrac{41}{10} - \dfrac{19}{5} = \dfrac{41}{10} - \dfrac{38}{10}$$
$$= \dfrac{3}{10} = 0.3$$

19. **(C)** To obtain the average of the test scores of the 2 excluded students, we subtract the sum of the scores of the 6 remaining students from the sum of the scores of all 8 students, and then divide by 2.

Sum of the 6 students' test scores = average score $\times$ the number of students = $78 \times 6 = 468$.

Sum of the 8 students' test scores = average score $\times$ the number of students = $82 \times 8 = 656$.

Therefore, the average of the test scores of the 2 excluded students = sum of those scores divided by 2:

$$\frac{656 - 468}{2} = \frac{188}{2} = 94$$

20. **(C)**

    In choice **A**, $-2^{-3} = -\frac{1}{2^3} = -\frac{1}{8} \neq 6$.

    In choice **B**, $-3^2 = -9$ not -6.

    In choice **D**, $13^{-1} = \frac{1}{13} \neq -13$.

21. **(A)** Convert millimeters to centimeters, centimeters to meters, meters to kilometers, then kilometers to miles as follows:

    $$5{,}000{,}000 \text{ mm} \times \frac{1 \text{ cm}}{10 \text{ mm}} \times \frac{1 \text{ m}}{100 \text{ cm}}$$

    $$\times \frac{1 \text{ km}}{1000 \text{ m}} \times \frac{1 \text{ miles}}{1.6 \text{ km}} = 3.1 \text{ miles}$$

22. **(C)** There are 16 ounces in a pound. Convert ounces to pounds, then pounds to kilograms as follows:

    $$44 \text{ ounces} \times \frac{1 \text{ pound}}{16 \text{ ounces}} \times \frac{1 \text{ kg}}{2.2 \text{ pounds}}$$

    $$= 1.25 \text{ kg}$$

23. **(C)** move the decimal five places to the left, to get 0.00006022.

24. **(D)** The factors of 24 and 36 are, respectively,

    $$24 = 2 \times 2 \times 2 \times 3$$
    $$36 = 2 \times 2 \times 3 \times 3$$
    $$60 = 2 \times 2 \times 3 \times 5$$

    Pick 3 2's from 24, pick 2 3's from 36, and pick a 5 from 60 to get:

    $$LCM = 2 \times 2 \times 2 \times 3 \times 3 \times 5 = 360$$

25. **(D)** There were $3 \times 3 + 1 = 10$ winners and $5610 - 10 = 5600$ non-winners. The ratio of winners to non-winners, therefore, is

    $$10 : 5600 = 1 : 560$$

26. **(D)** We set up the proportion:

    $$\frac{7 \text{ inches}}{3 \text{ inches}} = \frac{x \text{ miles}}{5645 \text{ miles}}$$

    Multiply both sides of the equation by 5,645 miles to get:

    $$x = \frac{7}{3} \times 5645 = 13{,}171 \text{ miles}$$

27. **(C)** If she paid off two-fifths of her credit card debt, she still owes three-fifths. The ratio she owes to the paid off amount is:

    $$\frac{3}{5} : \frac{2}{5} = 3 : 2$$

28. **(C)** The area of the shaded region is the difference between the area of the outer circle and inner circle. The area of the outer circle is:

    $$A_{Outer} = \pi r^2 = \pi (6)^2 = 36\pi \text{ in}^2$$

    where $r = 6$ because the radius of the outer circle is equal to the distance between the edge of the outer circle and its center, which is $3 + 3 = 6$.

    The area of the inner circle is:

    $$A_{Inner} = \pi r^2 = \pi (3)^2 = 9\pi \text{ in}^2$$

    Therefore, the area of the shaded region is:

    $$A_{Outer} - A_{Inner} = 36\pi - 9\pi = 27\pi \text{ in}^2$$

29. **(C)** Complementary angles are angles that add up to 90°. In choice **C**, $35° + 55° = 90°$.

30. **(C)** The area of a triangle is found by the formula $A = \frac{1}{2}bh$, where $b =$ base of triangle, and $h =$ height of triangle. In this case, we see from the figure that the height is

4 and the base is equal to 6 + 3 = 9. Plug in 4 and 9 into the formula to get:

$$A = \frac{1}{2}bh = \frac{1}{2}(9)(4) = 18 \text{ cm}^2$$

31. **(C)** The sum of the angles in a triangle is 180°. We are told that the triangle is isosceles, and side AB is equal to side AC. Therefore angle B is equal to angle C, and thus angle C is also equal to 43° degrees. So in the triangle above, ∠A + 43° + 43° = 180°. Therefore, ∠A = 180° − 43° − 43° = 94°.

32. **(C)** The sum of the 11 numbers in set A is

−5 + 3 − 1 + 0 − 3 − 3 − 3 + 6 + 9 + 12 − 4 = 11

Using the formula for the mean, we obtain:

$$\text{Mean} = \frac{\text{The sum of the data points}}{\text{The number of data points}} = \frac{11}{11} = 1$$

33. **(D)** The answer choices are all in the form $ax + by = c$. The y-intercept is −4. We can calculate the slope using the two points $(-3, 0), (0, -4)$ to be: $\frac{-4-0}{0-(-3)} = -\frac{4}{3}$. Therefore, the equation in slope-intercept form is $y = -\frac{4}{3}x - 4$. Multiply the entire equation by 3 to get $3y = -4x - 12$. Add $4x$ to both sides to get $4x + 3y = -12$.

34. **(B)** The factors of 36 other than 1 are:

2, 3, 4, 6, 9, 12, 18, 36

The factors of 72 are:

2, 3, 4, 6, 8, 9, 12, 18, 36, 72

The factors of 96 are:

2, 3, 4, 6, 8, 12, 16, 24, 48, 96

The greatest number that is common to all the factors is 12.

35. **(A)** The function decreases when, as the value of x increases, the value of y decreases. This occurs in the graph above in the intervals $(-\infty, -4]$, and $[0, 4]$.

36. **(A)** Let the area and the radius of Circle A be A_1 and r_1, respectively, and the area and the radius of Circle B be A_2 and r_2, respectively. Then since $A_1 : A_2 = 1 : 4$, we must have:

$$\frac{A_1}{A_2} = \frac{\pi(r_1)^2}{\pi(r_2)^2} = \frac{(r_1)^2}{(r_2)^2} = \frac{1}{4}$$

This tells us first that the radius and the area of a circle are not proportional, but rather, that the square of the circle's radius and the circle's area are proportional. Taking the square root of both sides, we find that the radii of the circles are proportional to the square roots of their areas:

$$\frac{r_1}{r_2} = \frac{1}{2}$$

The ratio of the circumference of Circle A to Circle B is:

$$\frac{2\pi r_1}{2\pi r_2} = \frac{r_1}{r_2} = \frac{1}{2} \text{ or } 1 : 2$$

37. **(C)** We have the equation now written in standard form and must convert it to slope-intercept form. Add $3x$ to both sides to get:

$$4y = 3x + 6$$

Now divide both sides of the equation by 4 to get:

$$y = \frac{3}{4}x + \frac{6}{4} = \frac{3}{4}x + \frac{3}{2}$$

Since the slope of a line in $y = mx + b$ form is m, we have $m = \frac{3}{4}$, the slope of the line.

38. **(C)** The population in 2015 was about 45,000 and in 2018 it was 60,000. The difference is 60,000 − 45,000 = 15,000, which is the growth in population.

39. **(D)** The difference in percentage between red and yellow is 18% − 14% = 4%. Let X be the number of students surveyed. Make an equation 4% of X = 30. So, $0.04 \times X = 30$. Divide both sides of the equation by 0.04 to get $X = \dfrac{30}{0.04} = 750$.

40. **(B)** We are told that the function is linear and therefore the equation is of form $y = mx + b$ where m is the slope and b is the y-intercept. You can plug 2 and 5 into x in each answer choice and see if you get the value for $f(x)$ for both conditions, or you can find the equation of the line using two points. We have the point (2, −2) and (5, 7). The slope is the change in $f(x)$ over the change in x, in this case:

$$m = \frac{7 - (-2)}{5 - 2} = \frac{9}{3} = 3$$

So, we know the equation is $y = 3x + b$, so only choices **B** is possible. To find b, plug in either point given, like (5, 7) to get $7 = 3(5) + b$, or $b = 7 - 15 = -8$. Therefore the equation is $y = 3x - 8$, choice **B**. With a linear equation, there will be only one possible equation, since there is only one way a line can connect two points. You should choose the method that is quickest for you.

To reach the editors of this book, please visit our website at
https://superlativepressbooks.com/
We encourage comments or suggestions.

www.ingramcontent.com/pod-product-compliance
Lightning Source LLC
Chambersburg PA
CBHW051208290426
44109CB00021B/2377